I0619970

Life
Changing
Words *from*
JESUS

A Daily Journey to an Abundant Life

Charles Hall

Copyright © 2024 by Charles Hall.

All rights reserved. No part of this publication may be reproduced, distributed, or transmitted in any form or by any means, including photocopying, recording, or other electronic or mechanical methods, without the prior written permission of the author, except in the case of brief quotations embodied in critical reviews and certain other noncommercial uses permitted by copyright law.

Printed in the United States of America

ISBN 979-8-89114-065-3 (sc)
ISBN 979-8-89114-066-0 (e)

Library of Congress Control Number: 2024903308

2024.03.14

MainSpring Books
5901 W. Century Blvd
Suite 750
Los Angeles, CA, US, 90045

www.mainspringbooks.com

To my wife Vivian,
my daughter, Emily and her husband Joe, my son, Bren and his wife, Austin,
and my grandchildren; Brynlee, Walker, Tatum, Reese, Luke, Anders, and Gracie.
May the Lord bless you and keep you,
May the Lord make His face to shine upon you and be gracious unto you,
May the Lord lift up His countenance upon you and give you peace.
Numbers 6:24-26

Acknowledgments

First and foremost, I want to thank God for entrusting me with the responsibility of writing a second devotional book. It is amazing how the Holy Spirit supplies a daily provision of ideas. As one of my favorite Christian authors said, "I thank God for allowing me to be the first person to read this book."

Second, I would like to thank my wife, Vivian, for her prayers, encouragement, and hours spent proofreading. Although we had a couple of disagreements on the wording, her wisdom, insight, and corrections were invaluable.

Lastly, I would like to thank Amy Baumgartner for the many hours she spent editing the manuscript. She readily volunteered, knowing from the first devotional the time and effort it would take on her part. I also appreciate the support given by her family allowing her time to spend editing the book.

Introduction

Paul writing in 2 Timothy 3:16-17 said, "All scripture is inspired by God and is useful to teach us what is true and to make us realize what is wrong with our lives. It corrects us when we are wrong and teaches us to do what is right. God uses it to prepare and equip His people to do every good work." I have always read the Bible through this lens of thought until our Men's Bible Study group, led by Nathan Sanders, took us on a year-long journey through the "Red Words." These are the actual words spoken by Jesus. Although I have read the Bible through a number of times, I had never participated in an in-depth study focused solely on the words of Jesus. It was during this study that Jesus' words began to speak to me. I found His words to be challenging, controversial, life-changing, and as Peter said in John 6:68 "offer eternal life to all who seek Him." I don't claim to be a Bible scholar or an expert on the words of Jesus; however, following this study, God planted a seed for this devotional book. That seed remained dormant until the fall of 2022, when God put the desire in my heart to begin writing a second devotional.

As you read the daily devotionals, focus on the words of Jesus. Let them speak to you in a new and fresh way. I promise they will change your life for the better. Jesus is coming soon. What better way to prepare for His return than to study and apply His words to your heart? If you don't know Christ as your personal Lord and Savior and have picked up this book out of curiosity, learn who Jesus is and His love for you. Find the words of eternal life. If nothing else, read Day 365 and ask Christ to forgive you of your sins and invite Him into your life today.

Prayer: May God richly bless you as you spend time in His Word.

> Matthew 4:4 But He answered and said, "It is written, 'Man shall not live by bread alone, but by every word that proceeds from the mouth of God.'"

Jesus had just been baptized by John in the Jordan River where the Spirit of God appeared and said, "This is My beloved Son, in whom I am well pleased." This is what's called "a mountaintop experience." Mountaintop experiences are when you encounter the presence of God so fully that your heart overflows with joy and your problems become insignificant. However, after His baptism, Jesus left to go into the wilderness for forty days to fast and pray. While He was there, Satan shows up and begins to tempt Jesus. Being human, Jesus was hungry. Satan uses Jesus' hunger to his advantage and says, "If you are the Son of God, command that these stones become bread." Jesus' first miracle was turning water into wine, so turning a few stones into bread would be no problem for Him. What would be wrong with creating a little bread to eat on the trip out of the wilderness? This is how Satan operates. You may have experienced God in a mighty way at a Sunday service, at a retreat, or in a Bible Study. However, Monday comes and you are back in the routine and the mountaintop experience begins to fade. Satan comes along and begins to plant ideas in your mind to distrust God's love for you and that your experience wasn't really real. Ideas such as, 'this one time won't hurt,' or 'no one will ever find out', or 'has God really forgiven me' begin to flood your mind. Satan's aim was to get Jesus to doubt that God could get Him through this time of hunger. How did Jesus answer Satan? He simply said, "It is written..." quoting Deuteronomy 8:3. How important is it to know God's word? God's word holds the answers to our doubts when Satan comes to tempt us. It is our lifeline to God. It teaches us His promises, His love, and His faithfulness. How much time are you spending in God's word? Are you using it when you are being tempted, or are you finding yourself agreeing with Satan? As you read through this book, you will see how much God loves you and wants to have a relationship with you. Don't allow Satan to plant those seeds of doubt in your mind. Get into God's word every day. Learn it, use it, and apply it.

Prayer: God give me the answers from Your word, so I can resist the temptations that Satan tries to use on me.

> *Matthew 4:10 Then Jesus said to him, "Away with you Satan! For it is written, 'You shall worship the Lord your God, and Him only you shall serve.'"*

Satan doesn't give up easily and always comes up with new ways to tempt us. Today's verse is about the third temptation of Jesus. The first was to change stones into bread. The second, Satan said to Jesus, "If You are the Son of God..." tempting Jesus to jump off the pinnacle of the temple and have angels catch Him, hoping Jesus would abuse His power. Jesus quoted scripture to Satan, saying "You shall not tempt the Lord your God." In the third and last temptation, Satan shows Jesus all the kingdoms of the world and said he would give them to Jesus, if Jesus would bow down and worship him. Satan is offering Jesus power and prestige. Jesus quotes scripture from Deuteronomy 6:13 to resist Satan's attack. Satan's attempts to draw us into sin are nothing new. He was pretty successful with Eve in the Garden of Eden where he said to her, "You will not surely die. For God knows that in the day you eat of it your eyes will be opened, and you will be like God, knowing good and evil." Sadly, both Adam and Eve believed Satan's lies and disobeyed God. What Satan had promised didn't turn out quite like he said. Most of my career, I have worked around money. I can't tell you the times that Satan has whispered in my ear, "you could use a couple of $20's, no one would ever miss them." It has been tempting, but I reply back, "God's word, says do not steal." What is Satan offering you? Is he offering you a better lifestyle, a promotion, or fame and fortune? The more important question is, what is Satan asking you to give up in exchange for it? Is he asking you to change your morals, values, or to turn your back on family or friends? Is Satan encouraging you to steal, kill, or even destroy your own body? How are you going to respond to temptation? Trust me, like Adam and Eve, wrong choices never turn out like Satan promises. Trust God's word. As James 4:7 says, "Therefore submit to God. Resist the devil and he will flee from you."

Prayer: God help me to resist the devil and his clever schemes that draw me away from You.

> *Matthew 5:3 Blessed are the poor in spirit, For theirs is the kingdom of heaven.*

Jesus' ministry had begun to generate very large crowds. He was teaching in the local churches and healing all kinds of sickness and disease. People were curious and wanted to hear more from this new teacher. Seeing the large crowd, Jesus went up on a mountain and began to teach. There Jesus turned the world upside down with His teaching, beginning with the Beatitudes which explains the happiness and joy of living a life according to God's plan. In the Beatitudes, we learn that God's way is totally opposite of what our society teaches. Jesus begins with saying the kingdom of heaven belongs to the poor in spirit. The Psalmist writes in Psalms 34:18, "The Lord is near to those who have a broken heart, and saves such as have a contrite spirit." Who are the poor in spirit, and does the kingdom of heaven only belong to someone who is poor? The poor in spirit understand that life in and of themselves is not enough. They are humble, empty of pride and accept the fact that without God, life is meaningless. One who is poor in spirit acknowledges a sinful nature and a need for God in their lives, humbly seeking God's forgiveness and His presence. Their trust is put in God for everything, including His provision, and His grace to get them through the circumstances of life. The poor in spirit are not necessarily poor. Someone who is not poor in spirit is one who has a difficult time acknowledging a need for God in their lives. Why? Because pride may have taken root and a feeling of self-sufficiency developed, pushing God out of their lives. Are you poor in spirit and humbly seeking God's grace and mercy each day? Perhaps you have never trusted God as your Savior or allowed your success to replace your trust in God with your own abilities. If you want to experience the kingdom of heaven, wholeness of life, fulfillment, blessings, and genuine joy then you must acknowledge your complete dependence on Him. Jesus said, "Blessed are the poor in spirit, for theirs is the kingdom of God."

Prayer: God teach me how to seek Your kingdom, not my selfish ambitions.

> *Matthew 5:4 Blessed are those who mourn, For they shall be comforted.*

Jesus didn't waste words as He was speaking to the crowd. Immediately after speaking about the 'poor in spirit', Jesus says, "blessed are those who mourn." Mourning is more than just crying, feeling sad about something, or moping around. *Merriam-Webster.com* defines mourning as "an act of feeling or expressing sorrow. A period of time during which signs of grief are shown." We mourn over the loss of something such as the death of a loved one, a tragedy, and even the loss of a special pet. In fact, we should mourn these things. In most cases, mourning lets others know how special the loss was to you and helps you cope. You don't have to know a person personally to express your grief. For example, people all over the world are mourning the loss of Queen Elizabeth II, who recently passed away at the age of 96. In John 11, we read about the death of Lazarus and how his sisters, Mary and Martha, mourned his loss. Jesus Himself wept at the tomb of Lazarus. However, Jesus is not talking about mourning the loss of a friend or loved one in this beatitude. This mourning has to do with our sin and the loss of fellowship with the Lord. This mourning comes from the Holy Spirit's work in our lives, convicting us of our sin and separation from a loving God. We recognize our spiritual poverty and unworthiness before a Holy and Righteous God. Conviction leads to mourning, which leads to forgiveness. There is no forgiveness of sins without remorse and repentance. We have to come to God and ask for His forgiveness. 1 John 1:9 states, "If we confess our sins, He is faithful and just and will forgive us our sins and purify us from all unrighteousness." In Psalms 51, David pours out his heart to God, asking for forgiveness and cleansing after he had committed adultery with Bathsheba. In verse 17, he writes, "The sacrifices of God are a broken spirit; a broken and contrite heart, O God, You will not despise." Are your sins causing you to mourn, or are they making your life miserable? Jesus said, those who mourn will be comforted. Confess your sins to Him today.

Prayer: God, please break my heart of pride and an unwillingness to confess my sins.

> *Matthew 5:5 Blessed are the meek, For they shall inherit the earth.*

How can the meek inherit the earth when they are taken advantage of, pushed around, and submissive? Wouldn't an aggressive, assertive, dominating personality be better suited to inherit the earth? Perhaps we should take a closer look at what Jesus means by meekness. Meekness does not equal weakness, but it does equate to a quiet and humble nature. It requires us to put everything in God's hand. It seeks another person's interest over the interests of our own. The meek understand how God wants them to live and interact with others. James 3:13 says, "Who is wise and understanding among you? Let him show it by his good life, by deeds done in humility that comes from wisdom." Great leaders can be meek. Moses was a famous leader, yet known as a humble person. Numbers 12:3 says, "Now the man Moses was very humble, more than all men who were on the face of the earth." We read in Numbers 12, that Moses' authority was challenged by of all people, his brother and sister, Aaron and Miriam. Instead of vigorously defending himself, or launching an attack on Aaron and Miriam, Moses puts his situation in God's hands. God steps in and confirms Moses as His servant and strikes Miriam with leprosy. Instead of gloating, Moses prays for Miriam's healing. Meekness is putting our faith in action with the confident assurance that God is in control. No matter our circumstances, God is working things out for our good. Romans 8:28 says, "And we know that all things work for the good of those who love Him, who have been called according to His purpose." When you put others' interests ahead of your own and allow God to work things out, you will inherit the earth. Jesus said those who are considered last in this world will be first in His kingdom. Matthew 20:16 "So the last will be first, and the first last. For many are called, but few are chosen." One last note about meekness. It should not be used as an excuse to avoid conflict. There are times when it is appropriate to take a stand. God will let you know when that time comes. However, taking a stand does not mean getting even with someone. Trust God for justice. Remember, blessed are the meek.

Prayer: God help me to have a quiet and humble nature, trusting You in all things.

> Matthew 5:6 Blessed are those who hunger and thirst for righteousness, For they shall be filled.

I enjoy watching survivalist shows. The survivalists' ability to survive difficult challenges with just the basic necessities is fascinating. However, at some point in their challenge, hunger and thirst set in and the survivalists drink the nastiest looking water, eat bugs, spiders, rats, snakes, and even tree bark. It proves when you get hungry and thirsty enough, things you would never have considered eating or drinking look enticing to you; such as, eating a rat or drinking muddy, warm water. Fortunately, I have never been this hungry or thirsty. However, Jesus said that just as we hunger and thirst for food and water, we should have a spiritual hunger and thirst for righteousness. What is righteousness? *Merriam-Webster. com* defines righteousness as, acting in accord with divine or moral law: free from guilt or sin. How do we achieve righteousness? Paul said in Romans 3:10, "As it is written, 'There is no one righteous, not even one;'" Without Jesus' death and resurrection, we have no chance at becoming righteous. Fortunately for us, Jesus has just spent the last three verses explaining how to achieve righteousness. It starts by becoming poor in spirit, acknowledging the sin in our lives and our need for God. Secondly, we mourn over our sin and separation from God. Our mourning leads to conviction, recognizing our spiritual poverty and unworthiness before a Holy and Righteous God. Lastly, we take on a spiritual nature of meekness, a quiet and humble nature, requiring us to leave everything in God's hands and seeking another person's interest over our own. Jesus said we should pursue righteousness every day as if we were starving for it. His promise to us is that as we pursue righteousness, we will be filled. But just like the amount and type of food we put into our bodies determines our fullness, so it is with our spiritual life. You can have a spiritual snack just to satisfy your hunger for God, or you can have a meal and be filled with His Spirit. Which do you want with your relationship with Christ? Do you want enough to get by, or do you want all that He has to offer? It is your choice. The menu is before you.

Prayer: God I want to be filled with Your presence, help me to hunger and thirst for righteousness.

A Biblical definition of mercy is not receiving the punishment we deserve for our sins. God demonstrated mercy, by sending His Son to die on the cross, paying the penalty for our sins and saving us from an eternity apart from Him. Paul said in Titus 3:5, "He saved us, not because of righteous things we had done, but because of His mercy..." However, mercy is not limited to God's plan of salvation. Mercy extends to anyone who has the power to help or punish. For example, parents have the responsibility of disciplining their children. Determining how to punish, when to punish, or when to show mercy can be difficult. Growing up, I had my share of well-deserved spankings. My parents were very fair when it came to discipline, but on occasion, my bottom wished they had been a little more merciful. In the Beatitudes, Jesus outlines the character traits of those who are ready for the kingdom of heaven. The traits we have studied so far are the inner traits of a believer. Being merciful is an outward or visible sign that someone believes and trusts in God. Why? Because God is merciful and instructs us to be. The more Christlike we become, the more merciful we are. Being merciful is more than just being kind. Being merciful is extending help to those who can't help themselves; the poor, the sick, the widow, the orphan, the addict, or the prisoner. The list is endless and opportunities are all around us. Jesus speaking in Matthew 25:37,40 said, "Then the righteous will answer Him, 'Lord, when did we see You hungry and feed You, or thirsty and give You something to drink?' The King will reply, 'I tell you the truth, whatever you did for one of the least of these brothers of Mine, you did for Me.'" How merciful are you? Are you caught up in your own life and don't have time for others? If so, you are missing out on the joy that comes with helping someone and God's mercy. Be thankful that you have the opportunity to help others and are not the one who needs help. As Jesus said, "blessed are the merciful."

Prayer: God help me to show mercy to those less fortunate than me.

> *Matthew 5:8 Blessed are the pure in heart, For they shall see God.*

Man has invented a number of medical devices to monitor and keep our hearts in rhythm. Without them, a number of people would have likely died from heart disease. Unfortunately, man has not come up with a solution to help our inner heart problem. Jeremiah 17:9 says, "The heart is deceitful above all things, and desperately wicked; who can know it?" King David understood he had a heart problem after he had sinned by committing adultery with Bathsheba and having her husband Uriah killed in battle. He cried out in Psalms 51:10, "Create in me a clean heart, O God, and renew a steadfast spirit within me." Also, Paul writing in Romans 7:24 said, "O wretched man that I am! Who will deliver me from this body of death?" How are we ever going to see God if we are born with an impure or sinful heart? The answer is Jesus Christ. Jesus came to pay the penalty for our sins and will forgive us if we confess our sins to Him. 1 John 1:9 says, "If we confess our sins, He is faithful and just to forgive us our sins, and to cleanse us from all unrighteousness." A pure heart begins with salvation. It is given to us as a free gift based on our faith in Christ. Secondly, we acknowledge the sin in our life that separates us from God. Thirdly, we confess our sins and are truly sorry that we have allowed them to sever our relationship with God. Lastly, like David, we remain steadfast, not falling back into the same sin. Does that mean I have to be perfect to see God? The short answer is no. No one is perfect. But the purer our heart is, the more we will see Him. But doesn't the Bible say in John 4:24, "God is spirit, and His worshipers must worship in spirit and truth?" How are we going to see God who is a spirit? We are quick to recognize God in the beauty of His creation. However, the benefit of a pure heart is that we recognize God is working in our lives by changing circumstances, making a way where there is no way. Even better, the more we pursue God, the more we see Him and His handiwork.

Prayer: God, please open the eyes of my heart, I want to see You.

> Matthew 5:9 Blessed are the peacemakers, For they shall be called the sons of God.

We are learning in the Beatitudes, that Jesus is instructing us on how a Christian should live. Today, we see that peacemakers are called the sons of God. God is a God of peace. 1 Corinthians 14:33 states, "For God is not a God of disorder but of peace." However, just because I am a peacemaker, it doesn't necessarily mean I am a Christian. We become the sons and daughters of God through our faith in Jesus Christ. Galatians 3:26 says, "You are all sons of God through faith in Christ Jesus." Just as we take on the nature of our earthly fathers, as children of God, we take on the nature of our heavenly Father. A friend of mine was telling me how he had begun to hang up a used paper towel to use later. He didn't realize it until his wife reminded him that his father had hung up paper towels to use again many years ago. My friend was doing the very same thing he had seen his father do. So, it is with our heavenly Father. If we are truly His son or daughter, we are going to imitate Him. What does a peacemaker look like? A peacemaker is one who prays for those they do not like or have had a 'run in' with. A peacemaker is one who tries to build bridges between people, seeking reconciliation. They prefer harmony and unity over discord and strife. They take the first step in trying to restore a relationship. Unfortunately, there are going to be people in your life, whether at work, at school, in your neighborhood, and even in your family that you may not like or they may not like you. You are going to have disagreements. Often times, the disagreements start over something very insignificant and can go one of two ways. The first is that the disagreement is able to be worked out and the relationship is restored. Second, things escalate into a major quarrel where things are said and done in anger. Perhaps you have seen or are even in a situation where this has happened. Family members stop speaking to each other. Neighbors build fences. Churches split. Feelings are hurt. Are you a peacemaker or a troublemaker? Do you try to mend relationships or split them apart? James 3:18 says, "Peacemakers who sow in peace raise a harvest of righteousness." What type of harvest are you raising?

Prayer: God help me to be a peacemaker, I want to be like You.

> Matthew 5:10 *Blessed are those who are persecuted for righteousness' sake, For theirs is the kingdom of heaven.*

Persecution is nothing new. Throughout history, people have been persecuted for their race, their political stance, social status, and religious beliefs. You can make the case that Cain killed his brother Abel as an act of persecution because of Abel's faith in God. Abel who offered God the best portions from the firstborn of his flock was looked on with favor by God. While Cain's offering of some random fruits of the soil, reflected an attitude of a thoughtless and careless offering. Cain was upset because Abel's offering was accepted and his was not. Jesus said, blessed are those who are persecuted for righteousness' sake, or those living a righteous life. Why would anyone want to punish or hurt someone who is living the way God intended? As my pastor recently taught us from Ephesians 6:12, "For our struggle is not against flesh and blood, but against the rulers, against the authorities, against the powers of this dark world and against the spiritual forces of evil in the heavenly realms." Satan and his demons will use every tactic including persecution to turn you away from God. Why are Christians persecuted? *Opendoorsusa.com* provides several reasons. First, there are governments that see Jesus as competition for power, especially in communist run nations like China and North Korea. A dictator or communist government wants complete allegiance to themselves and views a believer's commitment to Jesus Christ as a threat. Secondly, Christianity can conflict with the culture of an area where the worship of an idol, or even some type of demonic practice is common. Thirdly, in several third world countries, organized crime controls the country. A believer standing up for what is right gets in the way of their livelihood and exposes their greed. Lastly, in regions of the world where Islam and Hinduism are the primary religion, Christianity is seen as a threat. In these areas, Christians are threatened, jailed, and even killed. What do all these reasons have in common? It is the very thing that Jesus has been teaching us the last several days. As a follower of Christ, we are called to be different from the world and the world doesn't like it. You may not live in an area where persecution is currently taking place; however, that day may be coming. Be prepared. Pray for those who are being persecuted.

Prayer: God help us to be faithful to You in times of persecution.

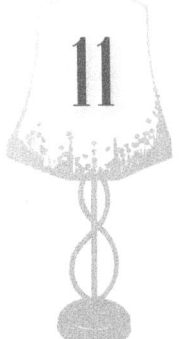

> *Matthew 5:11 Blessed are you when they revile and persecute you, and say all kinds of evil against you falsely for My sake.*

Persecution comes in many different forms, from being slandered, ostracized, having property confiscated, imprisonment, physical harm, and even death. Yesterday, we learned that living a Christlike life makes us different from the world. This difference is seen as a threat to the world's way of life and a main reason Christians are persecuted. Just because you live in an area where Christians are not physically threatened, it doesn't mean that you will escape persecution. Jesus said, "blessed are you when they revile and persecute you, and say all kinds of evil against you falsely for My sake." In other words, be prepared, someone is going to talk harsh to you, twist your words, and speak lies about you because of your faith in Christ. *Merriam-Webster.com* defines revile as, "to use abusive language." It was at a local *Right to Life* event that I witnessed first-hand the word revile put into action. Typically, I am not one who likes to venture very far out of their comfort zone. However, one Sunday afternoon, the churches in our area had planned a *Right to Life* rally by lining up on several major roadways within our city, peacefully displaying signs supporting the life of an unborn child. Vivian and I volunteered and took our place along with several hundred other people on Oleander Drive. As cars passed by, some were supportive and waved. Others shouted profanity and flashed obscene gestures. It wasn't difficult to pick out the ones who were just making fun of us from the ones who were truly angry of our support for the life of an unborn child. I also learned that when you take a stand for a cause opposite of what the world supports, people will "say all kinds of evil against you." You become a target of their hatred and frustration. Let someone speak the truth in love about God's word on homosexuality. That person instantly becomes a bigoted, homophobic, intolerant target of that community and the world in general. Your first reaction may be to stay quiet avoiding controversy and conflict. That may work for a while, but I also know that God will give you opportunities to stand for the truth of His word. Are you ready for the blessing of taking the heat that goes with speaking truth? Trust God, it is worth it.

Prayer: God help me to stand firm in the truth of Your Word.

> *Matthew 5:13 You are the salt of the earth; but if the salt loses its flavor, how shall it be seasoned? It is then good for nothing but to be thrown out and trampled underfoot by men.*

If you have ever had the pleasure of eating country ham, the first thing you notice is the saltiness of the meat. Why? Because country hams are hung up to dry, wrapped in a salt mixture. This process of curing meat has been around for thousands of years. Before refrigeration, meat had to be cured in salt or dried out into strips called jerky to prevent it from spoiling. Salt has many other uses. Before medical advances, salt was poured into wounds to prevent infection and stop bleeding. It also is used to create thirst and flavor food. In Jesus' day, salt was mined from the Dead Sea and wasn't as plentiful and pure as the salt we use. Today, salt can be found on every home and restaurant table. Jesus said that we (His followers) are the salt of the earth. Let's take a closer look at a couple of properties of salt to see how our role as Christians compare. Salt is a preservative. We live in world where sin is rampant. Psalm 14:3 says, "All have turned aside, they have together become corrupt; there is no one who does good, not even one." As followers of Christ, we are to preserve or keep ourselves and others from allowing the sin that is all around to infiltrate our lives. We are also called to preserve and spread the message of Christ. Salt adds flavor. Colossians 4:6 says, "Let your conversation be always full of grace, seasoned with salt, so that you may know how to answer everyone." In other words, our conversations should have a different flavor from the conversations of the world. They should be flavored with truth, encouragement, and life. Lastly, salt heals and prevents infection. Psalm 147:3 says, "He heals the brokenhearted and binds up their wounds." Jesus is calling us to minister to those who have lost hope. Just as salt heals wounds, He wants us to care for those who are hurting and lost. We are to bind up the wounds of broken relationships, discouragement, and hopelessness. Jesus concluded by saying that salt can lose its flavor and that flavorless salt has no value. Are you a "salty" Christian, or has your salt lost its flavor? If that is the case, take time today to renew your relationship with Jesus. Get your saltiness back.

Prayer: God, help me to live a salty life.

> Matthew 5:16 Let your light so shine before men, that they may see your good works and glorify your Father in heaven.

One of my favorite songs as a child growing up in church was, "This Little Light of Mine." The lyrics are very simple, but have a great message of living for Jesus. We have taught this song to our grandchildren who especially love the verse that says, "Don't let Satan blow it out! I'm going to let it shine." When we get to the part that says "blow it out," everyone begins to blow like they are blowing out a birthday candle. This song is not just for children. The last verse says, "Let it shine till Jesus, comes, I'm going to let it shine." We should be shining our light for Jesus throughout our entire life. What is the value of light? Go into a room without windows, close the door and cut off the light and you will quickly find out. Without light, there is complete darkness. Without light, you are cautious to move around for fear of running into something. Without light, there is no path to follow. Jesus said in John 8:12, "I am the light of the world. Whoever follows Me will never walk in darkness, but will have the light of life." Jesus said He is the light of the world. He lights the way through the darkness. In Christ, we have that light living within us. What are you going to do with His light? Are you going to hide it under a bushel or are you going to lift it up for all to see? Jesus said, that our light shines through our good works. How we live and act around others is our light. Paul said in Philippians 2:14-15, "Do all things without grumbling or disputing, that you may be blameless and innocent, children of God without blemish in the midst of a crooked and twisted generation, among whom you shine as lights in the world." Our light is going to be very dim if we are not living any different from the world. We should be gracious and caring with our words and sprinkle in good deeds along the way. Remember our purpose for doing good works is so that people would be able to see their way to God and give their life to Him. We shine so that people see God, not us.

Prayer: God, help me to shine Your light through my life each day.

> *Matthew 5:23–24 Therefore if you bring your gift to the altar, and there remember that your brother has something against you, leave your gift there before the altar, and go your way. First be reconciled to your brother, and then come and offer your gift.*

Jesus has a way of pointing out the issues of the heart. In Matthew 5:22, He said, "But I tell you that anyone who is angry with his brother will be subject to judgement. Again, anyone who says to his brother, 'Raca' is answerable to the Sanhedrin. But anyone who says, 'You fool!' will be in danger of the fire of hell." Jesus is speaking about the importance of our thoughts toward someone else. The path of anger, hatred, and name calling is sin just as murder is a sin. If we are to be the peacemakers as Jesus said in Matthew 5:9, then we have to be careful of our attitudes towards others. However, in today's verse, Jesus doesn't say "if you have something against your brother," instead He says, "if your brother has something against you," moving the conversation to our actions that may have damaged the relationship. How often has a careless word, or comment made in anger, ruined a relationship? How often has a bad choice split a family? Whatever the reason, the relationship has been damaged and a wedge has come between you. Jesus said that it was more important to try to restore that relationship than to offer sacrifices to God. He is prioritizing reconciliation, restoration and forgiveness over offering sacrifices. Isn't offering sacrifices an Old Testament requirement? Although we do not offer sacrifices, we have our own set of religious activities that are just as important. We go to church, we pray, we give, we study God's word, we tell others about Jesus, and we ask God for His blessings and His forgiveness. Do we really expect God to hear us, answer our prayers, forgive our sins, and shower us with blessings all the while we have left a trail of broken relationships behind us? How can we represent Christ, when we are the cause of hurt in someone's life? Jesus said, "go make it right, then come to Me." Is there someone who comes to mind that you need to mend a relationship with? It could be an old friend, a family member, or even someone at church. Take the time today to heal that relationship. If that person is not quite ready to forgive and move forward, pray for them and seek reconciliation as God leads you.

Prayer: God point out the relationships that I need to mend.

> Matthew 5:30 And if your right hand causes you to sin, cut it off and cast it from you; for it is more profitable for your that one of your members perish, than for your whole body to be cast into hell.

I don't ever recall seeing anyone who has cut their right hand off to prevent them from sinning. If Jesus had meant this literally, most every Christian would be one-handed following this command. To better understand Jesus' intent, we need to start reading at Matthew 5:27. There, Jesus begins talking about adultery and quotes the seventh commandment found in Exodus 20:14, "You shall not commit adultery." However, Jesus tears down another wall by saying, "But I tell you that anyone who looks at a woman lustfully has already committed adultery with her in his heart." It is easy to hide our true thoughts from the people around us, but not from God. Jesus is letting us know that it is not alright to think and act out in our minds adulterous thoughts even though we may never follow through with them. That is why it is so important to put up a guard to the things we allow into our minds. Jesus said in Matthew 15:19, "For out of the heart come evil thoughts, murder, adultery, sexual immorality, theft, false testimony, slander." Bad actions start from bad thoughts. If you are like me, it is not easy to keep these thoughts away. We are bombarded by sexual images every day on TV, online, and in social media. How do we do it? Do we pluck our eye out or cut our hand off? Of course not, but it does take a lot of effort and can be challenging. The first step is to pray and ask God's forgiveness and help. Ask Him to point out the areas of your temptation. Is it places you go, music you listen to, websites you look at, TV shows and movies you watch, or all of the above? Whatever it takes, you have to find a way to separate yourself from them. I can tell you from experience, just saying, 'I will never do that again,' doesn't work. Satan has a way of putting those things within easy reach. Replace the things you were looking at with something more appropriate. Try streaming options that include faith-based movies. Rightnow media and other Christian apps are a great source of uplifting and encouraging material. Pick up and read a book by a Christian author and limit your social media time.

Prayer: As David said in Psalm 51:10, "Create in me a pure heart, O God, and renew a steadfast spirit with me."

> Matthew 5:32 But I say to you that whoever divorces his wife for any reason except sexual immorality causes her to commit adultery; and whoever marries a woman who is divorced commits adultery.

According to *Surviveddivorce.com*, the most common reasons for divorce are financial issues, lack of intimacy, infidelity, abuse, and lack of compatibility. They also noted that the divorce rate has fallen from around 50% of marriages to 40%. They attribute the decline to two factors. First, people are waiting longer to get married and are making better decisions. Second, more couples are now choosing to live together and have a family without getting married. Divorce is nothing new. Moses wrote about issuing a certificate of divorce in Deuteronomy 24:1-4. Jesus referenced this scripture in the preceding verse in Matthew 5:31. However, He made it clear that He doesn't condone divorce. According to Jesus, marriage is a covenant between husband and wife. A covenant is more than just an agreement, or even contract. A covenant is a bond between two people. Jesus speaking in Matthew 19:4 said, "So they are no longer two, but one. Therefore what God has joined together, let not man separate." Vivian and I were married by her grandfather, Rev. Leonard B. Woodall who had a very commanding voice. When he got to the part of quoting Matthew 19:4 in our wedding, he added additional emphasis. I got the message, and thankfully we have been married 41 years. However, we are not untouched by divorce. We have witnessed it firsthand with friends, family, and neighbors. Divorce is painful. It affects not only the husband and wife, but children, parents and friends. Scars of divorce can last a lifetime and impact the next generation. Sadly, divorce seems to be the first answer to marital problems, instead of the last resort. Marriage is not easy. Over the 41 years of our marriage there have times when divorce seemed possible. Selfish choices, the busyness of jobs, children, and church, a poor choice of words, and a lack of communication took a toll on our marriage. Thankfully, we were able to work through those times and love each other more than when we first married. You may be in a marriage that is not going well and considering divorce right now. Just as it was in Jesus' day, obtaining a divorce is easy. Get a lawyer, sign a few documents, determine custody of the children, split up the assets and move on. It takes hard work, commitment, and perseverance to save a marriage. I can tell you it is worth it.

Prayer: God protect my marriage and help me do what it takes to make it better.

> Matthew 5:37 But let your "Yes" be "Yes," and your "No" be No."
> For whatever is more than these is from the evil one.

Lonesome Dove, starring Tommy Lee Jones and Robert Duvall is one of my all-time favorite western movies. The story revolves around several retired Texas Rangers driving a herd of cattle from Texas to Montana. In the story, Captain Woodrow Call makes a promise to the dying Augustus McCrae that he would take Augustus' body back to Texas from Montana and bury him by an orchard near San Antonio. Augustus dies in the dead of winter, so they put his body on ice until spring. When spring arrives, Captain Call packs the body in salt and charcoal, loads the coffin on a wagon and heads south towards Texas on a 1,500-mile trip. Needless to say, there were numerous obstacles that Captain Call encountered along the way. As he was burying Augustus, Captain Call said the following, "Well, Gus; there you go. I guess that will teach me to be more careful about what I promise people in the future." What a lesson on keeping a promise. Everyone can probably think back in their life to promises kept and unkept. For those unkept, I am sure there were very good reasons why they weren't. If you are like me, in many cases it was just that something better came along and took priority over the promise I had made. Although Lonesome Dove is just a fictional story, I often wonder if I would have kept the promise to make that trip. It is for certain that Augustus would have never known. It all comes down to what Jesus is saying in today's verse, "let your yes be yes, and your no be no." Are you a person of your word? When I was growing up, to make sure a person was telling the truth, someone say, "swear on a stack of Bibles." Unfortunately, I don't know if that would make any difference these days. Our yes and no has become a convenient means of getting what we want, instead of fulfilling a commitment. Proverbs 25:14 says, "Like clouds and wind without rain is a man who boasts of gifts he does not give." Are you as empty as a rainless cloud? Jesus can change that. Start by not making promises you don't intend to keep and keeping the promises you make. Let your yes be yes and your no be no.

Prayer: God help me to let my yes be yes and my no be no.

> *Matthew 5:39 But I tell you not to resist an evil person. But whoever slaps you on your right cheek, turn the other to him also.*

Did you know that slapping someone on the cheek has now become a sport? Slap fighting is an organized event, where two people stand across a table and take turns slapping each other. Obviously, this is not what Jesus meant by turning the other cheek. Also, turning the other cheek doesn't mean we can't defend ourselves. In Luke 22:36 Jesus tells the disciples to sell their cloak to buy a sword. Let's dig deeper into what Jesus is teaching here. In verse 38, Jesus said, "You have heard it said, 'Eye for eye, and tooth for tooth.'" He is referring to Exodus 21:23-25, The Law of Retaliation, given as a rule to help regulate the decisions of a judge or magistrate. This law was designed to prevent excessive punishment. Jesus is primarily talking to the Pharisees who had twisted the meaning of this law to personally seek revenge on someone. Jesus uses an example of a backhanded slap, which is meant as an insult. (A right-handed person slapping someone on the right cheek.) Several verses earlier, Jesus said in Matthew 5:11, "Blessed are you when they revile and persecute you, and say all kinds of evil against you falsely for My sake." Today, He is telling us how to respond to that persecution. Jesus said we are to turn the other cheek. The Sunday that Vivian and I were standing on the side of the road, supporting the Right to Life cause, my sinful nature wanted to take over and return the same gestures back to those passing by shouting obscenities at us. Putting our faith in action is not easy. Human nature wants to get even, and payback evil for evil. Jesus said, "let it go." Paul said in Romans 12:19-20, "Do not take revenge, my friends, but leave room for God's wrath, for it is written: 'It is Mine to avenge; I will repay,' says the Lord. On the contrary: 'If your enemy is hungry, feed him; if he is thirsty, give him something to drink. In doing this, you will heap burning coals on his head.'" When you face insults and unfair treatment, hang on and trust God. Don't return evil for evil. It may make you feel better in the short term, but it is not God's way. Turn the other cheek.

Prayer: God give me the patience and determination to turn the other cheek when faced with persecution, unfair treatment, and insults.

> *Matthew 5:41 And whoever compels you to go one mile, go with him two.*

Vivian and I attend Second Mile Church in Wilmington, NC, which was birthed out of this verse. Our Pastor, Adam Mew, and his family moved from Tennessee to Wilmington following the call of God to plant a church here. It was by God's providence that we met Pastor Adam and got involved. Leaving our comfortable pews, we set out to support this brand-new church. Our vision statement reads, "Jesus walked the first mile by coming to earth as the Son of God to live among us. That was motivated by law. He went the second mile by dying on the cross for our sin. He was resurrected from the dead overcoming death, hell, and the grave so that we could have life eternally. That was motivated by love. When we meet Jesus at His second mile, we can start living ours. One step into the second mile is when friendships grow deeper, God is revealed in a bigger way, and lives become more full." Initially I thought going the second mile was a nice catch phrase to get people's attention. However, over the last two years, I have learned that the second mile is where God really begins to work in your life. Jesus said, "if someone forces you to go one mile go with them two." In Jesus' day, a Roman soldier could grab anyone by law and make them carry his backpack one mile. The Jews hated this law. They saw it as demeaning, an inconvenience, and an interruption to their lives. They would drop the pack exactly at one mile and not take another step. Where are you in your walk with Christ? Are you on the first mile just doing what is required? Not to say the first mile is easy. Try walking a mile if you have not walked more than a block at a time. The second mile is by choice, but only made possible by finishing the first mile. The second mile is rewarding. It has been amazing to watch God work in our lives. He had given us opportunity upon opportunity and blessings. The second mile is hard work. There have been times when we have gotten weary, but God refreshes us. There are times when the second mile seems long, but God helps us persevere. Take a step of faith into the second mile, it is worth it.

Prayer: God help me to walk the second mile obediently with You.

> *Matthew 5:44 But I say to you, love your enemies, bless those who curse you, do good to those who hate you, and pray for those who spitefully use you and persecute you.*

The name Jim Elliott meant nothing to me until his story was shared at our Men's Bible Study one evening. Jim Elliott was a missionary in Ecuador in the 1950's. He and his wife, Elizabeth, met in college and moved to Ecuador to serve there. While there, Jim felt God call him to take the gospel to the Huaorani Indians who lived deeper into the interior of Ecuador. The Huaorani's were known as a very primitive and savage tribe. Leaving his wife and 10-month-old daughter behind, Jim and four other missionaries traveled to the Huaorani's village. Sadly, Jim and his companions were speared to death by the Huaorani's. However, Jim's death is not the end of the story, but the beginning. Elizabeth remained in Ecuador with her small child determined to bring the gospel to those who killed her husband. Approximately three years after Jim's death, Elizabeth and several others had an opportunity to visit the Huaorani Tribe. Not knowing their fate, Elizabeth and her three-year-old daughter set out on a two-day trip into the jungle. Elizabeth and the others were greeted by friendly Huaorani's and were able to make a difference in the lives of that village. Jim and Elizabeth's story is one of loving those who hate you. No one would have blamed Elizabeth for packing up and heading home after her husband's death. However, Elizabeth was quoted as saying, "As long as this is what the Lord requires of me, all else is irrelevant."[1] What a testimony of faith and obedience to God's word. In a world where we plan how to get even with someone who has wronged us, God says love your enemies. In a world where people hate you, curse you, and use you, God says to do good and pray for them. God's way requires faith, courage, and strength. Loving those who hate us is how we demonstrate that we belong to Him. I sometimes think to myself "But God, it is not easy. Do you know what they have done to me?" Jesus replies, "do you know what they did to Me?" As He was hanging on the cross, Jesus said, "Father forgive them, for they do not know what they do." Jesus set the example for us to follow. As Elizabeth Elliott said, "all else is irrelevant."

Prayer: God, please change my attitude towards those who hate me.

> *Matthew 6:1 Take heed that you do not do your charitable deeds before men, to be seen by them. Otherwise you have no reward from your Father in heaven.*

Early in my career with CP&L, TQM (Total Quality Management) was the latest and greatest management tool for improving work processes and overall work quality. In TQM, we learned there are four ways to complete a task. 1. Doing the wrong things the wrong way. 2. Doing the wrong things the right way. 3. Doing the right things the wrong way. 4. Doing the right things the right way. Our goal was for employees to evaluate what they were doing and how they were doing it to ensure they were efficient and productive. Employees were rewarded for their efforts. The awards were an acknowledgement of meeting goals and an incentive to continually 'raise the bar'. Jesus is introducing this TQM concept in today's verse. Charitable deeds are a good thing that should be done. However, the manner in which we do them has kingdom consequences. We called it, "Right things/Right." Jesus always seems to focus on doing things the right way. He looks at our heart and the motivation behind our actions. In this verse, Jesus has also given us three important lessons about giving. First, Jesus did not say "if you give", but "when you give." As a Christian, we are expected to give. Our first priority in giving should be our tithes and offering in support of the work of the church. Malachi 3:10 says, "Bring the full tithe into the storehouse, that there may be food in My house. And thereby put Me to the test, says the Lord of hosts, if I will not open the windows of heaven for you and pour down for you a blessing until there is no more need." Secondly, we should give to help others. Proverbs 19:17 states, "Whoever is generous to the poor lends to the Lord, and He will repay him for his deed." And lastly, our giving should not be done with a motivation of receiving recognition and praise from others but to glorify God and motivate others to follow our example. 2 Corinthians 9:8 says, "And God is able to make all grace abound to you, so that in all things at all times, having all that you need, you will abound in every good work." When done with the right motives, God rewards our generosity, so that we can continue to help others.

Prayer: God, help me to give generously with the right attitude.

> *Matthew 6:6 But when you pray, go into your room, and when you have shut your door, pray to your Father who sees in secret and will reward you openly.*

Just as we learned yesterday that giving is not optional, neither is prayer. Jesus said, "But when you pray," not "if you pray." Because prayer is so vital to our relationship with God, we are going to spend several days learning more about it. In Jesus' day, the Pharisees were committed to praying four times per day, at six, nine, twelve, and three o'clock.[2] On the surface, it seems like they had a very good prayer life. I try to pray twice a day, in the morning and at bedtime, with some shorter prayers mixed in throughout the day. I should be setting aside more time for prayer because the benefits are immeasurable. However, in the case of the Pharisees, they seemed to position themselves in the most public places when it came time to pray so they would be seen. Their purpose for praying was more to be recognized as a religious person rather than their love and devotion to God. Jesus said in verse 5, "...Assuredly, I say to you, they have their reward." Jesus is saying, the only answer to their prayer is the recognition from others they are seeking, because God has not heard them. As with giving, prayer is about our heart. Growing up in church, I heard some of the most eloquent prayers, packed with "Thee's and Thou's" from the King James Version Bible. I wished I could learn how to pray like that. However, I can't tell you if those prayers were sincere or just spoken to be heard. Only God and the person praying knows. There are times you may be asked to pray corporately, and that is okay. Just be sincere in your prayer. However, Jesus said when you pray, go to a quiet place to do so. First, a quiet place removes any distractions that would interfere with our time with God. Second, we get the privilege of being in the presence of our heavenly Father. In His presence is peace from the 'storms' of life that have tossed us around. Third, it is during those times that God meets our needs and answers our prayers. Jeremiah 33:3 says, "Call to Me and I will answer you and tell you great and unsearchable things you do not know." Are you getting alone with God each day?

Prayer: God help me to find a quiet place from the world's distractions to pray.

> Matthew 6:7 And when you pray, do not use vain repetitions as the heathen do. For they think that they will be heard for their many words.

One of the first prayers my parents taught me as a child was, "Now I lay me down to sleep, I pray the Lord my soul to keep. If I should die before I wake, I pray the Lord my soul to take." A different version of this prayer ends with, "Angels watch me through the night, and wake me with the morning light." Is Jesus saying we shouldn't be teaching our children bedtime prayers? Of course not. Jesus is speaking about using repetitious words and chants that have no meaning or reverence for God behind them. Inc.com lists "20 Awesome chants that will radically improve your life." They report that the most famous chant in the world is the Compassionate Buddha, "Om Mani Padme Hum," which is translated to "Hail to the jewel in the lotus." This chant is supposed to calm fears, soothe concerns and heal broken hearts. All I can say to that is, good luck. That chant may make your mind go numb from repeating it over and over, but only God can calm fears, soothe concerns and heal broken hearts. For our prayers to be heard, Jesus is teaching us how to pray, by starting with how not to pray. In Jesus' day pagan worship was very common. Their prayers contained repetitious chants and calls to their gods trying to get their attention. Jesus said that we don't have to repeat a bunch of mindless words for God to hear us when we pray. Jeremiah 29:12-13 says, "Then you will call on Me and come and pray to Me, and I will listen to you. You will seek Me and find Me when you seek Me with all your heart." God promises to hear and listen to our prayers with one condition, that our hearts are sincere in seeking Him. I could pray and ask God to forgive me of a particular sin in my life. However, God doesn't hear my prayer, when in the back of my mind, I am planning to do the very thing I am asking forgiveness for as soon as the prayer is over. Why? Because there is no sincerity in my prayer. Are your prayers filled with insincere, repetitious, mindless words just to fill up your prayer time? If so, God is not listening and you are wasting your time. Pray to Him with a sincere heart.

Prayer: God help my prayer time with You to be purposeful.

> *Matthew 6:9: In this manner, therefore pray: "Our Father in heaven, hallowed be Your name."*

Jesus taught us that our prayers should be different from the pagans and not a series of repetitious chants. He said, this is how you should pray, "Our Father in heaven..." First, we are to acknowledge God as our heavenly Father. Not only is God our creator, our provider, and our healer, He is most importantly our Father. 2 Corinthians 6:18 says, "I will be a Father to you, and you will be My sons and daughters, says the Lord Almighty." As His children, our desire should be to have a loving relationship with our heavenly Father. The Bible tells us that He loves us and wants the best for us. 1 John 3:1 says, "How great is the love the Father has lavished on us, that we should be called children of God." An article entitled, *The Importance of a Father in a Child's Life* in *www.pediatricsoffranklin.com*, states that "fathers are pillars in the development of a child's emotional well-being. Children look to their fathers to lay down the rules and enforce them. They also look to their fathers to provide a feeling of security, both physical and emotional. Studies have shown that a supportive father instills an overall sense of well-being and self-confidence." Imagine the impact a close relationship with your Heavenly Father would have. What are you missing out on because of a lukewarm relationship with God? Next Jesus said God's name is "hallowed," which means greatly revered and honored.[3] In our prayers, we should acknowledge that God's name is a holy name, one that should be revered, honored and respected. Sadly, today the names of God and Jesus are used in every way imaginable. They roll off our lips as swear words without any thought of reverence or respect. The third commandment says, "You shall not take the name of the Lord our God in vain..." We may be careful to obey this commandment by not using the Lord's name flippantly in our conversations or as a swear word; but, how are we approaching God in our prayers? Are we taking the time to give Him honor and reverence for who He is, or are we jumping into our wish list of requests for Him to answer? Is this not taking His name in vain as well? Take time at the beginning of your prayers to give honor and glory to your heavenly Father.

Prayer: God, how majestic is Your name in all the earth.

> *Matthew 6:10 Your kingdom come. Your will be done on earth as it is in heaven.*

After acknowledging God as our Heavenly Father and giving Him the glory and honor due, we are to pray for God's will to be done here on earth. But what is God's will and how do we know what to pray for? First, praying God's will be done is acknowledging that God is sovereign and in control. It also means that we accept God's plan, no matter the circumstances as right and good for us. Paul said in Romans 8:28, "And we know that all things work together for good to those who love God, to those who are called according to His purpose." Bad choices may not have been God's will for our lives; however, He can work them out for our good. The Bible has a lot to say about God's will. Romans 12:2 tells us how to know God's will for our lives. "And do not be conformed to this world, but be transformed by the renewing of your mind, that you may prove what is that good and acceptable and perfect will of God." We are to not think like the world, but renew our minds in the word of God to understand His perfect will for us. 1 Thessalonians 5:16-18 says, "Rejoice always, pray without ceasing, in everything give thanks; for this is the will of God in Christ Jesus for you." Even when we are having a bad day, we are to rejoice and give thanks for all things. Also in 1 Thessalonians 4:3-4, Paul writes, "It is God's will that you should be sanctified: that you should avoid sexual immorality; that each of you should learn to control his own body in a way that is holy and honorable." Another term for sanctified is "set apart." As a Christian, the way we live should be different from the way people who don't know God. Paul said it this way in Ephesians 5:15-18. "Be very careful, then, how you live – not as unwise but as wise, making the most of every opportunity, because the days are evil. Therefore do not be foolish, but understand what the Lord's will is. Do not get drunk on wine, which leads to debauchery. Instead, be filled with the Spirit." Praying for God's will on earth starts with you and I allowing His Spirit to lead us each day.

Prayer: Father, Your will be done on earth as it is in heaven.

> *Matthew 6:11 Give us this day our daily bread.*

Over the last several years, I have come to understand how important this short prayer can be and that our daily bread shouldn't be taken for granted. Since the Covid Pandemic, one crisis after another has led to food shortages and rising costs. In 2021, it was supply chain issues which led to shortages of all types of consumer products. In early 2022, it was a severe shortage in baby formula brought on by a major recall. Later in 2022, we began to feel the pinch of record inflation. The Bureau of Labor Statistics reported that, "over the 12 months ended June 2022, the price for food increased 10.4%, the largest increase since 1981 and energy prices rose 41.6%, the largest increase since 1980."[4] These are not the only areas affected by record inflation. The cost of everything has gone up, putting a strain on family budgets. For example, the same box of cereal I have eaten for the last several years increased in price $3.00 from one visit to the grocery store to the next. I had always thought that famine was a lack of rain to produce food. However, through this I have learned that famine can come in distribution breakdowns, the high cost of food, and a lack of income to pay for it. But most importantly, I have also learned that God provides no matter the circumstances. In 1 Kings 17:7-16, we find the story of Elijah with a widow and her son who were living in a time of severe famine. Elijah found the widow gathering sticks to cook the last bit of flour she had. Elijah told her to make a small cake of bread for him first, and then to make something for herself and her son. His request came with a promise that God would not let the jar of flour be used up and the jug of oil would not run dry until the Lord sent rain back to the land. She trusted God and the flour and oil never ran out. When we ask God for our daily bread, we are not asking for tomorrow's supply, only today's. The widow did not scoop out the flour to bake bread for tomorrow, just today. Like the widow and her son, God will supply your needs no matter the circumstances. Do you trust Him to provide your daily bread?

Prayer: God, thank You for supplying our daily bread.

> *Matthew 6:12 And forgive us our debts, as we forgive our debtors.*

Before we can learn how to forgive others, it is important to understand God's forgiveness to us. When you accepted Jesus Christ as your Lord and Savior, all your sins were forgiven at that moment. Colossians 2:13 says, "And you, being dead in your trespasses (sins) and the uncircumcision of your flesh, He has made alive together with Him, having forgiven you all trespasses (sins)." As a Christian we become a new person in Christ, leaving behind our past of sin and rebellion against God. 2 Corinthians 5:17 says, "Therefore, if anyone is in Christ, he is a new creation; the old has gone, the new has come!" If all our sins were forgiven and we are a new person in Christ, then why do we need to ask God to continue to forgive us? The answer is pretty simple, we still sin. Paul said in Romans 7:15, "I do not understand what I do. For what I want to do I do not do, but what I hate to do." Thanks be to God that sins committed after receiving Christ do not take away our salvation; but they will hamper our relationship with God. For example, over the 41 years of our marriage, there have been a few times when I may have done something which hurt Vivian's feelings. Sometimes I knew what I had done, and other times I didn't have a clue. However, until I recognized what I had done, apologized, and asked her forgiveness, our relationship just wasn't right. The same is with God. Sin is rebellion against God and separates us from a close relationship with Him. Just as my relationship with Vivian wasn't right, so does my relationship with God suffers because of sin. Recognizing our sins and asking God to forgive us restores our relationship with Him. Proverbs 28:13 says, "He who conceals his sins, does not prosper, but whoever confesses and renounces them finds mercy." However, in teaching us how to pray, Jesus adds another element to forgiveness. We are to ask God to forgive us in the same manner we forgive others. Is Jesus saying, we have to forgive others for our sins to be forgiven? Stay tuned, we will dive deeper into forgiveness on Day 29. Today it is important to understand that God is merciful and forgives all our sins if we ask Him to.

Prayer: God, please forgive me of my sin of _____.

> *Matthew 6:13 And do not lead us into temptation, but deliver us from the evil one. For Yours is the kingdom and the power and the glory forever. Amen.*

I'm confused. Doesn't James 1:13-14 say, "When tempted, no one should say, 'God is tempting me.' For God cannot be tempted by evil, nor does He tempt anyone; but each one is tempted when, by his own evil desire, he is dragged away and enticed." If God is not the source of temptation, who is and why are we asking God to not be led into it? In Luke 22:31 we read that Satan asked God permission to test the disciples, hoping to destroy their faith and ruin the ministry God had in store for them. Also, in Job 1:8-11, and Job 2:3-6, we read where Satan sought permission to put Job to the test to curse God by taking everything Job owned and ruining his health. Even Job's wife didn't help matters by saying, "Are you still holding on to your integrity? Curse God and die." (Job 2:9) Through these examples, we can understand that Satan is the source of our temptation. And quite often, Satan uses other people to set his trap. The good news is that Satan is under God's authority and God puts limits on what he can and cannot do. 1 Corinthians 10:13 says, "No temptation has seized you except what is common to man. And God is faithful; He will not let you be tempted beyond what you can bear. But when you are tempted, He will also provide a way out so that you can stand up under it." I have found this verse to be true in my life. However, there have been times when I didn't take the way out and suffered the consequences of falling to temptation. I have also learned that thinking my relationship with God is strong and secure without daily asking God to deliver me from the evil one is a recipe for failure. On my own, I can't fight the pull of temptation. Satan knows the right buttons to push to entice me into falling into sin. 1 Peter 5:8 says, "Be self-controlled and alert. Your enemy the devil prowls around like a roaring lion, looking for someone to devour." The only way to win against the devil is to be alert and seek God each day, asking Him to deliver you from the evil one. Trust God's word, resist the devil and his schemes.

Prayer: God, please lead me not into temptation and deliver me from the evil one.

> Matthew 6:14-15 *For if you forgive men their trespasses, your heavenly Father will also forgive you. But if you do not forgive men of their trespasses, neither will your Father forgive your trespasses.*

We learned on Day 27 that our sins were forgiven when we accepted Jesus Christ as our Lord and Savior. The slate of past sins was wiped clean and we became a new person in Christ. Unfortunately, we are still tempted to sin, and that is why Jesus taught us to pray, "Lead us not into temptation, but deliver us from the evil one." When we fall to temptation, our relationship with God becomes strained and we need His forgiveness. In today's verse, Jesus tells us that God's forgiveness of us is dependent on how we forgive others. Why should that matter? First, an important part of our relationship with God is to strive to become more like Him each day. Ephesians 5:1 says, "Be imitators of God, therefore, as dearly loved children." We also know that God forgave all our transgressions when we asked Him into our life. Ephesians 2:4 says, "But because of His great love for us, God who is rich in mercy, made us alive with Christ even when we were dead in transgressions. It is by grace you have been saved." Secondly, forgiveness heals. What exactly is forgiveness and how does it heal? *Christianity.com* defines forgiveness as "to pardon, give up resentment, and grant relief to an offender." Can I tell you that some offenses are easier to forgive than others and there are some that may take years to get beyond. I recall a time in my life when I was praying for God's judgement on someone instead of praying for God to help me forgive them. God convicted me of my attitude and turned my prayers around. Unforgiveness is like cancer. If left untreated, it will eat you up on the inside, causing a lack of sleep, stress, worry, anxiety, bitterness, and broken relationships. Forgiveness heals, brings peace back to your life, and restores your relationship with God. Lastly, why should a perfect God forgive me of the very thoughts of resentment, bitterness, anger, hatred, and revenge I am harboring towards someone that I do not want to let go of? Unless I truly repent, which is a complete change of mind, I am not looking for forgiveness. Is there someone in your life that you are finding hard to forgive? Ask God to teach you how to forgive as He forgave you. Enjoy the freedom and peace He gives you.

Prayer: God teach me how to forgive as You forgave me.

> *Matthew 6:17 But you, when you fast, anoint your head and wash your face.*

Is fasting incorporated into your pursuit of God? The way Jesus speaks about fasting in today's verse, He assumes it is. In his book, *The Fasting Edge*, Jentezen Franklin writes, "Fasting is not a requirement. Fasting is a choice. Whenever a believer chooses to begin a spiritual fast for one day or several days, he or she makes a choice to break out of the routine in order to draw closer to God."[5] Many churches will commit to a 21 day fast in January of each year. However, it doesn't matter when you choose to fast. Once you decide, it is important to have a purpose for your fasting. Fasting is not about losing weight. If that is your purpose, then go on a diet. Dieting is much easier. The last 20+ years, Vivian and I have participated in some type of fast in January. Our purpose for fasting is for God to prepare us for the upcoming year and to ask Him to intervene in the lives of our family. We write out a list of specific needs that we pray and fast over. The list should be things that are in accordance to God's will. Fasting and praying that God will provide you a new car could be appropriate if yours is on its last mile. However, if your purpose for a new car is to one up your neighbor, I don't think God would honor that request. Once you decide your purpose for fasting, you need to determine what you are fasting. I can tell you from experience, fasting is not easy no matter what you decide to fast. Perhaps the most popular fast is the "Daniel Fast," where meat, dairy, alcohol, and other rich foods are passed up for vegetables and water. If you have a sweet tooth like mine, giving up sweets can be monumental. Other fasts include social media, television, and movies. Most importantly, fasting works. It puts our dependence on God and draws us closer to Him. It also takes our attention off food and directs it to the things that are important in our life. Lastly, God rewards our fasting by answering our prayers in ways we never thought imaginable. Get closer to God, add fasting to your walk with Him.

Prayer: God help me to be purposeful in my fasting and prayer.

> Matthew 6:19 Do not lay up for yourselves treasures on earth, where moth and rust destroy and where thieves break in and steal.

During the year 2020 when the Covid virus was rampant, of all things, having enough toilet paper was a top priority. Shipments of toilet paper were unpredictable and whenever a new shipment arrived, people would line up to buy as much as the store would allow. I admit, Vivian and I felt more comfortable knowing we had a couple of extra rolls on hand. Covid taught me a lot about human nature. Many of us are hoarders, especially if there is a hint of something not being available. Let someone start a rumor of a shortage on a particular product, and the panic begins. I am certain Jesus is not talking about storing up toilet paper in today's verse. However, He is touching on an area where we as a nation have a problem; a selfish accumulation of wealth. First, let's clarify what Jesus is not saying. It is okay to plan for retirement. Solomon speaking about the ant in Proverbs 6:8 says, "Yet it stores its provisions in summer and gathers its food at harvest." Even ants plan ahead and store what they need for the future. It is also okay to be wealthy. Proverbs 10:22 says, "The blessing of the Lord brings wealth, and He adds no trouble to it." The problem with many of our material blessings is that we become too attached to them and hoard them up for ourselves. However, they can disappear in a moment. Ask anyone whose 401k was decimated by the collapse of the stock market in 2022. In an instant, your wealth and possessions can be gone. However, Jesus said to lay up treasures in heaven that cannot be taken away. What are heavenly treasures? Heavenly treasures are helping others with the right motive in mind. It is being the hands and feet of Jesus, caring, sharing, giving, and spending time with people. 1 Timothy 6:17-19 says, "Command them to do good, to be rich in good deeds, and to be generous and willing to share. In this way they will lay up treasure for themselves as a firm foundation for the coming age, so that they may take hold of the life that is truly life." Do you want to live a life that is truly alive, then start by helping someone in Jesus' name.

Prayer: God, help me to lay up treasures in heaven.

> Matthew 6:22 *The lamp of the body is the eye. If therefore your eye is good, your whole body will be full of light.*

Jackson Browne was one of my favorite artists in the 70's. He wrote a song, *Doctor My Eyes*, that has stuck with me throughout the years. The lyrics go, "Doctor, my eyes have seen the years, And the slow parade of fears without crying, Now I want to understand. I have done all that I could, To see the evil and the good without hiding, You must help me if you can. Doctor, my eyes, Tell me what is wrong, was I unwise to leave them open for so long?" The lyrics tell us we see both the evil and the good of this world, and that the evil seems to overshadow the good. Jesus said, our eyes are the gateway to our hearts and mind. Having a good eye will help us see everything more clearly. Jesus is not talking about having 20/20 vision. He is more concerned with how we discern what we see. Can we tell the difference between godliness and ungodliness? Unfortunately, there are no warning labels on what is presented to us on television and social media. Images and information are coming at us at an unbelievable pace. To make matters worse, Paul said in 2 Corinthians 11:14, "And no wonder, for Satan himself masquerades as an angel of light." Satan is out to deceive us. He wants us to think that the very things he uses to trap us are good for us. Sadly, if we get on the wrong path following Satan's light, our lives will actually fall further into darkness. All the more reason why our eyes should be trained to understand what we see. How do we discern which light is the light of Jesus and which light is from Satan? Psalm 119:105 says, "Your word is a lamp to my feet and a light for my path." Reading and knowing God's word is critical to recognizing God's light. Psalm 119:130 says, "The unfolding of Your words give light, it gives understanding to the simple." God's word illuminates. It shines in the darkness and fills our hearts and minds with understanding. It helps us discern good and evil. Is your vision getting a little blurry? If so, start spending time in God's word each day. Let His word clear your vision problems.

Prayer: God, help me to see things clearly through the lens of Your word.

Day 33

> Matthew 6:24 No one can serve two masters; for either he will hate the one and love the other, or else he will be loyal to the one and despise the other. You cannot serve God and mammon.

We learned in Day 31 that it was okay to be wealthy. Now it appears as if Jesus is condemning wealth. Is He contradicting himself just a few short verses later? What does Jesus mean by serving God or mammon? I have understood the word mammon described as simply wealth, money or riches. However, according to *Oxford dictionary.com*, mammon is defined as "wealth regarded as an evil influence or false object of worship and devotion." In other words, wealth, money and riches become our idol and take first place in our lives over our devotion to God. When our thirst for money is never satisfied, when we are envious of others wealth, or when we take matters into our own hands for unmet needs, we may be serving mammon. Solomon said in Ecclesiastes 5:10, "Whoever loves money never has enough; whoever loves wealth is never satisfied with his income. This too is meaningless." Sadly, the world of credit cards has made the pursuit of material things too convenient. According to *Lendingtree.com*, credit card debt in the United States in 2022, was $887 billion. The average unpaid balance on a credit card was $6,600, with 54% of credit card accounts carrying a balance. For the convenience of fulfilling your wants and needs, credit card companies are charging you an APR of 16.27%. The devil wants nothing more than for you to weigh yourself down with debt, so your devotion to God is overshadowed by a pursuit of money. Paul said in 1 Timothy 6:9, "People who want to get rich fall into temptation and a trap and into many foolish and harmful desires that plunge men into ruin and destruction." He went on to say in verse 10, "For the love of money is a root of all kinds of evil. Some people, eager for money, have wandered away from the faith and pierced themselves with many griefs." Who are you serving today? Have you wandered away from the faith, chasing after the "pot of gold at the end of the rainbow." Or perhaps your love for money has led you to do things you know are not right. God said, you can't serve Me if you are more interested in getting rich. The wonderful thing about putting God first and serving Him is that He will take care of your needs. Trust Him today with your money.

Prayer: God, I want to serve You, not mammon.

> *Matthew 6:25 Therefore I say to you, do not worry about your life, what you will eat or what you will drink; nor about your body, what you will put on. Is not life more than food and the body more than clothing?*

"Here's a little song I wrote, You might want to sing it note for note. Don't worry be happy. In every life we have some trouble, But when you worry you make it double. Don't worry be happy. Don't worry be happy." This memorable little song written by Bobby McFerrin, *Don't worry, Be Happy* tells us to stop worrying and be happy, because worry doubles your trouble. Life would be simple if it was that easy to do. However, when our world is crashing in around us, it is hard to be happy. Stress becomes a way of life and we become filled with anxiety about any number of things. We worry about finances, health, safety, relationships, and our future, just to name a few. Yet, Jesus makes it clear that we are not to worry about these and even the most basic necessities of life. Paul said in Ephesians 4:6, "Do not be anxious about anything, but in everything, by prayer and petition, with thanksgiving, present your requests to God." As God's children, we have the privilege of asking our Heavenly Father to provide for our needs. I have found that when I ask in faith, God delivers. Recently, our family planned a trip that would require a rental car that seats 6+ people. Unfortunately, the rental agencies did not have a large SUV or mini-van available during the dates of our trip. Naturally, my first inclination was to worry and fret over how we were going to get where we needed to go. We began looking at options to rent two smaller cars or even consider using a combination of Uber and a rental car. Vivian and I prayed, asking God to provide the transportation needed. The very next morning, God spoke to me through His word, letting me know He had heard our prayers. My daily Bible reading included Psalm 121:7-8, "The Lord will keep you from all harm, He will watch over your life; The Lord will watch over your coming and going both now and forever more." That verse jumped off the pages of my Bible and wiped away any anxiety about our transportation. 1 Peter 5:7 says, "Cast all your anxiety on Him because He cares for you." Giving your worries to God takes faith and a confidence that God will take care of them. Can you trust Him?

Prayer: God help me not to worry about the things of life.

> *Matthew 6:33 But seek first the kingdom of God and His righteousness, and all these things shall be added to you.*

Whenever I hear this verse quoted, the word "but" is often left out. However, this small word has a great purpose because it connects this verse with the previous verses. Jesus has just said, don't worry about what you are going to eat, drink and wear because life is more important than spending your time chasing after these. He promises to provide those things if our priorities are in order. Romans 8:32 says, "He who did not spare His own Son, but gave Him up for us all, how will He not also, along with Him, graciously give us all things?" Like a loving Father, God will take care of His children. However, there are things He expects of us. When our children were growing up, Vivian and I would give them an allowance. However, certain chores were expected of them before receiving it. They had a choice of whether or not to do their chores but only received an allowance when they were done right. Jesus instructs us to seek first the kingdom of God and His righteousness. Just as our children had a choice, God gives us a choice to seek Him. Jeremiah 29:13 says, "You will seek Me and find Me when you seek Me with all your heart." Seeking after God's kingdom requires our full effort. It is not something to do when it is convenient. What exactly is the kingdom of God? Daniel 7:27 says, "Then the sovereignty, power and greatness of all the kingdoms under heaven will be handed over to the holy people of the Most High. His kingdom will be an everlasting kingdom, and all rulers will worship and obey Him." Daniel 2:44 confirms this by saying "...God of heaven will set up a kingdom that will never be destroyed...it will endure forever." One day soon, Jesus is returning to set up His kingdom here on earth. As followers of Christ, Jesus is calling us to look for the coming of His kingdom and to begin living as if it were here. Psalm 119:172 defines God's righteousness as, keeping His commands. "...for all your commands are righteous." In other words, seeking His righteousness is obeying God's word. Revelation 22:14 tells us, "Blessed are those who do His commandments..." Jesus said, that if we seek after Him and obey His word, He will do His part to provide our every need.

Prayer: God, help me to seek after Your kingdom and Your righteousness.

> Matthew 7:2 *For with what judgement you judge, you will be judged: and with the measure you use, it will be measured back to you.*

Jesus has just said in Matthew 7:1, "Judge not, that you be not judged." We hear this verse quoted quite often in situations where a judgmental comment is made about someone. Does this mean we are not to judge someone? Without considering the full context of what Jesus said, the answer would be yes. In fact, this verse is often used to avoid conflict with someone who is living without any moral boundaries and accountability. However, Jesus continued with verse two saying, we will be judged with the measure we use to judge. He went on to explain what He meant in verses 3 – 5. There are occasions when we should discern between good and bad. If this involves another person, in essence we are judging them. 1 Thessalonians 5:21 says, "Test everything. Hold on to the good." 1 John 4:1 says, "Dear friends, do not believe every spirit, but test the spirits to see whether they are from God." For example, I would not want my grandchildren hanging around someone selling drugs because of the risk of them becoming addicted to drugs. In this situation, I have made a judgement about someone for the protection of my grandchildren. However, if I were to see someone who dressed similarly as the drug dealer and associated that person with selling drugs, then I have prejudged them. Without knowing the heart of this person, I have put them in a category below my standards. Unfortunately, we use standards that we compare ourselves with others. Naturally, we only use our standards when they make us 'look' better than someone else. When this happens, we overlook our shortcomings and flaws, and focus on what we perceive to be wrong with others. Jesus said this type of judgement is wrong. We become hypocritical, making a big deal of someone else's mistakes while doing the very same thing. Jesus tells us before looking at the 'speck of sawdust' in someone else's eyes, we should 'pay attention to the plank in our own eye.' In God's eyes, our life is no different from the person we are judging. Jesus is telling us to clean up our own lives before addressing the sin in the lives of others. This requires confession, repentance, and a commitment to live a Christlike life so we will have compassion, not criticism, for others.

Prayer: God, forgive me when I judge using my standards.

Matthew 7:6 *Do not give what is holy to the dogs; nor cast your pearls before swine, lest they trample them under their feet, and turn and tear you in pieces.*

Why is Jesus casting such a bad light on dogs and pigs? Most dogs are very friendly and make great companions. However, that was not the case in Jesus' day. Packs of dogs would roam the streets looking for anything to eat. For example, 1 Kings 16:4 says, "Anyone of Baasha who dies in the city the dogs will eat, and anyone of his who dies in the field the birds of the heavens will eat." This verse is not a very flattering depiction of dogs. However, there are some places in the world where not much has changed. I recall our mission trips to Nicaragua, where dogs roamed the streets of Los Brasiles. They were very skinny, malnourished, and always on the search for something to eat. In Jesus' day, pigs were worse off than dogs. According to Jewish law, pigs were considered unclean animals and were not to be eaten. They also had to scavenge for food and could become very aggressive when hungry. Obviously, Jesus is not speaking about feeding dogs and pigs. His message is pretty clear. We should not be wasting things of value on those who do not appreciate them or even angered by them. Sadly, there are some people who are not ready to receive the gospel message of salvation. In fact, there are some when approached will become argumentative and vicious towards you. Using discernment and not judging as we learned yesterday can be vital in our approach to someone with the gospel. 2 Timothy 2:25 says, "Those who oppose Him he must gently instruct, in the hope that God will grant them repentance leading them to a knowledge of the truth." Unless someone is hungry for the truth of God's word, they will put up some type of resistance to what you are sharing with them. I have heard comments such as, "I am just not ready," "I don't have time right now," and "God can't forgive me." Although it may not seem so, God is working on their hearts and your efforts are not wasted time. However, you may be 'casting pearls to swine' if you encounter someone who rejects the gospel message making fun of you and God's word. In those situations, it may be best to walk away and let God do His work in that person.

Prayer: God, help me to "cast my pearls" to those who are ready to receive them.

Day 38

Matthew 7:7 Ask, and it will be given to you; seek, and you will find; knock, and it will be opened to you.

Several days ago, I shared a story of an upcoming trip to visit our son, and needed transportation from the airport that would seat six people. Unfortunately, nothing of that size was available; but God made it clear, not to worry. (Psalm 121:7-8) Now the rest of the story. Being unsure of the availability of an Uber ride for six, I made reservations for a full-size car that would seat five. My plan was to send Vivian and the others in the rental and I would take an Uber. At the airport, I discovered there were no Uber rides available to my son's house. Standing in line at the car rental desk, I prayed, "Lord You promised that You have our coming and our going covered. I leave it in Your hands." As I was checking in, the rental agency representative happened to ask, if I would like an SUV instead of a car. I told him, unless the SUV could seat six, we may as well stick with the car. He said, let me check, I may have something that has just become available. Minutes later, we were driving out of the parking lot praising God with a Nissan Armada SUV that has third row seating. God answered my prayer for a larger vehicle. Jesus tells us to "ask and it will be given to you." Does this mean we can ask for a new car, a new house, or a million dollars and He will provide? James 4:3 says, "When you ask, you do not receive, because you ask with the wrong motives, that you may spend what you get on your pleasures." God loves to give us good things. However, we first have to ask. Secondly, we are not seeking what God can give, but we are seeking Him and His will for our lives. On Day 35, Jesus told us "To seek first the kingdom of God and His righteousness, then these things will be given to us." Lastly, we have to knock on the door of God's heart until He opens and allows us into His presence. Are you persistent in your prayer life, being specific with your requests to Him? I can share many stories of how God has answered my prayers. Trust God, He loves you and wants to give you good things that are in line with His will.

Prayer: God, teach me how to ask, seek and knock.

> *Matthew 7:12 Therefore, whatever you want men to do to you, do also to them, for this is the Law and the Prophets.*

Today's verse is known as the Golden Rule. You are probably more familiar with the version found in Luke 6:31, where Jesus is quoted, "Do to others as you would have them do to you." This basic principle on the treatment of others is not only established in Christianity, but can be found in most every other religion. Jesus said this was the essence of the Law given to Moses and the children of Israel when they were in the wilderness. Leviticus 19:18 says, "You shall not take vengeance, nor bear any grudge against the children of your people, but you shall love your neighbor as yourself; I am the Lord." In the early days of my career with CP&L, several new managerial philosophies were being introduced. I'll never forget one class where the Golden Rule was replaced with a "so called" newer, more people-friendly version which said, 'Treat others the way they want to be treated.' My first thought was, what is wrong with the Golden Rule? Jesus taught it and it has worked just fine for thousands of years. My next thought was, how am I supposed to know how others want to be treated? I have a pretty good idea how my close friends and family would like to be treated, but wouldn't have a clue for someone I hardly know. Lastly, what would I do if the treatment required me to compromise my Christian values. Needless to say, I stuck with the Golden Rule. So how do I live out the Golden Rule? First, it is important to understand the Golden Rule is more than being nice to someone so they will be nice to you. It is also not an excuse for seeking revenge; doing to others what they have done to you. The core of Jesus' message is loving your neighbor. In other words, we should treat others better than they have treated us. We should be honest to someone who is dishonest with us. We should be nice to someone who is not nice to us. We should show mercy to someone who has been unmerciful to us. Living out the Golden Rule is not quite as easy as it first appears. Jesus didn't say to do to those who love you as you would have them do to you. He included everyone.

Prayer: God help me to live out Your Golden Rule to all.

> *Matthew 7:13-14 Enter by the narrow gate; for wide is the gate and broad is the way that leads to destruction, and there are many who go in by it. Because narrow is the gate and difficult is the way which leads to life. And there are few who find it.*

My junior year of college, three friends and I decided to hike the Appalachian Trail during Spring Break. Our plan was to hike the trail from Clingman's Dome, TN to Fontana Dam, NC. We left Wilmington early one morning and drove into Virginia to get a pass to hike the trail. It was mid-afternoon when we finally arrived at Clingman's Dome to begin our hike. Carrying tents, sleeping bags, and food to last three days, we started the journey up the walk-way to Clingman's Dome where the Appalachian Trail passed by. Exhausted from the walk to the trail, we paused to make a decision, turn left or right. Unfortunately, no one had studied the map prior to leaving for our trip and there were no directional signs to point us in the right direction. Being great outdoorsmen, naturally we chose the wrong path. After hiking one mile in the wrong direction, we found ourselves back in the parking lot of Clingman's Dome and had to start all over again. Jesus said in life there are two gates, one that leads to the path of destruction and one to the path of life. In this journey called life, God gives us the choice of selecting the path we want to take. He said, the easiest and more attractive route is the one through the wide gate and many people chose this path. The narrow gate is more difficult to find and fewer people find it. Like our camping trip, you carry a lot of baggage with you. Also, the journey to reach the gates can be exhausting which makes the wide gate look even more enticing and choosing the wrong path much easier. However, at the end you will find yourself back in the same parking lot you started. Jesus said in John 10:10, "The thief comes only to steal and kill and destroy; I have come that they may have life, and have it to the full." Choosing the narrow path may be difficult, but it is worth it. Not only does it lead to eternal life, but He promises that we will live life to the full. What path are you on? If you are following everyone else down the wrong path, it is not too late to find the gate (Jesus) that leads to life. Ask Him into your life today.

Prayer: God, help me to find the narrow gate that leads to life.

> *Matthew 7:16;20 You will know them by their fruits. Do men gather grapes from thornbushes or figs from thistles? Therefore by their fruits you will know them.*

Jesus issued a warning about false prophets in verse 15 and goes on to explain how we can recognize them. According to _www.gotquestions.com_, "A false prophet is a person who spreads false teachings or messages while claiming to speak the Word of God." In Jesus' day, false prophets were motivated by self-interest and spoke what the people wanted to hear, rather than messages from God. Financial gain, greed, power and control seem to be the motivation of modern-day false prophets or preachers. This certainly was the case of Jim Jones who started a church called the People's Temple in the late 1950's. Ten years later, he moved his church to California where it grew rapidly. His message of faith healing and mind reading attracted a number of followers. However, Jim Jones openly engaged in adultery, drug use, and profanity. He also coerced members of his church to sign over their possessions, including their homes, to the church. Later, to avoid scrutiny by the press and the US government, Jones and over 900 followers moved to a compound in Guyana, named after himself, Jonestown. It was at Jonestown where, at his urging, 913 people including many children, committed suicide by drinking poison.[6] Jesus said, we would recognize a false prophet by their fruit. In Jim Jones' case, the fruit was pretty evident, but the people were captivated by his message and drank the kool-aid. Other false prophets may not be as easy to discern. They are very adept at twisting God's word to fit their message. That is why it is very important to know God's word, and to identify the fruit being produced by prophet. Galatians 5:22 says, "But the fruit of the Spirit is love, joy, peace, patience, kindness, goodness, faithfulness, gentleness, and self-control. Against such things there is no law." In comparison, the fruits of a sinful nature are found in Galatians 5:19 "...sexual immorality, impurity and debauchery; idolatry, and witchcraft; hatred, discord, jealousy, fit of rage, selfish ambition, dissensions, factions and envy, drunkenness, orgies and the like." If someone is a false prophet or preacher, the bad fruit will show up. Jesus said, you can't pick grapes off a thornbush or figs from thistles. They may have pretty blossoms, but all you get is thorns. Know your fruit.

Prayer: God help me to recognize the fruit of a false prophet or preacher and not be led astray.

Day 42

> *Matthew 7:21 Not everyone who says to Me, "Lord, Lord," shall enter the kingdom of heaven, but he who does the will of My Father in heaven.*

The old saying "there are two things you can count on, death and taxes," is missing the most important one: Judgement Day. At the end of everyone's life is an appointment called Judgement Day, where we will stand before Jesus and be told one of two things; "well done My good and faithful servant", or "depart from Me you who are cursed into the eternal fire." Regrettably, Jesus said that some who claim to be a Christian will learn they never had a relationship with Him. In a 2022 Barna survey, "69% of Americans said they identified themselves as a Christian. Yet, only 6% possess a biblical world view and demonstrate a consistent application of biblical principles. Even more frightening, 25% of the 6% say there is no absolute moral truth." That is why it is very important to know, that you know you are a child of God. First, the Bible tells us that through our faith in Jesus Christ, we have eternal life. Ephesians 2:8-9 says, "For it is by grace you have been saved, through faith, and this not from yourselves, it is the gift of God." We accept this gift by acknowledging we are a sinner in need of help, confessing our sins to God, repenting of those sins, and accepting Jesus as our Lord and Savior. Romans 10:9 says, "That if you confess with your mouth, 'Jesus is Lord,' and believe in your heart that God raised Him from the dead, you will be saved." Acts 2:21 tells us, "And everyone who calls on the name of the Lord will be saved." However, there is more to salvation. Jesus said in John 14:15, "If you love Me, you will obey what I command." James 2:17 tells us, "In the same way, faith by itself, if it is not accompanied by action, is dead." But didn't Jesus say that some of these He didn't know, prophesied in His name, cast out demons, and did many wonders? Wouldn't that count as good works? Well, it would to me, but God looks at a person's heart. Jeremiah 17:10, "I the Lord search the heart and examine the mind, to reward a man according to his conduct, according to what his deeds deserve." My prayer is that your heart is right with God and you are a good and faithful servant.

Prayer: God help me to be a faithful servant.

> *Matthew 7:24 Therefore whoever hears these sayings of Mine, and does them, I will liken him to a wise man who built his house on the rock.*

In the early 80's, my father and a long-time friend decided to build a beach house on North Topsail Island. They had a lot just behind a row of beach front homes and wanted to build the house completely by themselves. I would take off every weekend and go help them. Once built, the beach house became a favorite vacation spot for my family. However, in 1996, with wind gusts of 136 mph, Hurricane Fran made landfall just south of Wilmington, NC causing major damage to southeastern NC. Fran also brought a 12' tidal surge which washed away many homes on Topsail Island. In fact, the five homes in front of our beach house were completely washed away. Although tattered and torn, by the grace of God, our beach house survived the storm. Sadly, not much could have been done to prevent the other homes from being washed away. However, just like home construction, Jesus said the foundation we build our lives on matters. In verse 25 Jesus said, "the rain came down, the streams rose, and the winds blew and beat against the house; yet it did not fall, because it had its foundation on the rock." This should come as no surprise, but you are going to face storms in your lifetime. Some may be as bad as Hurricane Fran, destroying everything in its path; while others, may be a popup thunderstorm that unexpectedly comes out of nowhere. Jesus said whoever hears His words and puts them into practice is like a wise man. His house is built on a solid foundation and can withstand the storms of life. However, the foolish man hears God's words but chooses not to put them into practice and his house is washed away. James 1:22 says, "Do not merely listen to the word, and so deceive yourselves. Do what it says." The storms of life will quickly let you know if you are putting God's word into practice. For those who do, His promises will see you through any storm. Promises like, Lamentations 3:21-23, "Yet I call this to mind and therefore I have hope; because of the Lord's great love we are not consumed, for His compassions never fail. They are new every morning; great is Your faithfulness." What foundation are you building your life on?

Prayer: God help me to build my foundation on Your word.

> Matthew 8:3 Then Jesus put out His hand and touched him saying, "I am willing; be cleansed." Immediately his leprosy was cleansed.

"Shackled by a heavy burden, Neath a load of guilt and shame, then the hand of Jesus touched me, And now I am no longer the same. He touched me, oh, He touched me. And oh, the joy that floods my soul, something happened, and now I know, He touched me and made me whole." This song, *He Touched Me*, written by Milton Schafer and Ira Levin reminds us that just as Jesus reached out His hand to heal the leper, He still reaches out to touch and restore the sick and the hurting. In today's verse, Jesus had just finished speaking to the crowd when a person with leprosy came and knelt before Him. Having Jesus' attention, the leper said, "Lord if You are willing, You can make me clean." In Jesus' day, leprosy was a very contagious skin disease which made a person and anything they touched unclean. Lepers were considered outcasts and required to shout the word unclean whenever they approached someone. For this man to approach Jesus required a tremendous amount of faith. His faith was also demonstrated in how he asked Jesus for healing. He didn't say, "If You can heal me," but, "If You are willing." Although this was the first recorded miracle in the book of Matthew, it was not Jesus' first miracle. Perhaps, the leper had heard about Jesus' ability to heal and was certain that Jesus could heal him. Confident that Jesus could heal him, the leper approached Jesus and knelt before Him, showing respect and reverence to the Son of God. Jesus could have easily said, your leprosy is healed, go on your way. However, Jesus did the one thing no one expected, He touched the leper. This was likely the first time this leper had been touched by someone in many years. Can you imagine the joy and love the leper felt by this simple touch of healing, and the shock and disbelief of the crowd? Jesus knew what the leper needed. He also knows the heavy burden you are carrying. He knows the load of guilt and shame that are weighing you down. Can I tell you, there is power in the touch of Jesus. Just as Jesus told the leper, "I am willing; be cleansed," He is willing and able to heal and deliver you. Reach out to Him and ask.

Prayer: Lord if You are willing, please take this burden of _____ from me.

> *Matthew 8:10 When Jesus heard it, He marveled, and said to those who followed, "Assuredly, I say to you, I have not found such great faith, not even in Israel."*

The news of Jesus' ability to heal the sick and perform miracles rapidly spread throughout the region. As He was entering Capernaum, a Roman Centurion approached Jesus asking for help. He said to Jesus, "Lord, my servant lies at home paralyzed and in terrible suffering." Jesus told the Centurion, not to worry, He would go heal his servant. Then the story takes an unexpected turn. The Centurion told Jesus, "Lord, I do not deserve to have You come under my roof. But just say the word, and my servant will be healed. For I myself am a man under authority, with soldiers under me. I tell this one, 'Go,' and he goes; and that one, 'Come,' and he comes. I say to my servant, 'Do this,' and he does it." Although nothing takes Jesus by surprise, the Centurion's faith amazed Jesus to the point of Him saying, "I have not found anyone in Israel with such great faith." Jesus then told the Centurion to go home, "It will be done just as you believed it would." The Centurion's servant was healed because of his faith in Jesus' ability to heal him. The Centurion not only had tremendous faith, he was also humble and recognized his unworthiness to be in the presence of the Lord. As a Roman officer, he could have easily walked up to Jesus and demanded Him to come and heal his servant. However, he chose to humble himself and submit to Jesus' authority. What lessons can we learn from the Centurion? First, how we approach Jesus in our prayer life is important. Recognizing God's holiness and sovereignty affirms our belief in Him and His ability to act on our behalf. It also points to our unworthiness coming before a Holy God. In His model prayer, Jesus opened with, "Our Father, who is in heaven, hallowed or holy is Your name". Secondly, just as Jesus marveled over the faith of the Centurion, our faith pleases Him and He rewards us for it. Hebrews 11:6 says, "And without faith, it is impossible to please God, because anyone who comes to Him must believe that He exists and that He rewards those who earnestly seek Him." Do you want to increase your faith? Ask God to give you more. He will in ways you never thought possible.

Prayer: God help my faith to be as deep as the Centurion's.

Matthew 8:20 And Jesus said to him, "Foxes have holes and birds of the air have nests, but the Son of Man has nowhere to lay His head."

Many people were fascinated by Jesus' teaching and ability to heal the sick, and wanted to be one of His disciples. One such person was a scribe or teacher of the law who approached Jesus and said, "Teacher, I will follow You wherever You go." Jesus' reply was, I am essentially homeless, and you will be too if you follow Me. The Bible never mentions the scribe again. Evidently the cost of giving up his home and traveling around with Jesus was too much for him. The scribe probably committed to following Jesus because of His teaching and healing ministry, wanting to be a part of the excitement. Sadly, the scribe missed the most important aspect by not accepting Jesus as Lord and Savior. To be clear, salvation is a free gift from God. Ephesians 2:8 says, "For it is by grace you have been saved, through faith, and this is not from yourselves, it is the gift of God." There are not enough good deeds or money to buy salvation. Nor, can you work your way to heaven. Romans 6:23 says, "For the wages of sin is death, but the free gift of God is eternal life in Christ Jesus our Lord." However, when we ask Jesus into our hearts to be our Lord and Savior, we are also agreeing to live by His word. 1 John 1:5-6 says, "But if anyone obeys His word, God's love is truly made complete in him. This is how we know we are in Him: Whoever claims to live in Him must walk as Jesus did." It would be safe to say that no one lives like Jesus prior to being saved. Therefore, following Jesus will require us to make changes in our lives. Jesus may not be asking you to be homeless, but there will be a cost to follow Him. The cost is different for each person. You may have to make a complete lifestyle change, losing some close friendships. You may have to give up a habit that is controlling your life. You may find yourself on a different career path. Following Jesus can lead us in many directions. However, I can tell you from experience it is worth it. What the scribe didn't know is that Jesus can replace what he had to give up with something much better. Follow Jesus, see where He takes you.

Prayer: God help me to follow You each day.

> Matthew 8:26 But He said to them, "Why are you fearful, O you of little faith?" Then He arose and rebuked the winds and the sea, and there was a great calm.

In His short three-year ministry, Jesus traveled a number of miles either on foot or by boat. After speaking with the scribe who asked about following Him, Jesus and the disciples got into a boat and headed to the region of Gadarenes. According to the Book of Mark, it was late in the day. Jesus, tired from the day's activities, was asleep in the back of the boat when a fierce storm arose. The storm was so bad that it frightened the disciples who were experienced fisherman. As the waves were crashing over the boat, they woke Jesus, saying, "Lord, save us! We're going to drown." Jesus got up and before calming the storm, asked the disciples "what happened to your faith?" Were they going to let a storm cast doubt on who He was? Then Jesus simply said, "Peace, be still," and immediately there was complete calm. The disciples' response after Jesus calmed the storm is surprising. Mark 4:41 says, "They were terrified and asked each other, 'Who is this? Even the winds and the waves obey Him?'" They had just asked Jesus to save them, but were completely shocked that He did. How well do you know the peace speaker? Have you called Him by name to calm the storms of your life? There are storms of life that are not too bad and we think we have them under control, while others seem insurmountable with no way out. Jesus is there to speak peace into your life. Like the disciples, you may think Jesus is in the back of the boat asleep, oblivious to the pain you are going through. It is at that moment we begin to doubt if Jesus knows our situation or cares enough to do anything about it. Can I tell you that Jesus cares for you and can calm the storm that is raging in your life. He wants you to ask in faith, trusting that He knows what is best for you. Note that the disciples were still in the boat after the storm was calmed. God may not change the circumstances causing your storm; however, He can give you peace and the assurance you will make it through. Proverbs 3:5 says, "Trust in the Lord with all your heart and lean not on your own understanding." Do you really trust Him? If so call on Jesus today.

Prayer: Lord save me, I feel like I am going to drown.

> *Matthew 9:2 Then behold, they brought to Him a paralytic lying on a bed. When Jesus saw their faith, He said to the paralytic, "Son, be of good cheer; your sins are forgiven you."*

Jesus left the Region of Gadarenes and returned to His home base of Capernaum. Mark 2:2-5, tells us that Jesus was in a home teaching when four men carrying their paralytic friend, tried to get through the crowd to see Him. The crowds were so great, the men made an opening in the roof and lowered their friend down to Jesus. Matthew tells us that Jesus recognized their faith. A few days ago, we read about the faith of the Centurion who asked Jesus to heal his servant, and that faith pleases God. (Hebrews 11:6) Today, we witness the faith of four friends and a paralytic who went 'the second mile' to get to Jesus. What is faith? Faith is putting our beliefs into action, just as the four friends did. Hebrews 11:1 tells us, "Now faith is the confidence in what we hope for and assurance about what we do not see." Jesus then turned His attention to the helpless cripple laying before Him. The natural thing for Jesus to say would have been, "Get up, take your mat and go home." However, Jesus tells him to "cheer up, your sins are forgiven." We'll never know the condition of the paralytic's heart. He may have been more crippled by sin than his body was. Not only did he leave healed, his faith led to his sins being forgiven as well. God's answer to spiritual brokenness is forgiveness. What sin are you carrying around that has you spiritually and emotionally paralyzed preventing you to live a fulfilled life? Are you full of anger, depression, selfishness, jealousy, and hatred? Perhaps a lifestyle of sexual immorality, drunkenness, or addiction has enslaved you. How many times have you tried to change things on your own, only to find yourself right back where you were? Jesus is telling you, "Be of good cheer, your sins are forgiven. Just come to Me in faith, believing I can heal and set you free from your sin." Are you ready to make a change that will last? Put your faith into action by asking Jesus to heal and forgive you. Then allow the Holy Spirit to start working in your life, replacing the old ways with His ways. A word of caution, Satan will try to drag you back into your "old life." Don't fall for his tricks. Trust God and seek Him each day.

Prayer: In Jesus name, God please heal and forgive me.

> *Matthew 9:9 As Jesus passed on from there, He saw a man named Matthew sitting at the tax office. And He said to him, "Follow Me." So he arose and followed Him.*

In the movie, *Groundhog Day*, Bill Murray portrays a television weatherman named Phil Conners who is covering the annual Groundhog Day event in Punxsutawney, Pennsylvania. Conners becomes trapped in a time loop, causing him to relive February 2nd, over and over. Each day he wakes up and discovers it is Groundhog Day again. This is how I picture Matthew's life prior to meeting Jesus. Matthew was a tax collector, an occupation that carried with it hatred from his fellow Jews. Each day he would go to his tax booth, collect taxes and start all over again. Life for Matthew was dull, meaningless, and lacked purpose until one day, Jesus walked by and said, "Follow Me." Without hesitation, Matthew gets up, leaves everything, and follows Jesus. The same day, Matthew invites his friends who were considered notorious sinners by the religious leaders, to have dinner with Jesus. What can we learn from this story of Jesus choosing Matthew to be one of His disciples? First, Jesus loves us just as we are. Although Matthew's profession put him in a category of the worst of sinners, Jesus showed love and compassion towards him. Jesus, didn't tell Matthew to go clean up his life and check back with Me in a few years. He saw what Matthew could be and said, "Follow Me." Neither does Jesus require us to clean up our lives before we can be saved. I have heard some people use the excuse that they are too sinful, too messed up for God to love them. They can't possibly give their lives to Jesus the way they are living now. Jesus is saying to you, "I love you just as you are, come follow Me." Secondly, when Jesus called Matthew, he left everything and started following Jesus. Are you willing to leave your old lifestyle behind to follow Jesus? Jesus can't use you if you are more interested in holding on to your old ways instead of opening up to the life He has for you. Jeremiah 29:11 says, "For I know the plans I have for you, declares the Lord, plans to prosper you and not harm you, plans to give you hope and a future." What was Matthew's life like after he decided to follow Jesus? You can read all about it in the first book of the New Testament.

Prayer: Jesus, thank You for loving me as I am, and calling me to follow You.

> Matthew 9:12 When Jesus heard that, He said to them. "Those who are well have no need of a physician, but those who are sick."

Jesus and His disciples are at Matthew's house having dinner with Matthew and his tax collector friends. The Pharisees and other religious leaders stop by and see Jesus at the table, enjoying a meal with "those sinners." They ask the disciples, "Why does your Teacher eat with tax collectors and sinners?" The implication being that if Jesus was who He said He was, holy and righteous, He wouldn't be hanging out with those people. The Pharisees view was to let sinners like Matthew and his friends receive the judgement they deserved. The Bible doesn't tell us if Jesus overheard them talking or if the disciples told Jesus what the Pharisees had asked them. Nor does it tell us why the Pharisees asked the disciples and not Jesus. However, when Jesus heard what was asked, He answered with a short parable, "It is not the healthy who need a physician, but those who are sick." Jesus was with the spiritually sick, those in need of His help. Unfortunately, the Pharisees who looked down on everyone who were not as religious as they, were in just as much need of Jesus healing. They were good at keeping the letter of the law, but failed miserably with having compassion for others. Digging deeper into this story, we learn there are three categories of people. First, there are the tax collectors who are lost, sinners in need of a Savior. Second, there are the Pharisees who go through the motions of being religious, but in their hearts, are just as lost as the tax collectors. Even worse, they don't recognize their spiritual condition and think they are doing okay. Lastly, there is Jesus and His disciples, offering healing and hope to those who are lost. If you examine your life, you will find yourself in one of these categories. Hopefully, you have accepted Jesus as your Lord and Savior and follow Him daily, sharing God's love to the lost. Perhaps you are like the tax collectors, lost and in need of a Savior. Or, maybe you are like the Pharisees, putting on a good show, but inside you are spiritually dead. If you identify more with either of the last two categories, Jesus said in Matthew 11:28, "Come to Me, you who are weary and burdened, and I will give you rest." Come to Jesus today, He will change your life.

Prayer: God, please help me, I need You in my life.

> Matthew 9:13 But go and learn what this means: "I desire mercy and not sacrifice."

Jesus has just told the Pharisees, "It is not the healthy who need a doctor, but sick." Then He takes a jab at the Pharisees by quoting Hosea 6:6, telling them to go learn what it means. "For I desire mercy, not sacrifice, and acknowledgement of God rather than burnt offerings." This is the second time we find Jesus talking about mercy. The first was in Matthew 5:7 where Jesus said, "Blessed are the merciful, for they shall obtain mercy." Sadly, the Pharisees were not in the mercy business and Jesus knew it. They were all about setting a very high standard which would be impossible to follow. Then, they would look down in judgement on those who could not live up to their pious position. Before we start 'casting stones' at the Pharisees, perhaps we should take a closer look at ourselves. I confess I am guilty of the same thing. On our visits to New York City to spend time with our son and his family, we walk by a number of homeless people, living on the streets. I am ashamed to say that I don't have a lot of compassion for them and to be honest, somewhat nervous walking by. Closer to home, perhaps someone walks into your church, who doesn't fit the 'church mold.' Is that person welcomed or do you avoid them, hoping they don't come back? Too often we draw conclusions about someone based on their appearance, the way they talk, or their behavior. If any of these do not conform to our "standards," then like the Pharisees, instead of trying to find ways to engage with that person do we look down on them? As a Christian, we can get caught up trying to live a good life, while missing the mark on what is most important to God. We focus on the "do's and don'ts" rather than love and mercy. The Message Bible says it best in Micah 6:6,8, "How can I stand up before God and show proper respect to the high God? But He's already made it plain how to live, what to do, what God is looking for in men and women. It's quite simple, Do what is fair and just to your neighbor, be compassionate and loyal in your love, And don't take yourself too seriously, take God seriously."

Prayer: God help me to be merciful.

> Matthew 9:16 *No one puts a piece of unshrunk cloth on an old garment; for the patch pulls away from the garment, and the tear is made worse.*

It sounds like Jesus is giving us a sewing lesson today. However, with Jesus there is always an important message in His words. John the Baptist's disciples had come to Jesus and asked Him why His disciples did not fast like everyone else. From Moses' day, fasting is an important facet of the Jewish faith. According to *www.slife.org*, there are specific times of fasting dictated to all Jews. In all, there are six main fasts, seven customary fasts, and various times of private fasts the Jews celebrate. Fasting is used to express regret and seek atonement for wrongdoing, express mourning, and to express gratitude to God for His provision. Jesus told John's disciples, "How can the guests of the bridegroom mourn while He is with them? The time will come when the bridegroom will be taken away from them; then they will fast." When teaching a truth, Jesus rarely spoke directly about anything, but would use life examples and parables to get His message across. His teaching methods drove the Pharisees crazy, and at times confused His own disciples. What is Jesus teaching us about patching an old garment? The old garment represents our lives before coming to Christ. Like an old pair of jeans, the wear and tear of life has left them faded, with holes in the knees. Although this is in style today, it wasn't many years ago. As a child, I can remember my mother trying to patch up holes in my jeans. The problem with patching is that a new piece of cloth, never matched the old. The patch covered the hole, but the repair was very obvious. And, after a couple of washes, the patch would begin to peel away from the jeans. Following Christ requires more than trying to patch the holes in your life caused by sin. You can cover up the sin and get by for a while, but sooner or later your old life begins to show back up. Following Christ means that we allow Him to change us from the inside out. Paul writes in 2 Corinthians 5:17, "Therefore, if anyone is in Christ, he is a new creation; the old has gone and the new has come!" Yes, that means that we let go of the old habits, the old friends, the old language, the old lifestyle and follow Him. Are you a new creation?

Prayer: God, help me to be a new creation in You.

> Matthew 9:17 *Nor do they put new wine into old wineskins, or else the wineskins break, and the wine is spilled, and the wineskins are ruined. But they put new wine into new wineskins, and both are preserved.*

Jesus continues His conversation with John the Baptist's disciples with a second parable of the importance of putting new wine into new wineskins. In Jesus' day, wine was stored in leather pouches. Over time, the leather would age and become stiff and brittle. Putting new wine into an old pouch would rupture the pouch because of the pressure created by the fermenting wine. Yesterday we learned that when we accept Jesus as our Lord and Savior, we become a new person in Christ. We leave our old ways behind and begin living a Christlike life, following Jesus' teachings and example. Realizing that it is impossible for us to accomplish this on our own, God has given us His Holy Spirit to reside in our hearts. Jesus said in John 16:7, "But I tell you the truth: It is good that I am going away. Unless I go away, the Counselor (Holy Spirit) will not come to you; but if I go, I will send Him to you." It is only by the power of the Holy Spirit that God can change us, but most importantly, we must be willing to change. Too often this is the stumbling block for people who want to follow Jesus as their Lord and Savior. We still want to keep our 'old wineskin,' hanging on to our old sins. Paul said in Ephesians 5:18, "Do not get drunk on wine, which leads to debauchery. Instead, be filled with the Spirit." We have to be willing to let the Holy Spirit point out and convict us of the sins in our lives, creating a new wineskin. The Holy Spirit will not go where He is not invited or welcomed. We have to ask God to fill us with His Spirit. Jesus said in Luke 11:13, "If you then, though you are evil, know how to give good gifts to your children, how much more will your Father in heaven give the Holy Spirit to those who ask Him?" The Holy Spirit is a vital part of a Christian's life. Not only does the Holy Spirit convict us of sin, He is a teacher. John 14:26 says, "But the Counselor, the Holy Spirit, whom the Father will send in My name, will teach you all things and will remind you of everything I say to you." Have you invited the Holy Spirit into your life today?

Prayer: God, please fill me with Your Holy Spirit.

> Matthew 9:28 And when He had come into the house, the blind men came to Him. And Jesus said to them, "Do you believe that I am able to do this?"

Jesus has had a busy day and was headed back to the house where He was staying. Along the way, two blind men heard that Jesus was walking by and began calling out to Him, "Have mercy on us, Son of David." No doubt, they had heard the stories of Jesus healing others, and wanted to be healed of their blindness. However, Jesus didn't even acknowledge their plea for help and kept on walking. Although the Bible doesn't tell us, I am sure the blind men began to cry out even louder as Jesus walked away. It also doesn't tell us why Jesus didn't stop to speak to them or heal them. Perhaps, Jesus wanted to avoid healing them in public, or He wanted to test the level of their faith. In either case, the blind men didn't give up. They followed Jesus to the house and boldly went up to Him. Testing their faith a little more, Jesus asked them, "Do you believe that I am able to do this?" Just like a good drama series on TV, we will find out what happens tomorrow. In the meantime, there is an important lesson for us to learn about our relationship with Christ. There have been times when I have felt like the blind men, calling out to Jesus to answer my prayers, only to think they have gotten no farther than the ceiling. I begin to question God, is He even listening? Have you ever felt the same way? God's word tells us that He hears our prayers. Psalm 66:19-20 says, "But God has surely listened and heard my voice in prayer. Praise be to God, who has not rejected my prayer or withheld His love from me!" In Jeremiah 29:12-13 we read, "Then you will call upon Me and come and pray to Me, and I will listen to you. You will seek Me and find Me when you seek Me with all your heart." God hears our prayers like Jesus heard the cries from the blindmen. However, He may delay in answering them to accomplish His will, grow our faith, or to fit His perfect timing. Whatever the reason, we should not give up or doubt God. Psalm 40:1 says, "I waited patiently for the Lord; He turned to me and heard my cry."

Prayer: God, thank You that You hear my prayers even when I don't think You are listening.

> *Matthew 9:29 Then He touched their eyes, saying, "According to your faith let it be to you."*

Today we learn the rest of the story. Jesus has just asked the blind men, "Do you believe I am able to do this?" Their reply was pretty simple and straightforward, 'Yes, Lord.' Jesus touched their eyes and told them, based on their faith it shall be done and immediately they could see. Jesus then warns them to keep their healing a secret. However, in the excitement of being healed, they spread the news to everyone they saw. Sadly, we live in a world of spiritually blind people. They are blind to who Jesus is and blind to their own sin. They are blind to how they should live, blind to His Kingdom, and the life that Jesus offers. Even worse, many do not even know they are blind. We work with these people. We go to school with them. We live in the same neighborhood and even go to church with them. At times, we may even find ourselves blinded by the glamour of the world. Is there any hope for the blind? Just as Jesus healed these two men of their physical blindness, He can heal spiritual blindness as well. Psalm 146:8 says, "The Lord gives sight to the blind, the Lord lifts up those who are bowed down." The first step to healing is acknowledging our blindness. Rarely will someone take this first step on their own. However, God may be using you to lead your co-worker, your classmate, or your neighbor to Him. Next, we have to ask God in faith, believing He can restore our sight. The blind men were healed because they believed Jesus could heal them, not only because Jesus had compassion for them. Jesus loves us, but when we are separated from Him because of our spiritual blindness, He will not heal us if we don't want Him to. Lastly, we should be just as excited as the blind men Jesus healed, telling others the great things He has done for us. Yesterday we closed with Psalm 40:1, waiting patiently on the Lord. Today we close with Psalm 40:2, "He lifted me out of the slimy pit, out of the mud and mire; He set my feet on a rock and gave me a firm place to stand." Praise God for His healing touch on your life.

Prayer: God, please heal my spiritual blindness.

> *Matthew 9:37-38 Then He said to His disciples, "The harvest truly is plentiful, but the laborers are few. Therefore pray the Lord of the harvest to send out laborers into His harvest."*

Jesus begins traveling to all the surrounding towns and villages, teaching in the synagogues and preaching the good news of salvation. Matthew tells us Jesus also healed all types of sickness and disease. Because people had never heard teaching or witnessed the healing power of Jesus before, great crowds gathered where ever Jesus was. Matthew 9:36 says, "When He saw the crowds, He had compassion on them, because they were harassed and helpless, like sheep without a shepherd." Jesus had compassion on the crowds because the religious leaders of the day lacked kindness and mercy. They were more interested in forcing people to follow their made-up rules, rather than shepherding the people. Are we the same as the religious leaders of Jesus day? Do we have compassion on the lost and hurting, or are we more interested in getting them to act like us? Jesus said, there is a ripe harvest of spiritually lost people who are hungry to know God, not to follow a bunch of rules. He also said the laborers are few. Nothing has changed in the 2000+ years since Jesus spoke these words. People are still lost and hurting and His laborers are few. However, Jesus offers us a solution to meet the need of more workers. Jesus said, pray that God would send out more believers to help in His harvest. Pray that God would plant seeds of ministry into mission minded people to go and minister to the lost. This could mean someone feels led to go to a foreign country. However, not everyone is called to go to serve in a foreign country. I am seeing God's calling on young men and women to go and plant churches in already church saturated communities. Not only should you pray that God send others, you should pray that God would send you. Ask Him to open doors to give you opportunities to share the good news with a neighbor, co-worker, family member, or classmate. As you pray that God will use you, be willing to follow His call. I have found that the opportunities can take you out of your comfort zone, or not be at a convenient time. Isaiah 6:8 says, "Then I heard the voice of the Lord saying, 'Whom shall I send? And who will go for us?' And I said, 'Here am I Lord. Send me.'" Are you an Isaiah?

Prayer: Here am I Lord, send me.

> Matthew 10:7-8 And as you go, preach, saying, "The kingdom of heaven is at hand." Heal the sick, cleanse the lepers, raise the dead, cast out demons. Freely you have received, freely give.

In the Book of Mark, we find more details about the mission trip Jesus is sending His twelve disciples on. Mark 6:7 says, "Calling the Twelve to Him, He sent them out two by two and gave them authority over evil spirits." Jesus then told them to preach the kingdom of heaven is at hand, heal the sick, cleanse the lepers and cast out demons. Jesus empowered them to do the very same things He was doing. When I was in high school, our church youth leader taught our youth group how to share the plan of salvation with someone. We spent several months training and practicing on each other. Then one night, she said it was time to put our training into practice. We were paired up, two by two, and dropped off on a street corner in a neighborhood near our church. The plan was to knock on doors and after a brief introduction, ask them if they had thought much about spiritual matters, hoping to share the plan of salvation with them. Needless to say, we didn't get invited into very many homes. Although we weren't very successful reaching our community for Christ, there were a few people whose lives were changed. However, in today's world I wouldn't even attempt something like this. Having a lasting impact on the lost, requires relationship building. Most people want to know you care, before they care what you have to say. While our methods for reaching the lost and hurting have changed over the years, the mission is still the same. Jesus is sending us out to reach them. He has empowered you and I to share the good news, that He has come to give us eternal life. He has called us to minister to the sick, by lifting them up in prayer, and taking care of them. He has called us to cleanse those who suffer with an addiction. He has called us to raise those who were dead in their sins, to be given a new life in Christ. And lastly, He has called us to cast out demons. We can offer hope to those who are suffering from mental bondages of depression, guilt, and fear. Why should we do these things? Because Jesus said, you have received these very same things from Me, give them to others.

Prayer: God, give me opportunities to help the lost and hurting.

> *Matthew 10:16 Behold, I send you out as sheep in the midst of wolves. Therefore be wise as serpents and harmless as doves.*

Prior to sending the disciples on their journey, Jesus gives them some practical instruction on how to approach people they will encounter. Some will be like wolves, who are natural predators of helpless sheep. They travel in packs, view sheep as an easy meal and attack at a moment's notice. Sadly, people are no different today than they were 2000 years ago. There are some who are looking for an innocent, unaware person to take advantage of. This is never more evident than the epidemic of human trafficking that is taking place today. According to www.safehorizon.com, Human trafficking is defined as, "the illegal trade in human beings through recruitment or abduction by means of force, fraud, or coercion for the purposes of forced labor, debt bondage or sexual exploitation." They report that nationally, 24.9 million people are victims of forced labor in the private economy or used for sexual exploitation. Sadly, this is the world we are living in today. Just as Jesus sent the disciples, He is sending us out into the world to reach the lost. His instructions are just as relevant to us, "Therefore be wise as serpents and harmless as doves." I am okay with trying to be harmless as a dove, but being like a snake has always had a negative connotation. I can remember my father saying, "that person is a snake in the grass." They pretend to be your friend all the while trying to take advantage of you. That is why Jesus linked having the practical wisdom of a snake, with the traits of a dove. A dove is seen as innocent, having pure motives. Jesus is telling us that practical wisdom will help us avoid the traps set by the world, but as we go, our motives and actions should model Him. John 2:24 says, "But Jesus would not entrust Himself to them, for He knew all men." Practical wisdom includes getting to know someone before fully trusting them. How many people have been scammed by trusting someone who is offering them "something too good to be true." Ask God for wisdom each day to be able to discern good from evil. Proverbs 2:6 says, "For the Lord gives wisdom, and from His mouth come knowledge and understanding." Use His wisdom to avoid the traps set by the devil and to help others.

Prayer: God give me wisdom and understanding so that I can help others.

> *Matthew 10:18 You will be brought before governors and kings for My sake, as a testimony to them and to the Gentiles.*

Without a doubt, the most influential Christian to U.S. Presidents and many world leaders in my lifetime was the late Billy Graham. According to *Decision Magazine. com*, "Graham has touched millions of people around the world, young, old, rich, poor, ordinary, and powerful. From Harry Truman to Donald Trump before he entered politics, Mr. Graham met 13 of the last 14 presidents and was able to develop a personal friendship with half of them. Regardless of political party, Mr. Graham accepted invitations to meet with any president, sharing the Gospel of Jesus Christ." Very few will ever have the opportunity Billy Graham had to witness to multiple presidents. However, Jesus told His disciples, don't be surprised when you are brought before governors and kings. Jesus is foreshadowing a time much later in the disciples' ministry when they would face persecution. According to *Christianity.com*, many of the disciples were killed for their faith. Peter and Paul were martyred during the persecution of Nero. Peter was crucified upside down, and Paul beheaded. Andrew was also believed to be crucified. Phillip was put to death by a Roman Proconsul. John was exiled to the Island of Patmos where he later wrote the Book of Revelation. Jesus' message is for us as well. There will come a day when Christians are brought before rulers and kings. Unfortunately, the meeting will not be the type of invitation Billy Graham received to meet with the presidents. As our world heads towards the return of Jesus, persecution of Christians will continue to increase. Even today, in some parts of the world Christians are driven from their homes, jailed, and killed for their faith. Revelation 2:10 says, "Do not be afraid of what you are about to suffer. I tell you the devil will put some of you in prison to test you, and you will suffer persecution for 10 days. Be faithful, even to the point of death, and I will give you life, as your victor's crown." I don't know that we are ever prepared to endure persecution. However, God tells us to endure and to persevere because there is a reward at the end. 2 Timothy 2:10, "If we endure, we will also reign with Him. If we disown Him, He will also disown us." My prayer is that God will strengthen you for the road ahead.

Prayer: God help me to be prepared to stand for You when persecution comes my way.

> *Matthew 10:19-20 But when they deliver you up, do not worry about how or what you should speak. For it will be given to you in that hour what you should speak; for it is not you who speak, but the Spirit of your Father who speaks in you.*

Some people seem to have a gift when it comes to public speaking. They can speak effortlessly on any subject with very little preparation. On the other hand, I tend to relate with Moses when it comes to speaking. Exodus 4:10 says, "Moses said to the Lord, 'O Lord, I have never been eloquent, neither in the past nor since You have spoken to Your servant. I am slow of speech and tongue.'" When called upon to speak, I prepare, I memorize, and try to keep to my notes. I also have a tendency to be a little blunt in spur of the moment conversations. That is why I am so thankful that Jesus gave us His promise of the Holy Spirit speaking through us "in the hour that you should speak." There have been several occasions when I know that the Holy Spirit has guided my words. Earlier this year, our church participated in the Religious Fair Day on the campus of UNC Wilmington. We set up a table in the Student Center with other churches and religious organizations to give students the opportunity to share Christ and to get to know us. Pastor Adam was busy talking with another student when the head of the LBGQT Student Group stopped by our table and asked if members of their community were welcome at our church. I said a quick prayer, "Lord, give me the words," and began to answer. My first comment was that everyone is welcome at our church. Then I told her, our church believes that the Bible is God's inerrant word, and our Pastor preaches God's word. That being the case, some may not like what they hear, but all are welcome to come and worship with us. The student coordinator, said "okay" and went on to the next table. I can only trust God, that my comments were the right ones for that time. On another occasion, a friend was sharing some personal problems that went well beyond my capability of helping him. Again, I asked God for help. Without getting into details, my primary response was that I am praying for him and recommended counseling. While I like to be prepared and have my comments preplanned, Jesus is telling us not to worry about what to say; He will give us the words. Ask Him to guide your conversations.

Prayer: God give me the right words to say in those difficult conversations.

> *Matthew 10:22 And you will be hated by all for My name's sake.*
> *But he who endures to the end will be saved.*

My sister is an avid runner. She has recently completed a full marathon of 26.2 miles in every state. That is over 1,360 miles, not to mention the many miles of training she has put in. She said, at some point in a marathon, many runners will "hit the wall." This occurs when there is a sudden loss of energy and fatigue quickly sets in. The runner's pace slows down dramatically and is tempted to quit. However, those that push through get their "second wind," when their body finds the strength and energy to continue on and complete the run. Following Jesus is like a marathon. Along the way, we will "hit the wall" with all types of challenges, including those who will hate us for being a Christian. Jesus promised that if we endure, "get our second wind" and complete this race called life with Him, we will be saved. Paul said in 2 Timothy 4:7-8, "I have fought the good fight. I have finished the race. I have kept the faith. Now there is in store for me the crown of righteousness, which the Lord, the righteous Judge, will award to me on that day, and not only to me, but also to all who have longed for His appearing." What is the secret to enduring to the end? First, we should avoid becoming weary. Refresh yourself in God's word each day and spend time with Him. Quality time in His presence is like getting your second wind. Second, be an encourager to others and find someone that will pick you up when you are struggling. Hebrews 3:13, "But encourage one another daily, as long as it is called 'Today,' so that none of you may be hardened by sin's deceitfulness." Next, understand that the trials of life can help you become a stronger Christian by making you more dependent on God. James 1:2-3 says, "Consider it pure joy, my brothers, whenever you face trials of many kinds, because you know that the testing of your faith develops perseverance." Lastly, keep on doing good. Galatians 6:9 tells us, "Let us not become weary in doing good, for at the proper time we will reap a harvest if we do not give up." Let your motto be a quote from Jim Valvano's famous speech at the ESPY's, "Don't give up, don't ever give up."

Prayer: God help me to faithfully run this race called life.

> *Matthew 10:26 Therefore do not fear them. For there is nothing covered that will not be revealed, and hidden that will not be known.*

Jesus is continuing His instructions to the disciples before sending them out on their mini-mission trip. He has already told them that they were going out as sheep among wolves, but not to fear because one day He will expose every evil plan and judge with righteousness. There have been several times when I wish Jesus would go ahead and reveal the truth. For example, what is the truth behind the COVID vaccines? Have they been helpful in saving lives? Or, does the vaccine have harmful side effects that have cost lives and ruined people's health? I am also interested in the truth behind the 2020 presidential election. Was there voter fraud and election tampering in several states as some have claimed? Or was the election a legitimate landslide for Joe Biden? I also want to know if Jeffrey Epstein committed suicide or was he murdered to cover up the debauchery that took place on his private island? It is easy to name things for God to reveal as long as they don't involve me. Jesus said, all that is hidden will be made known. One day everyone will stand before God and give an account of their life, the good, the bad and the ugly. I am so thankful that my sins are covered by the blood of Jesus. 1 John 1:7 says, "But if we walk in the light, as He is in the light, we have fellowship with one another, and the blood of Jesus, His Son, purifies us from all sin." Psalms 103:12 says, "As far as the east is from the west, so far has He removed our transgressions from us." However, Jesus is talking about revealing something far more important. In the very end, all will agree that Jesus is Lord. Everyone who has denied Christ and fought against Christianity and the gospel will acknowledge Jesus as the Son of God, the Messiah. This includes every atheist, Muslim, Buddhist, and Hindu. Philippians 2:10-11 says, "That at the name of Jesus, every knee should bow, in heaven and on earth and under the earth, and every tongue confess that Jesus Christ is Lord, to the glory of God the Father." My prayer is that you have acknowledged Jesus Christ as Lord and accepted Him as your personal Savior. Don't put if off until it is too late.

Prayer: Lord, I pray for Your kingdom to come, Your will be done.

> Matthew 10:28 And do not fear those who kill the body but cannot kill the soul. But rather fear Him who is able to destroy both soul and body in hell.

What does Jesus mean by killing the body and the soul? In Genesis 1:27 we read that God created "man" in His own image, both male and female. We know that God exists as three entities in one: God the Father, the Son, and the Holy Spirit. Likewise, God has created us with a body, soul, and spirit. 1 Thessalonians 5:23 says, "May God Himself, the God of peace, sanctify you through and through. May your whole spirit, soul, and body be kept blameless at the coming of our Lord Jesus Christ." Let's take a closer look at all three. Our physical bodies give us the ability to see, hear, taste, touch and function. They were designed by God to last us while we are alive on earth. Talking about our bodies, 1 Corinthians 15:44 says, "It is sown a natural body, it is raised a spiritual body. If there is a natural body, there is also a spiritual body." Our soul on the other hand is our inner being or spiritual body. Sometimes we refer to it as our heart, which is made up of our mind, emotions, and free will. Our souls will live forever, either in heaven or in hell. Lastly, our spirit is our connection to God. It is that inner drive that keeps us searching for purpose in life. Those who accept Jesus as their Lord and Savior activate their spirit and are made alive in Christ. Colossians 2:13, "When you were dead in your sins and in the uncircumcision of your sinful nature, God made you alive with Christ." It is through our spirit that we pray and commune with God. Jesus speaking in John 4:24 said, "God is Spirit, and His worshipers must worship in spirit and in truth." After we accept Christ into our lives, the process of conforming our soul to the image of Jesus begins. Romans 12:2 says, "Do not conform any longer to the pattern of this world, but be transformed by the renewing of your mind. Then you will be able to test and approve what God's will is, His good, pleasing, perfect will." Jesus said, not to fear those who could only harm your physical body because there is an enormous loss if we allow the fear of this world to prevent us from following Him.

Prayer: God help me to not fear those who could harm me for following You.

> *Matthew 10:29 Are not two sparrows sold for a copper coin? And not one of them falls to the ground apart from your Father's will.*

Jesus has just told His followers, not to fear those who could harm them for following Him. Now He lets them know how much God cares for them by sharing two examples. First, Jesus said that "not one sparrow falls to the ground apart from your Father's will." Luke also recorded Jesus' statement in chapter 12:6 as, "Yet not one of them is forgotten by God." What is the value of a sparrow? Not very much. In Jesus' day, two were sold for a copper coin or the equivalent of one cent. In Leviticus 14:4, we find sparrows were used for a cleansing sacrifice by someone healed of an infectious skin disease. For sparrows to be so insignificant, they have to be very plentiful. According to _www.zoologicalworld.com_, the sparrow can be found in every part of the world. They estimate there are over 1.6 billion sparrows in the world and have a lifespan of four to seven years. That means that God is aware of approximately 400 million sparrows that die each year. It is incomprehensible how much God cares for you. If He is watching over each sparrow that falls, how much more is He watching over you? Jesus continued by saying in Matthew 10:31, "So don't be afraid, you are worth more than many sparrows." Jesus wants you to know that a life lived for Him is not meaningless in His eyes. Every sacrifice you make or trouble you encounter while serving Him, whether big or small, is seen by Him. God is with you all the way. Jesus didn't promise His disciples an end to their suffering. He was encouraging them not to fear persecution because He would take it away, but that He would be with them. The same promise is for us. God promises to be with us through every trial of life. Let the lyrics of the following song encourage you today. "Why should I feel discouraged, why should the shadows come, Why should my heart be lonely, and long for heaven and home, When Jesus is my portion? My constant friend is He: His eye is on the sparrow, and I know He watches me; His eye is on the sparrow, and I know He watches me. I sing because I'm happy, I sing because I'm free, For His eye is on the sparrow, And I know He watches me."[7]

Prayer: God thank You for watching over me.

> *Matthew 10:30 But the very hairs on your head are all numbered.*

After telling the disciples that God is aware of every sparrow that falls to the ground, Jesus then tells them "the very hairs on your head are all numbered." How many hairs is God keeping track of? According to *www.healthline.com,* our heads hold approximately 100,000 hairs. They also report that hair grows at a rate of approximately six inches per year and we lose between 50 to 100 hairs per day depending on our hair care routine. Just in my family alone, God has numbered 1.3 million hairs. How does God keep track of 1.6 billion sparrows and trillions upon trillions of hair? He is God. Jeremiah 32:27 says, "I am the Lord, the God of all mankind. Is anything too hard for Me?" However, if we focus on the how and not the why God keeps up with every little detail, then we have missed what Jesus is telling us. God loves you. He loves you so much that He knows and cares about every detail of your life, inside and out. David said in Psalm 139:1-4; 13, "O Lord, You have searched me and You know me. You know when I sit and when I rise; You perceive my thoughts from afar. You discern my going out and my lying down; You are familiar with all my ways. Before a word is on my tongue You know it completely... For You created my inmost being, You knit me together in my mother's womb." It doesn't matter what you are going through, what you have done or even what you have said, God loves you. Nothing can separate you from His love. Romans 8:35;38-39 says, "Who shall separate us from the love of Christ? Shall trouble or hardship or persecution or famine or nakedness or danger or sword?...For I am convinced that neither death nor life, neither angels nor demons, neither the present nor the future, nor any powers, neither height nor depth, nor anything else in all creation will be able to separate us from the love of God that is in Christ Jesus our Lord." When you begin to doubt God's love for you, let the hair you see in your hair brush or in the shower remind you of God's love for you and that 'the very hairs on your head are numbered.'

Prayer: God, let the hairs on my head remind me of Your love for me.

> Matthew 10:32 *Therefore whoever confesses Me before men. Him I will also confess before My Father who is in heaven.*

Jesus said for Him to recognize us before God the Father, we must confess Him before men. In other words, we are to tell or make known to others that we have accepted Him as Lord and Savior of our lives. Why is that so important? Because salvation is just more than believing. James 2:19 says, "You believe that there is one God. Good! Even the demons believe that and shudder." According to a Gallop Poll found in USA Today, 81% of Americans say they believe in God. Although pretty high, this number is down six points from a 2017 poll.[8] However, approximately 56% of Americans say they seldom or never attend church and only 22% say they attend weekly.[9] It is easy to say "I believe in God" but there is very little commitment to serving Him without confessing Him as Lord. Paul said in Romans 10:9-10, "That if you confess with your mouth, 'Jesus is Lord,' and believe in your heart that God raised Him from the dead, you will be saved. For it is with your heart that you believe and are justified, and it is with your mouth that you confess and are saved." To paraphrase Paul, if we really believe God sent His only Son to die for our sins and raised Him from the dead, how can we be silent about it? What are some ways we can confess Christ? First and most importantly when we accept Jesus as Lord and Savior, we make a public profession or declaration that we have decided to follow Him. We announce our decision to others. We then seal this decision by being baptized. Baptism is a step of obedience after salvation as a public profession of faith in Christ and identification with Him. Baptism doesn't save us. It is a symbolic act of Jesus' death and resurrection. Romans 6:3-4 says, "Or don't you know that all of us who were baptized into Christ Jesus were baptized into His death? We were therefore buried with Him through baptism into death in order that, just as Christ was raised from the dead through the glory of the Father, we too may live a new life." Our profession of Christ does not stop after baptism. We then begin to tell our friends, neighbors and family members what Jesus has done for us. Are you sharing the good news?

Prayer: God help me to daily confess You.

Day 67

> Matthew 10:33 But whoever denies Me before men, him I will also deny before My Father who is in heaven.

Is Jesus saying that if I slip up one time and deny Him, that I will not go to heaven? I sure hope not. Because I have been guilty of it many times. Several years ago, Vivian and I attended a conference in San Antonio. The conference was to begin on Sunday evening, so we traveled early Saturday and had planned to go to Cornerstone Church, where John Hagee was pastor. We had a great day at church and lunch on the River Walk. Later that day at the conference, someone asked me what we did that day. Instead of saying we went to church, I simply said we hung around downtown San Antonio for the day. Moments later, guilt ran through my body. I had the perfect opportunity to say we were at church and speak about Christ. Instead, I was intimidated by the situation and failed. That day was over 10 years ago, and it still bothers me. Perhaps you can relate to my story. Take heart, God can still use you. Let's look at the life of Peter. Jesus has just been arrested and Peter had followed the crowd to the High Priest's house where a mock trial was conducted. There, confronted by three different people, Peter denied knowing Jesus. Luke 22:61-62 tells us, "The Lord turned and looked straight at Peter. Then Peter remembered the word the Lord had spoken to him: 'Before the rooster crows today, you will disown Me three times.' And he went outside and wept bitterly." Peter had two choices after that evening. He could run away and never be heard of again, or he could seek God's forgiveness and be stronger the next opportunity he had. A few weeks later, we read about Peter in Acts 2. Verse 14 says, "Then Peter stood up with the Eleven, raised his voice and addressed the crowd..." Verse 41 says, "Those who accepted his message were baptized, and about three thousand were added to their number that day." Yesterday we learned that 81% of Americans believe in God, but only 22% attend church regularly. While church attendance doesn't guarantee salvation, it is a step of acknowledging the need for Christ in your life. Also, the words we use and the life we live lets others know that we are Christians. Are you acknowledging Christ in your life or denying Him?

Prayer: God, please forgive me for denying You before men.

> *Matthew 10:38 And he who does not take his cross and follow after Me is not worthy of Me.*

Quite often, we associate a sickness or burden in our lives as our "cross to bear." These may challenge us from reaching our full potential but cannot be compared to the cross Jesus bore. The cross was a painful and horrible means of executing criminals. Those being crucified were forced to carry the beam of their cross to a place of execution. There, they were nailed to the beam, and left to hang until their eventual death from either exhaustion or asphyxiation. Jesus knew He would be forced to carry His own cross to Golgotha, where He would be crucified. John 19:17-18 says, "Carrying His own cross, He went out to the place of the Skull (which in Aramaic is called Golgotha.) Here they crucified Him, and with Him two others, one on each side and Jesus in the middle." The Book of Matthew also tells us that Simon of Cyrene was forced to help Jesus carry the cross because Jesus was too weak to continue. Taking up a cross in Jesus' day meant certain death. If we are going to follow Jesus, He expects us to die to our old self and become a new person. Paul said in 2 Corinthians 5:17, "Therefore, if anyone is in Christ, he is a new creation. The old has passed away; behold the new has come." Galatians 2:20 also tells us, "I have been crucified with Christ and I no longer live, but Christ lives in me. The life I now live in the body, I live by faith in the Son of God, who loved me and gave Himself for me." Jesus is saying, to follow Me requires more than just inviting Me into your life. You must be willing to let go of your own agenda, personal dreams, and way of life to follow Me. 1 John 2:5-6 says it this way, "But if anyone obeys His word, God's love is truly made complete in him. This is how we know we are in Him: Whoever claims to live in Him must walk as Jesus did." Following Christ and allowing Him to direct your steps requires us to surrender to His will. The beauty of it, is that God replaces what we give up with something much more valuable, an inner satisfaction and a purpose to our lives.

Prayer: God help me to take up my cross daily and follow You.

> Matthew 10:39 He who finds his life will lose it, and he who loses his life for My sake will find it.

Have you ever heard someone say, "I have got to find myself?" Most likely that person was either unhappy or may have reached a point where they felt like something was missing, questioning the meaning of life. To find themselves, they begin a journey of self-reflection, thinking about their past life experiences. They also look at past and present relationships, their accomplishments or lack of accomplishments. Out of this self-reflection comes a new and motivated person ready to take on the world, only to find themselves back in the same unhappiness. Why do people find themselves caught up in this cycle of unhappiness? Perhaps we are looking for the wrong things. Jesus said, "those who find their lives will lose it." What are we looking for? Things such as social status, the right relationship, a new house, a new car, and a large bank account can bring momentary pleasure; however, they are not lasting. The newness wears off and then we want something different. The thing about things is that we are never satisfied with them. But Jesus also said, "He who loses his life for My sake, will find it." Jesus had a way of conveying the same message in several different ways. Yesterday, He said, "anyone who does not take up his cross and follow Me is not worthy of Me." We learned that in order to follow Him, we have to be willing to die to our old way of life. Today, He promises that we will find our true purpose in life by choosing to follow Him. In fact, He has created you and I with a specific purpose in mind and given us His Spirit to help us achieve it. 2 Corinthians 5:5 says, "Now it is God who has made us for this very purpose and has given us the Spirit as a deposit, guaranteeing what is to come." You may be at a point where you have your life planned out and don't think you need to listen to God. Proverbs 19:21 tells us, "Many are the plans of a person's heart, but it is the Lord's purpose that prevails." In other words, your life will be a vicious circle of unhappiness until you submit to His purpose, because His purpose prevails. Find real life, put yours in His hands.

Prayer: God, teach me how to lose my life for Your sake.

> *Matthew 10:42 And whoever gives one of these little ones only a cup of cold water in the name of a disciple, assuredly, I say to you, he shall by no means lose his reward.*

Jesus has just told His disciples to "take up their cross and follow Him," and "he who loses his life for My sake will find it." Following Jesus requires that we sacrifice our own wants and desires in submission to His will for our lives. As we do, God fills us with a sense of purpose, satisfaction and contentment. Then, Jesus tells His disciples in Matthew 10:40-41, "He who receives you receives Me, and he who receives Me receives the one who sent Me. Anyone who receives a prophet will receive a prophet's reward, and anyone who receives a righteous man because he is a righteous man will receive a righteous man's reward." Meaning that as the disciples are going out, anyone who helps them, even something as simple as giving them a cup of cold water will be rewarded by God. On Day 19, I shared that Vivian and I attend Second Mile Church in Wilmington, NC. Our Pastor and his wife, living in Tennessee at the time, were led by God to start a church in the Wilmington area. They prayed, prepared, and moved to Wilmington at God's direction without knowing anyone here. Through God's divine providence, Vivian learned of a new family moving to Wilmington to start a church. She reached out to them on social media, inviting their family of six to our home for dinner. From that meeting, God led us to become a part of a brand-new church. Being a part of a new church is not easy and it has stretched us. However, God has blessed us and given us a purpose for serving there. God has called you to a specific purpose. We are all disciples, sent by God to share the good news of Jesus Christ. It could mean talking about Christ to the person sitting next to you at work, or someone you see at the grocery store every week. It could mean supporting a missionary in a foreign country, financially and through prayer. It could even mean lifting up a fellow believer who is going through a difficult time. The list is endless. Jesus said in Matthew 25:40, "The King will reply, 'I tell you the truth, whatever you did for one of the least of these brothers of Mine, you did for Me.'" It is time to get busy fulfilling your purpose.

Prayer: God, open doors for me to serve others.

> Matthew 11:4 Jesus answered and said to them, "Go and tell John the things which you hear and see."

The Bible tells us that John the Baptist and Jesus were cousins. Luke 1:15-17 speaks about John's purpose, "And he will go on before the Lord, in the spirit and power of Elijah, to turn the hearts of the fathers to their children and the disobedient to the wisdom of the righteous, to make ready a people prepared for the Lord." John lived in the desert, preaching repentance for the coming of the Messiah was at hand, and baptized many people. Luke 3:16 tells us, "John answered them all, 'I baptize you with water. But one more powerful than I will come, the thongs of whose sandals I am not worthy to untie. He will baptize you with the Holy Spirit and with fire.'" Jesus also came to John to be baptized. However, John was reluctant to baptize Jesus because he felt unworthy. Jesus told John "Let it be so now; it is proper for us to do this to fulfill all righteousness." (Matthew 3:15) In today's verse, John is now in prison, put there by King Herod for speaking against Herod's marriage to his brother's wife. Knowing that his ministry was coming to an end, John had sent his disciples to Jesus to ask Him, "Are You the one who was to come, or should we expect someone else?" He wanted to know for sure that Jesus was the Messiah, the one who he had preached was coming. Jesus' answer is found in Matthew 11:4-6, "Go back and report to John what you hear and see: The blind receive sight, the lame walk, those who have leprosy are cured, the deaf hear, the dead are raised, and the good news is preached to the poor. Blessed is the man who does not fall away on account of Me." Like John, have you ever wondered if Jesus was really who He said He was? Is He the Messiah, the only path that leads to salvation? The world will tell you there are many ways to find God and salvation. For Islam, salvation is based on the deeds of a person. For Buddhism, salvation is self-awareness. In Hinduism, salvation is achieved through a series of reincarnations. Jesus said in John 14:6, "I am the way and the truth and the life. No one comes to the Father except through Me." Look closely at the evidence and make your own decision.

Prayer: God, thank You for sending Your Son Jesus.

> *Matthew 11:11 Assuredly, I say to you, among those born of women there has not risen one greater than John the Baptist; but he who is least in the kingdom of heaven is greater than he.*

John the Baptist was a prophet sent to prepare the people's heart for the coming of the Messiah. He preached repentance and baptized all who received his message. Both Isaiah and Malachi prophesied the coming of John. Isaiah 40:3 says, "A voice of one calling: 'In the desert prepare the way for the Lord, make straight in the wilderness a highway for our God.'" Malachi 3:1 says, "See, I will send My messenger, who will prepare the way before Me. Then suddenly the Lord you are seeking will come to His temple; the messenger of the covenant, who you desire, will come, says the Lord Almighty." As far as being a vital part of the kingdom of God, it is hard to find anyone else greater than John the Baptist. Jesus even said that John was the greatest person born on earth. However, Jesus then said, "but he who is least in the kingdom of heaven is greater than he." How can that be possible? John the Baptist preached repentance. Acts 18:24-25 tells us about Apollos who was baptized by John, "Meanwhile a Jew named Apollos, a native of Alexandria, came to Ephesus. He was a learned man, with a thorough knowledge of the Scriptures. He had been instructed in the way of the Lord, and he spoke with great fervor and taught about Jesus accurately, though he knew only the baptism of John." Apollos knew who Jesus was, but had not accepted Jesus as Lord and Savior. Paul then said in Acts 19:4-5, "'John's baptism was a baptism of repentance." He told the people to believe in the one coming after him, that is, Jesus. On hearing this, they were baptized into the name of the Lord Jesus.' John the Baptist was a great prophet and fulfilled his mission of preparing the way. When Jesus came to die on the cross for our sins, He made a way for us to become not only repentant but righteous in His sight and joint heirs with Him. John 1:12 says, "Yet to all who received Him, to those who believed in His name, He gave the right to become children of God." God loves us so much that we are more to Him than repentant sinners, but His very own children. Rejoice today, you are a child of God.

Prayer: God, thank You for making me a joint heir with Your Son, Jesus Christ.

> Matthew 11:24 But I say to you that it shall be more tolerable for the land of Sodom in the day of judgement than for you.

Sodom and Gomorrah are known for being destroyed by God because of their great wickedness. God rained down fire and brimstone and completely wiped out both cities. However, before executing judgment, God went to see for Himself if the cities were deserving of destruction. Genesis 18:20 says, "Then the Lord said, 'The outcry against Sodom and Gomorrah is so great and their sin so grievous that I will go down and see if what they have done is as bad as the outcry that has reached Me. If not, I will know.'" Abraham begged the Lord not to destroy them if He could find as few as ten righteous people. Only Lot, Abraham's nephew, and his two daughters were spared. Who could be more wicked and deserving of punishment than Sodom and Gomorrah? Jesus said in Matthew 11:23-24, "And you, Capernaum, will you be lifted up to the skies? No, you will go down to the depths. If the miracles that were performed in you had been performed in Sodom, it would have remained to this day." Capernaum was Jesus' adopted home. The Sermon on the Mount was preached in that area. Jesus performed many miracles there, including raising a little girl from the dead. (Luke 8:40-56) In spite of all that Jesus did in Capernaum, there was no revival, no acceptance of Him as the Messiah. Even the religious leaders questioned Him and accused Jesus of blasphemy for healing on the Sabbath and forgiving people of their sins. What would Jesus say about your city, your state, or even our country? Isaiah 13:11 says, "I will punish the world for its evil, the wicked for their sins. I will put an end to the arrogance of the haughty and will humble the pride of the ruthless." Do you think He would come to condemn our nation for rejecting His word? Most importantly, what is your response to the word of God? God loves you and has given you an opportunity to repent and accept Him as Lord and Savior. However, God is also a God of justice. His word tells us that our sin has consequences. Romans 6:23 says, "For the wages of sin is death, but the gift of God is eternal life in Christ Jesus our Lord." Where will you stand on the day of judgement?

Prayer: God, I accept You as my Lord and Savior, please come into my life today.

> Matthew 11:25 *At that time Jesus answered and said, "I thank You, Father, Lord of heaven and earth, that You have hidden these things from the wise and prudent and have revealed them to babes."*

As I was growing up, I can remember my parents telling me, "You are getting too big for your own britches." According to *www.idomsthefreedictionary.com*, this phrase means "overconfident in one's importance, skill, and authority; behaving as if one is more important or influential than one actually is." I also remember coming to the realization I wasn't as smart and important as I thought I was. Life has a way of quickly bringing us back to reality. Jesus' prayer today implies that it takes a child-like faith to know Him. He also said the minds of the wise and more educated have been blurred to who He was. Not much has changed in 2000 years. According to *www.pewresearch.org*, "Highly educated Americans are less inclined than others to say they believe in God with absolute certainty and to pray on a daily basis. And, when asked about their religious identity, college graduates are more likely than others to describe themselves as atheists or agnostics." To be clear, I am not saying that salvation is based on your level of education. I know many Christians who have a college education. I am one of them. However, I am speaking about the type of education that promotes worldly wisdom and intelligence leading to self-dependence and a false sense of confidence. Sadly, this type of wisdom causes people to think there is no God, or they don't need God in their life. The Bible is irrelevant to them and they have no understanding of Jesus and the sacrifice He made. Our grandson, Anders, just turned one year old. He is still dependent on his parents to take care of all his needs. He trusts them to give him food, change his diapers, and to comfort him because he can't do those things on his own. God wants us to have that type of trust in Him. Worldly wisdom says, "There is no God." Godly wisdom says, "In the beginning was God." Worldly wisdom says, "I can make it on my own." Godly wisdom says, "I need You, Lord." Worldly wisdom says, "I am a good person, I am going to heaven." Godly wisdom says, "I am saved by grace through faith, and not by myself, it is the gift of God, not of works." Are you listening to the world's wisdom or God's wisdom? Don't let your education and knowledge confuse you.

Prayer: God, thank You that it takes child-like faith to know You.

> *Matthew 11:28 Come to Me, all you who labor and are heavy laden, and I will give you rest.*

At one point in my career with Progress Energy, I was a supervisor in our newly opened Customer Service Center. We had just closed our local business offices and transitioned all customer support to a centralized Call Center. To say the least, there was a huge learning curve. As soon as I walked in the door each morning, my "feet hit the ground running." We were resolving customer complaints, employee concerns, hiring new employees due to a high turnover rate, and developing new guidelines and procedures. It was one of the most demanding times of my career and had me on the brink of giving up and leaving the company. Thankfully, we got better at what we were doing and things began to improve. Later, I became thankful for that experience because it helped me to be successful in another job at the Call Center. Life is not easy and rarely goes as planned. On many days, it can be a struggle just to get through it. Vivian and I have a saying, "It is a good thing we didn't know what was going to happen today. If we did, we would not have gotten out of the bed." Nowhere in the Bible does God promise anyone an easy life. We are going to have problems, face hardships, and experience pain in our lives. Some of our burdens can even be self-inflicted. The question becomes, how do we respond when trouble comes our way? Which of the following options best fits you? 1. Withdraw and let life overwhelm you. 2. Take out your frustrations on those closest to you. 3. Numb your mind with drugs or alcohol. 4. Run away from your problems. 5. Give your life and your problems to God. The Bible tells us to give our problems to God. Psalms 50:15 says, "And call upon Me in the day of trouble; I will deliver you, and you will honor Me." Psalms 9:9 also tells us, "The Lord is a refuge for the oppressed, a stronghold in times of trouble." Jesus tells us today, "Come to Me, all you who labor and are heavy laden, and I will give you rest." Jesus knows that you are facing struggles. He knows that your problems are more than you can handle on your own. He is giving you an invitation today to come to Him. His promise is rest.

Prayer: God, thank You for Your promise of rest.

> *Matthew 11:29 Take My yoke upon you and learn from Me, for I am gentle and lowly in heart, and you will find rest for your souls.*

A yoke is a wooden device that is attached to an animal's neck and connected to a plow or cart for pulling. In Jesus' day, a yoke was also used as a frame to hang over someone's shoulders for carrying heavy loads. It was a common piece of equipment and everyone could relate to the hard work it represented. Jesus said, "take My yoke and learn from Me...you will find rest for your souls." Jesus knew that the people were overwhelmed and struggling to get by. On one side of their yoke was the harsh rule of the Romans and the other was the oppressive laws and regulations created by the religious leaders. That was over 2,000 years ago and things have changed. In America, we have religious freedom and are not governed by foreigners who make life difficult for us. We have it made, or do we? In spite of all our freedom, do we still find ourselves burdened with a load of stress, anxiety, depression, financial problems, addictions, health issues, and worry about our future? Jesus knows the challenges you face and the stress that comes with the responsibilities of life. He wants you to replace them with His purpose and plan for your life. He promises blessings, renewed strength, and rest for your soul when you do. 1 Peter 5:7 says, "Cast all your anxiety on Him because He cares for you." Psalms 55:22 also says, "Cast all your cares on the Lord and He will sustain you; He will never let the righteous fall." Both of these verses tell us to 'cast all our cares' on the Lord. When I hear the word cast, I think of fishing. When fishing, I am casting a line with a hook and bait or a fishing net with plans to catch something. The Bible tells us to throw our problems on the Lord. Just as a hook or net catches a fish, our burdens become attached to Him. If you have ever caught a fish, you know the excitement and anticipation of pulling the fish out of the water. As you cast over your burdens to Jesus, He draws closer to you. You experience the anticipation and excitement of His presence in your life. What burdens do you need to surrender to God and trust Him with today? Go fishing, cast your cares on Him.

Prayer: God, I cast all my cares on You today.

> Matthew 12:3 But He said to them, "Have you not read what David did when he was hungry, and he and those who were with him."

One Sabbath day as Jesus and His disciples were walking through a grainfield, they picked a few heads of grain and ate them. The Pharisees saw them picking the grain and said to Jesus, "Look! Your disciples are doing what is unlawful on the Sabbath." The Pharisees were referring to the Laws of Moses found in Exodus 34:21, "Six days you shall labor, but on the seventh day you shall rest; even during the plowing season and harvest you must rest." Jesus' reply was to remind them of the story of David and his men found in 1 Samuel 21:6. On the run from Saul, they ate some of the consecrated bread in the temple, which according to Jewish Law was unlawful for them to do. Jesus teaches us two valuable lessons today. First, He asks the Pharisees, "Have you not read?" That question applies to us as well. Have you not read God's word? The Bible is God's written word, given to us so that we can know Him better and live according to His plan. 2 Timothy 3:16-17 says, "All scripture is God-breathed and is useful for teaching, rebuking, correcting and training in righteousness, so that the man of God may be thoroughly equipped for every good work." Psalms 119:105 also tells us, "Your word is a lamp to my feet and a light for my path." There are a number of Bible reading plans available which can help get you started. Make time to read God's word each day. Daily devotionals are good, but getting into God's word is invaluable. Secondly, Jesus teaches us is to avoid getting caught up in following the legalistic requirements of being a Christian, but following the heart of God. If our faith becomes a list of do's and don'ts then we are not following His heart. If we are more concerned about how we look on the outside rather than the condition of our hearts, we may not be following the heart of God. If we put going to church over helping others, then we may not be following God. Jesus went on to say in Matthew 12:7, "...I desire mercy not sacrifice..." He is telling us that God wants us to love people over following religious rituals. He wants us to come to Him and experience His love and share it with others.

Prayer: God, help me to read and follow Your word.

> *Matthew 12:12 Of how much more value then is a man than a sheep? Therefore it is lawful to do good on the Sabbath.*

Yesterday, we read where Jesus and His disciples were accused of breaking the Law of Moses by picking a few kernels of grain and eating them. Jesus' day did not end there. Matthew 12:9-10 tells us, "Going on from that place, He went into their synagogue, and a man with a shriveled hand was there. Looking for a reason to accuse Jesus, they asked Him, 'Is it lawful to heal on the Sabbath?'" Jesus could have easily said to the man with the shriveled hand, come back tomorrow and I will heal your hand. Instead, He asks the Pharisees, "If any of you has a sheep and it falls into a pit on the Sabbath, will you not take hold of it and lift it out?" The Pharisees did not answer Jesus, because the obvious answer was yes. No one would leave their sheep in a pit to suffer all day or fall prey to a wolf. Jesus then asks them, "How much more valuable then is a man than a sheep?" Jesus is not suggesting that observing the Sabbath was wrong; however, the requirement not to work was intended to give people a break from work, not to add to their burden. Jesus concludes by telling the Pharisees, the Sabbath was a day for doing good, to help someone in need. Again, Jesus is trying to tell us love is greater than legalism. I can tell you from experience, some church denominations love to create rules. In the early 80's, the church Vivian and I attended, had plenty of rules. Men couldn't wear short pants. Women had to wear dresses, use no make-up, no jewelry, and not cut their hair. Boys and girls could not go swimming together. Going to the beach was not allowed because of mixed bathing. These rules have become obsolete and dropped by the wayside. However, deep inside, we all desire to have a list of rules to know what is permissible and still be a Christian. We want to know the gray areas. Is smoking permissible? What about alcohol? Do I have to go to church every Sunday? Jesus is telling us, enough of this nonsense, "I desire mercy not sacrifice." He wants you to learn how to love Him more than anything else. When we do, everything else will fall into place.

Prayer: God, help me to learn the value of a sheep.

> Matthew 12:13 Then He said to the man, "Stretch out your hand."
> And he stretched it out, and it was restored as whole as the other.

The Bible doesn't tell us if the man with a crippled hand was born that way or if his hand had been injured in an accident. Nor does it tell us if the man just happened to be at the synagogue that day, or if the Pharisees had him there to set a trap for Jesus. In either case, Jesus wasn't intimidated by the Pharisees and their rules. His concern was for the man who needed healing. After addressing the Pharisees on what was more important, following their rules or being merciful, Jesus turns His attention to the man. Notice Jesus just didn't say to him, your hand is now healed. He tells the man to 'stretch out your hand.' His hand, which was likely a source of embarrassment and ridicule, had now become the focus of attention. The man had a choice. He could listen to Jesus or try to win the approval of the religious leaders and walk away. Paul said in Galatians 1:10, "Am I now trying to win the approval of men, or of God? Or am I trying to please men? If I were still trying to please men, I would not be a servant of Christ." The man trusted Jesus and stretched it towards Him. Matthew tells us that as he stretched out his hand, "it was restored as whole as the other." Trusting Jesus brought healing and restoration. Although the Bible doesn't tell us, no doubt he left rejoicing. Our lives are no different from the man with the crippled hand. We live with things that paralyze us such as, doubt, fear, negativity, addictions, depression, oppression, hate, unforgiveness, and unforgiven sin. Not only can these be a source of embarrassment, but they also prevent us from living a fulfilled life. Just as Jesus required an act of obedience and faith from the man with the crippled hand, He requires that of us if we want to be healed. Paraphrasing today's verse, Jesus said, "show Me...", and in Matthew 11:28 He says, "Come to Me..." The question becomes do we trust Him enough to share the ugliness and pain in our lives, or do we decide to live with it? His word tells us in Psalms 147:3 says, "He heals the brokenhearted and binds up their wounds." Whatever you are carrying, give it to God. He can heal you.

Prayer: God, please heal my stretched forth hand.

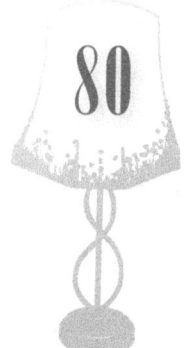
> *Matthew 12:25 But Jesus knew their thoughts, and said to them: "Every kingdom divided against itself is brought to desolation. And every city or house divided against itself will not stand."*

Jesus had just healed a demon-possessed man who was blind and mute. All the people were amazed and began to ask each other if Jesus was the Messiah. Not so with the Pharisees. When they learned about the healing, they said, "It is only by Beelzebub, the prince of demons, that This fellow drives out demons." Matthew tells us, "But Jesus knew their thoughts." Let's stop here for a minute. Jesus knows our thoughts? I have had some thoughts that were not too pleasant, so disgusting that I pray no one will ever know. David writes in Psalm 139:2, "You know when I sit and when I rise; You perceive my thoughts from afar." Perhaps that is why Paul said in Philippians 4:8, "Finally, brothers, whatever is true, whatever is noble, whatever is right, whatever is pure, whatever is lovely, whatever is admirable – if anything is excellent or praiseworthy – think about such things." I am so thankful that God is a loving God who forgives. Jesus then asks the Pharisees, 'If Satan drives out Satan, he is divided against himself. How can his kingdom stand?" Simply put, division causes ruin. Despite the consequences, division is rampant in our country, our churches and our families. The last time I recall our country being unified resulted from the events of September 11, 2001. Sadly, that spirit of unity did not last long and our nation has continued to split into two completely opposite directions. In past years, I have also witnessed churches split over disagreements about Pastors, color of the carpet, and type of music. Churches are now beginning to split over social issues such as homosexuality. Families are not immune from division either, fighting over finances, sibling rivalries and disagreements with in-laws. The Bible has a lot to say about unity. Paul writing in Ephesians 4:1-6 sums it up pretty well, "I therefore, a prisoner for the Lord, urge you to walk in a manner worthy of the calling to which you have been called, with all humility and gentleness, with patience, bearing with one another in love, eager to maintain the unity of the Spirit in the bond of peace. There is one body and one Spirit—just as you were called to the one hope that belongs to your call— one Lord, one faith, one baptism."

Prayer: God help me to walk in the manner in which You have called me.

> Matthew 12:29 Or how can one enter a strong man's house and plunder his goods, unless he first binds the strong man? And then he will plunder his house.

Vivian and I have taken several mission teams to serve in Nicaragua. While there, we would stay at a facility developed by Michael and Sue Buzbee with Open Hearts Ministry. The compound was gated and as most Latin American businesses, had an armed guard. We felt safe and secure while staying there. However, one morning after our team had left, the compound was robbed at gunpoint. Fortunately, no one was hurt in the incident. The question on everyone's mind was how did the robbers get past the armed guard at the gate without being detected? Either by coincidence or good planning, the robbers were driving the same type of vehicle that made weekly deliveries to the compound. The guard thought this was another routine delivery. Once inside, the robbers knew where to go and quickly took all loose cash and left without being confronted by the guard. Jesus, talking to the Pharisees, used an analogy of a strong man protecting his house. Unless someone were to overtake the strong man and tie him up, how could they enter and plunder his house? Just as the robbers tricking the guard at the gate in Nicaragua, they would have had no chance of getting inside. Who is Jesus talking about? Satan and his demons represent the strong man. Satan's house is the power and influence he has over everyone on the earth. 2 Timothy 2:26 says, "And that they will come to their senses and escape from the trap of the devil, who has taken them captive to do his will." Jesus said in John 8:43, "I tell you the truth, everyone who sins is a slave to sin." Without Christ in our lives, we belong to Satan and are slaves to sin. Being a slave to sin leads to death and eternal separation from God. However, Jesus has come to plunder Satan of his captive property, our souls, and to offer us eternal life with Him. Isaiah 42:7, prophesying about Jesus says, "To open eyes that are blind, to free captives from prison and to release from the dungeon those who sit in darkness." On our own, we are completely unable to escape the consequences of sin. However, through the sacrifice Jesus made on the cross, we are set free from sin and have eternal life with Him. Give Him praise today for overcoming Satan and the world.

Prayer: God, thank You for overpowering Satan and setting me free.

> Matthew 12:30 *He who is not with Me is against Me, and he who does not gather with Me scatters abroad.*

When someone is unable to make a decision or take a stand between two opposing ideas, they are "straddling the fence." There have been times when I have been guilty of straddling the fence. I have a tendency to analyze both sides of an idea, and not wanting to disappoint anyone, remain undecided. Jesus said, "He who is not with Me is against Me." He made it pretty clear that straddling the fence was not an option if we are going to follow Him. Romans 8:5 says, "Those who live according to the sinful nature have their minds set on what that nature desires; but those who live in accordance with the Spirit have their minds set on what the Spirit desires." We can't have it both ways. Either we are living and serving our sinful nature, or we are living and serving Christ. God doesn't allow us to live by the 80/20 rule. In 1 Samuel 15, we read the story of Saul, who was commanded by God to attack and totally destroy the Amalekites. Why did God want the Amalekites destroyed? The answer is found in Exodus 17. The Amalekites had attacked the Israelites after God freed them from slavery in Egypt. The Amalekites were defeated by Moses and the Israelites, but God made a promise in Exodus 17:14, "...I will erase the memory of Amalek from under heaven." Hundreds of years later, King Saul was given the task to fulfill God's promise. Saul and his army attacked and defeated the Amalekites as God commanded. However, Saul lived by the 80/20 rule and did not completely destroy them. He brought back the best of the Amalekite flocks and allowed King Agag to live. Because of his disobedience, God rejected Saul as King of Israel, and had Samuel anoint David as King. Are you living by the 80/20 rule, trying to serve God, but keeping one foot in the world? 1 John 2:15-17 says, "Do not love the world or anything in the world. If anyone loves the world, the love of the Father is not in him. For everything in the world – the cravings of sinful man, the lust of his eyes and the boasting of what he has and does – does not come from the Father but from the world. The world and its desires pass away, but the man who does the will of God lives forever."

Prayer: God help me to follow You completely.

> Matthew 12:31 Therefore I say to you, every sin and blasphemy will be forgiven men, but the blasphemy against the Spirit will not be forgiven men.

Jesus speaking to the Pharisees, describes what many have called, "the unpardonable sin." Of all the verses in the Bible, this one gave me the most concern as a young Christian. Not yet strong in my faith, I often worried if I had committed the unpardonable sin. Had I committed some grievous sin that I really didn't know what I had done? If so, since it was unpardonable, was there any chance of forgiveness or was I doomed for hell? Satan loves to put doubt and fear in a young believer's mind. Thankfully as I grew older and matured in my faith in God, I better understood what "blasphemy against the Spirit" meant. First, let's understand what the word blasphemy means. *www.merriam-webster.com* defines blasphemy as, "the act of showing contempt or lack of reverence for God." In this verse, it is a defiant irreverence of the Holy Spirit. Jesus speaking in John 16:8 tells us about the Holy Spirit, "When He comes, He will convict the world of guilt in regard to sin and righteousness and judgment." John 14:26 adds, "But the Counselor, the Holy Spirit, whom the Father will send in My name, will teach you all things and will remind you of everything I have said to you." The Holy Spirit is God in spirit form here on earth. To the person who has not accepted Christ as his or her Lord and Savior, the Holy Spirit is that inner voice that is leading them to make that decision. For the Christian, the Holy Spirit teaches us how to live a Christ-like life. The Sunday evening when I accepted Jesus as my Lord and Savior, my heart was pounding. Pastor Stines, had just given an invitation for anyone to come and receive Christ into their heart. I felt the Holy Spirit's urging to step out and make that profession of faith. I had two choices, stand still and wait for another time, or step forth. I thank God that I made that decision over 50 years ago. The Holy Spirit gives us opportunities throughout our life to make that decision. However, the more we reject His calling, the easier it becomes the next time until our hearts become callused. At some point, we totally put God out of our lives and reject (blaspheming) the work of His Spirit, condemning ourselves.

Prayer: God, help me to listen to the voice of Your Spirit.

> Matthew 12:33 *Either make the tree good and its fruit good, or else make the tree bad and its fruit bad; for a tree is known by its fruit.*

My great-uncle owned an apple orchard in Rockingham County, NC. As a young child, I can remember visiting him and enjoying apples right off the tree. My grandmother had a press that we would fill with apples and make fresh apple juice. It seemed his apple trees were always plentiful. However, as a child I didn't realize the amount of work it took to have healthy apple trees. There was pruning, spraying, fertilizing, mulching, and watering to name a few. If my great-uncle had tried to take a shortcut and leave out one step, his crop could have not developed properly. His apples would have been infested with insects, their growth stunted, or his trees would produce a much smaller crop. Needless to say, maintaining a productive apple orchard is a year-round process. Speaking about us, Jesus said, "a tree is known by its fruit." Just as all flowering trees produce fruit, we produce fruit as well. Is our fruit good or bad? Today, we are going to focus on the bad fruit. If we are being driven by our sinful nature, the Bible says we are producing bad fruit. Galatians 5:17 says, "For the sinful nature desires what is contrary to the Spirit, and the Spirit what is contrary to the sinful nature. They are in conflict with each other, so that you do not do what you want." Paul goes on to list some of the bad fruit we produce in Galatians 5:17-21, "The acts of the sinful nature are obvious: sexual immorality, impurity and debauchery; idolatry, and witchcraft; hatred, discord, jealousy, fits of rage, selfish ambition, dissentions, factions and envy; drunkenness, orgies, and the like. I warn you, as I did before, that those who live like this will not inherit the kingdom of God." If you can see to one or more of these attributes regularly demonstrated in your daily life, you are not living as God would have you live. You may even profess to be a Christian, but are producing this type of fruit. Paul said, those who live like this will not inherit the kingdom of God. He also said in 2 Corinthians 5:10, "Godly sorrow brings repentance that leads to salvation and leaves no regret, but worldly sorrow brings death." If you are truly sorry for your sins, ask God for forgiveness.

Prayer: God, forgive me for any bad fruit I have produced.

> *Matthew 12:35 A good man out of the good treasure of his heart brings forth good things, and an evil man out of the evil treasure brings forth evil things.*

On Day 63 we learned that God created us in His image, with a body, soul and spirit. Our soul or heart is made up of our mind, emotions, and free will. Jesus said that it is out of our hearts, that either good or bad things originate. Speaking in Mark 7:21-22 Jesus also said, "For from within, out of men's hearts, come evil thoughts, sexual immorality, theft, murder, adultery, greed, malice, deceit, lewdness, envy, slander, arrogance and folly." It doesn't take any effort on our part for our sinful nature to dominate our thoughts and actions. Unfortunately, we are born with it. How do we break the chains of our sinful nature? Paul said in Galatians 5:24-25, "Those who belong to Christ Jesus have crucified the sinful nature with its passions and desires. Since we live by the Spirit, let us keep in step with the Spirit." When we accept Jesus as our Lord and Savior, our spirit connects with the Spirit of God. It is through our spirit that we pray and commune with God. It is also by the Holy Spirit that our sinful nature is replaced with the fruits of the spirit. Galatians 5:22-23 says, "But the fruit of the Spirit is love, joy, peace, patience, kindness, goodness, faithfulness, gentleness, and self-control. Against such things there is no law." Paul went on to say in verse 25, "Since we live by the Spirit, let us keep in step with the Spirit." Keeping in step with the Spirit takes a daily commitment to follow Him. It requires spending time in God's word and in prayer. Being a Christian doesn't mean I am immune from being controlled by my sinful nature. Yesterday, I told you about the work my great-uncle did to help his trees bear fruit. God wants us to bear good fruit as well. Jeremiah 17:8 says, "He will be planted like a tree by the water that sends out its roots by the stream. It does not fear when heat comes; its leaves are always green. It has no worries in a year of drought and never fails to bear fruit." Allow your roots to grow deep into God's word. Trust Him when the storms of life come. Become that tree that produces love, joy, peace, patience, kindness, goodness, faithfulness, gentleness and self-control no matter the circumstances of your life.

Prayer: God, help me to bring forth good things out of my heart.

> Matthew 12:36 But I say to you that for every idle word men may speak, they will give account of it in the day of judgement.

Jesus continued to say in verse 37, "For by your words you will be acquitted, and by your words you will be condemned." These verses also gave me a lot of concern as a young Christian. Was Jesus saying that Christians couldn't laugh, tell jokes, and have fun because they may say an idle word? Should I just keep my mouth shut and not say anything in fear of saying the wrong thing? Thankfully, I had it wrong and this is not at all what Jesus meant. We read yesterday that it is out of our hearts that either good or bad things come. This includes our words and their intention. If our lives are being controlled by our sinful nature, the words we use will reflect that. At the end of our lives, our words will come back to condemn us. Even as Christians, being led by the Holy Spirit, we need to be careful with our words. The words we say can build someone up or tear them down. This is especially true of parents and grandparents talking to their children. Word such as, "you can't do anything right," or "why can't you be like your brother or sister," take root in our children's lives and produce what is planted. Words can also stir up anger or bring peace to a situation. Proverbs 15:1 says, "A gentle answer turns away wrath, but a harsh word stirs up anger." James 3:2 says, "We all stumble in many ways. If anyone is never at fault in what he says, he is a perfect man, able to keep his whole body in check." Since no one is perfect, we are going to make mistakes and say the wrong thing. Then how do we keep from saying the wrong thing at the wrong time? 1 Peter 3:10 tells us, "For, whoever would love life and see good days must keep his tongue from evil and his lips from deceitful speech." Colossians 4:6 tells us to, "Let your conversation be always full of grace, seasoned with salt, so that you may know how to answer everyone." David's answer was to pray this prayer found in Psalms 19:14, "Let the words of my mouth and the meditation of my heart be pleasing in Your sight, O Lord, my Rock and my redeemer." Stop and ask God to guide your conversations.

Prayer: God, I pray my words would be pleasing in Your sight.

> *Matthew 12:40 For as Jonah was three days and three nights in the belly of the great fish, so will the Son of Man be three days and three nights in the heart of the earth.*

Jonah was running away from a mission God had given him to go to Nineveh and preach repentance. He was thrown into the sea, because of a great storm God had caused to get his attention. No sooner than he hit the water, a great fish swallowed Jonah. Jonah 1:17 says, "But the Lord provided a great fish to swallow Jonah, and Jonah was inside the fish three days and three nights." Was it a coincidence that Jonah spent three days and three nights inside the belly of that fish? Perhaps it took Jonah three days and three nights to come to his senses and repent while sloshing around in that dark, wet, nasty fish stomach. Jonah 2:1 only tells us, "From inside the fish Jonah prayed to the Lord his God." After hearing Jonah's prayer, Jonah 2:10 says, "And the Lord commanded the fish, and it vomited Jonah onto dry land." Once the Lord commanded the fish, it could have taken a couple of days for the fish to swim towards land, where he vomited up Jonah. Or was Jonah in the belly of the fish for three days and three nights for this very moment, to prophesy about Jesus' death and resurrection? The Pharisees had just asked Jesus in Matthew 12:38, "... Teacher, we want to see a miraculous sign from You." Although the Pharisees had seen Jesus give sight to the blind, heal the sick and lame, and bring Jairus' daughter back to life, they wanted more proof that He was the Messiah. Jesus told them in Matthew 12:39, "A wicked and adulterous generation asks for a miraculous sign! But none shall be given except the sign of the prophet Jonah." Jesus knew His mission was to die on the cross and to rise three days later. Unlike Jonah, Jesus was undeterred in accomplishing His mission. He wasn't going to allow the 'so called' religious leaders of the day to slow Him down. Sadly, it was the religious leaders who had Jesus crucified. Jesus told them in Matthew 12:41, "The men of Nineveh will stand up at the judgment with this generation and condemn it; for they repented at the preaching of Jonah, and now one greater than Jonah is here." Even the sign of Jonah didn't convince the Pharisees and other religious leaders that Jesus was the Messiah. What sign do you need?

Prayer: God, thank You for completing Your mission here on earth.

Day 88

> *Matthew 12:50 For whoever does the will of My Father in heaven is My brother and sister and mother.*

Jesus was speaking to a crowd when someone told Him, "Your mother and brothers are standing outside, wanting to speak to You." Matthew 12:48-49 records Jesus reply, "'Who is My mother, and who are My brothers?" Pointing to His disciples, he said, "Here are My mother and My brothers.'" He also said that anyone who did the will of the Father was also His brother and sister. As a Christian, we become a member of a larger family, with brothers and sisters we may never meet until we get to heaven. Ephesians 2:19 says, "So then you are no longer strangers and aliens, but you are fellow citizens with the saints and members of the household of God." Vivian and I were members of the Princeton Church of God for many years. They took being a part of the family of God very seriously. Everyone had either brother or sister attached to their name. I was Brother Charlie and Vivian, Sister Viv. Everyone was treated like family. How do we become a member of the family of God? A family that reaches past race, social status, political affiliation, the way a person looks, and even our past mistakes. Jesus said it is anyone who does the will of My Father. Our first step to becoming a member of this family is found in 1 Timothy 2:3-4; "This is good and pleases God our Savior, who wants all men to be saved and to come to a knowledge of the truth." What is the knowledge of truth? Jesus said in John 14:6, "I am the way, the truth and the life. No one comes to the Father except through Me." We must have repented of our sins and accepted Jesus as Lord and Savior of our lives. Ephesians 5:15-17 tells us, "Be very careful, then, how you live – not as unwise but as wise, making the most of every opportunity because the days are evil. Therefore do not be foolish, but understand what the Lord's will is." God wants us to live differently from the world around us avoiding the same old sins that held us captive before coming to Him and to understand His will for us. 1 John 5:3 says, "This is the love of God: to obey His commands. And His commands are not burdensome.' My prayer is that you have joined the family of God.

Prayer: God, thank You for adopting me into Your family.

> *Matthew 13:9 He who has ears to hear, let him hear.*

Jesus had just shared a parable about a farmer who went to sow seed. As He did with most parables, Jesus ended with, "He who has ears to hear, let him hear." Jesus was telling them, listen closely, pay attention to what I am saying. Don't just enjoy a good story, but understand the meaning behind it. Vivian and I have been married over 40 years. Like many husbands, I have selective hearing. When watching something on TV or working on a project, Vivian will say something to me. I pick up about every third word, and try to intelligently respond to what she is saying. Unfortunately, that doesn't work out too well, because my response clearly lets her know I wasn't listening. It is at that point, I am told, 'you need hearing aids.' I probably do, but more importantly, I needed to devote my full attention to what she was saying. (Husbands, please learn from my mistakes and do a better job of listening to your wife.) We are surrounded by voices trying to get our attention. Businesses use advertisements to shape our thoughts about their products and our need for them. Artists promote their ideas through the words of their music. Social media has become a platform for many to share their opinions. Celebrities, who have large numbers of people following them have become self-declared experts on various subjects. The people we are close to such as our parents, friends, and co-workers pour their ideas into our lives. However, there is one more voice that is speaking to us. It can be heard in a number of ways. 1 Kings 19:11-12 we read about the Lord appearing to Elijah, "The Lord said, 'Go out and stand on the mountain, in the presence of the Lord, for the Lord is about to pass by. Then a great and powerful wind tore the mountains apart and shattered the rocks before the Lord, but the Lord was not in the wind. After the wind there was an earthquake, but the Lord was not in the earthquake. After the earthquake came a fire. And after the fire came a gentle whisper." God will not speak over the voices in our lives, but often speaks to us in a still small voice, saying, listen to what I am saying. What voices are you listening to?

Prayer: God, help me to hear Your still small voice.

> Matthew 13:12 *For whoever has, to him more will be given, and he will have abundance; but whoever does not have, even what he has will be taken away from him.*

After Jesus had finished speaking, the disciples asked Him, "Why do you speak to the people in parables?" Jesus, told the disciples, "The knowledge of the secrets of the kingdom of heaven has been given to you, but not to them." This may sound unfair, but Jesus is talking about the level of faith people have when hearing the message of the gospel. Some will hear the good news and let it take root and grow. Others, will hear the word, but have selective hearing and not grasp its true meaning. Jesus said, to those who have faith, more will be given; while those who don't will continue to fall further away. I read a statement that sums this verse up. The same warming sun that softens wax will harden clay. It all depends on what our hearts are made of. A good example is the story of Moses when he went to Pharoah to ask for the release of the Israelites from slavery. Pharoah, whose heart was hardened towards God, suffered through nine plagues without letting the Israelites go. However, after the 10th plague, which killed every first born in the land of Egypt, Pharoah was ready to get rid of Moses and the Israelites. A few days later, Pharoah changed his mind and gathered his army to pursue them. We know the rest of the story. Pharoah's hardened heart cost him his life and the lives of his army, all drowning in the Red Sea. Who do you identify with in today's reading? Are you comparable to the disciples who have heard and accepted the good news of the gospel? Through prayer, reading God's word, and meeting with other believers your faith continues to grow. Perhaps you are more like Pharoah. Friends or family members have shared their faith with you, but you want no part of it. You may have even attended church and felt God's spirit moving in your heart. However, there was always an excuse not to respond to God's call on your life. Either the time wasn't right or you needed to clean up some things first. Or perhaps, you wanted to "sow your wild oats" first. Whatever the reason, the more you reject God's call on your life, the fewer opportunities you may have. Don't delay, give your life to God, you will not regret it.

Prayer: God, please let me be one to whom more is given.

> *Mathew 13:13 Therefore I speak to them in parables, because seeing they do not see, and hearing they do not hear, nor do they understand.*

Talking about the religious leaders of the day, Jesus went on to say in verse 14, "In them is fulfilled the prophecy of Isaiah: 'You will be ever hearing but never understanding; you will be ever seeing but never perceiving. For this people's heart has become calloused; they hardly hear with their ears, and they have closed their eyes. Otherwise they might see with their eyes, hear with their ears, understand with their hearts and turn, and I would heal them.'" A similar word was given to the prophet Ezekiel, "Son of man, you are living among a rebellious people. They have eyes to see but do not see and ears to hear but do not hear, for they are a rebellious people." We find the same reasons why the religious leaders, the people of Ezekiel's day, and even many today have a hard time accepting God's word. First, God's word convicts us of our lifestyle and challenges us to make a change. Sadly, we grow very accustomed to the way we live our life. We would rather overlook the verses of scripture that speak to our lifestyle instead of changing our lifestyle to match God's word. Secondly, we develop a rebellious attitude towards God and His word, and refuse to accept it. We also rebel against God's authority, perceiving Him as a tyrant trying to control our life. Deuteronomy 32:4 says, "He is the Rock, His works are perfect, and all His ways are just." God's purpose is not to control us, but as a loving Father, He only wants the best for us. Lastly, if we are not listening to the Holy Spirit, God's word will sound like foolishness to us. 1 Corinthians 2:14 says, "The natural person does not accept the things of the Spirit of God, for they are folly to him, and he is not able to understand them because they are not spiritually discerned." Those who don't want to see, hear, or understand the word of God will remain spiritually blind. However, for those seeking to know more about God's word, it will be revealed to them. Romans 15:4 says, "For everything that was written in the past was written to teach us, so that through endurance and encouragement of the scriptures we might have hope." My prayer is that you are learning more about God and His word.

Prayer: God, help me to see, hear, and understand Your word.

> *Matthew 13:17 For assuredly, I say to you that many prophets and righteous men desired to see what you see, and did not see it, and to hear what you hear, and did not hear it.*

Jesus talking to His disciples in verse 16 said, "But blessed are your eyes because they see, and your ears because they hear," because many before them longed to see and hear what they are witnessing. Can you imagine sitting around a campfire, listening to the very Son of God speak? Even better, you of all the people in the world, have been given the ability to understand what Jesus is talking about, while the Biblical scholars of the day are clueless. The times you don't understand, you are able to ask Jesus as we find in Luke 8:9. Jesus said, even the prophets wanted to see and hear what you are hearing. We could dwell on how blessed the disciples were to hear the words of Jesus. However, these words are meant for us as well. We can read in the Bible what they saw, and hear the words they heard. Better yet, we have the Holy Spirit to guide us to the truth. Jesus speaking in John 16:13 said, "But when He, the Spirit of Truth, comes, He will guide you into all truth. He will not speak on His own; He will speak only what He hears, and He will tell you what is yet to come." Although it would be nice, God's word is not going to come to us in an audible voice, unless we are listening to it on the Bible App. We have to take the time to read and absorb what His word is telling us. Paul said in Colossians 2:2-4, "My purpose is that they may be encouraged in heart and united in love, so that they may have the full riches of complete understanding, in order that they may know the mystery of God, namely, Christ, in whom are hidden all the treasures of wisdom and knowledge. I tell you this so that no one may deceive you by fine-sounding arguments." Paul packs a lot in these three short verses. He wants us to have a complete understanding of Christ, where wisdom and knowledge are found. He also wants us to know God's word, so we are not deceived by fine-sounding arguments. Today, more than ever we need to have a deeper understanding of God's word. Set aside time each day to read and study God's word.

Prayer: God, help me to see and hear Your words.

> *Matthew 13:18 Therefore hear the parable of the sower.*

The Parable of the Sower is located in Matthew 13:3-9. It is one of the few parables Jesus provides an explanation and is found in verses 19-23, "When anyone hears the message about the kingdom and does not understand it, the evil one comes and snatches away what was sown in his heart. This is the seed sown along the path. The one who received the seed that fell on the rocky places is the man who hears the word and at once receives it with joy. But since he has no root, he lasts only a short time. When trouble or persecution comes because of the word, he quickly falls away. The one who received the seed that fell among thorns is the man who hears the word, but the worries of this life and the deceitfulness of wealth choke it, making it unfruitful. But the one who received the seed that fell on good soil is the man who hears the word and understands it. He produces a crop, yielding a hundred, sixty, or thirty times what was sown." Jesus is pointing out that it is the condition of the soil, not the seed that brings results. Just as one seed of corn is capable of producing four or five ears of corn that average 800 kernels each, it is the condition of the soil that determines how the corn develops on the stalk. Our hearts are compared to the four types of soil. Like a trodden down path, some have a hard heart towards God's word. They hear it, but it goes in one ear and out the other. Satan comes along quickly and erases what was heard. Rocky soil represents those who hear God's word and are initially excited about it; but when trouble comes along, they give up because of a lack of faith. The seed that is choked out by thorns represents someone who hears the word, but has let the cares of life and pursuit of wealth take priority in their lives. Lastly, the seed that falls on good soil, takes root, grows and produces an abundant yield. Sadly, there is only a 25% chance that God's word will take root in someone's life and grow. As Christians, our goal should be to help prepare the soil in someone's life so they will be ready to receive God's word.

Prayer: God, help me to prepare the soil in someone's life.

> Matthew 13:24 Another parable He put forth to them, saying: "The kingdom of heaven is like a man who sowed good seed in his field."

In Matthew 13:24-30 we read the parable of the "Wheat and the Tares." It says "The kingdom of heaven is like a man who sowed good seed in his field. But while everyone was sleeping, his enemy came and sowed weeds among the wheat, and went away. When the wheat sprouted and formed heads, the weeds also appeared. The owner's servants came to him and said, 'Sir, didn't you sow good seed in your field? Where then did the weeds come from?' 'An enemy did this,' he replied. The servants asked him, 'Do you want us to go and pull them up?' 'No,' he answered, 'because while you are pulling the weeds, you may root up the wheat with them. Let both grow together until the harvest. At that time I will tell the harvesters: First collect the weeds and tie them in bundles to be burned; then gather the wheat and bring it into my barn.'" This parable helps answer the age-old question, "why is there so much evil and bad in the world, and what should be done about it?" In the parable, there are two planters. The first is God, who plants the good seed. The other is Satan, who comes along at night and plants weeds among the good seed. The plants looked very similar when they first began to grow. So much so, that it was not clear which ones were the wheat or the tares, until the plants matured and the wheat stalks began to produce kernels. Tares on the other hand were a useless weed. The worker's response was to pull up the weeds and get rid of them. They wanted to make a judgment call on each plant and pull the bad one's out. However, the farmer who planted the good seed (God) told them to let both grow together, because they may damage the wheat, pulling out the weeds. No one is perfect, so judging a person against someone else may cause more damage than good. Lastly, we learn that a harvest of the good and bad wheat will take place. God will send His angels, the reapers, to separate the tares from the wheat. The tares would be burned, and the wheat gathered into the barn. Are you a wheat or a useless weed in God's kingdom? If you are unsure, ask God to show you.

Prayer: God, I pray that I would be among the wheat on Judgment Day.

> Matthew 13:31 Another parable He put forth to them saying: "The kingdom of heaven is like a mustard seed, which a man took and sowed in his field."

Jesus tells six parables in a row to describe the kingdom of heaven. Today we are reading the Parable of the Mustard Seed. Jesus continued in verse 32 saying, "which indeed is the least of all seeds; but when it is grown it is greater than the herbs and becomes a tree, so that the birds of the air come and nest in its branches." The people in Jesus' day were looking for a Messiah who would overthrow the Roman's and set up an earthly kingdom like King David's. However, through these parables, Jesus is telling them His kingdom would be very much different. His kingdom is a spiritual rule over the hearts and lives of those who choose to follow Him. Those who deny God's authority and refuse to accept Him as Lord and Savior are cast out of His kingdom. Today Jesus uses a tiny, insignificant, mustard seed to describe His kingdom. Let's take a look at the mustard seed. Mustard is made by combining mustard seeds with vinegar, salt, lemon, and other ingredients to form a paste or sauce. It has a very tart and tangy flavor. According to _www.realsimple.com_, mustard is rich in protein, fiber, vitamin C and many of the B-complex vitamins. All in all, there is nothing very special about mustard. However, when a tiny mustard seed takes root and grows, it becomes a tree that reaches approximately 20 feet in height and has branches that extend out about 20 feet. Many great things have very humble beginnings. For example, the world was waiting for an earthly king to be born. However, the Messiah, the Savior of the world, was born in a manger, unnoticed by most except a few shepherds. His ministry began with 12 uneducated disciples, who after His death, changed the world. Even today, God uses small, insignificant people to change the world. People like Billy Graham, the son of a dairy farmer who grew up in rural North Carolina, and Mother Teresa, born of Albanian heritage in Macedonia, have made lasting impacts in the world. Perhaps God is calling you to do something for His kingdom, and you feel incapable of doing it. Remember that God can use the most insignificant person, to accomplish great things. Let that mustard seed take root and grow in your life.

Prayer: God, here am I, use me.

> *Matthew 13:33 Another parable He spoke to them: "The kingdom of heaven is like leaven, which a woman took and hid in three measures of meal till it was all leavened."*

In this short parable, Jesus compares the Kingdom of Heaven to leaven. Leaven, commonly known as yeast, is a single cell fungus that is only visible with a microscope. (*www.thespruceeats.com*) Yeast is a living organism that converts its food, sugar and starch into carbon dioxide. Because bread dough is elastic and stretchable, the carbon dioxide cannot escape causing the bread to expand or rise. Without leaven, the dough remains flat. My mother used to make the best yeast rolls. She would prepare the dough with yeast, and set it aside for several hours. It was fun to watch the dough triple in size. However, the best part was eating a hot roll with melted butter and strawberry preserves. Without the yeast, my mother's rolls would have been a dry, flat, piece of bread. The yeast transformed the dough into a delicious piece of bread. Notice that Jesus went into great detail about how the leaven was used. First, He draws attention to the woman, who in Jesus' day was often overlooked and taken for granted. Secondly, He tells how much flour was used. Why are these details so important? Couldn't Jesus have easily said, 'the kingdom of heaven is like leaven, when mixed with flour, will cause the bread to rise.' Like yesterday, Jesus is pointing out that anyone can do great things for His Kingdom. He doesn't require every believer to have a Masters of Divinity degree to be a part of His Kingdom. He just wants us to be "leaven" in our sphere of influence. As leaven is mixed in with the dough and slowly changes it into bread, Jesus wants us to impact those around us. Jesus also said the leaven was mixed in with "three measures of meal." This is equivalent to four gallons of flour, which would make enough bread to feed over 100 people. When we accept Christ as Lord and Savior, we are changed from the inside out. Our transformed life should have an impact on someone. Once it does, that person's transformed life has an impact on someone else. This is how the leaven spreads. Paul said in 2 Corinthians 3:18, "And we, who with unveiled faces all reflect the Lord's glory, are being transformed into His likeness with ever-increasing glory, which comes from the Lord, who is the Spirit." Go spread some leaven today.

Prayer: God, help me to reflect Your glory.

> *Matthew 13:44 Again, the kingdom of heaven is like treasure hidden in a field, which a man found and hid; and for joy over it he goes and sells all that he has and buys that field.*

Growing up, we had a saying, "finders keepers, losers weepers." Therefore, if I happened to find a dollar bill, it was mine. However, if we found something more valuable, such as a wallet or pocketbook, naturally we tried to find the rightful owner. In Jesus' day, it was very common to hide money and other valuables in the ground since banks did not exist. This practice is still around for a few who don't trust financial institutions. I can recall my grandmother hiding money in a cake in her freezer. She also kept money under her mattress in her bedroom. When she passed away, the family turned the house upside down, trying to find money she had hidden. By law in Jesus' day, treasure found on a piece of property could not be removed and belonged to the property owner. If the property was sold, the land and any valuables on it belonged to the new owner. In this parable, Jesus likens the kingdom of heaven as someone discovering a valuable treasure in a field. Upon finding it, he hides it and sells all he has to buy the field so the treasure would be his. Jesus' message is that the kingdom of heaven is worth trading off everything we own in order to possess it. This sounds pretty easy, but is it? In Matthew 19:16-22, we read about the Rich Young Ruler who came to Jesus and asked Him, "Teacher, what good thing must I do to get eternal life?" Jesus told him he needed to obey the commandments, to which the young man told Him, he had done so. Jesus then said, "If you want to be perfect, go sell your possessions and give to the poor, and you will have treasure in heaven. Then come, follow Me." Verse 22 says, "When the young man heard this, he went away sad, because he had great wealth." Is the pursuit of worldly wealth preventing you from following Christ? It is very easy to get caught up spending all your time and energy chasing after wealth. It can become an obsession with no limits on how much is enough. All the while, missing out on something much more valuable that pays eternal dividends. Proverbs 21:21 says, "He who pursues righteousness and love finds life, prosperity and honor." My prayer is that you have your priorities in order.

Prayer: God, help me to put You first in my life.

> Matthew 13:45-46 *Again, the kingdom of heaven is like a merchant seeking beautiful pearls, who, when he had found one pearl of great price, went and sold all that he had and bought it.*

A pearl begins as a small irritant that becomes trapped in an oyster's shell. The oyster senses the object and begins to coat it with the materials its shell is made of. Over time, the irritant becomes a beautiful pearl. Living on the coast, Vivian and I get invited to an oyster roast from time to time. On rare occasions, someone will find a small pearl formed in one of the oysters. Unfortunately, none are of any value such as the one mentioned in today's parable. In yesterday's parable, someone stumbled upon a great treasure by accident and sold all he had to obtain it. Today, a merchant is looking for pearls of great value and finds the one of greatest value and sells all he has to buy it. We are all searching for something. According to a recent study the University of Minnesota[10], "everyone needs to experience the healing power of love from others, self, and an ultimate source. We need a sense of meaning and hope in the midst of losses, tragedies, and failures. We need spiritual resources to help heal the painful wounds of grief, guilt, resentment, unforgiveness, self-rejection, and shame. Spiritual resources are also needed to deepen our experiences of trust, self-esteem, hope, joy and love of life." The question we have to ask ourselves is "are we looking in the right place and do we settle for less than the best?" According to _www.pewresearch. com_, most Americans rate family, career, and money ahead of spirituality and faith when asked, "What makes life meaningful?" There is nothing wrong with these, except how we prioritize them. Proverbs 8:17 says, "I love those who love Me, and those who seek Me will find Me." God is not hard to find. However, many chose to try everything else before giving their life to Him. Jesus said in Matthew 6:33, "But seek ye first the kingdom of God, and His righteousness, and all these things will be added unto you." Like the merchant in today's parable, seek out the pearl of greatest value, the kingdom of God. Put Him first and He will take care of family, career and money. Paul said in Philippians 4:19, "And my God will meet all your needs according to His glorious riches in Christ Jesus." Trust God today, sell out to Him and find true happiness, peace, and meaning to life.

Prayer: God, help me to fully trust You.

> *Matthew 13:47 Again, the kingdom of heaven is like a net that was cast into the sea and gathered some of every kind.*

Jesus continued the parable in verses 48-50 saying, "When it is full, the fisherman pulled it up on the shore. Then they sat down and collected the good fish in baskets, but threw the bad away. This is how it will be at the end of the age. The angels will come and separate the wicked from the righteous, and throw them into the fiery furnace, where there will be weeping and gnashing of teeth." Jesus packed several lessons into this short parable. The most obvious is there will be a judgment day where the good and bad are separated. However, Jesus also tells us that the net will gather some of every kind. This should be great news to you and me. Although Daniel writes otherwise, the Jewish concept of the Messiah was that He was coming only to deliver them. At times, I think we may even get caught up in that same type of thinking. Daniel 7:14 tells us, "He was given authority, glory and sovereign power; all peoples, nations and men of every language worshipped Him. His dominion is an everlasting dominion that will not pass away, and His kingdom is one that will never be destroyed." Jesus came to offer salvation to everyone. As Jesus said, there will be "some of every kind" when we get to heaven. However, for some the gathering will not be happy occasion. Those who have not accepted Jesus as their Lord and Savior and had their names written in the "Lamb's Book of Life," will not enter heaven. They will be found guilty, and thrown into the lake of fire. It doesn't matter how good a person's life was, how often they attended church, or how many people they helped. None of those things will get a person to Heaven. We all must have prayed a similar prayer, "Lord Jesus, I believe in God and that You are the Son of God as Your Word says. I realize that I am a sinner, and I believe You died for my sins. I now turn from my sins and ask You to come into my heart. I receive You as my Lord and Savior. Thank You for saving me." If you have prayed this prayer for the first time, please let a pastor or Christian friend know so they can encourage and help you with the next steps.

Prayer: God, thank You for saving my soul.

> *Matthew 13:51 Jesus said to them, "Have you understood all these things?"*

Our grandchildren have grown up in the modern age of technology. Its influence on them has been interesting to watch. When they are playing outside and need to stop to get something to drink, they will say "pause it" just as if they were pausing a video. Today, Jesus pauses to do a listening check. Paraphrasing verse 51, Jesus said, "Hey guys, have you got all this?" Surprisingly, they replied, "yes." Jesus then said in verse 52, "Therefore every teacher of the law who has been instructed about the kingdom of heaven is like the owner of a house who brings out of his storeroom new treasures as well as old." Jesus has been teaching on the kingdom of heaven, using parables to describe it. Now that the disciples understand the basics, Jesus teaches them that while becoming a part of the kingdom of heaven is an important first step, it is not the only step to following Him. They were now to become teachers of the gospel, using what they had learned and were going to experience after His death and resurrection. We see Peter doing this in Acts 2:14-41, where he quotes from the Prophet Joel, talks about King David, and speaks about Jesus' death and resurrection. Verse 41 says, "Those who accepted his message were baptized, and about three thousand were added to their number that day." Jesus words apply to us as well. He may not have called you to be a Peter and stand before thousands to speak, but you have a role in His kingdom. As Christians, we become His disciples and have been given an assignment to make disciples and teach others God's Word. Jesus said in Matthew 28:19-20, "Therefore go and make disciples of all nations, baptizing them in the name of the Father, and of the Son and of the Holy Spirit, and teaching them to obey everything I have commanded you. And surely I am with you always, to the very end of the age." Your role may be to lead a small group in your home. Perhaps God wants you to teach your children and grandchildren about Him. Or maybe He is calling you to reach out to those who feel isolated and disconnected from society. We each have a role and a story to tell.

Prayer: God, help me to understand Your word so that I can share it with others.

> Matthew 13:57 So they were offended at Him. But Jesus said to them, "A prophet is not without honor except in his own country and in his own house."

Jesus has gone back to His hometown of Nazareth where He began teaching in the synagogue. Matthew 13:54 says, "...and they were amazed. 'Where did this Man get this wisdom and these miraculous powers?'" They knew Jesus and His entire family. Jesus had grown up there. He was the son of a carpenter with four brothers and two sisters. There was nothing special about Jesus when He was growing up. However, no ordinary kid from Nazareth would be able to do these things on their own. Where did He get this ability to teach and do miracles? Deep down they knew that Jesus' wisdom and power could only have come from God. They had a choice to believe that Jesus was the Messiah, the Son of God, or reject Him. Sadly, they allowed the power of familiarity to take over and did not want to believe in Him, so they were "offended at Him." This story teaches us that an unbelieving heart will always find a reason to reject Christ. It also reminds us that some will be offended because God doesn't do what they think He should do. For example, "If God cares about me, why did He allow this sickness or tragedy happen to my family?" Or, "Serving God cramps my lifestyle, with all its rules and regulations." The list goes on and on. However, for those who can get by the excuses, John 1:12 says, "Yet to all who received Him, to those who believed in His name, He gave the right to become children of God." Just as Jesus found it difficult to be accepted in His hometown, the hardest place to be a Christian is in your own home and among those who know you best. Once you accept Christ as Lord and Savior, people are watching you. Especially family and friends who are not Christians. They want to see if you have really changed. Don't worry, you will slip and mess up from time to time. All you can do is your best to live a faithful life for Christ, but confess and apologize when you make a mistake. Present the gospel to them by your changed life, new attitude, and devotion to Christ. Trying to win them to Christ by overcoming their offenses at God is almost impossible. Allow God to work on them from the inside out.

Prayer: God help me to present the gospel to my unsaved family and friends.

Matthew 14:16 But Jesus said to them, "They do not need to go away. You give them something to eat."

The day was getting late and thousands of people had followed Jesus into a remote area where He taught them and healed the sick. The disciples came to Jesus and said, "This is a remote place, and it is already getting late. Send the crowds away, so they can go to the villages and buy themselves some food." Jesus then told His disciples, "You give them something to eat." Mark 6:37 records the disciples' reply, "That would take eight months of a man's wages! Are we to go and spend that much on bread and give it to them to eat?" Jesus then asked the disciples, how much food did they have. They found five loaves of bread and two small fish and brought them to Jesus. Jesus took the loaves and fish, looked towards heaven and gave thanks. Then He began to break the bread and fish into pieces and handed them to the disciples to distribute to the people. Matthew 14:20 says, "They all ate and were satisfied, and the disciples picked up twelve basketfuls of broken pieces that were left over." In all, there were 5,000 men plus women and children who were fed that day. How does God turn a little basket of food into enough to feed over 5,000? Moreover, how did He feed over 1 million Israelites in the wilderness each day with manna for 40 years? Psalms 107:9 tells us, "For He satisfies the thirsty and fills the hungry with good things." The answer, He is God. The more important question is, why does God do these things? Matthew 14:14 tells us, "...He had compassion on them." Jesus' compassion moved Him to do things for people. God loves us unconditionally. God didn't wait for a time when most everyone was living right before He sent His Son, Jesus, to pay the penalty for our sins. He doesn't ask if we are Jewish, American, African, Asian, or Hispanic before accepting us into His kingdom. He doesn't ask if we are rich or poor, young or old. God welcomes us all. Jesus said in John 6:35, "I am the bread of life. He who comes to Me will never go hungry, and he who believes in Me will never be thirsty." Psalms 34:8 says, "Taste and see that the Lord is good..." Have you tasted the bread of life? Let Him satisfy the hunger of your soul.

Prayer: God, thank You for satisfying our hunger.

> *Matthew 14:27 But immediately Jesus spoke to them, saying, "Be of good cheer! It is I; do not be afraid."*

Today's verse sounds like a nice, routine greeting from Jesus. My interpretation of it is, "Hey guys cheer up, it's Me, don't be afraid." However, the timing and location of this greeting is not so routine. The disciples are in the middle of the Sea of Galilee, rowing a boat in a fierce storm around 3:00 am in the morning. Jesus was not with them because He had stayed behind to spend time alone in prayer. During their struggle against the storm, the disciples catch a glimpse of a figure walking on the water and were terrified. Thinking they see a ghost; they all cry out in fear. Jesus then calls out to let them know it is, Me, Jesus. Earlier that day, the disciples had just witnessed Jesus multiplying five loaves and two fishes into enough food to feed over 5,000 people, with left-overs. As the crowd was dispersing, Jesus told the disciples to get in the boat and go on ahead of Him to the other side. As they were making their way across, a terrible storm hit. Isn't this so much like life? The disciples were in the middle of God's will, doing exactly what He had told them to do, yet they find themselves caught up in a terrible storm. To make matters worse, Jesus knew the storm was coming. Like the disciples, following God's will doesn't exempt us from being caught up in life's storms. In fact, some of life's biggest challenges occur when we are following God's will. Also, the disciples didn't recognize Jesus in the storm. Who would have expected Jesus to come walking to them on the water? Instead, the disciples jumped to the conclusion that they had seen a ghost. How often do we look for Jesus in the middle of our storms? What we perceive to be something that adds chaos to our storm, may actually be Jesus. He will not let you face the storm alone. However, have we allowed fear to override our faith and blind our eyes to the presence of the Lord in our storms? Nahum 1:7 tells us, "The Lord is good, a refuge in times of trouble. He cares for those who trust in Him." Trust Jesus to be with you in the storms of life.

Prayer: God, thank You for being with me in the storm.

> *Matthew 14:31 And immediately Jesus stretched out His hand and caught him, and said to him, "O you of little faith, why did you doubt?"*

Yesterday, we left the disciples struggling against a terrible storm. Jesus came walking towards them on the water and called out, "Be of good cheer. It is I. Take courage." At first, the disciples thought Jesus was a ghost. Then Peter spoke up in verse 28 saying, "Lord, if it is You, tell me to come to You on the water." Jesus simply said "Come." Verse 29 says, "Then Peter got down out of the boat, walked on the water and came toward Jesus." Can you imagine that first step? I would have been holding on to the boat with both hands as I put one foot in the water. Only after I felt I wasn't sinking, would I let go of the boat and begin walking very slowly. Peter was walking on water until something happened. Verse 30, "But when he saw the wind, he was afraid and, beginning to sink, cried out, 'Lord, save me!'" The moment Peter took his eyes off Jesus and began to focus on the storm, he began to sink. When Peter cried out, Jesus reached out His hand and pulled him to the safety of the boat. Matthew 14:32 tells us, "And when they climbed into the boat, the wind died down." The moment Peter stopped focusing on the one who called him to step out, he began to panic. Can you relate with Peter? The moment I begin to focus more on my problems instead of my Creator, the more insurmountable they appear until I become paralyzed with fear and anxiety. Isaiah 41:13 says, "For I am the Lord, your God, who takes hold of your right hand and says to you, 'Do not fear; I will help you.'" Just as Jesus was there to reach out and pull Peter out of the water, He is with us through the storms that are raging in our lives. However, this requires great faith. From my experience, some storms may last for years and you may wonder, will they ever end. Deuteronomy 31:8 tells us, "The Lord Himself goes before you and will be with you, He will never leave you nor forsake you. Do not be afraid; do not be discouraged." Remember God is always with you. Don't let the storms of life take your eyes off Him.

Prayer: God, thank You for never leaving or forsaking me.

> Matthew 15:4 For God commanded, saying, "Honor your father and your mother; and, he who curses father or mother, let him be put to death."

Jesus is talking to the Pharisees who had asked Him why didn't His disciples follow the ceremonial tradition of washing their hands before eating. Jesus' reply to them was, "And why do you break the command of God for the sake of your tradition?" Jesus then quotes one of the Ten Commandments about honoring your father and mother found in Exodus 20:12, which says "Honor your father and mother, so that you may live long in the land the Lord Your God is giving you." He also added a second part about being put to death for cursing them which is found one chapter later in Exodus 21:17, "Anyone who curses his father or mother must be put to death." The tradition of the Pharisees Jesus is referring to is one where a grown child can declare some property as a "gift to God", so that the child would not have to use the property to care for their elderly parents. Being a parent is not easy. That little bundle of joy when first born, becomes "a round the clock" needy creature that will go through many stages before reaching adulthood. Along the way, a lot of mistakes will be made and some parents will do a much better job than others at raising children. Ephesians 6:4 provides some parental guidance, "Fathers, do not provoke your children to anger by the way you treat them. Rather, bring them up with the discipline and instruction that comes from the Lord." Also Proverbs 22:6 tells us, "Train up a child in the way he should go, and when he is old he will not turn from it." Wouldn't it be great if all parents followed that advice? Sadly, that is not the case. Some parents have not grown up themselves and are still living out their youth. Others are non-existent in their children's lives, while others turn to abuse and threats to control their children. The Bible tells us, no matter how we were raised, we should treat our parents with dignity and respect. This command doesn't end when we become adults. As Jesus pointed out, it becomes even more important as our parents get older. At some point, there will be things our parents are not capable of doing for themselves anymore. What are you going to do when that time comes?

Prayer: God, help me to honor my father and my mother.

Day 106

> Matthew 15:10-11 When He had called the multitude to Himself, He said to them, "Hear and understand; Not what goes into the mouth defiles a man; but what comes out of the mouth, this defiles a man."

Yesterday, Jesus scolded the Pharisees for their man-made traditions that contradicted the commandment of honoring our father and mother. Jesus went on to tell them in verses 7-9, "Hypocrites! Well did Isaiah prophesy about you saying: 'These people draw near to Me with their mouth, And honor Me with their lips, But their heart is far from Me. And in vain they worship Me, Teaching as doctrines the commandments of men.'" Jesus did not play around with those who pretended to make God first in their lives and then do whatever they wanted. God has not changed. He will not tolerate us when we pretend we are devoted to Him, all the while doing what we want to do replacing His will with our own. Jesus speaking in John 14:15 said, "If you love Me, keep My commandments." That sounds like a pretty simple request; yet, it is much easier said than done. We have a sinful nature that flares up from time to time wanting to take control of our lives. Paul said in Romans 12:2, "And do not be conformed to this world, but be transformed by the renewing of your mind, that you may prove what is that good and acceptable and perfect will of God." The world's pattern says it is okay to live together before marriage. Get to know each other and make sure things will work out. God's word says in Ephesians 5:31, "For this reason a man shall leave his father and mother and be joined to his wife, and the two shall become one." The world says, grab all you can while you can. God's word says in Matthew 6:33, "But seek first the kingdom of God and His righteousness, and all these things shall be added to you." The world says you get to choose what gender you want to be. God's word says in Genesis 5:2, "He created them male and female, and blessed them and called them Mankind in the day they were created." Jesus said we will know a person by what comes out of his mouth. If our hearts align with the way the world thinks, it will be pretty evident. Jesus wants our thoughts, words, and actions to come from a heart that is committed to Him, not the world.

Prayer: God, let the words of my mouth and the meditation of my heart be acceptable to You.

> *Matthew 15:18 But those things which proceed out of the mouth come from the heart, and they defile a man.*

This is the second time Jesus has spoken about the things that come from our heart. As a reminder, our heart is made up of our mind, emotions, and free will. Still not quite understanding what Jesus meant, Peter said to Him in verse 15, "Explain the parable to us." Jesus told them it wasn't the food we eat that defiles us, but the words we speak that originate from our hearts. If our hearts are not right, it will be reflected in our words and our actions. As much as we try to hide our inner self, it will come out from time to time. Our problem is that what was already in our hearts prior to being saved fights against our new nature. Galatians 5:17 says, "For the sinful nature desires what is contrary to the Spirit, and the Spirit what is contrary to the sinful nature. They are in conflict with each other, so that you do not do what you want." Can you feel this war going on within you? I struggle with this daily. My sinful nature tells me, it's okay to do this. While the Holy Spirit is telling me, "You don't need this in your life." Romans 7:15-19 tells us, "I do not understand what I do. For what I want to do, I do not do, but what I hate I do. And if I do what I do not want to do, I agree that the law is good. As it is, it is no longer I myself who do it, but it is sin living in me. I know that nothing good lives in me, that is, in my sinful nature. For I have the desire to do what is good, but I cannot carry it out. For what I do is not the good I want to do; no, the evil I do not want to do – this I keep on doing." How do we break this vicious cycle? We have to daily allow the Holy Spirit to lead our lives. Romans 8:9 says, "You, however, are controlled not by the sinful nature but by the Spirit, if the Spirit of God lives in you. And if anyone does not have the Spirit of Christ, he does not belong to Christ." Who is in control of your life?

Prayer: God, help me to be controlled by Your Holy Spirt.

> *Matthew 15:28 Then Jesus answered and said to her, "O woman, great is your faith! Let it be to you as you desire." And her daughter was healed that very hour.*

Today we read another example of someone's faith, persistence, and understanding of Jesus that resulted in Him granting their request for healing. Faith or the absence of faith seem to be the key element in Jesus' ability and willingness to heal. The conversation Jesus just had with this woman demonstrates her faith and was the reason for her daughter's healing. We read the account in Matthew 15:22-27, "A Canaanite woman from that vicinity came to Him, crying out, 'Lord, Son of David, have mercy on me! My daughter is suffering terribly from demon-possession.' Jesus did not answer a word. So His disciples came to Him and urged Him, 'Send her away, for she keeps crying out after us.' He answered, 'I was sent only to the lost sheep of Israel.' The woman came and knelt before him. 'Lord, help me!' she said. He replied, 'It is not right to take the children's bread and toss it to their dogs.' 'Yes, Lord,' she said, 'but even the dogs eat the crumbs that fall from their master's table.'" This woman was not a Jew. She was not brought up in a synagogue, where the Word of God was taught. She lived in the area of Tyre and Sidon where Jesus had not traveled before now. Yet, she understood who Jesus was and what He could do. Even though Jesus kept silent, she kept crying out to Him, to the point of the disciples asking Jesus to send her away because she was worrying them. Jesus speaks up and tells her, He was sent to look after His own people. Her reply was priceless. She was willing to accept the "crumbs off the table," knowing that was enough to heal her daughter. As a believer, we know Jesus and what He is capable of doing. However, does that affect the way we pray to Him? Do we pray in faith for things in our lives and the lives of others? Do we continue to press in and persevere with our prayers, even though He remains silent? Hebrews 4:16 says, "Let us then approach the throne of grace with confidence, so that we may receive mercy and find grace to help us in our time of need." As His children, God wants to give us more than the crumbs that fall to the floor. Pray with faith.

Prayer: God, help me to ask in faith believing You will answer.

> *Matthew 15:34 Jesus said to them, "How many loaves do you have."*

Jesus had just returned from Tyre and Sidon, where He healed the Canaanite woman's daughter. He was walking along the Sea of Galilee and went up on a mountainside to teach and heal. Verse 30 says, "Great crowds came to Him, bringing the lame, the blind, the crippled, the mute and many others and laid them at His feet; and He healed them." The people did not want to leave. Verse 32 tells us, "Jesus called His disciples to Him and said, 'I have compassion for these people, they have already been with Me three days and have nothing to eat. I do not want to send them away hungry, or they may collapse on the way.'" It was only a few days earlier when Jesus fed the large crowd of 5,000 men plus women and children with five loaves and two fish. Can you imagine spending three days in the middle of nowhere to hear someone preach? When you are in the presence of God as these people were, you do not want to leave. This very thing is happening at Asbury College in Wilmore, KY. What began as a scheduled chapel service on February 8, 2023 has turned into a continual time of worship and prayer that has lasted for weeks, drawing tens of thousands of people from all over the world. The presence of God filled the room as a group of approximately 20 students stayed and began to worship and pray for one another. No one left and others began to join them. Evangelist Jon Burdette was quoted as saying, "Attending the revival at Asbury was an unforgettable experience. We could literally feel the 'weighty' presence of God as soon as we walked into the building."[11] To those who stay and earnestly seek Him, God will feed, physically and spiritually. Matthew tells us there were four thousand, beside the women and children who were with Jesus that day. The disciples had found seven loaves of bread and a few small fish. Jesus took the bread and fish, blessed it, and gave it to His disciples to distribute to the people. Verse 37 says, "They all ate and were satisfied. Afterward the disciples picked up seven basketfuls of broken pieces that were left over." Mostly importantly, God satisfies our soul when we are in His presence. Seek His presence today and be filled.

Prayer: God, my soul longs for Your presence.

> *Matthew 16:4 A wicked and adulterous generation seeks after a sign, and no sign shall be given to it except the sign of the prophet Jonah. And He left them and departed.*

The Pharisees are back asking Jesus to show them a sign from heaven. We read on Day 87 where they had asked Jesus for a similar sign. Jesus' reply at that time was, "but none shall be given except the sign of the prophet Jonah." This time Jesus told them, "When evening comes, you say, 'It will be fair weather, for the sky is red,' and in the morning, 'Today it will be stormy, for the sky is red and overcast.' You know how to interpret the appearance of the sky, but you cannot interpret the signs of the times.'" (Matthew 16:2-3) In other words, the religious leaders had seen the signs and had either ignored them or refused to believe who Jesus was. Like the religious leaders' doubt of Jesus, many today doubt the existence of God. The atheist and agnostic will say, "prove to me there is a God." They are looking for physical or scientific evidence, while ignoring the evidence all around, demanding something more concrete. They refuse to believe the Bible, not taking the time to see the number of prophesies the Bible has revealed. We find the Bible has foretold the future with incredible detail and accuracy. They also refuse to see the creation of the universe as the handiwork of God. They are convinced our universe began with one enormous explosion of energy and light, called the Big Bang. However, they ignore the complex details that sustain life in every plant and animal. Most importantly, they have refused to believe that Jesus is the Son of God, who came to pay the penalty for our sin, by dying on the cross and being raised on the third day. Despite the evidence of Jesus appearing to over 500 people after His death, many still think Jesus was just a good man with a great message. Why is it so difficult for people to accept Jesus? The main problem is our rebellious heart. As long as a person's heart remains skeptical, they will come up with excuses to not believe. Jesus is telling us, there is enough evidence for you to believe. Paul said in Romans 10:9, "That if you confess with your mouth, 'Jesus is Lord,' and believe in your heart that God raised Him from the dead, you will be saved." Have you surrendered your heart to Him?

Prayer: God, thank You for dying for my sins.

> *Matthew 16:15 He said to them, "But who do you say that I am?"*

At this point in Jesus' ministry, many still did not understand who He was. According to Matthew 16:14, some people thought He was John the Baptist reincarnated, others thought He was either Elijah, Jeremiah, or one of the Old Testament prophets. However, Jesus wanted to know what His Disciples, those closest to Him, thought. If they did not understand who He was, then how could they present the gospel to the world when He was gone? Although Jesus was talking to His disciples, everyone will make up their own minds who He is. Some will decide that Jesus was just a moral person, who went around doing good things for others. Some will say that Jesus was a charismatic teacher, who drew large crowds to hear Him. Still others will say He was just another in a great line of prophets and religious leaders. Even some will say that Jesus was martyred for His beliefs. If this is the extent of your knowledge of Jesus Christ, you really do not know Him. Paul, once a persecutor of Christians, best described Jesus in Colossians 1:13-20, "For He (God) has rescued us from the dominion of darkness and brought us into the kingdom of the Son (Jesus) He loves, in whom we have redemption, the forgiveness of sins. He (Jesus) is the image of the invisible God, the firstborn over all creation. For by Him (Jesus) all things were created; things in heaven and on earth, visible and invisible, whether thrones or powers or rulers or authorities; all things were created by Him (Jesus) and for Him (Jesus). He (Jesus) is before all things, and in Him (Jesus) all things hold together. And He (Jesus) is the head of the body, the church; He (Jesus) is the beginning and the firstborn from among the dead, so that in everything He (Jesus) might have the supremacy. For God was pleased to have all His (God) fullness dwell in Him (Jesus), and through Him (Jesus) to reconcile to Himself (God) all things, whether things on earth or things in heaven, by making peace through His (Jesus) blood, shed on the cross." Jesus is our Savior, Deliverer, and Redeemer. He overcame the grave having defeated sin and death. For all who receive Him, He gives eternal life and the right to become children of God. Who do you say Jesus is?

Prayer: God, help me to know You more.

> Matthew 16:17 Jesus answered and said to him, "Blessed are you, Simon Bar-Jonah, for flesh and blood has not revealed this to you, but My Father who is in heaven."

Peter answered Jesus' question from yesterday's verse, saying, "You are the Christ, the Son the of living God." Paraphrasing Jesus' reply, "great answer Simon-Bar Jonah, because this is not something you could have figured out on your own." Jesus continued speaking in verses 18-19, "And I tell you that you are Peter, and on this rock I will build My church, and the gates of Hades will not overcome it. I will give you the Keys of the Kingdom of Heaven; whatever you bind on earth will be bound in heaven, and whatever you loose on earth will be loosed in heaven." Prior to this conversation with Jesus, Peter was known as Simon, Bar-Jonah, or son of Jonah. Jesus calls Simon, Peter or "Petros" in Greek, which means "detached stone." Was Jesus planning to build His church on Peter? Of course not. While Petros means detached stone, Jesus said He was building His church on "this rock" or "Petra," which is a bedrock or cornerstone. In other words, Christ is the foundation of His Church. Simon or Peter's confession that Jesus was the Christ, was a building block on that foundation. Peter speaking about Jesus in Acts 4:11-12 said, "He is the stone you builders rejected, which has become the cornerstone. Salvation is found in no one else, for there is no other name under heaven given to men by which we must be saved." What is so significant about Christ being the cornerstone? If I am going to put my life, my future, and complete trust into something, I want it to be a firm foundation that I can depend on. Let the words of the hymn written by Edward Mote speak to you today, *My Hope is Built on Nothing Less*, that goes: "My hope is built on nothing less than Jesus' blood and righteousness. I dare not trust the sweetest frame, but wholly lean on Jesus' name. In every rough and stormy gale, my anchor holds within the veil. When all around my soul gives way, He then is all my hope and stay. When He shall come with trumpet sound, oh, may I then in Him be found, dressed in His righteousness alone, faultless to stand before the throne." My prayer today is that He is your foundation.

Prayer: On Christ the solid rock I stand, all other ground is sinking sand. God, put my feet on solid ground.

> *Matthew 16:23 But He turned and said to Peter, "Get behind Me, Satan! You are an offense to Me, for you are not mindful of the things of God, but the things of men."*

Husbands, have you ever done something extra special for your wife and began feeling pretty good about yourself, only to say or do the wrong thing and wind up in the "dog house" a few days later? Around my house, this is called going from "Hero to Zero." Today, we learn that Peter has first-hand experience of going from "Hero to Zero." Yesterday, Jesus commended Peter for his answer, "You are the Christ, the Son of the living God," and told him, the Church would be founded on this acknowledgment. Peter had to be feeling pretty good about himself. However, Jesus begins to tell the disciples in verse 22, "...that He must go to Jerusalem and suffer many things at the hands of the elders, chief priests and teachers of the law, and that He must be killed and on the third day be raised to life." Verse 23 tells us, "Peter took Him aside and began to rebuke Him. 'Never Lord!' he said. 'This shall never happen to You!'" Jesus then turns to Peter and said, "Get behind Me, Satan!, You are an offense to Me, for you are not mindful of the things of God, but the things of men." That had to smack Peter right between the eyes. Jesus left no doubt that Peter's comments were not acceptable. The Bible doesn't make it clear if Jesus is calling Peter, "Satan," or speaking directly to Satan for his role in influencing Peter's comments. In either case, Jesus wasn't going to allow Satan to create any doubt about His purpose for coming to the earth. The good news is that Peter learned a valuable lesson from this experience. He later wrote in 1 Peter 5:8, "Be self-controlled and alert. Your enemy the devil prowls around like a roaring lion looking for someone to devour." As with Peter, Satan is looking to damage our faith and trust in God. He wants nothing more than to destroy our testimony and make us ineffective followers of Christ. As Peter learned, we have to be alert and vigilant at all times. The good news is that if we stumble and fall into temptation like Peter, God can forgive us and still use us for His Kingdom. Whenever you feel Satan begin to tempt you, tell him to "Get behind me Satan, You are an offense to me."

Prayer: God, help me to be self-controlled and alert to Satan's schemes.

> Matthew 16:24 Then Jesus said to His disciples, "If anyone desires to come after Me, let him deny himself, and take up his cross, and follow Me."

After scolding Peter for saying that Jesus would never be handed over to the religious leaders, killed, and on the third day, be raised to life; Jesus turns to the disciples and tells them, that anyone who desires to be His disciple, must deny himself, take up his cross, and follow Him. In this short verse, Jesus gives us clear instructions on what it means to be His disciple. First, we must understand that discipleship is not limited to the twelve men Jesus called to be His disciples. Jesus speaking in John 8:31-32, "To the Jews who had believed Him, Jesus said, 'If you hold to My teaching, you are really My disciples. Then you will know the truth and the truth will set you free.'" Jesus also said in Matthew 28:19, "Therefore go and make disciples of all nations, baptizing them in the name of the Father, and of the Son, and of the Holy Spirit." When we accept Jesus Christ as our Lord and Savior, we become His followers or disciples. As a disciple, one of our responsibilities is to make other disciples. However, today we focus on the three principles of discipleship Jesus gives us; Self-Denial, Sacrifice, and Submission. Many Christians today have following Christ all wrong. We want the benefits, but are not willing to pay the price of discipleship. Self-denial, sacrifice, and submission are just the opposite of our human nature. That is why Luke 9:23 tells us, "If anyone would come after Me, he must deny himself, and take up his cross <u>daily</u> and follow Me." What does a life of self-denial, sacrifice, and submission look like? Can I tell you that it is easier said than done. First, following Jesus requires us to daily renew our hearts and minds to be subject to His will not ours. We do that through daily prayer and reading God's word so that He can show us His will and purpose. Next, we have to deny the urge to indulge in the sinful desires we have. This is a constant battle that rages inside of us, denying the desires that our carnal sinful flesh loves. Lastly, we utilize self-control, which is a fruit of the Holy Spirit, to help us with the fight against our earthly nature. The Holy Spirit is present in our lives to help us. Ask Him to give you self-control.

Prayer: God, help me to be a true disciple of Yours.

> Matthew 16:26 For what profit is it to a man if he gains the whole world, and loses his own soul? Or what will a man give in exchange for his soul?

I heard a story about a rich man on his death bed, making his wife promise to empty their bank account and put his millions in the casket with him. When asked if she complied with her late husband's request, she replied, "of course, I wrote him a check and placed it in the casket." In all seriousness, whatever wealth and possessions we accumulate in our lifetime become worthless to us at our death. How sad it will be for those whose priority in life is to acquire wealth at any cost to themselves and to others. They have traded their very souls for a few years of earthly pleasure. Today, Jesus asks several thought-provoking questions, "What does it profit a man if he gains the whole world? Or, what will a man give in exchange for his soul?" In Genesis, chapter 25 we read that Esau gave up his birthright for a bowl of soup. Judas betrayed Jesus for 30 pieces of silver. Even more sad are those who profess to know Christ as their Savior, yet prefer to chase after the riches of this world. Jesus spoke of them in Matthew 13:22, "Now he who received seed among the thorns is he who hears the word, and the cares of this world and the deceitfulness of riches choke the word, and he becomes unfruitful." John writing in 1 John 2:15 said, "Do not love the world or the things in the world. If anyone loves the world, the love of the Father is not in him." The things of this world have a strong pull on our lives. How do we overcome this desire to chase after the world? Jesus said in John 16:33, "These things I have spoken to you, that in Me you may have peace. In the world you will have tribulation; but be of good cheer, I have overcome the world." The only way we can overcome the world is through our complete faith and trust in Jesus. 1 John 5:4-5 says, "For whatever is born of God overcomes the world. And this is the victory that has overcome the world – our faith. Who is he who overcomes the world, but he who believes that Jesus is the Son of God?" Jesus knows the temptations we face and will see us through as long as we trust Him.

Prayer: God, give me the faith to overcome the world.

> *Matthew 16:27 For the Son of Man will come in the glory of His Father with His angels, and then He will reward each according to his works.*

Jesus has just told the disciples that He will be handed over to the chief priests and be killed, but on the third day He will be raised back to life. Today, Jesus makes it clear that He will make a triumphal return to earth, not as a baby born in a manger, but in all His glory with a multitude of angels. After His return, Jesus will set up court to reward each believer according to their works. Paul writes about this judgement of believers in 2 Corinthians 5:10, "For we must all appear before the Judgement Seat of Christ, that each one may receive the things done in the body, according to what he has done, whether good or bad." Just to be clear, this is not the Great White Throne of Judgment mentioned in Revelation 20:11-15. That judgment is reserved for those who have not accepted Christ as their Savior. The Judgement Seat of Christ is a time of examination and rewards. It is a time for each believer to give an account of their lives and what they have done for Him. Jesus will ask what we did with the resources He entrusted us with. How faithful were we? Did we miss opportunities to serve? Did we follow the leading of the Holy Spirit in our lives? Each person is given different opportunities and abilities. As Paul said in 1 Corinthians 3:8, each person is rewarded based on what we did with what God gave us. "Now he who plants and he who waters are one, and each one will receive his own reward according to his own labor." Paul goes on to say that our rewards will be based on the quality of our service to God. Some of our works may not pass the test. 1 Corinthians 3:12-15 says, "If any man builds on this foundation using gold, silver, costly stones, wood hay or straw, this work will be shown for what it is, because the Day will bring it to light. It will be revealed with fire, and the fire will test the quality of each man's work. If what he has built survives, he will receive his reward. If it is burned up, he will suffer loss; he himself will be saved, but only as one escaping through the flames." What are you building your foundation on?

Prayer: God, I pray that my works are acceptable to You.

> Matthew 17:20 So Jesus said to them, "Because of your unbelief; for assuredly, I say to you, if you have faith as a mustard seed, you will say to this mountain, 'Move from here to there,' and it will move; and nothing will be impossible for you."

A father had just come to Jesus asking Him to have mercy on his son. He told Jesus he had brought the boy to Jesus' disciples, but they couldn't heal him. Jesus rebuked the demon that was possessing the boy and he was immediately healed. Later the disciples came to Jesus and asked why they couldn't drive out the demon. Jesus had already sent the disciples out to preach and heal in His name. They had cast out demons before; yet, they were unable to heal this boy. The disciples may have been over confident based on past experiences and took this situation too lightly thinking they could handle it on their own. Jesus tells them they were unable to heal the boy because of their unbelief and lack of faith. Jesus also told them that even a small amount of faith can do great works, such as moving a mountain. Before you try telling a mountain to move, that was not Jesus' intention. He is just illustrating how even a small amount of faith can accomplish the impossible. Hebrews 11:1 defines faith as, "Now faith is being sure of what we hope for and certain of what we do not see." Faith is the key to successfully serving Christ. Without faith, we are as helpless as the disciples who could not heal the young boy. There have been times when I have prayed in faith for God to move in a certain situation and nothing happened, or so I thought. What I failed to see was that God was working, but not on my time schedule. Also, His answer to my prayer was completely different from what I had in mind. I have learned that God will answer our prayers only in ways that glorify Him, not fulfill our wish list. I have also seen prayers lifted in faith for healing. Some were answered and some not as intended. Should that stop us from praying in faith? Of course not. Hebrews 11:6 tells us, "And without faith it is impossible to please God, because anyone who comes to Him must believe that He exists and that He rewards those who earnestly seek Him." What mountains are you facing in your life today? Take them to your Heavenly Father in faith believing He will move them. Then allow Him to move it in the way that glorifies Him.

Prayer: God, grow my faith in You.

> *Matthew 17:22-23 Now, while they were staying in Galilee, Jesus said to them, "The Son of Man is about to be betrayed into the hands of men, and they will kill Him, and the third day He will be raised up." And they were exceedingly sorrowful.*

This is the second time Jesus has specifically told the disciples that He was going to be handed over to those who hated Him, killed and raised on the third day. The first time did not go so well with Peter rebuking Jesus for saying that He was going to be killed. Today, the disciples get the message and are greatly distressed and sorrowful. However, the fact that Jesus is going to be raised back to life, as a good friend of mine says, 'floated away like a balloon.' Luke 24 tells us that Mary Magdalene and some other women had gone to the tomb where Jesus body was laid, to finish preparing His body for burial. They found an empty tomb and went to tell the disciples who were huddled together, unaware that Jesus has risen. Luke 24:12 tells us, "But Peter arose and ran to the tomb; and stooping down, he saw the linen cloths lying by themselves; and he departed, marveling to himself at what had happened." Just as the disciples didn't want to hear or understand Jesus' plan for salvation, how often do we miss what He has planned for us. Isaiah 55:8 tells us, "For My thoughts are not your thoughts, Nor are your ways My ways, says the Lord." I recall a time in my career with Progress Energy when I knew for sure God was opening a door for me to become the Manager of the Fuquay-Varina Office. I had high hopes on going there. However, someone else was offered the job and I was left disappointed and wondering why God closed that door. Little did I know God had a better plan waiting for me. Six months later, I was offered the Area Manager position in the Selma Business Office in Johnston County. Oh, by the way, that is where my wife's family lives. God's plan was so much better than what I had in mind and well worth the disappointment and frustration I felt by not getting the first job. We worship a God of hope, who loves us and wants the best for us even though that may mean going through some valleys to get there. Jesus had to suffer a horrible death, but was raised to everlasting life on the third day. Don't miss out on the promises God has in store for you. Trust in His plan.

Prayer: God, I am thankful for Your way.

> *Matthew 17:27 Nevertheless, lest we offend them, go to the sea, cast in a hook, and take the fish that comes up first. And when you have opened its mouth, you will find a piece of money; take that and give it to them for Me and you.*

When Jesus and His disciples returned to Capernaum, collectors of the temple tax approached Peter and asked, "Does your Teacher not pay the temple tax?" The temple tax was established in Exodus 30:13-16, where every male 20 years and older was required to pay the tax once a year towards the upkeep of the temple. We find reference to the temple tax in 2 Kings 12:5-17 and Nehemiah 10:32-33. The tax was equivalent to two days wages. Peter answered them simply saying, "Yes," and went on his way. Verse 25-26 tell us, "And when he (Peter) had come into the house, Jesus anticipated him, saying, 'What do you think, Simon? From whom do the kings of the earth take customs or taxes, from their sons or from strangers.' Peter said to Him, 'From strangers.' Jesus said to Peter, 'Then the sons are free.'" Jesus was making the point that as the Son of God, He was not bound by earthly regulations and taxes. However, to avoid offending anyone, Jesus sends Peter on a fishing expedition to find the money to pay the tax for both. Jesus is setting the example for us to avoid offending others. How in the world do we avoid offending someone these days, when offense is taken at the slightest comment? Paul tells us in Romans 12:17-18, "Do not repay anyone evil for evil. Be careful to do what is right in the eyes of everybody. If it is possible, as far as it depends on you, live at peace with everyone." Being careful means to always think before speaking. Proverbs 16:23-24 says, "A wise man's heart guides his mouth, and his lips promote instruction. Pleasant words are like a honeycomb, sweet to the soul and healing to the bones." If you have to give or receive constructive criticism, correct the behavior, not the person. Proverbs 15:31-32 tells us, "He who listens to a life-giving rebuke will be at home among the wise. He who ignores discipline despises himself, but whoever heeds correction gains understanding." There is value in correction done the right way. However, our words and actions should be motivated by a love for others, not revenge. 1 Peter 4:8 says, "Above all, love each other deeply, because love covers a multitude of sins." Allow the love of God to fill your heart today to see the person not their actions.

Prayer: God help me to love others.

> *Matthew 18:3-4 Assuredly, I say to you, unless you are converted and become as little children, you will by no means enter the kingdom of heaven. Therefore whoever humbles himself as this little child is the greatest in the kingdom of heaven.*

The disciples came to Jesus and asked, "Who then is greatest in the Kingdom of Heaven?" They were wondering what role in Jesus' Kingdom each was going to be assigned. Who was going to be named Vice President, Secretary of State, Secretary of the Treasury and so on. This was not the only time this type of question was posed to Jesus. In Matthew 20, we find the mother of James and John approaching Jesus and asking for her sons to sit, one on the right hand and one on the left. Naturally, that did not go well with the other 10 disciples. Jesus knew that pride can be a stumbling block to following Him; so, He settles the issue by calling a little child to come over and stand beside Him. He then gave them an object lesson in humility. Pride, the opposite of humility is thinking too highly of oneself or their accomplishments. Pride is all about me, myself, and I. Pride puts our own desires for recognition above others. Proverbs has a lot to say about the pitfalls of pride. Proverbs 29:3 tells us, "A man's pride will bring him low, but a humble spirit will bring honor." Jesus tells us that unless we become as children, dependent on Him, we will not enter the Kingdom of Heaven. Just as a child recognizes their need for their parents to provide food, clothing, and shelter, we must realize our hopelessness without God. Pride says I can make it on my own. Humility says, I can't make it without God in my life. How do we humble ourselves? Humility is something you do for yourself. God can put circumstances in your life to help break you of pride, but choosing to be humble is a personal decision. Using Jesus' example, being humble is putting others ahead of ourselves. Philippians 2:6-8 tells us, "Who, being in very nature of God, did not consider equality with God something to be grasped, but made himself nothing, taking the very nature of a servant, being made in human likeness. And being found in appearance as a man, He humbled Himself and became obedient to death – even death on a cross!" Paul also writes in Philippians 2:3, "Do nothing out of selfish ambition or vain conceit, but in humility consider others better than yourselves." If you want to be great, become small.

Prayer: God, help me to put others ahead of myself.

> *Matthew 18:6 Whoever causes one these little ones who believe in Me to sin, it would be better for him if a millstone were hung around his neck, and he were drowned in the depth of the sea.*

We read yesterday in Matthew 18:4 where Jesus had called a little child over to use as an object lesson on faith and dependence in Him. Based on this verse, I assumed that the little ones Jesus was talking about today, were also children. In my thinking, a child molester, a human trafficker, or an abusive parent was in big trouble with God. Their eternal punishment was going to be so severe, that being drowned in the sea would be preferred over what was in store for them. However, God considers a new believer, regardless of age, as a "little one" in His eyes. Jesus speaking in Luke 17:1 said, "Things that cause people to sin are bound to come, but woe to that person through whom they come." The things that cause the "little ones" to sin are also known as stumbling blocks. Vivian and I take walks on a nature trail near our house. The trail goes through the woods and there are tree roots hidden under the leaves on the trail. Occasionally, one of us will stump our toe on a root causing us to trip and fall. Jesus said that anyone who leads someone else to sin or keeps them from having a relationship with Him is a stumbling block. A stumbling block would be similar to Vivian and me blindfolding someone and leading them on a walk on the trail and allowing them to trip and fall. Romans 14:13 says, "Therefore let us stop passing judgment on one another. Instead, make up your mind not put any stumbling block or obstacle in your brother's way." What are some examples of a stumbling block? A stumbling block could be a set of rules we make up and impose on a new Christian that are not found in the Bible. It could also be someone observing our participation in something that, while it may not be specifically be considered a sin, has the appearance of sin. Instead, we should be a role model to young Christians. Titus 2:7-8 says, "In everything set them an example by doing what is good. In your teaching show integrity, seriousness and soundness of speech that cannot be condemned, so that those who oppose you may be ashamed because they have nothing bad to say about us."

Prayer: God, help me to be a role model, not to be a stumbling block to someone else.

> *Matthew 18:9 And if your eye causes you to sin, pluck it out and cast it from you. It is better for you to enter into life with one eye, rather than having two eyes, to be cast into hell fire.*

Jesus speaking in Matthew 18:8 said, "If your hand or foot causes you to sin, cut it off and cast it from you. It is better for you to enter into life lame or maimed, rather than having two hands or two feet, to be cast into the everlasting fire." Jesus takes sin very seriously. It is the very reason He came to earth to die a painful death on the cross. Thankfully, His commands to cut our hand or foot off, pluck an eye out, and cast them from us are not to be taken literally. However, they do express the gravity of sin and the impact it can have on our life. We should not take sin lightly, because it leads to judgment and eternal suffering. As bad as it would be to lose a hand or foot, it would be much worse to lose our very souls. Our hands, feet, and eyes are the instruments that lead us into sin. As William Shakespeare said, "our eyes are the window to our soul." They take in millions of images each day. A question we need to ask ourselves is, "Do I tend to focus more on the images that lead me down the path of lust, or have I like Job, 'Made a covenant with my eyes not to look lustfully at a girl?'" (Job 31:1) The Internet has put the availability and privacy of pornography within easy reach of anyone with a telephone. Sadly, pornography has become an epidemic around the world. According to _www.visitthpastorsstudy.org_, 28,250 people are viewing pornography every second. The statistics for professing Christians are roughly the same as non-Christians when it comes to viewing porn, with approximately 50% of church-going men admitting to problems with pornography. Increasingly, pornography is becoming an addiction for women as well, with over 9.3 million women accessing adult websites each month. James 1:14-15 says, "But each one is tempted when, by his own evil desire, he is dragged away and enticed. Then, after desire has conceived, it gives birth to sin, and sin, when it is full grown, gives birth to death." Pornography drags a person away from God's plan for love, marriage and sex and distorts their view of the opposite sex. If you are struggling with pornography, please reach out to someone for help. Don't let it ruin your life.

Prayer: God, help to be careful where my eyes take me.

> Matthew 18:11 For the Son of Man has come to save that which was lost.

In this simple but profound statement, Jesus tells His purpose for coming to suffer a horrible death, and be raised to life again on the third day; to save the lost. Everyone regardless of race, ethnicity, social status and age are lost. However, many either don't know they are lost or don't trust Jesus to be their Savior. It is like the story of when a hurricane came ashore, bringing high winds and flooding. The flood waters continued to rise until a husband and his wife were forced to climb on the roof of their house. They earnestly prayed that God would save them from the flood. A short time later, a man came by with a boat and offered them assistance. They replied, "Thanks, God's got this. The water is going to recede and we can get back into our house." An hour later, a helicopter hovered over their house and offered assistance. They replied, "Thanks, God's got this and we are doing okay." A few hours later, the rising flood waters swept them away and they drowned. Upon reaching the pearly gates, they complained to God for letting them drown. God told them, "I sent a boat and helicopter to rescue you. Why didn't you take it?" God loves us so much that He sent His only Son to die for our sins. (John 3:16) Sadly, many are looking for something other than His Son to save them. Why can't they see that Jesus is the answer? Then there are those who don't even know they are lost. A friend of mine shared a conversation he had with a young man in his mid-20's. My friend had gotten to know this person and asked what his interests were outside of work. The young man replied, playing video games. My friend then asked if he went to church. The young man looked at him strangely and began to avoid the conversation. My first reaction to this conversation was how sad. This young man's life primarily consisted of work and video games. He didn't seem to be seeking anything more for his life, and even worse was clueless he was lost. How many people do I come in contact with each day are just like this young man? How can I offer hope to this lost and dying world we live in?

Prayer: God, help me to point others to Your Son for salvation.

> *Matthew 18:12 What do you think? If a man has a hundred sheep, and one of them goes astray, does he not leave the ninety-nine and go to the mountains to seek the one that is straying?*

Yesterday Jesus told us, "For the Son of Man has come to save that which was lost." Today, Jesus lets us know that He is also concerned about the welfare of His sheep, those who have accepted Him as Lord and Savior. In this parable known as the "Parable of the Lost Sheep" we read in verses 13-14, "And if he finds it, I tell you the truth, he is happier about the one sheep than about the ninety-nine that did not wander off. In the same way your Father in heaven is not willing that any of these little ones should be lost." To better understand what Jesus is telling us, let's break down the key points to this parable. First, Jesus is not referring to a shepherd, but the owner of the sheep, God. Psalm 100:3 says, "Know that the Lord is God. It is He who made us, and we are His; we are His people, the sheep of His pasture." As His sheep, God deeply cares for us. He doesn't want anyone to perish. He is even willing to leave the others to search after the lost sheep, and finding it brings Him much joy. Secondly, the sheep is lost because it made a choice to wander away from the rest of flock. Whether it was lured to another area by greener grass or it just decided to follow a path that led away from the flock, the sheep became lost. Isaiah 53:6 says, "We all, like sheep, have gone astray, each of us has turned to his own way; and the Lord has laid on Him the iniquity of us all." Being a Christian doesn't mean we are never tempted or that the lure of the things of this world will not take us away from our relationship with Christ. Satan wants nothing more than to separate us from the body of believers. Lastly, verse 13 reads, "And if he finds it." The wandering sheep may or may not be found. In its wandering, the sheep may have gotten swept away by a swift flowing stream. I have had always heard that sin will take you farther than you want to go, and make you stay longer than you want to stay. If you have wandered away, know that God loves you and is searching for you.

Prayer: God, thank You that you care enough to search after the one lost sheep.

> Matthew 18:15 Moreover if your brother sins against you, go and tell him his fault between you and him alone. If he hears you, you have gained your brother.

In today's study, Jesus provides believers a guide for resolving conflicts. He continued in verses 16-17 saying, "But if he will not listen, take one or two others along, so that 'every matter may be established by the testimony of two or three witnesses.' If he refuses to listen to them, tell it to the church; and if he refuses to listen even to the church, treat him as you would a pagan or a tax collector" Jesus tells us, if a fellow Christian steals, spread lies, verbally or physically attacks you, or does anything to harm you, the responsibility for reconciliation and forgiveness belongs to you. For those of us who prefer to avoid confrontation, it is easier to ignore and accept the offense rather than confronting the other person. However, that can lead to bitterness towards the offender. For others, it might be easier to take the matter to your friends who then develop a biased or unfair view about this fellow believer. This is how the rumor mill and gossip get started. Jesus said, first in a private conversation, humbly confront the person who has offended you. Leviticus 19:17 says, "Do not hate your brother in your heart. Rebuke your neighbor frankly so you will not share in his guilt." In most cases, the two in private conversation can work things out and prevent the conflict from expanding. If that step fails, then the offended party should take one or two witnesses and talk to the offender again. Deuteronomy 19:15 says, "One witness is not enough to convict a man accused of any crime or offense he may have committed. A matter must be established by the testimony of two or three witnesses." I have learned there are three sides to every story, yours, mine, and the actual. Having witnesses brings objectivity to the issue. It step two fails, the offended party should bring the offense to the whole church. Hopefully, the leadership of the church can mediate and resolve the conflict, bringing the offending party to repentance. Lastly, if the offending party is still unrepentant, remove him/her from the fellowship of the church. Hopefully, this will help the individual to understand the seriousness of their behavior and come to repentance. Dealing with conflict is never easy, but it is necessary to keep unity within the body of believers.

Prayer: God, help me to address conflict according to Your word.

> Matthew 18:18 Assuredly, I say to you, whatever you bind on earth will be bound in heaven, and whatever you loose on earth will be loosed in heaven.

As I dig deeper into God's Word, I realize my concept of some scripture is not entirely accurate. Today's verse is one of those occasions. I always considered binding and loosing as coming into agreement on a prayer need with others and giving it or releasing it to God. This is not the case, and not the first time Jesus has mentioned the concept of binding and loosing. Speaking to Peter in Matthew 16:19 He said, "And I will give you the keys of the Kingdom of Heaven, and whatever you bind on earth will be bound in heaven, and whatever you loose on earth will be loosed in heaven." In Jesus' day, the terms bind and loose were common legal phrases that meant to declare something forbidden or to declare it allowed. Jesus has just finished giving the disciples instructions on dealing with conflict and persistent sin in the church. The last step in verse 17 says, "And if he refuses to hear them, tell it to the church. But if he refuses to even hear the church, let him be to you like a heathen and a tax collector." The decision of whether the church should disassociate from this person is the process of binding and loosing. Jesus is confirming that the decision is recognized and approved in heaven. Just to be clear, the disassociation doesn't mean the church should wash their hands clean of that person, but should be praying for them to be made right with God again. Why is church disciple important? Because purity and righteousness in God's church is important. Does this mean the church should not welcome sinners? Of course not; however, it does mean that Christians should be living differently from others. 2 Corinthians 5:17, "Therefore, if anyone is in Christ, he is a new creation; the old has gone and the new has come!" Church discipline is also important for the wellbeing of the church. How many lives have been ruined by a church leader who was allowed to stay in their position, although being repeatedly reported for sexual misconduct? We should not be afraid to address deliberate sin in the church. Galatians 6:1, "Brothers, if someone is caught in a sin, you who are spiritual should restore him in a spirit of gentleness. Keep watch on yourself, lest you too be tempted."

Prayer: God, give me boldness to address blatant sin in the church.

> Matthew 18:19 *Again I say to you that if two of you agree on earth concerning anything that they ask, it will be done for them by My Father in heaven.*

Although today's verse follows Jesus' teaching on church discipline, it also applies to the power of believers praying together in unity. There is nothing more exciting than praying in agreement and witnessing God answer those prayers in miraculous ways. I attend a weekly Bible Study where time is allotted for sharing and praying over different requests from the men. Men with serious health issues have come to the class to be prayed for. They were anointed with oil and had hands laid on them, following the instructions found in James 5:14. "Is anyone among you sick? Let him call for the elders of the church and let them pray over him, anointing him with oil in the name of the Lord." We have also prayed for our local, state, and national leaders and for spiritual renewal and revival. During the week, prayer requests are daily sent to our group leader, who then forwards them through an email distribution list to over 300 people who are committed to praying. I receive on average, four emails a week with multiple prayer requests on each. Why are so many prayer requests sent out each week? As our leader says, "Not because we are good prayer's, but because of a good God who has been faithful in answering our prayers." Although God does not always answer our prayers in the way we had hoped for, we have witnessed several who have been miraculously healed of cancer and kidney stones. Jesus said there is power when two of you agree on earth about something. That is why unity between believers is so important. With unity there is authority in prayer. Our leader will often quote today's verse before we pray for someone to bring our hearts and minds in one accord with each other. At the conclusion of our prayers, we say in unison, "it shall be done," affirming God's promise to answer our prayer. 1 Corinthians 1:10 says, "I appeal to you brothers, in the name of our Lord Jesus Christ, that all you agree with one another so that there may be no divisions among you and that you may be perfectly united in mind and thought." Why is unity so important? "...For there the Lord bestows His blessing, even life forevermore," Psalm 133:3. Do you want to experience the power of prayer? Pray in agreement with others.

Prayer: God, help me pray and live in unity with other believers.

> *Matthew 18:20 For where two or three are gathered together in My name, I am there in the midst of them.*

Don't let this verse confuse you. God is not implying that it requires a group of two or three to be in His presence. God is always with us. 1 Corinthians 3:16 says, "Do you not know that you are the temple of God, and that the Spirit of God dwells in you?" Today's verse is often used to encourage the gathering of believers; however, it actually concludes Jesus' comments on church disciple. He assures the disciples that He would be with them as they gather to meet with the wrongdoer. This is encouraging because we live in a time when it is not fashionable to confront someone's lifestyle as sinful. Suppose I have a friend whose marriage is on shaky ground. He has become very friendly with another woman who sympathizes with him and shares the problems in her marriage as well. One conversation leads to another, until the two are sneaking away to be with each other. As a brother in Christ and friend, I notice what is taking place and go to my friend to talk with him about it. He admits things are not going well between him and his wife, and that the woman he is seeing, really understands and loves him. To make matters worse, the woman leads the praise team at church. He admits his actions are not right, and agrees to work things out with his wife. Weeks later, his behavior has not changed, and in fact has gotten worse. I get another friend to go with me this time to confront him. He now begins to defend his actions, saying, "I never loved my first wife and she makes my life miserable. I am going to end our marriage and develop a relationship with my new lover. Nothing you can say will change my mind." What do you do? Do you tell your friend good luck and pray for him. Or do you do the hard thing, and take the issue before the church or your church leadership with your witness? If your friend has no remorse or concern about his marriage and family, I can assure you this action will end your friendship. Now matter how painful the experience, God wants you to know that if you are doing the right thing with the right motive, He is there with you to support you.

Prayer: God, help to me save a lost brother or sister in Christ.

> *Matthew 18:21-22 Then Peter came to Him and said, "Lord, how often shall my brother sin against me, and I forgive him? Up to seven times?" Jesus said to him, "I do not say to you up to seven times, but up to seventy times seven."*

According to www.bibleref.com, Jewish Law required someone to forgive a person who was guilty of the same offense three times. After three offenses, the guilty party was not likely to change their behavior, so there was no need to continue forgiving them. Peter, aware of the Rabbinic Law, posed a question to Jesus about forgiveness. Perhaps trying to impress Jesus, Peter doubled the number of times one should forgive and added one more. Jesus' reply quickly let Peter know that there was no limit to forgiveness. Jesus shares a parable of the "Unforgiving Servant" in verses 23-34. In summary, a servant owed his king 10,000 talents which represented a huge sum of money that the servant was unable to pay back. In order to settle the debt, the servant's family was to be sold into slavery; however, the servant pleaded with the king for mercy and more time to pay. The king was moved with compassion on his servant and forgave him the huge debt. After being forgiven his debt, the servant left and confronted one of his fellow servants who owed him a couple of hundred dollars. The fellow servant begged for mercy and more time to pay off his debt; however, the man would not and threw his fellow servant in prison until the debt was paid. The king heard about his servant not forgiving the small debt his friend owed him. He called the servant back and told him, "Should you not also have had compassion on your fellow servant, just as I had pity on you?" The king delivered the servant to prison to be tortured until his debt was paid. Everyone appreciates being forgiven; however, they may find it difficult to forgive someone else when offended. Typically, it is what the other person did that makes it a struggle to forgive. For lesser offenses, we just simply refuse to forgive because of pride. Jesus tries to help us understand the "why" we should forgive others with the parable. The more we understand that God continues to forgive us of a staggering debt of pride, anger, lust, bitterness, rebellious behavior, and hurt we have caused others, the easier it should become to forgive someone else. Forgiveness starts when we let go of the bitterness and resentment towards someone. Are you ready to let it go?

Prayer: God, help to forgive as You forgave me.

> *Matthew 18:35 So My heavenly Father also will do to each of you,*
> *from his heart, does not forgive his brother his trespasses.*

I heard a great example of forgiveness at a recent funeral. A woman and her husband had been married for 39 years when he died of an Aortic Aneurysm that was misdiagnosed as heartburn. Naturally, the family was very upset with the doctor and wanted to take legal action against him. However, the wife refused, telling her family that it was just their father's time to go, and they should forgive the doctor. Hopefully, he would learn from his mistake and save someone else in the future. As I heard this story, I wondered if the doctor had even realized his mistake and the grief this family experienced. Yet, this simple act of forgiveness released the family from years of bitterness and hatred. It allowed them to move on with their lives with fond memories of their father and husband. The more I read about forgiveness in the Bible, the more I understand how important it is. Jesus tells us that God will not forgive those who are unwilling to forgive others. Not that forgiveness of others is a requirement for salvation, but because it is a by-product of being saved. In the past, I have wanted to put stipulations on forgiveness based on what the person did and if they were sorry for doing it. However, Jesus didn't put stipulations on the men who spit in His face, and struck Him at His mock trial. Nor did He say anything to the soldier who was ripping His back open with a whip made of sharp pieces of bone and metal. He said nothing to the soldier who was hammering the spikes in His hands and feet. He didn't even rebuke the one thief who was insulting Him while dying on the cross. No, the only thing Jesus said was, "Father forgive them, for they do not know what they are doing." Jesus even taught us to pray, "Forgive us our debts, as we forgive our debtors." I am not going to pretend that forgiveness is easy. It requires every bit of humbleness, compassion, and patience you have. Colossians 3:12-13 says, "Therefore as God's chosen people, holy and dearly loved, clothe yourselves with compassion, kindness, humility, gentleness and patience. Bear with each other and forgive whatever grievances you may have against one another. Forgive as the Lord forgave you." Ask God today to teach you more about forgiveness.

Prayer: God, teach me how to forgive.

> Matthew 19:4 And He answered and said to them, "Have you not read that He who made them at the beginning made them male and female."

Jesus is talking to the Pharisees who had just asked Him, "Is it lawful for a man to divorce his wife for just any reason?" Quoting Genesis 2:24, He answered them saying, "'Have you not read that He who made them at the beginning 'made them male and female.' For this reason a man shall leave his father and mother and be joined to his wife, and the two shall become one flesh?" God's plan is very simple. A man leaves his father and mother and becomes one with his wife. Unfortunately, as broken people, we have turned something simple, into a big mess. Marriage has become an agreement not a binding covenant. According to _www.brides.com_, the average marriage in the US lasts approximately eight years. However, becoming more prevalent is same sex marriages. For centuries, some men have sexually desired to be with another man instead of a woman. The same for women. Sodom and Gomorrah were destroyed by fire and sulfur because of their perverted lifestyle. Jude 7 says, "In a similar way, Sodom and Gomorrah and the surrounding towns gave themselves up to sexual immorality and perversion. They serve as an example of those who suffer the punishment of eternal fire." You can find more details about God's thoughts on homosexuality in Romans 1:26-27, 1 Corinthians 6:9, and 1 Timothy 1:9-10. The gay and lesbian lifestyle is now fully accepted, protected by the law and celebrated in some churches. To speak the truth of God's word about that lifestyle is considered hate speech and bigotry. Although nothing is hateful about God's word, it often does not align with our wants and desires. It also exposes our sin and rebellion against Him, which makes us uncomfortable. Perhaps you, a family member, or someone you know has chosen the LGBTQ lifestyle. God loves you and has a wonderful plan for your life. However, God is holy and despises sin of any kind. Hebrews 10:26-27 tells us, "If we deliberately keep on sinning after we have received the knowledge of truth, no sacrifice for sins is left, but only a fearful expectation of judgment and of raging fire that will consume the enemies of God." My prayer is that you will search God's word and let Him to speak to you. Ask Him to make your heart like His. Allow Him to change you from the inside out.

Prayer: God, help me to live a life that pleases You.

> *Matthew 19:9 And I say to you, whoever divorces his wife, except for sexual immorality, and marries another, commits adultery; and whoever marries her who is divorced commits adultery.*

After Jesus response to the Pharisee's first question about divorce, they followed up with a second question found in Matthew 19:7, "Why then did Moses' command to give a certificate of divorce, and to put her away?" Jesus' first answer had pointed to God's original plan for marriage, that divorce did not reflect the true plan of creation. However, the Pharisees, who were knowledgeable of the Law, brought up the Rules for Divorce written by Moses in Deuteronomy 24. Essentially, if marriage was to be a lifetime commitment, why did Moses allow certificates of divorce? Moses permitted divorce because it was an option to resolve a sinful, indecent act that had destroyed the marriage. Marriage hasn't gotten any easier since Moses' day. Vivian and I have been married almost 42 years. Like most marriages, ours has gone through some rough times as well. Most issues have been around selfishness, busyness of life, and lack of attention for each other. By God's grace, we have been able to work through our issues and remain "in love" with each other. Although there were some difficult days, for us, divorce was never an option. However, today, it seems as if divorce is used as an escape plan when the marriage gets difficult. I can only speak to my situation, but I am so thankful that Vivian and I made the effort to work through our differences. However, many were not resolved overnight. In fact, some took years, but it was worth it. There are a number of self-help ideas designed to improve your marriage. However, none of them will work unless both husband and wife are committed to staying married. Remember, you chose the person you married for a very good reason and working on your marriage is a life-long process that begins on your wedding day. Don't wait until it is too late to start working on your marriage. Things such as respecting and valuing your spouse, setting aside time to have a conversation, sharing financial expectations and goals, have date nights and most importantly, forgive quickly are all helpful suggestions. If all else fails, seek professional help. Use Ephesians 5:33 as a good foundation to your marriage, "However, each one of you also must love his wife as he loves himself, and the wife must respect her husband." Very simply, love and respect go a long way.

Prayer: God, please help me protect my marriage.

> Matthew 19:14 But Jesus said, "Let the little children come to Me, and do not forbid them; for of such is the kingdom of heaven."

Jesus was becoming very popular, with large crowds showing up wherever He was teaching. He had just finished a conversation with a group of Pharisees who had tested Him on marriage and divorce. Now, some parents were bringing their children to Jesus for Him to lay His hands on them and pray for them. The disciples, thinking they were helping Jesus, rebuked the parents and told them to move on. Mark 10:14 tells us, "When Jesus saw this, He was indignant." He had just taught the disciples a few days earlier in Matthew 18 about how precious children are to God. Now, the disciples are turning them away? Jesus wanted the children to come to Him, and told the disciples, "Let the little children come to Me, and do not hinder them, for the kingdom of heaven belongs to such as these young children." (Luke 18:16) Underlying in this story is the love these parents had for their children. Psalm 127:3 says, "Behold, children are a heritage from the Lord. The fruit of the womb is a reward." We can learn some valuable lessons from the parent's example. Children are dependent on their parents to love them, care for them, provide for them, and teach them about life. Every family is different, and go about meeting those needs in a variety of ways. However, in this story, the parents were taking their children to Christ. They wanted their children to be blessed by Jesus. It is our role as a parent is to point our children to Christ. We shouldn't leave that responsibility to a children's church worker or a pastor. Proverbs 22:6 says, "Train up a child in the way he should go; even when he is old he will not depart from it." Read God's word to your children, pray with them, for them, and discipline them with the goal of showing them the way to Jesus. Ephesians 6:4 says, "Fathers, do not provoke your children to anger, but bring them up in the discipline and instruction of the Lord." Make learning God's word fun, not a punishment. Incorporate lessons from the Bible in your daily conversations. However, one of the best methods for teaching our children is not in words, but by actions. Be a "Do what I do, not, do what I say" parent.

Prayer: God, help me to lead my children to You.

> *Matthew 19:17 So He said to him, "Why do you call Me good? No one is good but One, that is God. But if you want to enter into life, keep the commandments."*

A rich young ruler came up to Jesus and asked, "Good Teacher, what good thing shall I do that I may have eternal life?" Jesus answered him saying, "Why do you call Me good? No one is good but One, that is God." Was Jesus implying He wasn't good? Not at all. Jesus is God, and He is incapable of sinning. However, the young ruler only knew Jesus as a Teacher, not the Son of God. So, Jesus gave him the standard of goodness, which is God. No one has lived up to God's standard, that is why He sent His only Son to make us right with Him. I heard someone share a testimony, about a being called good. He and a friend were on an airplane and the friend became airsick. The man went out of his way to take care of his friend. Later at the airport, a lady came up to the man and said, "I can tell you are a good man, the way you looked after your friend." The man replied, "Thank you, but there is no one that is truly good except God." This opened up a conversation with the woman about Jesus and the plan of salvation. The woman's perception of good, was the kindness shown to the sick friend. The young ruler's perception of "good" was to obey the commandments. Keeping them was his ticket to heaven. Jesus even said, "But if you want to enter into life, keep the commandments." Don't let Jesus' response confuse you, trying to live a good life will not save you. That is the point He is leading the young ruler to discover. The young man thinking he has lived a very good life, asks Jesus, "Which ones?" Jesus said, "'You shall not murder,' 'You shall not commit adultery,' 'You shall not steal,' 'You shall not bear false witness,' Honor your father and your mother,' and, 'You shall love your neighbor as yourself.'" The young man had to be feeling pretty good, when he said to Jesus, "All these things I have kept from my youth. What do I still lack?" We will find out tomorrow. Romans 3:10 says, "There is no one righteous, not even one." As hard as we may try, we can't live a good enough life measured up to God's standards.

Prayer: God, I am thankful that I don't have to try to be good to be saved.

> *Matthew 19:21 Jesus said to him, "If you want to be perfect, go, sell what you have and give to the poor, and you will have treasure in heaven; and come, follow Me."*

Jesus now turns the conversation to the condition of the young man's heart. All too often we want to make following Christ a list of do's and don'ts. I recall growing up hearing some people who professed to be Christians saying, "I don't' drink, I don't smoke, I don't steal, I haven't committed adultery, and I don't lie," thinking those actions were ensuring their salvation. All the while Jesus is asking, "What about humility, being a servant, giving generously, helping the poor, visiting the sick, and ministering to those in prison?" Jesus knew that the young man's heart was devoted to keeping the rules, rather than following Him. He also knew that the young man found security in his riches over trusting God. He wanted both his money and God as long as God didn't get in the way. Verse 22 says, "But when the young man heard that saying, he went away sorrowful, for he had great possessions." Money and possessions in themselves are not a bad thing. Its takes both to survive in today's world. However, when acquiring and holding on to them become more important to us than serving God, we have a problem. This not only applies to money and possessions, but to our time and activities as well. Where does going to church, reading God's word, and prayer, fall on our list of priorities for the week? Think about these real-life situations and answer how you would handle them. Our friend has a four-year-old grandchild involved in a recreational soccer league. However, his games were scheduled for Sunday morning during the normal church hours. What would you do? Allow the child to participate in the league, thinking it will be good experience and it only lasts eight weeks. Or, would you pull the child out of this league and sign him up for another that doesn't play on Sunday morning? Another friend has invested in a boat. He works long hours and the only available time he has to use it is on Sundays. Because of the crowded conditions on the water, he likes to get out on the water early on Sunday morning. What do you do? Take your boat out and enjoy God's creation, sell it, or try to squeeze in other opportunities to use it. We all face these kinds of decisions. Jesus wants to know where our hearts are.

Prayer: God, help me to put You first in my life.

> Matthew 19:24 *And again I say to you, it is easier for a camel to go through the eye of a needle than for a rich man to enter the kingdom of God.*

Did Jesus say that it was impossible for a rich person to enter the kingdom of God; or, was He implying that it was just very difficult? If He was talking about a real needle, then it would be impossible. However, if He was referring to a lower gate in Jerusalem where a camel had to squirm on their knees to get through, then there is hope for a rich person. Another important matter is Jesus' definition of a rich person. Mine has always been someone who has more than I do. But that definition doesn't hold water because, I would be considered rich by someone else's standards. I think the disciples' response in Matthew 19:25 sums it all up, "When the disciples heard this, they were greatly astonished and asked, 'Who then can be saved?'" If a rich person can't be saved, then who can? Many equate riches to God's blessings on someone. Therefore, if God has blessed that person, then why is it impossible for them to be saved? God does bless people with wealth; however, some acquire it through dishonest and ruthless means. Others devote their lives to obtaining it above everything else. In the process of achieving the millionaire or billionaire club, they fail to see their need for God. What do they need God for? Wealth has become their god. Billy Graham said, "The ground is level at the foot of the cross.[12]" In other words, our riches mean nothing to God. We are all sinners in need of a Savior. Unless we humble ourselves, repent of our sins, and ask Jesus to be the Lord and Savior of our lives, we can't be saved. Our riches cannot buy our way into heaven. There is hope for the rich person who trusts God with their riches and their lives. 1 Timothy 6:17-19 says, "Command those who are rich in this present world not to be arrogant nor to put their hope in wealth, which is so uncertain, but to put their hope in God, who richly provides us with everything for our enjoyment. Command them to do good, to be rich in good deeds, and to be generous and willing to share. In this way they will lay up treasure for themselves as a firm foundation for the coming age, so that they may take hold of the life that is truly life."

Prayer: God, help me to be rich in good deeds.

> *Matthew 19:26 But Jesus looked at them and said to them, "With men this is impossible, but with God all things are possible."*

Jesus answered the disciples' question of, "Who then can be saved?", with today's verse, "With men this is impossible, but with God all things are possible." He is teaching that no matter how hard we try, our good works aren't sufficient to gain salvation and no amount of riches can buy our way into heaven. Think about how frustrating it would be to try to live a perfect life to earn your salvation. One slip of the tongue, one careless mistake and you are guilty of sin and therefore cannot enter the kingdom of God. Once the mistake is made there is no turning back. Now you fall short of the righteous requirement of the Law. However, Jesus is preparing to introduce a five-letter word that will turn everyone's world completely upside down. Through His life, death, and resurrection man's concept of salvation will go from works to faith. Ephesians 2:4-6, "But God, who is rich in mercy, because of His great love with which He loved us, even when we were dead in trespasses, made us alive together with Christ (by grace you have been saved), and raised us up together and made us sit together in heavenly places in Christ Jesus." That five-letter word is "Grace." God's unmerited favor and love for a people who do not deserve it. Grace is God willing and able to forgive us and make us right with Him, in spite of the fact we don't deserve to be treated with such goodness. Romans 3:10 says, "There is none righteous, no, not one." Romans 3:23 plainly tells us, "For all have sinned and fall short of the glory of God." How does grace work? Ephesians 2:8, "For by grace you have been saved through faith, and that not of yourselves; it is the gift of God, not of works, lest anyone should boast." God's grace is a free gift that saves us from our sins. All we have to do is accept His gift of grace through faith in His son, Jesus Christ. Although God's gift of grace is free to us, it cost Him His very own Son who suffered and died a cruel death on the cross. Although we celebrate God's gift of grace each year at Easter, take time today to thank Him for His grace and wonderful plan of salvation.

Prayer: God, I am thankful that with You, all things are possible.

> Matthew 19:30 But many who are first will be last, and the last first.

In the movie, *Talladega Nights*, the main character Ricky Bobby, is a NASCAR race driver. As a boy, Ricky Bobby's father was never around, but left him with a saying that stuck with him throughout his racing career, "If you ain't first, you are last." Ricky Bobby is not alone. Much of the world lives by this motto, wanting to be first and doing whatever it takes to be out front. Jesus turns this concept completely upside down, saying "many who are first, will be last, and the last first." Yet, we live in a world where we are bombarded with messages that we have to have more. Billions of dollars are spent each year to convince us we have to have nicer, bigger, and better. To be considered successful, we need to drive this type of vehicle, wear a certain type of clothes, and make ourselves look youthful again. Jesus makes it clear, that one day when it is too late, many will come to realize they have lived for what did not matter. The things they were pursuing will have no value in His kingdom. Does this mean that poor people will be first in heaven and rich people last? Not necessarily. Jesus looks at what is in our hearts. 1 Samuel 16:7, "But the Lord said to Samuel, 'Do not consider his appearance or his height, for I have rejected him. The Lord does not look at the things man looks at. Man looks at the outward appearance, but the Lord looks at the heart.'" What do our lives resemble in relation to humbleness versus pride or selfishness versus servanthood? Proverbs 4:23 says, "Keep your heart with all diligence, for out of it spring the issues of life." Is it time to change the way you think? Perhaps selfishness, self-promotion, and self-advancement have overtaken your priorities. Pray for God to guard your heart and change your attitude to one of being His servant, advancing His Kingdom. Ask Him to change your priorities, not living for the money and fortune of this world, but laying up treasures in heaven. Allow Him to change your definition of success and to discover what is most important to Him. As you turn your life over to Him, you will discover how satisfying His plan is over chasing after the riches of this world.

Prayer: God, help me to reprioritize my life to live according to Your plan.

> Matthew 20:22 But Jesus answered and said, "You do not know what you ask. Are you able to drink the cup that I am about to drink, and be baptized with the baptism that I am baptized with?"

The mother of James and John has just asked Jesus when He comes into His kingdom, if her two sons could sit on His right and left hand. This is a very bold request considering there are ten other disciples who would like to have those positions of power and recognition as well. It is even more astonishing she would ask this of Jesus right after He has told them in Matthew 20:18-19, "Behold, we are going up to Jerusalem, and the Son of Man will be betrayed to the chief priests and to the scribes; and they will condemn Him to death, and deliver Him to the Gentiles to mock and to scourge and to crucify. And the third day He will rise again." It is very likely; this conversation had been planned by James and John who were standing with their mother as she made her request. Jesus' answer was not one of rebuke, but turning to James and John, He said, "You do not know what you are asking. Can you drink from the cup I am going to drink?" They quickly answered, "We are able." Jesus did not promise those positions to them, but told them, "You will indeed drink from My cup." James would later be the first disciple martyred for the faith. John would be beaten, tortured, and exiled to the Isle of Patmos where he wrote the Book of Revelation. Jesus wants us to know that following Him is not about fame and glory, but sacrifice, perseverance, and servanthood. All too often, we want the honor and glory of the title rather than the work that comes with it. Elder, Deacon, Worship Leader, Ladies' Ministry Leader, Small Group Leader, etc., are very important roles in today's church. With them come responsibility and hours of hard work no one knows about, except you and God. However, what is our motivation for aspiring to these positions? Is it to serve and use the talents God has given us, or is it for the recognition that role provides? Philippians 2:3 says, "Do nothing out of selfish ambition or vain conceit, but in humility consider others better than yourselves." Jesus said, following Him comes with a price. Don't worry about your status in the kingdom of God, but that you are faithfully serving Him. Life may be a competition, but the kingdom of God is not.

Prayer: God, help me to focus on following You.

> *Matthew 20:26 Yet it shall not be so among you; but whoever desires to become great among you, let him be your servant.*

The disciples heard the conversation James and John's mother had with Jesus. Up to this point, Peter seemed to be taking a position of leadership within the group, and now, James and John are asking for the top two spots. The other disciples were upset because they were also vying for positions in Jesus' kingdom. Matthew 20:24, "And when the ten heard it, they were greatly displeased with the two brothers." I can only imagine the conversations that were taking place. However, Jesus steps in and teaches the disciples a revolutionary concept about leadership. Jesus said, "Whoever desires to be great among you, let him be your servant." According to Jesus, there is nothing wrong with achieving greatness. The desire to achieve or excel in something is God given. While God plants the seeds of desire, it is up to each individual how deep those roots go. I have always wanted to be the best in something, but I have found that there will always be someone bigger, faster, smarter, and more talented. However, what separates the great from the good, the good from the mediocre, and the mediocre from the bad is desire. What is a person willing to sacrifice to achieve greatness? Athletes are blessed with God given talent, but no one sees the hours of training. In the gym you hear terms like, "No pain, no gain" or "sweat equity." The same for great musicians. They do not walk out on stage and perform without hours and hours of practice before hand. However, Jesus said, greatness is not found in position, wealth, athletic achievements, and power. In His kingdom, greatness is found in being a servant. This may sound contradictory, but Jesus also makes it clear that it is not wrong to seek positions of leadership and influence. In fact, we need more Christians to fill those roles. But the way you lead should be through humbly serving others. 1 Peter 4:10 says, "Each one should use whatever gift he has received to serve others, faithfully, administering God's grace in its various forms." A servant leads by example rather than trying to control and manipulate others. A servant doesn't flaunt their authority and influence over others to get their way. A servant doesn't seek self-glorification. What changes do you need to make to achieve greatness in God's eyes?

Prayer: God, teach me how to be a servant.

> *Matthew 20:28 Just as the Son of Man did not come to be served,*
> *but to serve, and to give His life a ransom for many.*

While the disciples are still jockeying for position in Jesus' kingdom, He plainly tells them that He "did not come to be served, but to serve, and give His life for many." Philippians 2:5-11, "Your attitude should be the same as that of Christ Jesus; who, being in very nature God, did not consider equality with God something to be grasped, but made Himself nothing, taking the very nature of a servant, being made in human likeness. And being found in appearance as a man, He humbled Himself and became obedient to death – even death on a cross! Therefore, God exalted Him to the highest place and gave Him a name that is above every name, that at the name of Jesus every knee should bow, in heaven and on earth and under the earth, and every tongue confess that Jesus Christ is Lord, to the glory of God the Father." These verses sum up the gospel, the good news of Jesus Christ who humbled Himself and came to earth to die a violent death on the cross. He took on the very nature of a servant, yet God exalted Him to the highest position and gave Him a name that is above all names. Romans 8:34 tells us that He has not stopped serving, but is at the right hand of God, always interceding for us. "Who is He that condemns? Christ Jesus, who died – more than that, who was raised to life – is at the right hand of God and is also interceding for us." What do you need from Christ today who is interceding for you? He can give you strength to get through a difficult day. He provides wisdom to help you make sound decisions. He can provide peace in the midst of the storms of life. He comforts those who are hurting. He supplies your daily bread. He gives you the air you breathe. He heals your sicknesses. Think about it, God is at work in your life even when you don't realize it. A servant relies on his master for everything. A good test of our servanthood, is our dependence on Him. Are we too proud and haughty to ask God for help? Or, have we humbled ourselves before Him and, cried out "Abba Father, I need You?" Jesus is waiting to hear from you.

Prayer: God, thank You for coming to serve. Help me to have a servant's heart.

> *Matthew 21:13 And He said to them. "It is written, 'My house shall be called a house of prayer,' but you have made it a 'den of thieves.'"*

Jesus has just ridden into Jerusalem, with a large crowd spreading their cloaks and palm branches on the road before Him, shouting, "Hosanna to the Son of David! Blessed is He who comes in the name of the Lord! Hosanna in the highest!" This fulfills the prophecy found in Zechariah 9:9 that reads, "Rejoice greatly, O Daughter of Zion! Shout, Daughter of Jerusalem! See, your King comes to you, righteous and having salvation, gentle and riding on a donkey, on a colt, the foal of a donkey." Matthew writes in verses 10-11, "all the city was moved, saying, 'Who is this?' So the multitudes said, 'This is Jesus, the prophet from Nazareth of Galilee.'" This was Jesus' announcement to the world, that He was the Messiah; however, they missed the message, recognizing Him as only a prophet. Jesus then enters the courtyard area of the temple where many had set up businesses for exchanging currencies and selling animals for sacrifice. Angry at what He sees, Jesus overturns their tables and benches, quoting Isaiah 56:7 "... for My house will be called a house of prayer," and Jeremiah 7:11 "...you have made it a den of thieves." It is pretty clear that Jesus is passionate about the temple of God being a place of prayer to God, one of seeking after God, and one of glorifying God. Yet, the very place in the temple that has been designated as a place of prayer was turned it into a marketplace. I am not sure what Jesus' reaction would be if He walked into our churches today. At times it is difficult to tell if they are a place of worship or just a place of fellowship. But more importantly, what would Jesus' reaction to our own temple be? 1 Corinthians 6:19, "Do you not know that your body is a temple of the Holy Spirit, who is in you, whom you have received from God? You are not your own." Jesus is just as passionate about our lives as He is the church. What are we more focused on: prayer, giving glory to God, and seeking after Him, or seeking after our own self-interests? Have we put personal gain and benefit above Him? Ask Him to make you a person of prayer and to be the temple He created you to be for His Kingdom.

Prayer: God, cleanse my temple and make it holy in Your sight.

> Matthew 21:19 And seeing a fig tree by the road, He came to it and found nothing on it but leaves, and said to it, "Let no fruit grow on you ever again." Immediately the fig tree withered away.

Telling this fig tree to wither is the only miracle Jesus performed as a curse. It also shows the human side of Jesus. Matthew 21:18 says, "Now in the morning, as He returned to the city, He was hungry." After His triumphal entry into Jerusalem the previous day, Jesus and the disciples were headed back there. Being hungry, Jesus saw a lone fig tree up ahead that looked promising. However, when He reached the tree, He discovered there was no fruit on it and said, "Let no fruit grow on you ever again." Was Jesus just mad at the tree for not having fruit and took out His frustration on it, or is there a deeper message? This incident took place in early spring at the time of Passover. Although figs do not ripen until late summer, early fall, there should have been some buds or even unripen figs on the tree. There were none. The tree looked healthy from a distance, but close up it had no fruit and wouldn't be producing any later on. Because the tree was not producing fruit like it should, Jesus caused it to wither. A modern-day example would be the love my mother had for buttercup flowers. She planted hundreds of them in her yard. However, many of them have not bloomed in several years. In researching the reason for not blooming, we learned that buttercups only last about 10 years. After then, they look more like a weed than a flower. Since they were never going to bloom again, we dug them up. Although, Jesus' immediate lesson to the disciples was the judgment coming to the religious leaders who had the appearance of being fruitful, but were not, there is a message for us as well. Are we bearing fruit or are we more focused on looking like a Christian than actually serving and living like one? Jesus said in John 15:5-6, "I am the Vine; you are the branches. If a man remains in Me and I in him, he will bear much fruit; apart from Me you can do nothing. If anyone does not remain in Me, he is like a branch that is thrown away and withers; such branches are picked up and thrown into the fire and burned." To be fruitful, we need to be connected to God. Spend time with Him each day.

Prayer: God, help me to bear fruit for Your kingdom.

Day 144

> *Matthew 21:22 And whatever things you ask in prayer, believing, you will receive.*

When the disciples saw the withered fig tree, Matthew 21:20-21 says, "They marveled saying, 'How did the fig tree wither so soon?' Jesus answered them saying, 'Assuredly, I say to you, if you have faith and do not doubt, you will not only do what was done to the fig tree, but also if you say to this mountain, be removed and be cast into the sea, it will be done.'" Jesus then tells the disciples they will receive anything they ask as long as they ask in faith believing. Is Jesus saying we can ask for anything in prayer believing, and He is required to give it to us? If so, my life would be entirely different from what it is right now. There are some things I have prayed for that were really selfish in nature and would have led me away from Christ instead of to Him. God is not Santa Claus, whose main purpose is to fulfill our wish lists. Praying in faith means that we trust God to do what is best for us and His will for us. When I was 15 years old, I told my father I wanted a MG Midget for my first car. The MG Midget is a very small, two passenger, convertible, 5-speed, sports car. My idea was to look "cool" driving around Wilmington. My father had other ideas. The vehicle wasn't safe for a young, inexperienced driver. It was a foreign made car, so repairs and maintenance would be more expensive, not to mention insurance on a 16-year-old. So, for my 16th birthday, my father brings home a 1969 Toyota Corolla for me to drive. It was not the fancy sportscar I had asked for, but it was a very functional car that lasted through my college years. Just as my father knew what vehicle was best for me at the time, we need to trust in God's wisdom, love, knowledge, and goodness to know what is best for our lives. But what about my prayers for healing that go unanswered? They are asked in faith. How about the prayers for my failing marriage, or my job that I just got laid off from? All I can tell you is to trust God. Pray with faith and for His will to be done. Things may not work out the way you wanted, but know that God is in control.

Prayer: God, help me to ask in faith.

> *Matthew 21:31 Which of the two did the will of his father?*

Jesus talking with the Pharisees, shares a parable of two sons. Matthew 21:28-30 says, "But what do you think? A man has two sons, and he came to the first and said, 'Son, go, work today in my vineyard.' He answered and said, 'I will not,' but afterward he regretted it and went. Then he came to the second and said likewise. And he answered and said, 'I go sir,' but he did not go." Jesus then asks the Pharisees, "which of the two did the will of his father?" They answered, "the first." Although the first son complained and even said he wouldn't work in the vineyard, he started feeling guilty and obeyed his father. The second son never intended to obey his father. He was more interested in talking about it rather than actually doing it. More than anything else, God wants our obedience. He accepts anyone into His kingdom who hears His Word, believes, and responds by obeying Him. This parable is great news for anyone who has not accepted Christ as Lord and Savior. You may have made some shameful choices in your past and your life is a complete mess. Jesus tells us, it is never too late to change. Today, you can invite Jesus into your life and begin following Him. Like the first son, following Jesus requires repentance and changes in your life. However, these changes will bring you into an intimate and personal relationship with Him. This parable is also a warning to those who claim to be a Christian, but are not living in obedience to God's word. It is for those who say all the right things, make the right promises, but fail to do the right things. It is for those who think they don't need to repent. Jesus said in Matthew 7:21, "Not everyone who says to Me, 'Lord, Lord,' will enter the kingdom of heaven, but only he who does the will of My Father who is in heaven." The lesson of the fig tree and the parable of the two sons are clear reminders that God can see through the image we try to portray to others. He knows our motives, plans, ambitions, and our actions. Have you become more like the second son, saying yes to God's will, but not following through? If so, take time today to renew your relationship with Him.

Prayer: God, help me to do Your will.

> *Matthew 21:33 Hear another parable: There was a certain landowner who planted a vineyard and set a hedge around it, dug a winepress in it and built a tower. And he leased it to vinedressers and went to a far country.*

Jesus continued speaking to the Pharisees and religious leaders, sharing another parable known as the "Parable of the Tenants." In this parable, a landowner plants a vineyard and invests a great amount of time, resources, and labor into it, anticipating a rich harvest. The owner then rented the vineyard to some farmers and left on a journey. When harvest time approached, the owner sent his servants to collect his fruit. The tenants beat one, killed another and stoned a third servant. The owner then sent more servants to collect. However, they were treated the same way. Lastly, the owner said, "I will send my son to collect, surely they will respect him." But when the tenants saw the son, they conspired together and said, "This is the heir, Come, let's kill him and take his inheritance." So, the tenants threw the son out of the vineyard and killed him. Jesus then asks, "Therefore, when the owner of the vineyard comes, what will he do to those tenants?" The crowd answers, "He will bring those wretches to a wretched end, and he will rent the vineyard to other tenants who will give him his share of the crop at harvest time." Jesus then said to them, "Have you never read in the scriptures: 'The stone the builders rejected has become the capstone; the Lord has done this, and it is marvelous in our eyes?' Therefore, I tell you that the kingdom of God will be taken away from you and given to a people who will produce its fruit." In this parable, God is the owner of the vineyard, the religious leaders are the tenants, the prophets are the owner's servants, and Jesus is the owner's son. Not until the Pharisees condemn themselves, do they realize the parable is about them. They are furious and wanted to arrest Jesus, but were afraid to do it because of the crowds who thought Jesus was a prophet. God is still looking for faithful tenants who produce fruit for Him and will continue to pronounce judgement on unfaithful ones. We see this principle play out today in the rise and fall of church denominations and ministries. God removes His anointing from ministries that have become unfaithful and births new churches that are faithful and fruitful. Are you attending a fruitless church? If so, it may be time for a change.

Prayer: God, help me to be a faithful tenant.

> Matthew 21:42 Jesus said to them, "Have you never read in the Scriptures: 'The stone which the builders rejected has become the chief cornerstone. This was the Lord's doing, and it is marvelous in your eyes?'"

Continuing His conversation with the Pharisees, Jesus rhetorically asks if they have ever read Psalm 118:22-23, about the stone the builders rejected. This stone would become the cornerstone, the most important stone in the construction of a building. This stone (Jesus) would be the Lord's doing and the rejection of Him by the builders (religious leaders) could not stop it from happening. Isaiah 28:16 prophesies about this cornerstone saying, 'So this is what the Sovereign Lord Says: 'See, I lay a stone in Zion, a tested stone, a precious cornerstone for a sure foundation; the one who trusts will never be dismayed.'" Jesus then told the Pharisees in Matthew 21:43-44, "Therefore I say to you, the kingdom of God will be taken from you and given to a nation bearing the fruits of it. And whoever falls on this stone will be broken; but on whomever it falls, it will grind him to powder." Jesus doesn't hold back His condemnation of the Pharisees, saying the kingdom of God will be taken from them. Just as we learned yesterday, God will remove His anointing and favor from those who have become unfaithful and give it to someone else who is earnestly seeking Him. Jesus then gives a warning about opposing this stone. "Those who fall on it will be broken, and whoever it falls on will be crushed." Isaiah 8:14 says, "And He will be a sanctuary; but for both houses of Israel He will be a stone that causes men to stumble and a rock that makes them fall. And for the people of Jerusalem, He will be a trap and a snare." For the believer, Jesus is the Rock of our Salvation. Psalm 18:2 says, "The Lord is my rock, my fortress and my deliverer; my God is my rock, in whom I take refuge. He is my shield and the horn of my salvation, my stronghold." When we fall on the Rock (Jesus), He breaks our old lives and makes us new in Him. Yet for those who reject Jesus, He is a stumbling block and eventually a stone that crushes them. Jesus is warning every one of the consequences for defying and rejecting Him. They will encounter the Rock, not as a stronghold, but one that falls and crushes them. My prayer is that He is the Rock in whom you take refuge.

Prayer: God, thank You for being the Rock of my salvation.

> Matthew 22:2 *The kingdom of heaven is like a certain king who arranged a marriage for his son.*

Jesus shares another parable, comparing the kingdom of heaven to a great wedding banquet given by a king for his son. The king sent his servants out to remind the invited guests to come to the wedding feast. However, the guests refused to come. So, the king sends out more servants to get the guests to come to the wedding. But some of the guests made light of it and went on their way. Others seized the king's servants, mistreated them, and killed them. The king was enraged and sent his army to destroy the murderers and burn down their city. The king then said to his servants, "The wedding banquet is ready, but those I invited did not deserve to come. Go to the street corners and invite anyone you can find." The servants went out and gathered all the people they could find, both good and bad until the wedding hall was filled with guests. The parable continues with the king noticing one of the guests not wearing the appropriate wedding clothes which was an insult in those days. We will learn what the king does about this situation tomorrow. For today, we are going to focus on the guest list for this great party. This parable was directed to the nation of Israel, in particular, the religious leaders of the day. They were invited to the greatest wedding party of all time found in Revelation 19:7,9, "Let us rejoice and be glad and give Him glory! For the wedding of the Lamb has come and His bride has made herself ready." Verse 9, "Then the angel said to me, 'Write: Blessed are those who are invited to the wedding supper of the Lamb!' And he added, "These are the true words of God."' Sadly, they had torn up their invitations, murdered the messengers, and went back to their lives. We also read they were punished for rejecting the king's invitation. Because of Israel's rejection of Christ, this invitation has been extended to everyone. What have you done with your invitation to this great celebration? Did you throw it in the trashcan when it arrived in the mail? Or, perhaps you set it aside planning on responding later on. My prayer is you were excited about the invitation and sent your RSVP back right away, posting it on the refrigerator as a daily reminder of your decision to attend.

Prayer: God, thank You for inviting me into Your kingdom.

Matthew 22:14 *For many are called, but few are chosen.*

We are continuing with the Parable of the Wedding Feast in Matthew 22:11-13, "But when the King came in to see the guests, he noticed a man there who was not wearing wedding clothes. 'Friend,' he asked, 'how did you get in here without wedding clothes?' The man was speechless. Then the king told the attendants, 'Tie him hand and foot, and throw him outside, into the darkness, where there will be weeping and gnashing of teeth.'" Jesus concludes by saying, "For many are called, but few are chosen." According to my NIV Study Bible, it was the custom for the host to provide guests with the proper wedding garments. This would have been necessary since the guests in the parable had been invited to the banquet right off the streets. For some reason, this one guest decided not to put on the provided garment, which would have been an insult to the host. It also is likely why the guest was speechless. He knew he was wrong for being improperly dressed. The king was not happy and had the guest tied up and kicked out of the banquet. Jesus makes the point that everyone is invited to the wedding feast, but only those wearing the appropriate wedding clothes are chosen to participate and celebrate with the king. Anyone who hears the gospel and are offered the opportunity to accept Jesus as their Lord and Savior are called. They have heard God's word and have been given an opportunity to respond. When we accept Christ, we take on His righteousness. Isaiah 61:10, "I delight greatly in the Lord; my soul rejoices in my God. For He has clothed me with garments of salvation and arrayed me in a robe of righteousness, as a bridegroom adorns his head like a priest, and as a bride adorns herself with her jewels." Sadly though, there are people who come to church regularly who listen to the sermon, participate in worship, and even tithe. But they have not given their heart to Christ and are still clothed in their own self-righteousness and sin. They may be able to fool others, but God recognizes them by their garments. Those chosen, or the ones who have put on the righteousness of Christ will enter heaven. Those who are pretending and refuse to repent, will find themselves speechless at judgement.

Prayer: God, cloth me in Your righteousness.

> *Matthew 22:21 They said to Him, "Caesar's." And He said to them, "Render therefore to Caesar the things that are Caesar's, and to God the things that are God's."*

There are a number of theories on paying taxes. Vivian's grandfather was very proud to be able to pay taxes. He grew up during the Great Depression and became a Free Will Baptist minister. He also farmed on the side. Finances were very tight and to make enough money to even pay taxes was a blessing. So, it was a very good year financially when he had to pay taxes. On the other hand, many feel the government is taking too much of their income or disagree with how the government is spending their tax dollars and look for every available deduction and loophole. The Pharisees had come to Jesus in hopes of tricking Him into saying something they could use against Him. They asked Him, "Teacher, we know You are a man of integrity and that You teach the way of God in accordance with the truth. You aren't swayed by men, because You pay no attention to who they are. Tell us then, what is Your opinion? Is it right to pay taxes to Caesar or not?" The Jews hated the Roman's and the required taxes they imposed upon them. If the Pharisees could get Jesus to say "Yes," then they would use His answer to denounce Him as disloyal to the people. If He said, "No," they would report Him to the Roman governor who would have Him executed for treason. Jesus said, "show Me the coin used for paying taxes," and asks, "Whose portrait is this? And whose inscription?" The Pharisees replied, "Caesar's." Jesus then said, "Give to Caesar the things that are Caesar's and to God the things that are God's." Jesus' answer left them speechless. It also raises the question, what is God's? Caesar's picture and inscription were on the coin, so the taxes belonged to him. What bears the image of God? Genesis 1:27 tells us, "God created man in His own image, in the image of God He created him; male and female He created them." Each person bears the image of God. Bearing His image, we belong to Him. Psalm 100:3 says, "Know that the Lord is God. It is He who made us, and we are His; we are His people, the sheep of His pasture." Have you rendered your life to God? Today would be a great day to do so.

Prayer: God, I surrender my life to You.

> Matthew 22:30 For in the resurrection they neither marry nor are given in marriage, but are like angels of God in heaven.

In hopes of trapping Him, Jesus was asked a hypothetical question about marriage by the Sadducees who did not believe in the resurrection. His answer gives us a glimpse of what life is like in heaven. For some, Jesus' answer could be disappointing because of a great, life-long relationship with your spouse. For others, this comes as a relief after years of living with a nagging or unloving spouse. Yet, why would something that God put so much importance on in this life, not even be a part of the next? This is one of those situations where we will better understand God's plan when we get to heaven. However, we do know that God created marriage for companionship and procreation. In Genesis 2:18,24, we read, "And the Lord God said, 'It is not good that man should be alone; I will make him a helper comparable to him.' Therefore, a man shall leave his father and mother and be joined to his wife, and they shall become one flesh." Earlier in Genesis 1:28 God said, "Be fruitful and multiply; fill the earth and subdue it; have dominion over the fish of sea, over the birds of the air, and over every living thing that moves on the earth." In heaven, having children will not be necessary. Everyone lives for eternity and those entering heaven have done so because of their faith in Jesus Christ. Although Jesus said marriages will not take place in heaven, there will still be love and unity, but on a much deeper level. We will experience an entirely new relationship between other resurrected believers. He also said, we will take on the likeness of angels, but not become angels. 1 Corinthians 2:9 says, "However, as it is written: 'No eye has seen, no ear has heard, no mind has conceived what God has prepared for those who love Him.'" Isaiah 65:11 also says, "Behold, I will create new heavens and a new earth. The former things will not be remembered, nor will they come to mind." We have a promise from God's word that we cannot begin to comprehend how great heaven will be. It will be so wonderful, that our former life on earth will not be remembered or even stored in our memories. Trust God and His plan.

Prayer: God, help me to better understand Your plan for us as believers when we join You in heaven.

> Matthew 22:37 Jesus said to him, "You shall love the Lord your God with all your heart, with all your soul, and with all your mind."

Jesus, when asked by a Pharisee, "Teacher, which is the greatest commandment in the law?", replied, "You shall love the Lord God with all your heart, soul, and mind." Very simply, God wants our total commitment to Him. Our problem is that we view love as an emotion or feeling that can change based on circumstances. I love you as long as you do what I want you to do, or you are friendly to me. Or in the context of marriage, I will love you until someone better comes along or you no longer fulfill my needs. In these examples, love is conditional. However, Jesus said that love for God is much more than that. It is not a feeling or emotion, but a decision that starts from our inner most being to have a deep, permanent, desire and affection towards Him. The desire to love Him doesn't come naturally. We are born with a sinful nature, that makes it impossible for us to love God with all our heart, soul, mind and strength 24 hours a day, seven days a week. Only by the forgiveness of sins and the presence of the Holy Spirit in our lives drawing us closer to God, do we learn to love Him. It is also impossible to love a God we don't know. Loving God unconditionally requires a relationship with Him. We develop that relationship through spending meaningful time in prayer, studying His word, obeying His commands, praising Him for the things He has done, and sharing His love for us to others. 1 Thessalonians 5:17 simply says, "Pray continually." In other words, our prayer time should not be limited to one short prayer per day. Pray throughout the day. Allow time to listen to God. 2 Timothy 2:15 says, "Do your best to present yourself to God as one approved, a workman who does not need to be ashamed and who correctly handles the Word of truth." Get into God's word, learn who He is, and read from the Book of Psalms each day. It will fill your heart with praise. Psalm 150:2 says, "Praise Him for His acts of power; praise Him for His surpassing greatness." Get to know God and learn how to love Him more each day. Then share the love you have for Him with others.

Prayer: God, help me to learn to love You with my heart, my soul, and with all my mind.

Day 153

> *Matthew 22:39 And the second is like it: You shall love your neighbor as yourself.*

When Jesus was asked what the greatest commandment was, He responded, "You shall love the Lord your God with all your heart, with all your soul, and with all your mind." But then He adds, "The second is like it: You shall love your neighbor as yourself." Loving God should be our first priority. If our relationship with Him is not right, then it is impossible for our relationship with others to be right. 1 John 4:7-8 says, "Dear friends, let us love one another for love comes from God. Everyone who loves has been born of God and knows God. Whoever does not love does not know God, because God is love." In Luke 10:25-37, we read where a lawyer asked Jesus what he needed to do to inherit eternal life. Jesus asked the lawyer his interpretation of the scriptures. The lawyer said to love the Lord your God and to love your neighbor as yourself. Jesus told the lawyer he had answered correctly, and all he needed to do was live it. The lawyer then asks the question that we all want to know the answer to, "Who is my neighbor?" In the story of the "Good Samaritan," we learn that our neighbor is not only those who live in our neighborhood, but anyone we come in contact with, such as a young man named Dallas who was pacing back and forth on a street corner near our church one Sunday morning. He was dressed in a sleeveless T-shirt with shorts and shoe strings for a belt. His possessions included two large garbage bags and a skateboard. Vivian and I arrived early for church to help set up and were a little apprehensive as we passed by Dallas. I saw our pastor and asked if he had seen the young man outside. He said yes and that he had fed him breakfast. Later as we held our pre-service, Serve Team prayer time, Dallas came near. Several of us walked over and began talking with him. We learned that Dallas was homeless, without a vehicle, and looking for work. We invited him to join us and introduced him to one of our members who is the Operational Director for a homeless shelter. We also provided him transportation and helped meet some of his immediate needs. Have you met a Dallas?

Prayer: God, help me to love my neighbor, no matter who they are.

> Matthew 23:11-12 But he who is greatest among you shall be your servant. And whoever exalts himself will be humbled, and he who humbles himself will be exalted.

In 1996 I was selected as the Smithfield/Selma Area Chamber of Commerce's Citizen of the Year for my involvement with the local United Way Chapter and the Johnston County Education Foundation. After receiving that award, I was feeling pretty good about myself and a bit prideful. It was a short six months later that my job as Area Manager in Johnston County for Progress Energy was eliminated and I was offered a job at our newly formed Customer Service Center in Raleigh. I went from what I considered an important person in the community to the low person on the proverbial "Totem Pole." God has a way of getting our attention when we become too prideful. James 4:10 says, "Humble yourselves before the Lord, and He will lift you up." God's way is completely opposite of man's way. Those who chase after honor and position will be humbled. While those who humble themselves will be lifted up. Micah 6:8 tells us, "He has showed you, O Man, what is good. And what does the Lord require of you? To act justly and to love mercy and to walk humbly with your God." How do I walk humbly with God? Jesus said, be a servant. Being a servant is valuing others more than yourself. In his book, "The Purpose Driven Life," Rick Warren lists five characteristics of a servant's heart. The first is availability. A servant is one who allows God to interfere with their schedule. Serving only when it is convenient for you is not true servanthood. Secondly, true servants are perceptive and look for ways they can serve others. They also have to be flexible to respond to that need. Next, true servants are dedicated to giving their best to the task no matter how great or small. No act of service is too small or beneath you. God is looking for your effort, not perfection. Fourthly, servants are reliable. They do what they say they are going to do. They follow through on their promises. Lastly, servants serve with humility. They are not looking for recognition or the limelight. Philippians 2:3-4 says, "Do nothing out of selfish ambition or vain conceit, but in humility consider others better than yourselves. Each of you should look not only to your own interests, but also to the interests of others." Look for ways to be a servant today.

Prayer: God, help me to be a humble servant.

> Matthew 23:23 Woe to you, Scribes and Pharisees, hypocrites! For you pay the tithe of mint, and anise and cumin, and have neglected the weightier matters of the law: justice and mercy and faith. These you ought to have done, without leaving the others undone.

In Matthew 23, Jesus pronounces eight woes or judgments on the Scribes and Pharisees. Today Jesus accuses them of missing the forest for the trees. They were more focused on certain aspects of the law and negligent with others. James 2:10 says, "For whoever keeps the whole law and yet stumbles at just one point is guilty of breaking all of it." The Scribes and Pharisees had taken tithing to the next level. In today's world, they were great at determining their total gross income and paying tithes down to the very last penny, but had missed the most important things to God; justice, mercy, and faith. Jesus isn't saying that paying tithes was unimportant or unnecessary. Tithing honors God and demonstrates our obedience and trust in Him to provide our needs. Tithing also reminds us that God is the source of all our blessings. However, if we are only paying tithes out of a feeling of obligation rather than gratitude, we may be like the Pharisees who were motivated by duty not love. God's desire for His children is that our actions are motivated by love. He desires for us to relate to Him from our hearts. Our obedience should come from a knowledge that God loves us and has our best interest at heart. Yesterday we read in Micah 6:8 that God requires that we act justly, love mercy, and walk humbly. Jesus said today that justice, mercy, and faith are the more important matters of the law. Justice meaning that we treat everyone equally, not showing favoritism to those we like and disregarding those who may be less fortunate. Mercy is having a genuine care and concern for others. Forgiving them for their mistakes rather than piling on the punishment. Faith is trusting God in the good times and the bad. Hosea 6:6 says, "For I desire mercy, not sacrifice, and acknowledgment of God rather than burnt offerings." Throughout God's word we read that He is more interested in the condition of our heart, than our works. No one is perfect and will get it completely right all the time. Romans 3:23 says, "For all have sinned and fall short of the glory of God." However, a good start would be asking God each day to help us live a life of love, just as Christ loved us.

Prayer: God, help me to live a life of love, just as You loved me.

> *Matthew 23:28 Even so you also outwardly appear righteous to men, but inside you are full of hypocrisy and lawlessness.*

The Pharisees were good at playing church. On the outside they looked like the epitome of someone who loved and obeyed God. They attended every service. They prayed the most flowery prayers. They raised their hands during the worship songs. They even put something in the offering plate each week. Yet something was not right and Jesus called them out on it. Sadly, everything they did was just for show and God was not fooled by their religious acts. They had a serious heart problem. They had a form of godliness, but their hearts were far from Him. God knows our inner thoughts and sees us as we really are, not as we appear to others. Psalm 139:1-3 says, "O Lord, You have searched me and You know me. You know when I sit and when I rise; You perceive my thoughts from afar. You discern my going out and my lying down; You are familiar with all my ways." What is the condition of your heart? I read a quote from www.sharingbread.com that says, "The main business of a believer lies within them." In other words, it is easier to address those big sins that are out there for everyone to see. Yet, the harder battle is dealing with the sins that only God sees. The Pharisees downfall was that they loved themselves far more than they loved God. What nagging sin lurks in your heart? Is it lust, envy, greed, hatred, idolatry, rage, or selfishness? If left alone, any one of these sins will take you further away from God. Eventually, He will call you out on them. David had the right answer when he recognized things were not right with his life. He wrote in Psalm 139:23-24, "Search me, O God, and know my heart; test me and know my anxious thoughts. See if there is any offensive way in me, and lead me in the way everlasting." Ask God to search your heart today to see if there is any offensive sin there. If so, confess that sin and ask Him to remove it from your life. Don't allow it to take root and grow in your heart. Then ask God to do for you like David wrote in Psalm 51:10, "Create in me a pure heart, O God, and renew a steadfast spirit within me."

Prayer: God, search me and know my heart today.

> Matthew 24:4-5 And Jesus answered and said to them: "Take heed that no one deceives you. For many will come in My name, saying, 'I am the Christ,' and will deceive many."

Jesus and the disciples take a hike to the Mount of Olives to be alone. There, they ask Him, "Tell us, when will these things be? And what will be the sign of Your coming, and of the end of the age?" Just to be clear, the things Jesus tells the disciples over the next several verses are not about the rapture, but what will occur immediately before He comes to set up His kingdom on earth. Jesus first gives some general signs that will precede His second coming. In today's verse, Jesus tells them, that "many would come in My name, saying 'I am the Christ,' and will deceive many." Should the rapture occur prior to the Tribulation as many believe, think about the confusion caused by millions of people disappearing. Also, consider the void left by those who preached and taught the truth of God's word. Those days will be even more difficult than they are now. 2 Timothy 3:1-5 says, "But mark this: There will be terrible times in the last days. People will be lovers of themselves, lovers of money, boastful, proud, abusive, disobedient to their parents, ungrateful, unholy, without love, unforgiving, slanderous, without self-control, brutal, not lovers of the good, treacherous, rash, conceited, lovers of pleasure rather than lovers of God – having a form of godliness but denying its power. Have nothing to do with them." You may be thinking, people are already acting like this and you would be correct. However, it will be on a much larger scale. For those reasons, many will be looking for stability, and direction in their lives. According to Jesus, there will be plenty to step up to fill that void, claiming they are the Christ. Their teaching will sound Biblical, but as Timothy says, "it has a form of godliness, but denies God's power." Romans 10:3 says, "Since they did not know the righteousness that comes from God and sought to establish their own, they did not submit to God's righteousness." They will teach what people want to hear, not the true way to salvation. Sadly, many will stand before the Lord, deceived by the teaching of these false teachers and hear the words of Jesus, "I never knew you." False teaching is not limited to the Tribulation. Test the word you are being taught. Make sure it is not just a form of godliness.

Prayer: God, help me to know and discern Your word.

> Matthew 24:6 *And you will hear of wars and rumors of wars. See that you are not troubled; for all these things must come to pass, but the end is not yet.*

World War I or the Great War was truly a world-wide conflict involving the nations of Europe, Russia, the United States, the Middle East, and Japan.[14] It was fought from 1914 to 1918 and named the "War to end all wars" by the British Author, H.G. Wells. Over 8.5 million soldiers and 13 million civilians were killed during World War I.[15] Since World War I, the website *www.war-memorial.net* lists over 200 wars that have occurred around the world, with the latest being the war in Ukraine. Like the war in Ukraine, the reasons wars start varies; but they are usually very complicated and political in nature. War is typically won when one opposing side overpowers the other by destroying their will to fight. In order to overpower each other, man has continued to develop new and more efficient ways of killing each other. Jesus said, don't be troubled when you hear of wars and rumors of wars, the end is still to come. God has told us about the final battle to come in Revelation 16:12-16, "The sixth angel poured out his bowl on the great river Euphrates, and its water was dried up to prepare the way for the kings from the East. Then I saw three evil spirits that looked like frogs; they came out of the mouth of the dragon, out of the mouth of the beast and out of the mouth of the false prophet. They are the spirits of demons performing miraculous signs, and they go out to the kings of the whole world, to gather them for the battle of the great day of God Almighty. 'Behold, I come like a thief! Blessed is he who stays awake and keep his clothes with him, so that he may not go naked and be shamefully exposed.' Then they gathered the kings together to the place that in Hebrew is called Armageddon." In Revelation 19, Jesus wearing a robe with this name written on it, "King of Kings and Lord of Lords," rides out to meet the kings of the earth and their armies who have gathered to make war against Him. Jesus captures the beast and the false prophet and throws them into a fiery lake of burning sulfur. The rest of the armies are killed by the rider of the white horse, Jesus. Game over. God wins.

Prayer: God, I thank You that You have already won the final battle.

> *Matthew 24:7 For nation will rise against nation, and kingdom against kingdom. And there will be famines, pestilences, and earthquakes in various places.*

Next on the list of the signs of Jesus return is famines, pestilences, and earthquakes in various places. Jesus made it clear in Matthew 24:8, that these do not signal the end, they are merely the beginning of sorrows. They form the backdrop of what is to come, and will increase in intensity until He does. As believers, we should take heart because we know the greater meaning of these events and there is nothing stopping God from bringing His word to conclusion. Revelation chapter 6 tells us about the Seals of Judgment opened by the Lamb of God during the beginning of the Tribulation. These judgments coincide with Jesus' warning to the disciples. Let's take a look at some of these events. Famine is a wide-spread scarcity of food. It can be the result of weather conditions, war, crop failure and poverty. We read about the war in Ukraine yesterday. Because of its fertile soil, the Ukraine produces an abundance of grain and is known as the Breadbasket of Europe. According to the UN Food and Agriculture Organization, Ukraine is the 5th largest exporter of wheat in the world. Because of the war, fuel, fertilizer, and the ability to export crops have been affected. We are already seeing the impacts with higher food costs. Eventually, because of grain shortages, famine will begin to spread. With COVID-19 we have already seen how quickly and deadly a world-wide pandemic can be. According to the World Health Organization, there have been almost 764 million cases of COVID reported world-wide, with 6.9 million deaths. According to the CDC, another issue with COVID is that the virus constantly changes through mutation. These changes allow the virus to spread more easily or make it resistant to treatments or vaccines. As the virus changes, it becomes harder to stop. Lastly, on Jesus' list is earthquakes. The National Earthquake Information Center reports there are approximately 20,000 earthquakes a year or 55 per day. They happen all over the world, and in the case of the recent earthquake in Turkey where over 50,000 people were killed, can be devasting. As believers, we are not protected from the effects of these events. The question is how will we respond when they occur? Will we trust God in His Sovereignty or will we respond as those in Revelation 16:9?

Prayer: God, help me to trust You in times of trouble.

Day 160

> Matthew 24:9 *Then they will deliver you up to tribulation and kill you, and you will be hated by all nations for My name's sake.*

Jesus' description of the signs of His return are a warning to us. He doesn't want anyone to be taken by surprise by the troubles of this broken world. He makes it clear; believers will experience martyrdom and hatred by everyone. Revelation 6:9-11 says, "When He opened the fifth seal, I saw under the altar the souls of those who had been slain for the word of God, and for the testimony which they held. And they cried with a loud voice, saying, 'How long, O Lord, holy and true, until You judge and avenge our blood on those who dwell on the earth?' Then a white robe was given to each of them; and it was said to them that they should rest a little while longer, until both the number of their fellow servants and their brethren, who would be killed as they were, was completed." Persecution and martyrdom for faith in Christ is already taking place in many parts of the world. It is sure to become more widespread as Jesus' return draws near. The day may come when you find your faith tested by persecution. It is during those times; we learn the depth of our faith. Isaiah 7:9 says, "...If you do not stand firm in your faith, you will not stand at all." Today is a day of prayer for strength to face persecution and prayer for those who are experiencing persecution right now:

- Pray for the strength to stand firm in persecution.
- Pray for the power to witness to those who hate you.
- Pray for the physical safety of Christians facing violent attacks. Ask God to protect them.
- Pray for the spiritual strength of Christians challenged for their faith. Ask God to give them hope.
- Pray for the families of persecuted Christian leaders. Ask God to bring comfort and support to them.
- Pray for the oppressors and persecutors of Christians. Ask God to change their hearts.

Prayer: God, help me to become united in prayer with persecuted brothers and sisters all over the world.

Day 161

Matthew 24:10 And then many will be offended, will betray one another, and will hate one another.

Jesus told us yesterday that His followers would face persecution. Today He tells us, "Many will be offended, will betray one another, and will hate one another." As the time of Jesus' return gets closer, persecution of Christians will become more widespread. Jesus is saying, like the Parable of the Sower in Matthew 13, there will be some who receive the Word of God, but it has fallen on stoney ground and doesn't take root. When they see the trials and persecution affecting the lives of other believers, they will become discouraged and fall away from the faith. But it gets worse. Those who have fallen away from the faith, betray those who have not, in order to avoid persecution themselves. They will turn the names of believers over to the persecutors, or inform them where they are. Those who have turned their backs on Christ and His gospel, will become the most bitter enemies and persecutors of Christians. Jesus speaking in Luke 21:16-19 gives us a better idea who these people are. "You will be betrayed even by your parents, brothers, relatives and friends, and they will put some of you to death. All men will hate you because of Me. But not a hair on your head will perish. By standing firm, you will gain life." This is another reason to pray for strength to face persecution. It will come from people we know and love. The Apostle Paul was imprisoned several times, flogged, received 39 lashes five times, beaten with rods, stoned, sleep deprived, shipwrecked, hungry, cold, always on the move and lived in constant danger. Yet he was able to say in Romans 8:18, "I consider that our present sufferings are not worth comparing with the glory that will be revealed in us." Paul is not trying to minimize the pain we experience. He had suffered much more than most. However, he is trying to put it in an eternal perspective. Paul is saying, be strong, the pain you are suffering now is no comparison to the glory of God that will be revealed in us. Sadly, those whose faith doesn't take root, have nothing to support them when things get hard. Psalms 37:39 says, "The salvation of the righteous comes from the Lord; He is their stronghold in time of trouble." Ask God to be your stronghold today.

Prayer: God, be my stronghold and help today.

> Matthew 24:12 And because lawlessness will abound, the love of many will grow cold.

Today's news is filled with reports of violent crime and lawlessness. I could quote article after article of crime in the US. Just a couple of examples include the hundreds of teens who recently stormed the streets of Chicago, destroying property, and attacking bystanders. Or Audrey Hale, walking into Covenant School in Nashville, TN, killing three children and three adults. Every week, we read of someone who has been killed in the United States as a result of gun violence. Jesus said, before His return, lawlessness would only continue to increase. Paul writing to Timothy, warns us that people's love for God would diminish, and they would become lovers of themselves. 2 Timothy 3:1-5 says, "But mark this: There will be terrible times in the last days. People will be lovers of themselves, lovers of money, boastful, proud, abusive, disobedient to their parents, ungrateful, unholy, without love, unforgiving, slanderous, without self-control, brutal, not lovers of the good, treacherous, rash, conceited, lovers of pleasure rather than lovers of God – having a form of godliness but denying its power. Have nothing to do with them." What in the wide, wide, world is going on here? Sadly, this falling away and increase in lawlessness didn't happen overnight. It has been taking place for years, with a slow but steady drifting away from God's Word. As a nation, we have begun to push God out of the picture, leaving behind a society where evil along with its lies and consequences is tolerated. Jesus warned that "the love of many would grow cold." As Christians, we have to be very careful not to become numb and uncaring about the evil that is overtaking our society. Hebrews 2:1, "We must pay more careful attention, therefore, to what we have heard, so that we do not drift away." What can we do? Humbly repent before God. Cry out in repentance for God's mercy. Remain strong in our faith. Don't accept what is evil as good, and good as evil. Pray for spiritual renewal. Replace the darkness that is around you with light. Jesus said in Luke 21:34, "Be always on the watch, and pray that you may be able to escape all that is about to happen, and that you may be able to stand before the Son of Man."

Prayer: God, help my faith to remain strong and not grow cold.

> *Matthew 24:13 But he who endures to the end shall be saved.*

Endurance, perseverance, persistence, resolution, and fortitude are traits we typically associate with a long-distance runner. Quick bursts of energy and power along with a strong resolution to win are needed by a sprinter. Both types of athletes sacrifice and train hard to win. However, I would compare our walk with Christ to a marathon rather than a sprint. Faith, endurance, perseverance, and persistence are required to remain strong in our faith through the trials of life. Hebrews 12:1-3 reminds us, "Therefore, since we are surrounded by such a great cloud of witnesses, let us throw off everything that hinders and the sin that so easily entangles, and let us run with perseverance the race marked out for us. Let us fix our eyes on Jesus, the author, and perfector of our faith, who for the joy set before Him endured the cross, scorning its shame, and sat down at the right hand of the throne of God. Consider Him who endured such opposition from sinful men, so that you will not grow weary and lose heart." Is Jesus saying that our salvation is somehow dependent on our personal ability to remain saved by enduring? Absolutely not! We have to take into context what Jesus said in verse 12, that "the love of many will grow cold." Those who endure to the end are those who are the opposite of the ones whose love grows cold. They will stand firm in their faith despite the trials and persecutions they may face. 1 Peter 1:3-7, "Praise be to the God and Father of our Lord Jesus Christ! In His great mercy He has given us new birth into a living hope through the resurrection of Jesus Christ from the dead, and into an inheritance that <u>can never perish, spoil or fade</u> – kept in heaven for you, who through faith are shielded by God's power until the coming of the salvation that is ready to be revealed in the last time. In this you greatly rejoice, though now for a little while you may have had to suffer grief in all kinds of trials. These have come so that your faith – of greater worth than gold, which perishes even though refined by fire – may be proved genuine and may result in praise, glory and honor when Jesus Christ is revealed." Keep your eyes fixed on Jesus and resolve to stand firm in your faith.

Prayer: God, help me to endure to the end.

> *Matthew 24:14 And this gospel of the kingdom will be preached in all the world as a witness to all the nations, and then the end will come.*

Jesus promises the gospel will be preached all over the world before the end of time, giving everyone an opportunity to accept Him as Lord and Savior. 2 Peter 3:9, "The Lord is not slow in keeping His promise, as some understand slowness. He is patient with you not wanting anyone to perish, but everyone to come to repentance." Although we serve a loving God who doesn't want anyone to perish; we also serve a just God who will judge those who do not receive the truth. The time period just prior to Jesus' return is called the Tribulation. At the beginning of the tribulation, a world leader will emerge that promises peace, prosperity, and a solution to the world's problems. Just prior to the Tribulation, many believe that Christians will be taken up to heaven in the rapture. If all Christians have been raptured, then who would be around to preach the gospel to all the world? First, God sends two witnesses found in Revelation 11. They will prophesy 1,260 days, until they are killed by the Anti-Christ, or the new world leader. Some will believe and accept Jesus as Lord and Savior because of their preaching. Others grow to hate them and celebrate their death. Also, Revelation 7:4 tells us there will be 144,000 Spirit filled Jews who have been sealed for God's service during this period. They will testify of salvation in Christ during this Tribulation period. Revelation 14:6 says, "Then I saw another angel flying in the midst of heaven, having the everlasting gospel to preach to those who dwell on the earth – to every nation, tribe, tongue, and people." However, those who accept Christ during this period will not have it easy. The Anti-Christ will rise to power and require everyone to worship him, receiving his mark on their forehead or hand. Those who accept the mark, will be condemned to hell. Revelation 14:9-10, "Then a third angel followed them, saying with a loud voice, 'If anyone worships the beast and his image, and receives his mark on his forehead or on his hand, he himself shall also drink of the wine of the wrath of God, which is poured out full strength into the cup of His indignation. He shall be tormented with fire and brimstone in the presence of the holy angels and in the presence of the Lamb.'"

Prayer: God, thank You for wanting everyone to be saved.

> *Matthew 24:15 Therefore when you see the "abomination of desolation," spoken of by Daniel the prophet, standing in the holy place, (whoever reads, let him understand).*

Today's verse generates a lot of questions. What is the "abomination of desolation?" Where is the holy place he is standing? Has this event already occurred as some Bible scholars believe? How does this relate to what Daniel prophesied in Daniel 9? What are we to understand? First, an abomination is something that causes hatred or disgust. Desolation is a complete state of destruction. Putting those together in the context of this verse, it would be something or someone that is so disgusting, that their very presence destroys the holiness of the place they are standing. The most holy place for the Jews is the Temple. The Temple has been destroyed, desecrated, and rebuilt several times throughout history. In fact, some Bible scholars believe the abomination of desolation occurred in 167 BC, when Antiochus Epiphanes sacrificed a pig on the altar and set up a statute of Zeus in the Temple for people to worship. However, Daniel 9:27 speaking of a ruler to come says, "He will confirm a covenant with many for one seven. In the middle of the seven, he will put an end to the sacrifice and offering. And on a wing of the temple, he will set up an abomination that causes desolation, until the end that is decreed is poured out on him." It is pretty evident Daniel is speaking about the seven-year Tribulation. The ruler to come or the Anti-Christ will make a treaty with Israel, rebuilding the Temple at its original location. This occurs at the beginning of the seven-year Tribulation period. It is not clear how this will be done because this location is currently a very holy site to the Arabs. After three and one-half years, the Anti-Christ breaks his covenant with the Jews by erecting a statute of himself in the temple to be worshiped. Revelation 13:15 says, "He was granted power to give breath to the image of the beast, that the image of the beast should both speak and cause as many as would not worship the image of the beast to be killed." Life is not going to be easy for those who accept Christ during the tribulation. Don't put off that decision. Luke 21:36 says, "Be always on the watch, and pray that you may be to escape all that is about to happen, and that you may be able to stand before the Son of Man."

Prayer: God, help me to watch and pray.

Matthew 24:21 *For then there will be great tribulation, such as has not been since the beginning of the world until this time, no, nor ever shall be.*

If things are bad now, you do not want to be around when the great tribulation period begins. This period will be marked with lawlessness and judgments. Revelation 9:20-21, "But the rest of mankind, who were not killed by these plagues, did not repent of the works of their hands, that they should not worship demons, and idols of gold, silver, brass, stone and wood, which can neither see nor hear nor walk. And they did not repent of their murders or their sorceries or their sexual immorality of their thefts." During this period, the restraint of evil will be lifted and lawlessness will take over. People will do whatever their evil heart's desire. Despite the judgement and terrible catastrophes God leashes on the earth, mankind will become more defiant rather than repentant. God's final judgments are found in Revelation 15 – 16. 15:1, "Then I saw another sign in heaven, great and marvelous; seven angels having seven last plagues, for in them the wrath of God is complete." 16:1, "Then I heard a loud voice from the temple saying to the seven angels, 'Go and pour out the bowls of wrath of God on the earth.'" 16:2, "So the first went and poured out his bowl upon the earth, and a foul and loathsome sore came upon those who had the mark of the beast and those who worshipped his image." 16:3, "Then the second angel poured out his bowl on the sea, and it became blood as of a dead man; and every living creature in the sea died." 16:4, "Then the third angel poured out his bowl on the rivers and springs of water, and they became blood." 16:8, "Then the fourth angel poured out his bowl on the sun, and power was given to scorch people with fire." 16:10, "Then the fifth angel poured out his bowl on the throne of the beast, and his kingdom became full of darkness; and they gnawed their tongues because of the pain." 16:12, "Then the sixth angel poured out his bowl on the great river Euphrates, and its water was dried up, so that the way of the kings from the east might be prepared." 16:17, "Then the seventh angel poured out his bowl into the air, and a loud voice came out of the temple of heaven, from the throne, saying, 'It is done.'" Thank God for His mercy on us.

Prayer: God, may Your will be done.

> *Matthew 24:27 For as the lightning comes from the east and flashes to the west, so also will the coming of the Son of Man be.*

The seventh bowl of judgment found in Revelation 16:17-21 literally shakes the entire earth. There will be thunder and lightning along with a great earthquake that pushes the needle on the Richter Scale to levels never seen before. Entire cities will be destroyed, islands disappear in the ocean, and mountains crumble. Hailstones weighing 100lbs each, will fall from the sky. Then just as sudden as lightning flashes across the sky or an earthquake occurs without warning, Jesus will appear. The first time Jesus came to the earth, He was in the form of a baby, born in a stable to the virgin Mary. His birth was announced by the angels to shepherds, who were out in the fields watching their flocks. Only the Maggi recognized someone special had been born by observing a new star, the Star of Bethlehem. Throughout His ministry, many considered Jesus a great prophet, but few recognized Him as the Messiah. John 1:10-11, "He was in the world, and the world was made through Him, and the world did not know Him. He came to His own, and His own did not receive Him." The religious leaders of the day saw Jesus as a threat and had Him crucified. The centurion and those who helped crucify Jesus only recognized Jesus as the Son of God after He died. Matthew 27:54, "So when the centurion and those with him, who were guarding Jesus, saw the earthquake and the things that had happened, they feared greatly, saying, 'Truly this was the Son of God.'" Jesus' return to earth will be completely different the next time. No one will miss it. Like lightning, it will be unmistakable, quick and powerful. He will come as a king to judge the world. Are you looking for His return? 2 Peter 3:4 says, "They will say, 'Where is this coming He promised? Ever since our fathers died, everything goes on as it has since the beginning of creation.'" Life gets busy and we often let it take priority over our relationship with God. Jesus said in Luke 21:36, "Watch therefore, and pray always that you may be counted worthy to escape all these things that will come to pass, and to stand before the Son of Man." Spend time in God's word each day. Get to know Him and recognize Him as your Lord and Savior and soon coming King.

Prayer: God, help me to look for Your return.

> *Matthew 24:29 Immediately after the tribulation of those days the sun will be darkened, and the moon will not give its light; the stars will fall from heaven, and the powers of the heavens will be shaken.*

Just prior to Jesus' return, there will be an upheaval in the skies. The sun will be darkened causing the moon to redden until it is unable to reflect the light of the sun. Stars and meteor showers will fall across the sky. There are several theories as to what may cause this phenomenon to happen. One explanation is that volcanic activity will increase spewing vast clouds of cinder and ash. They will overtake the sky, darkening the sun and moon. Another is a gravitational disturbance in the solar system, disrupting the normal view of the sun and moon. The last theory is that nuclear war will create clouds of dust and debris which block out the sky. It really doesn't matter how it will happen. But we can be sure that it will. The Bible speaks of this occurrence in several places. Isaiah 13:9-10, "See, the day of the Lord is coming – a cruel day, with wrath and fierce anger – to make the land desolate and destroy the sinners within it. The stars of the heaven and their constellations will not show their light. The rising sun will be darkened and the moon will not give its light." Joel 2:30, "The sun will be turned to darkness and the moon to blood before the coming of the great and dreadful day of the Lord." Lastly Revelation 6:12-13, "I watched as he opened the sixth seal. There was a great earthquake. The sun turned black like sackcloth made of goat hair, the whole moon turned blood red, and the stars in the sky fell to the earth as late figs drop from a fig tree when shaken by a strong wind." These will be dreadful days. Revelation 6:15, "Then the kings of the earth, the princes, the generals, the rich, the mighty, and every slave and every free man hid in the caves and among the rocks of the mountains." People go into hiding, fearful of what may take place next. The good news is that God's children will not be around to watch this unfold. That should motivate us to make sure our family, friends, and co-workers know Jesus as their Lord and Savior. However, trying to scare them out of hell or the events of the last days is not the best approach. Simply share God's love for them.

Prayer: God, help me to lead others to You.

> Matthew 24:30 *Then the sign of the Son of Man will appear in heaven, and then all the tribes of the earth will mourn, and they will see the Son of Man coming on the clouds of heaven with power and great glory.*

At the end of the tribulation period, a sign will appear in the heavens announcing Jesus' return. Jesus doesn't tell us what the sign is, nor did the disciples ask. The Pharisees had previously asked Jesus for a sign to show them that He was the Messiah. Jesus told them they would have no further sign other than the sign of Jonah, which referenced His death, burial and resurrection over a three-day period. Sadly, the Pharisees did not recognize the sign Jesus had given them. However, this sign will be unmistakable. Jesus said all the tribes of the earth will mourn when they see it. Although they will be full of sorrow and regret, they will not repent. After the sign, Jesus will be seen by all coming on the clouds with great authority. Revelation 19:11-16 describes Jesus' second return, "Now I saw heaven opened, and behold, a white horse. And He who sat on him was called Faithful and True, and in righteousness He judges and makes war. His eyes were like a flame of fire, and on His head were many crowns. He had a name written that no one knew except Himself. He was clothed in a robe dipped in blood, and His name is called 'The Word of God.' And the armies in heaven, clothed in fine linen, white and clean, followed Him on white horses. Now out of His mouth goes a sharp sword, that with it He should strike the nations. And He Himself will rule them with a rod of iron. He Himself treads the winepress of the fierceness and wrath of Almighty God. And He has on His robe and on His thigh a name written, 'KING OF KINGS AND LORD OF LORDS.'" Hebrews 4:12 gives us more details about this sword, "For the word of God is living and active. Sharper than any double-edged sword, it penetrates even to dividing soul and spirit, joints and marrow; it judges the thoughts and attitudes of the heart." It is God's word, powerful and infallible, that will defeat Satan and his followers. God's word will also bring justice and peace to the remaining believers. Isaiah 55:11, "So is My word that goes out from My mouth: It will not return to Me empty, but will accomplish what I desire and achieve the purpose for which I sent it." You can depend on God's word.

Prayer: God, help me to trust Your powerful word.

> *Matthew 24:35 Heaven and earth will pass away, but My words will by no means pass away.*

Yesterday, we learned that God's word is powerful and infallible. It can also be polarizing. Either you love it, despise it, or ignore it. Some see it as a book of hope and salvation, while others refuse to accept God's truth and exposure of our sin and rebellion. Throughout the centuries, many have tried to physically destroy and discredit the Bible. Instead of recognizing the Bible as the inerrant word of God, they claim it is a book of myths and an unreliable work of men. Despite the efforts to eliminate the Bible, organizations like the Gideons distribute over 70 million copies of it worldwide each year. (*Wikipedia.org*) In Nicaragua, a ministry is providing every child in public school with an illustrated children's Bible and over 11,500 Bibles have been distributed so far. In places like China where Christianity is banned, Bibles have to be smuggled into the country. *www.christiantoday.com* tells the story of how 20 Christians smuggled 1 million Bibles into China in one night. People are hungry for the word of God. Isaiah 55:10-11 tells us, "As the rain and the snow come down from heaven, and do not return to it without watering the earth and making it bud and flourish, so that it yields seed for the sower and bread for the eater, so is My word that goes out from My mouth; it will not return empty, but will accomplish what I desire and achieve the purpose for which I sent it." No matter the efforts of those who despise God's word, it will get to those who need it and accomplish His purpose. David writing in Psalm 19:7-10 said, "The law of the Lord is perfect, reviving the soul. The statutes of the Lord are trustworthy, making wise the simple. The precepts of the Lord are right, giving joy to the heart. The commands of the Lord are radiant, giving light to the eyes. The fear of the Lord is pure, enduring forever. The ordinances of the Lord are sure and altogether righteous. They are more precious than gold, than much pure gold; they are sweeter than honey, than honey from the comb." God's word revives our soul and brings joy to our hearts. It opens our eyes to His truth. But most important, God's words are eternal. Isaiah 40:8, "The grass withers and the flowers fall, but the word of our God stands forever."

Prayer: God, thank You for Your precious word.

> *Matthew 24:36 But of that day and hour no one knows, not even the angels of heaven, but My Father only.*

Jesus plainly tells us that only the Father knows the day and hour of His return. However, that hasn't stopped many from trying to pin down the month and year of His return. In the late 1980's, Edgar Whisenant published a book, "88 *Reasons the Rapture Will Occur in 1988.*" I had a copy of his book and struggled with the evidence he presented; knowing Jesus said, no one knows the day or hour of His return. Whisenant argued that the rapture would occur in 1988 because it marked 40 years or one generation since Israel had become a nation. This would have fulfilled Jesus words in Matthew 24:34, "I tell you the truth, this generation will certainly not pass away until all these things have happened." He also claimed the rapture would occur between the days of September 11 through the 13th coinciding with the Jewish Holiday, Rosh Hashana. This is the beginning of the Jewish New Year, and celebrated with the blowing of a shofar or hollowed out ram's horn. The blowing of a trumpet or shofar in conjunction with the rapture is mentioned in 1 Corinthians 15: 52, "In a flash, in the twinkling of an eye, at the last trumpet. For the trumpet will sound, and the dead will be raised to imperishable, and we will be changed." Obviously, Mr. Whisenant was wrong. Thirty-five years later, the rapture nor Jesus' return has occurred. One thing we do know is that the signs of His return are ever increasing. 2 Peter 3:9-10, "The Lord is not slow in keeping His promise, as some understand slowness. He is patient with you, not wanting anyone to perish, but everyone come to repentance. But the day of the Lord will come like a thief. The heavens will disappear with a roar, the elements will be destroyed by fire, and the earth and everything in it laid bare." If the Lord tarries, those of us in the last quarter of our lives may not witness the rapture and His return. Yet, everyone is just an instant away from the end of their earthly life. We are not guaranteed tomorrow. Jesus doesn't want anyone to perish. Have you accepted Him as Lord and Savior? If not, don't continue to put that decision off. today would be a great day to give your life to Him.

Prayer: God, help me to be prepared for Your return.

> Matthew 24:44 *Therefore you also be ready, for the Son of Man is coming at an hour you do not expect.*

Jesus makes it clear; His return will be when we least expect it. He illustrates our readiness with the story of Noah found in Genesis 6-7. Jesus said in Matthew 24:37-39, "As it was in the days of Noah, so it will be at the coming of the Son of Man. For in the days before the flood, people were eating and drinking, marrying and giving in marriage, up to the day Noah entered the Ark; and they knew nothing about what would happen until the flood came and took them all away. That is how it will be at the coming of the Son of Man." Although Noah and his sons took 120 years to build the Ark, his neighbors gave little or no thought to the reason the Ark was being built and went on about life as normal. Then one day the Bible tells us, "All the springs of the great deep burst forth, and the floodgates of the heavens were opened. And rain fell on the earth forty days and nights." Everyone except Noah and his family were clueless and swept away by the flood. Jesus warns us not to be like the people of Noah's day, but to be looking for His return. For, just as suddenly as the rains began to fall, so will Jesus' return be. Jesus also describes our readiness with a story about keeping watch for a burglar found in Matthew 24:43, "But understand this: If the owner of the house had known at what time of night the thief was coming, he would have kept watch and would not have let his house be broken into." Jesus even refers to Himself as a thief coming in the night in Revelation 16:15, "Behold I am coming as a thief. Blessed is he who watches, and keeps his garments, lest he walk naked and they see his shame." In other words, blessed is the person who is watching for My return and as the old saying goes, "Doesn't get caught with their pants down." Jesus' intent is not for us to live carelessly, but in expectant hope of His return. Don't allow the daily grind of life to take precedence over your relationship with Christ. Jesus is telling us to be strong in our faith, be alert, trust Him in all things, and finish strong.

Prayer: God, help me to remain faithful, always on watch for Your return.

> Matthew 24:45-46 *Who then is a faithful and wise servant, whom his master made ruler over his household, to give them food in due season? Blessed is that servant who his master, when he comes, will find so doing.*

Jesus shares a parable of a faithful and evil servant to illustrate the difference between those who are faithfully anticipating His return and those whose philosophy is "while the cat's away, the mice will play." A modern-day example of this parable is when a teacher gets called to the principal's office for a few minutes. She leaves the class an assignment to work on while she is gone. Not knowing how long the teacher will be gone, some begin to diligently work on the assignment. Others, decide it is play time and begin shooting spit balls at one another. The teacher returns unexpectedly and catches those who are playing around. The students who were working on the assignment are rewarded for following her instructions and those who didn't are sent to detention. In this parable, the servants are given duties and responsibilities while the master is away. We are those servants. God has a plan for you and I and has given us the skills and ability to accomplish His work. Ephesians 2:10, "For we are God's workmanship, created in Christ Jesus to do good works, which God prepared for us to do." There is nothing more fulfilling in life than to know God's will for your life and feel like you are contributing to the work of His kingdom. Everyone's role is different but equally important to God. What matters to God is our faithfulness in the assignment He has given us. Those who are faithful and persevere are rewarded with greater responsibilities in God's eternal kingdom. However, there is another type of servant in this parable. This servant doesn't think his master is coming back anytime soon and begins to slack off. Falling into temptation, he begins to mistreat his fellow servants; those God has given him to look after. He falls even further by eating and drinking with drunkards. This drifting away from Christ is a slow but steady progression. It can happen to anyone who takes their eyes off Christ and His return, putting their own wants and desires ahead of Him. For those who choose to continue down the path of unfaithfulness, every thought, attitude, and action will be laid before Christ. 2 Corinthians 5:10, "For we must all appear before the judgment seat of Christ..." Sadly, the unfaithful servants will find this to be a time of great sorrow and pain.

Prayer: God, help me to be a faithful servant.

> Matthew 25:1 *Then the kingdom of heaven shall be likened to ten virgins who took their lamps and went out to meet the bridegroom.*

Jesus shares another parable about a wedding processional to illustrate our readiness for His return. In Jesus' day, the groom and his friends would first travel to the bride's home where part of the ceremony would take place. Then the wedding party would travel to the groom's home, usually at night, where they would finish the wedding and enjoy the reception. Guests would follow the wedding party to the groom's house; however, everyone was expected to have their own light. Anyone without a light was not allowed into the wedding. In this parable, ten virgins were invited to the wedding and had prepared their lamps. Both the wise and foolish virgins had full lamps, so there is no way to distinguish between the two. The wait became longer than expected, and the virgins fell asleep. Falling asleep was not a problem because they all immediately woke up when they heard the announcement that the groom was coming. However, due to the lateness of the hour, all the lamps were beginning to run out of oil. Five of the virgins had brought extra oil and refueled their lamps. Five did not, and asked the others to share their oil with them. They were told, no because there would not be enough oil to refuel all the lamps to keep them burning during the wedding. While those without oil went into town to buy more, the others were allowed into the reception. Those without oil hurried back to the groom's house and knocked on the door. Instead of being told they were too late, Jesus said, "Assuredly, I say to you, I do not know you," very much like Jesus words found in Matthew 7:23, "Then I will tell them plainly, 'I never knew you. Away from Me you evil doers!'" There are several lessons to be learned from this parable. First, we need to check our faith level. If our faith is based on trying to get into heaven by being good, we are going to run out of fuel. We will never have enough goodness to get us into heaven. Secondly, our faith is not transferable. The faith of our parents or grandparents will not get us into heaven. We are saved by grace, through our own faith in Christ. Lastly, a crisis will expose our level of faith. It will distinguish those who "walk the walk" or just "talk the talk."

Prayer: God, help me to be faithful.

> *Matthew 25:14 For the kingdom of heaven is like a man traveling to a far country, who called his own servants and delivered his goods to them.*

The Parable of the Talents is the last of three parables Jesus shares to prepare us for His return. In this parable, the master before leaving on a long journey, gives five talents to one servant, two to another, and one to the last. The master eventually returns to settle the accounts with his servants. In Jesus' day, one talent was worth two years wages, so each servant was entrusted with a great sum of money. However, each servant is given different amounts based on their abilities. The one who received more wasn't insulted with managing a trivial amount, while the one who received less wouldn't be overwhelmed by the task. The master also shows a lot of trust in his servants by not telling them how to invest the talents he has given them. The one who received five talents got busy and gained five more talents. Likewise, the one who received two talents did the same thing. However, the one who received one talent "went off, dug a hole in the ground and hid his master's money." A long time later, the master returns to settle the accounts with his servants. The servants who received the five and two talents, proudly return ten and four to their master. The master tells them, "Well done, good and faithful servant! You have been faithful with a few things; I will put you in charge of many things. Come and share your master's happiness." Then the servant who was given one talent, returned it back to his master saying, "I knew you are a hard man, harvesting where you have not sown and gathering where you have not scattered seed. So, I was afraid and went out and hid your talent in the ground, See, here is what belongs to you." The master was not happy with this servant's handling of the talent. He calls the servant "wicked and lazy" and takes the talent away from him and gives it to the one who had gained five more. God has given each of us opportunities and the ability to serve Him in various capacities. Are you using those opportunities He has given you, or have you hidden them in the ground? As this parable reminds us, God will hold His servants accountable for what they have done or not done.

Prayer: God, help me to be faithful with the opportunities You have given me.

Matthew 25:31-32 When the Son of Man comes in His glory, and all the holy angels with Him, then He will sit on the throne of His glory. All the nations will be gathered before Him, and He will separate them one from another, as a shepherd divides his sheep from the goats.

We can dismiss and ignore talk of judgment; but it is coming. There will be a day of reckoning. God created us with a conscience that helps us identify right from wrong. Paul writes that our conscience also bears witness to the consequences or judgment of our thoughts and actions. Romans 2:15-16, "Since they show that the requirements of the law are written on their hearts, their consciences also bearing witness, and their thoughts now accusing, now even defending them. This will take place on the day when God will judge men's secrets through Jesus Christ, as My gospel declares." The Bible clearly speaks about judgment as well. Hebrews 9:27 tells us, "Just as man is destined to die once, and after that to face judgment." Dr. David Jeremiah is perhaps one of the most knowledgeable persons I know on end times prophecy. In his study Bible, Dr. Jeremiah writes about the three major upcoming judgments of mankind. The first is the Judgment Seat of Christ which occurs following the Rapture of the Church. It takes place during the seven-year tribulation and is where believers receive rewards for their faithfulness. This judgment is described in 1 Corinthians 3:11-15. The second judgment is the Judgment of Nations or the separation of the sheep and goats, which Jesus is speaking about in today's verse. The last judgment is the Great White Throne Judgment found in Revelation 20, where unbelievers will stand before a just God and give an account for their sins. The Judgment of the Nations takes place at Christ's return, just prior to the beginning of His Millennium Reign. Jesus tells us, "All the nations will be gathered before Him," so this judgment is for those who have survived the Tribulation period. Just as a shepherd separates his flock, Jesus places those who are His sheep on His right, and the goats on His left. The sheep being those who were saved during the Tribulation and the goats are the unsaved. This is a judgment you and anyone you care for do not want to be around for. During this time, Christians will face tremendous persecution and trials. If you have not received Christ as Lord and Savior, today is a great day to do so. If you are saved, share the Gospel with those close to you.

Prayer: God, my prayer is for all to be saved.

> Matthew 25:34 Then the King will say to those on His right hand, "Come, you blessed of My Father, inherit the kingdom prepared for you from the foundation of the world."

After separating the sheep from goats, Jesus turns to those on His right and welcomes them into His Kingdom, calling them blessed. He tells them, "Inherit the kingdom prepared for you..." Everyone who enters the Kingdom of Heaven is an heir and a child of God. However, having been born with a sinful nature, into a sinful world, we are all slaves to sin. Jesus said in John 8:34, "I tell you the truth, anyone who sins is a slave to sin." Sadly, those who have not repented will face God's judgment. The good news is that God had a plan to rescue us from our life of sin and make us His heirs. Galatians 4:7 says, "So, you are no longer a slave, but a son; and since you are a son, God has made you an heir." Jesus goes on to tell those on His right, how He identified them as His sheep in verses 35-36, "For I was hungry and you gave Me food; I was thirsty and you gave Me drink; I was a stranger and you took Me in; I was naked and you clothed Me; I was sick and you visited Me; I was in prison and you came to visit Me." Is Jesus saying our works lead to salvation? Absolutely not. His Word tells us if we are truly His disciples, our works will align with His character and we will follow His example. Jesus said in Mark 10:45, "For even the Son of Man came not to be served, but to serve and to give His life as a ransom for many." However, Jesus lets us know that serving others is not just a check the box and move on type of attitude. While it would be easy to hand a burger and bottle of water to someone on the street corner and say mission accomplished, that is not what servanthood looks like. Jesus displayed true servanthood by washing the disciples' feet at the Last Supper. He got down on His hands and knees and scrubbed. He invested in those He was serving. As His heirs, we are called to help those in need and be the hands and feet of Jesus. Praying for those in need is good, but love is found in deeds, not words. Take time today to invest into someone's life who needs help.

Prayer: God, help me to be a faithful servant.

> Matthew 25:41 Then He will also say to those on His left hand, "Depart from Me, you cursed, into the everlasting fire prepared for the devil and his angels."

Those on Jesus' left, the goats, are listening to Jesus praise the group on the right for their good works, welcoming them into the Kingdom of Heaven. Very likely, many are beginning to feel pretty good about themselves and think they are the **G**reatest **O**f **A**ll **T**ime (GOAT). Why? Because some have done a lot of the good deeds mentioned by Jesus. They have contributed money to worthwhile causes, helped eradicate disease, or spearheaded reforms to benefit the needy. They regularly donate clothes to the Salvation Army, and volunteer annually at a homeless shelter to serve a Thanksgiving meal. They are well known and respected throughout the community because of their generosity. No doubt, these are great causes and worthwhile endeavors that have helped a lot of people. However, there is one thing separating the fate of the sheep and the goats. The sheep have received Jesus Christ as Lord and Savior and are motivated to do good works because of their love for Christ and obedience to His word. While the goats are primarily doing good deeds for recognition or to "feel good" about themselves. Sadly, no amount of money or the number of good deeds they accomplish will gain them salvation. Ephesians 2:8-9, "For it is by grace you have been saved, through faith – and this not from yourselves, it is the gift of God – not by works, so that no one can boast." The fate of those on Jesus' left is very clear. They will be sent to the place of punishment that was originally prepared for Satan and his angels. We learn several things about hell from Jesus' words to the condemned. First, their punishment will separate them from the presence of a loving, but just God. Secondly, they are cursed. Their souls condemned because of their decision not to trust Him. Lastly, the separation is everlasting. There is no coming back, no options for redemption. They are condemned to spend eternity in a place of everlasting torment. My friend, do not listen to those who would say, God is a loving God and would never send anyone to hell. Yes, God is a loving God and desires that all would be saved. However, He is a just God who cannot condone sin. He has prepared a place for those who do not accept Him as Lord and Savior.

Prayer: God, I pray that my works are motivated out of a love for You.

> Matthew 26:13 Assuredly, I say to you, wherever the gospel is preached in the whole world, what this woman has done will also be told as a memorial to her.

Jesus is now in Bethany at the home of Simon the leper, enjoying a meal with His disciples and a few friends. John 12 tells us that Lazarus, Martha, and Mary were also there at Simon's house. Since everyone had gathered there, many believe Simon was one of the lepers Jesus had previously healed. Yet, unknown to all except Jesus, it is one week away from His crucifixion. While the guests are reclining at the table enjoying the food and fellowship, John 12:3 tells us, "Then Mary took about a pint of pure nard, an expensive perfume; she poured it on Jesus' feet and wiped His feet with her hair." The disciples were indignant, saying "why this waste? This fragrant oil might have been sold for much and given to the poor." Jesus heard the disciples and told them, "Why trouble the woman? For she has done a good work for Me...For in pouring this fragrant oil on My body, she did it for My burial." While the disciples saw Mary's act as an extravagant and inappropriate waste, Jesus recognized it as worship for the Messiah who would soon die, be buried, and resurrected. Jesus not only defends her actions; He elevates it as a moment that will be remembered throughout history and preached around the world. Jesus' words are even being fulfilled today. Mary will ever be remembered for this selfless act of worship of her Lord and Savior. However, there have been other people throughout history who are remembered for doing evil deeds. John Wilkes Booth assassinated Abraham Lincoln. Lee Harvey Oswald assassinated John F. Kennedy. Adolf Hitler started World War II and exterminated millions of Jews. I could name many more. However, the more important question is what do you want to be remembered for? Each day we make choices that will build on the legacy we leave behind. Like everyone else, there are some things I have done and said, that I wish would never be remembered again. Philippians 3:13-14 says, "Brothers, I do not consider myself yet to have taken hold of it. But one thing I do: Forgetting what is behind and straining toward what is ahead, I press on toward the goal to win the prize for which God has called me heavenward in Christ Jesus." Don't look back at past mistakes, but press forward serving Christ.

Prayer: God, help me to be remembered for the good things I have done.

Matthew 26:21 *Now as they were eating, He said, "Assuredly, I say to you, one of you will betray Me."*

Jesus and the disciples are celebrating the Passover meal, when He plainly tells them, "One of you will betray Me." The disciples are saddened, then one by one begin to ask Him, "Lord is it I?" with the exception of Judas who asks, "Rabbi, is it I?" Judas' response reveals his true devotion to Jesus. While the others have accepted Jesus as Lord, Judas only thinks of Him as Rabbi, or teacher. Judas' motives for betraying Jesus are not recorded in the Bible. Perhaps he thought Jesus' earthly ministry wasn't going in the direction he felt it should. Or, maybe he wanted to force Jesus into declaring His Lordship and set up His earthly kingdom right away. We do know Judas was given 30 pieces of silver for handing Jesus over to the religious leaders, fulfilling a prophecy found in Zechariah 11:13, "And the Lord said to me, 'Throw it to the potter' – the handsome price at which they priced me! So I took the thirty pieces of silver and threw them into the house of the Lord to the potter." After betraying Jesus, Judas became remorseful for his actions and tossed the 30 pieces of silver into the temple. The money was later used by the priests to buy the potter's field to bury strangers. After telling the disciples that one would betray Him, Jesus continued saying in Matthew 26:23, "...but woe to that man by whom the Son of Man is betrayed! It would have been good for that man if he had not been born." Was Judas born to deny Jesus, or could he have chosen a different path? John 6:64 tells us, "...For Jesus had known from the beginning of time which of them did not believe and who would betray him." This is where God's sovereignty and human choice is made clear. Jesus speaking in John 7:17 said, "If anyone chooses to do God's will, he will find out whether My teaching comes from God or whether I speak on My own." Judas had a choice to acknowledge Jesus as Lord, or to betray Him. Yet he chose to see Jesus as just another teacher. Jesus had warned Judas not to go through with his actions because of the consequences. Even after betraying Jesus, there was still hope for Judas. However, Judas chose remorse over repentance. What choices are you making today?

Prayer: God, help me to choose to serve You, not betray You.

> Matthew 26:26 And as they were eating, Jesus took bread, blessed and broke it, and gave it to the disciples and said, "Take, eat, this is My body."

At this moment, the disciples had no idea what Jesus meant by the broken bread representing His body. They were simply celebrating the Passover meal with Jesus. However, Jesus' meaning would become much clearer in the next few days after His death and resurrection. Luke 19:22 adds a little more detail to the words of Jesus saying, "This is My body given for you; do this in remembrance of Me." Jesus is establishing an ordinance known as communion or the "Lord's Supper" which has been celebrated by Christians ever since that night. Today, we focus on the breaking of bread, representing the body of Christ. Jesus said in John 6:35, "I am the bread of life. He who comes to Me shall never hunger, and who believes in Me shall never thirst." Our physical life needs bread or food to survive. In the same manner, Jesus' broken body is the source of nourishment for our spiritual life. The body of Christ represents life and forgiveness. Just as Jesus broke the bread and handed the pieces to the disciples, Jesus' body was broken and torn apart for the forgiveness of our sins. Isaiah 53:4-7 says, "Surely He took up our infirmities and carried our sorrows, yet we considered Him stricken by God, smitten by Him, and afflicted. But He was pierced for our transgressions, He was crushed for our iniquities; the punishment that brought us peace was upon Him, and by His wounds we are healed." This is why we celebrate communion with deep reverence and thankfulness. Jesus was pierced for our disobedience, His body was broken for our immoral behavior, He was punished for our sins. Artists' rendition of the crucifixion do not give justice to the tearing of His body. Isaiah 52:14, "Just as there were many who were appalled at Him – His appearance was so disfigured beyond that of any man and His form marred beyond human likeness." Jesus' body was torn beyond recognition, yet He bore that pain and suffering for our salvation and the forgiveness of our sins. The next time you participate in communion, take time to thank Jesus for sacrificing His body, the Bread of Life. Reflect on the whip as it was drug across His back. Think of the spikes that were driven through His hands and feet. Then, take the bread and do this in remembrance of Him.

Prayer: God, thank You for the body of Christ which was given for me.

> *Matthew 26:27-28 Then He took the cup, and gave thanks, and gave it to them saying, "Drink from it, all of you. For this is My blood of the new covenant, which is shed for many for the remission of sins."*

In the Bible, blood represents life. Before Christ, the shedding of blood for animal sacrifices was necessary to atone for people's sins. Hebrews 9:22 says, "In fact, the law requires that nearly everything be cleansed with blood, and without the shedding of blood there is no forgiveness." Blood was also used to seal a covenant between God and His people. Exodus 24:8, "Moses then took the blood, sprinkled it on the people and said, 'This is the blood covenant that the Lord has made with you in accordance with all these words.'" Blood was used to mark the homes of the Israelites living in Egypt on the night of Passover when the death angel killed all the first born of Egypt. Exodus 12:22-23, "Take a bunch of hyssop, dip it into the blood in the basin and put some of the blood on the top and on both sides of the doorframe. Not one of you shall go out the door of his house until morning. When the Lord goes through the land to strike down the Egyptians, He will see the blood on the top and sides of the doorframe and will pass over that doorway and, and He will not permit the destroyer to enter your houses and strike you down." In His last sacrificial act on the cross, the blood of Jesus replaces the need for shedding the blood of animals. He fulfilled all the Old Testament requirements with His blood. He established a new covenant, one that does not require the obedience of the Law to receive salvation. He covered our sins with His shed blood. His blood seals us from death and destruction. 1 Peter 1:18-19 says, "For you know that it was not with perishable things such as silver or gold that you were redeemed from the empty way of life handed down to you from your forefathers, but with the precious blood of Christ, a lamb without blemish or defect." Reflect on the lyrics of the song written by Thomas and Mary Miller, "*O The Blood*." 'O the blood, Crimson love, Price of life's demand, Shameful sin, placed on Him, The hope of every man, O the blood of Jesus washes me, O the blood of Jesus shed for me, What a sacrifice that saved my life, Yes, the blood, it is my victory."

Prayer: God, thank You for the blood that washes me whiter than snow. The blood that saved my life.

> *Matthew 26:34 Jesus said to him, "Assuredly, I say to you that this night, before the rooster crows, you will deny Me three times."*

Vivian and I have a saying, "Don't ever say, what you are not going to do." Invariably the very thing you said you would never do; you find yourself doing. Such is the case of Peter. Jesus tells Peter that before the night is over, Peter will deny Him three times. Peter's response to Jesus is found in verse 35, "Even if I have to die with You, I will not deny You." A little later when Judas and the mob arrived to arrest Jesus, it was Peter who struck the high priest's servant with a sword, cutting off his ear. Peter was ready to fight and die for Jesus. Yet, a few minutes later as Jesus was being led away, all the disciples deserted Him and ran away. Peter and John turned around and followed the mob from a distance to see what would happen to Jesus. As Peter was sitting around a fire in the courtyard of the high priest, a servant girl said to him, "You also were with Jesus of Galilee." Peter told her, "I do not know what you are saying." Peter moved to another location, when another girl saw him and said to those around him, "This fellow also was with Jesus of Nazareth." Peter again denied with an oath, "I do not know the Man." A little later those who were standing around said to Peter, "Surely you also are one of them, for your speech betrays you." Matthew 26:74-75, "Then he began to curse and swear, saying, 'I do not know the Man!' Immediately a rooster crowed. And Peter remembered the words of Jesus..." Matthew tells us that Peter went away and wept bitterly. Thankfully, this is not the last we hear about Peter. Peter repents and finds redemption and purpose. He goes on to be a great leader in the faith, leading thousands to Christ on the Day of Pentecost. However, Peter had to learn a very painful lesson. He was over-confident in his own abilities rather than trusting in God's strength. When put to the test, Peter relying on his own strength failed. Proverbs 3:5-6 says, "Trust in the Lord with all your heart and lean not on your own understanding; in all your ways acknowledge Him, and He will make your paths straight." Ask God to fill you with His power and strength each day.

Prayer: God, teach me to lean on You.

> Matthew 26:39 He went a little farther and fell on His face, and prayed, saying, "O My Father, if it is possible, let this cup pass from Me; nevertheless, not as I will, but as You will."

Jesus and the disciples leave the upper room and go to pray at the Garden of Gethsemane, which is located at the foot of the Mount of Olives. Jesus leaves the disciples in the garden and takes Peter, James, and John a little further to pray and watch with Him. It is in this prayer we see the human side of Jesus. Matthew 26:37-38 tells us, "...He began to be sorrowful and deeply distressed. Then He said to them, 'My soul is exceedingly sorrowful, even to death. Stay here and watch with Me.'" Jesus knew what was about to take place and felt intense grief and anguish. Luke 22:44, "And being in anguish, He prayed more earnestly, and His sweat was like drops of blood falling to the ground." According to www.webmd.com, this condition is known as "Hematidrosis" which is a very rare condition that causes one to sweat or ooze blood from their skin when they are not cut. It is triggered by extreme distress or fear. The human side of Jesus did not want to experience the humiliation, torture, and painful death on the cross. His prayer was that if it was any way possible to avoid it, please allow it to happen. Had Jesus' prayer stopped here, He would have sounded selfish and unwilling to fulfill His mission on earth. However, Jesus closes His prayer with these selfless words "nevertheless, not as I will but as You will." Jesus was committed to obeying the Father, and following through with His mission. Philippians 2:8, "And being found in appearance as a man, He humbled Himself and became obedient to death – even death on a cross." Jesus' prayer is a great model for us. In all situations, it is okay to ask God for exactly what we want. Philippians 4:6 says, "Do not be anxious about anything, but in everything, by prayer and petition, with thanksgiving, present your requests to God." We can come boldly before the throne of God with our requests; however, like Jesus, our prayers should include our willingness to accept and obey God's will in all circumstances. This includes times when God's answer is no or not yet and our faith and obedience to Him is tested. My prayer is that you will trust His will for you in every situation.

Prayer: God, help me to accept Your will for my life.

> Matthew 26:45 Then He came to His disciples and said to them, "Are you still sleeping and resting? Behold, the hour is at hand, and the Son of Man is being betrayed into the hands of sinners."

After pouring out His heart to God, Jesus returns to find Peter, James, and John asleep. He woke them up and told Peter, "What! Could you not watch with Me one hour? Watch and pray, lest you enter into temptation. The spirit is indeed willing, but the flesh is weak." Jesus went away and began to pray the same prayer again, that this cup would pass from Him, but God's will be done. After praying, He came back to find the disciples asleep again. This time Jesus did not wake them, but left to pray a third time. The last time He returned, Judas and the mob were coming to arrest Jesus. Jesus wakes the disciples and tells them, "Behold, the hour is at hand..." This hour meant different things to different people. For Jesus, this hour was the beginning of His journey to the cross. It was the culmination of His mission on earth. For the disciples, it was an hour of testing. Earlier that evening, Jesus had warned the disciples they would desert him. Peter very adamant at the time, said he was willing to die with Jesus. Jesus knew the key to overcoming temptation was prayer. That is why He warned them earlier, saying, "Watch and pray, lest you enter into temptation." Sadly, the disciples had been sleeping when they should have been praying and abandoned Jesus in His greatest time of need. How often do we make commitments to ourselves and God like the disciples, only to fall into the same sins over and over. Our intentions are great, but our follow through is weak. Having a willing spirit is a good start, but it is just not enough to overcome our fleshly desires. Jesus tells us to watch and pray, because trials and temptation are inevitable. They show up unexpectedly, without warning when we are most vulnerable. That is why prayer is so important. It prepares us and gives us strength when the trials of life do show up. I can tell you from personal experience, trying to overcome trials and temptation on your strength does not work. I am thankful for a forgiving God, who can make something worthwhile out of the mess we make of our lives. However, God wants us to watch and pray to avoid the pitfalls of life.

Prayer: God, help me to watch and pray.

> *Matthew 26:52 But Jesus said to him, "Put your sword in its place, for all who take the sword will perish by the sword."*

Some Biblical scholars believe that Peter was actually trying to take a swing at Judas, when he cuts off the ear of the high priest's servant, Malchus. Yet, even in the midst of the confusion of the moment, Jesus has compassion on the man who came to arrest Him. Luke 22:51, "But Jesus answered, 'No more of this!' And He touched the man's ear and healed him." Jesus tells Peter to put his sword up and that He could have easily called down 12 Legions of angels to defend Him. Jesus knew Peter would have no chance surviving a sword fight with the trained soldiers who were in the crowd. More importantly, Peter would play a big part in building the church after His death and resurrection. This was all part of God's plan. Jesus also told Peter, "All who draw the sword will die by the sword." In other words, violence produces violence. Those who are violent, will likely come to a violent end. Jesus is teaching Peter, that violence is not always the answer to solving our problems. Perhaps one of the most famous proponents of non-violent demonstrations was Dr. Martin Luther King. During his short life, Dr. King led eight peaceful protests against racism and injustice, beginning with the Montgomery Bus Protest in 1955, and culminating with the March on Washington in 1968 to address the issues of economic justice and housing for the poor.[16] Dr. King wrote about six principles of non-violence in his 1958 book, "*Stride Toward Freedom: The Montgomery Story.*"[17] Although, Dr. King's protests were often met with violence, he never retaliated. Non-violence takes strength and resolve. Sadly, the protests of today seem to be rooted in violence. The actions of groups such as Antifa, Black Lives Matter, and the Siege on the Capital have done more to harm their cause than help it. They have created new victims in the wake of their actions and lost the sympathy of many who could have helped them make positive changes. It is also important to point out, Jesus just said to put the sword away. He did not say, it should never be used. There are times and places when a response to violence is needed. Ask God for insight to know when it is necessary.

Prayer: God, help me to put my sword away, and only use it when the situation calls for it.

> *Matthew 26:64 Jesus said to him, "It is as you said. Nevertheless, I say to you, hereafter you will see the Son of Man sitting at the right hand of the Power, and coming on the clouds of heaven."*

Jesus is on trial at the house of Caiaphas, the High Priest, where the religious leaders are trying to gather enough evidence to convict and sentence Him to death. Matthew tells us that many false witnesses came forward, but they couldn't get their testimony straight. Seeing that the trial was going nowhere, Caiaphas asks Jesus directly, "I put You under oath by the living God: Tell us if You are the Christ, the Son of God." Notice, Jesus had not responded to any accusations until He was put under oath by Caiaphas. Under oath, Jesus answers him saying, "It is as you said." This is an odd response to a simple yes or no question. However, it is the same reply Jesus gave to Judas when he asked if he was the one who was going to betray Him. It was Jesus' way of telling Caiaphas and the other religious leaders, yes, I am the Messiah, the Son of God, and deep down you know the answer to your question. You are afraid to admit it, because My words have exposed your religious charade. Not only that, the next time you see Me, I will be seated on the right side of God, the Mighty One. Instead of standing in front of you as a defendant on trial, I will judge the nations. Killing Me will not be the end of Me and your troubles. You will see Me alive and coming back on the clouds. Daniel prophesies about this declaration in Daniel 7:13-14, "In my vision at night I looked, there before me was one like a Son of Man, coming with the clouds of heaven. He approached the Ancient of Days and was led into His presence. He was given authority, glory and sovereign power; all peoples, nations and men of every language worshipped Him. His dominion is an everlasting dominion that will not pass away, and His kingdom is one that will never be destroyed." Upon hearing this declaration from Jesus, Caiaphas and the religious leaders had a choice whether to accept Jesus as the Son of God, or reject Him. Sadly, they chose to reject Him and would be held accountable for their decision. You and I are faced with the same decision to accept or reject Jesus as Lord and Savior. My prayer is that you have chosen wisely.

Prayer: God, I choose Your Son, Jesus Christ as my Lord and Savior.

> *Matthew 26:75 And Peter remembered the word of Jesus who had said to him, "Before the rooster crows, you will deny Me three times." So he went out and wept bitterly.*

We read several days ago that Jesus told Peter he would betray Him. He would also be reminded of his denial by the crowing of a rooster. Luke tells us that just as soon as Peter had uttered his last and most stern denial of Jesus, the rooster crowed. To add to Peter's pain, Luke 22:61 says, "The Lord turned and looked straight at Peter. Then Peter remembered the word the Lord had spoken to him..." After hearing the rooster crow, Peter left weeping bitterly. But we also learned that Peter repented and was later used mightily by God. Just as Peter's actions in that courtyard severed his relationship with Christ, our sins do the same to our relationship with Him. Isaiah 59:2, "But your iniquities have separated you from your God; your sins have hidden His face from you, so that He will not hear." After being confronted with his failure, Peter was very sorrowful and sought forgiveness and restoration. Our sins should cause us to do the same. Seeking repentance is more than just praying, "God forgive me of my sins." I have to admit, I will often take this shortcut in prayer, not being specific with God about my sins. This may be okay for corporate prayer, but it is important to identify our sins privately before the Father. How can we have remorse and Godly sorrow for our sins, when we don't even recognize what they are? It is also important to know what we are asking God to forgive us for, so that we can take steps to remove those things from our lives. Colossians 3:8 says, "But now you must rid yourselves of all such things as these: anger, rage, malice, slander, filthy language from your lips." Paul lists more sinful behaviors in Galatians 5:19-20, "The acts of the sinful nature are obvious: sexual immorality, impurity, and debauchery; idolatry and witchcraft; hatred, discord, jealousy, fits of rage, selfish ambition, dissensions, factions and envy; drunkenness, orgies, and the like." God's word promises us mercy and forgiveness when we confess our sins. Proverbs 28:13, "He who conceals his sins does not prosper, but whoever confesses and renounces them finds mercy." Unconfessed sin can hinder your relationship with the Father and make you ineffective in trying to serve Him. Be like Peter, confess, repent, remove, restore, and rejoice.

Prayer: God, please forgive me of _____.

> *Matthew 27:46 And about the ninth hour Jesus cried out with a loud voice, saying, "Eli, Eli, lama sabachthani?" that is, "My God, My God, why have You forsaken Me?"*

It is about three o'clock in the afternoon and a strange darkness has covered the land for three hours as Jesus hung on the cross. Jesus cries out in a loud voice, quoting from Psalm 22:1, "My God, My God, why have You forsaken Me?" Matthew tells us that some misunderstood Jesus, thinking He was calling for the Prophet Elijah to come help Him. However, the truth is Jesus was calling out to God who had truly forsaken Him, because He was bearing the weight of our sins. God in His holiness could not bear to look upon all the sins of world Jesus was carrying at that moment. Although He felt abandoned, Jesus trusted in God's plan and endured the pain and suffering, dying on the cross. It is amazing how descriptive David's words were in Psalm 22 about Jesus' death. Psalm 22:15-18, "My strength is dried up like a potsherd, and My tongue sticks to the roof of My mouth; You lay Me in the dust of death. Dogs have surrounded Me; a band of evil men has encircled Me, they have pierced My hands and My feet. I can count all My bones; people stare and gloat over Me. They divide My garments among them and cast lots for My clothing." David included words of encouragement that we can trust God and His plans. Psalm 22:3-5, "Yet You are enthroned as the Holy One; You are the praise of Israel. In You our fathers put their trust; they trusted You and You delivered them. They cried out to You and were saved; in You they trusted and were not disappointed." There have been times in my life when I have cried out to God these very same words. I have felt abandoned and that God was nowhere to be found. The truth is that I deserve to be forsaken by the Father. However, Jesus chose to suffer the separation I deserve and took my sins with Him to the cross. That is why I have the assurance that no matter how I feel, I know that God will never forsake me. Deuteronomy 31:8 tells us, "The Lord Himself goes before you and will be with you; He will never leave you nor forsake you. Do not be afraid; do not be discouraged." Praise God, He is always with us.

Prayer: God, I thank You for never leaving or forsaking me.

> *Matthew 28:18-20 And Jesus came and spoke to them saying, "All authority has been given to Me in heaven and on earth. Go therefore and make disciples of all the nations, baptizing them in the name of the Father and of the Son and of the Holy Spirit, teaching them to observe all things I have commanded you; and lo, I am with you always, even to the end of the age." Amen.*

Known as the Great Commission, Jesus entrusts His disciples and all those who will follow them, the task of making disciples all over the world. In His mandate, Jesus shares three key elements to achieving this mission, "Go and make disciples, Baptize, and teach." Let's take a closer look at each. "Go," does not mean that Jesus has called everyone to be a missionary to a foreign country. "Go" simply means, as you are going about your daily life, reach out to those you see every day. Get to know people and share your faith in Jesus Christ with them. Invite them to church to hear the word of God and to get plugged into a community of believers. However, we must be careful. Jesus didn't say make church goers of everyone; but make disciples. We have plenty of church goers whose total spiritual life consists of spending an hour or two at church on Sunday. Being a disciple is so much more. It is an on-going process of growing in our faith and becoming more Christlike through the power of the Holy Spirit. Discipling someone, means we are sharing and teaching them how to follow Christ through our actions and sometimes our words. Next, Jesus said to baptize them in the name of the Father and of the Son and of the Holy Spirit. Why is baptism important? Baptism is on outward testimony of an inward change in a person's life. It represents the burial or washing away of our old life and the transformation to a new person in Christ. Colossians 2:12, "Having been buried with Him in baptism and raised with Him through your faith in the power of God, who raised Him from the dead." Most importantly, baptism is an act of obedience, signifying I am a follower or disciple of Christ. Lastly, Jesus said to teach the new disciples to observe the things He commanded. Paul said in Romans 10:14, "How, then can they call on the one they have not believed in? And how can they believe in the one of whom they have not heard? And how can they hear without someone preaching to them?" Likewise, how can someone know the word of God without being taught? God doesn't expect us to be Bible scholars, but He does expect us to teach what we know to others.

Prayer: God, help me to disciple others.

> Mark 1:17 Then Jesus said to them, "Follow Me, and I will make you become fishers of men."

Jesus would never ask us to do anything He hasn't already done. Yesterday, we learned that Jesus has called each one of us to go and make disciples of those we see daily. According to Mark, Jesus is walking along the Sea of Galilee and sees Simon and his brother Andrew casting a net into sea. Fishing for a living in Jesus' day was very hard work and often done at night. Like most jobs, it fed the family and paid the bills. However, Jesus comes along and offers Simon and Andrew something that causes them to drop their nets and leave their occupation. Jesus offered them a purpose, and a meaning to life. Jesus simply said, "I will make you become fishers of men." When we accepted Jesus as Lord and Savior of our lives, He called you and I to a greater purpose. We have a choice of "dropping our nets," and following Jesus or stand on the shore and watch others fulfill His call. Knowing God's will for your life may not be as clear as Jesus' call to Simon and Andrew. In fact, Jesus' purpose for our life is more often found through spending time in prayer and in God's word, walking in obedience to Him. As we do, God begins to reveal His purpose and plans to us. Hebrews 13:20-21, "May the God of peace, who through the blood of the eternal covenant brought back from the dead our Lord Jesus, that great Shepherd of the sheep, equip you with everything good for doing His will, and may He work in us what is pleasing to Him through Jesus Christ, to whom be glory for ever and ever. Amen." God has a different plan and purpose for each of us. Some are called to work directly in ministry like missionaries and pastors, while others are called to be a witness through an occupation or simply being a Christian parent. God's purpose for our lives may not be wrapped up in big moments that are world changing. Instead, His purpose could be laid out for us in random acts of kindness, divine appointments, and being there for a loved one who is struggling with life. Are you struggling to know God's purpose for your life? Take time today to seek the God of peace, who equips us for doing His will.

Prayer: God, help me to find my purpose in life.

> *Mark 12:43-44 So He called His disciples to Himself and said to them, "Assuredly, I say to you, that this poor widow has put in more than all those who have given to the treasury; for they all put in out of their abundance, but she out of her poverty put in all that she had, her whole livelihood."*

Jesus and the disciples are in the temple by the offering box, observing how the people were putting money into the treasury. Mark 12:41 says, "...And many who were rich put in much." A poor widow comes along who only put in two mites, the equivalent of two pennies in today's currency. By any standards, that would not be enough to keep the lights on at the church. However, Jesus said she has put in more than the others. What was the difference in her giving as compared to those who were wealthy? It was her attitude in giving. Jesus said, she put in all she had. She trusted God over the two pennies she had left to provide for her needs. Perhaps she had heard Proverbs 3:9-10, "Honor the Lord with your wealth, with the first fruits of all your crops; then your barns will be filled to overflowing, and your vats will brim over with new wine." Or maybe she had read Malachi 3:10, "Bring the whole tithe into the storehouse, that there may be food in My house. Test Me in this, says the Lord Almighty, and see if I will not throw open the floodgates of heaven and pour out so much blessing that you will not have room enough for it." I'll have to admit putting everything in the offering plate would be a true test of faith that I have never done. However, Vivian and I have trusted God throughout our marriage with our tithes and offerings. There were times early in our marriage when paying the bills was a challenge, but our tithes came first. We may never have had the best of everything, but we wanted for nothing. Like the widow, trusting God in your giving requires true faith, but it may also require you to change the way you are currently spending your/ God's money. For example, our first Christmas presents were hand-made Christmas ornaments and cross-stitched pictures. Each year, God provided and things got much better. I can truly say Jesus' words in Luke 6:38 have come to pass in our lives, "Give, and it will be given to you. A good measure, pressed down, shaken together and running over, will be poured into your lap. For with the measure you use, it will be measured to you." Trust God, be faithful in your giving to Him.

Prayer: God, help me to trust You in my giving.

> *Luke 2:49 And He said to them, "Why did you seek Me? Did you not know that I must be about My Father's business?"*

Having a young child disappear from sight in a public place will raise the anxiety level of any parent. When our children were young, they loved to play hide and seek around the clothes racks at Belks. One moment, they are right beside Vivian who is looking some clothes for them, and the next they are gone. Panic sets in as Vivian is running around the store looking for them. The children on the other hand are playing and having a good time. When they are finally found there is a mixture of emotions; relief that they are okay, and anger that they decided to hide. Jesus is twelve years old when His parents make their annual trip to Jerusalem to celebrate the Feast of the Passover. After the festival, Mary and Joseph left to go home with many other friends and family who had also come to Jerusalem. After traveling a day's journey, they begin to look around for Jesus whom they thought had been walking back with friends. When they couldn't find Him anywhere, they head back to Jerusalem to look for Him. Three days later they find Jesus in the temple sitting among the teachers, listening and asking questions. Mary's response is typical of any loving mother. She said in Luke 2:48, "...Son, why have You treated us like this? Your father and I have been anxiously searching for You." Jesus does not ask her why they were looking for Him, but He suggests the temple is the only place they should expect to find Him. It is also not surprising at the early age of 12, Jesus references God as His Father. Luke 2:40 says, "And the Child grew and became strong in spirit, filled with wisdom; and the grace of God was upon Him." Most 12-year-olds I know are mainly focused on playing video games, participating in sporting activities, and looking at social media. Jesus was intent on learning and growing, preparing Himself for ministry that would not officially begin until 18 years later. What can we learn from Jesus' experience as a child? No one is too young to learn and study God's word. We should be providing our children opportunities, resources, and encouragement to grow in their faith. Make Bible study a part of your weekly family time. Show them the importance of learning God's word.

Prayer: God, help me to challenge my children and grandchildren to study and learn Your word.

> *Luke 4:12 And Jesus answered and said to him. "It has been said, 'You shall not tempt the Lord your God.'"*

Never doubt the fact that Satan is very smart. He knows scripture and how to manipulate it to plant seeds of doubt. Once he has you questioning God's word and faithfulness, his job becomes very easy. Satan also seems to move in with temptation when we are most vulnerable. He is very patient, waiting for the right moment to strike. 1 Peter 5:8, "Be self-controlled and alert. Your enemy the devil prowls around like a roaring lion looking for someone to devour." In today's verse, Satan has taken Jesus to Jerusalem and set Him on the pinnacle of the temple, daring Him to jump off. Satan quotes Psalm 91:11-12 saying, "For He shall give His angels charge over You, To keep You in all Your ways. In their hands they shall bear You up, lest You dash your foot against a stone." Satan was in effect, trying to force Jesus to fulfill God's word by jumping off the pinnacle. In other words, let's see if God will really send His angels to catch You. In the playground, we used to call this, "I dare you." "Let's see if you can really skip three bars on the monkey bars or jump from the top of slide." If the person you dared hesitated, then it was, "I double-decker dare you." Basically, we were trying to force the other person to do something a little dangerous, by making them feel guilty for not doing it. Similarly, Satan may be saying something like this to you: "Doesn't 1 Corinthians 6:12 say, 'Everything is permissible to me.' Go ahead, enjoy that drink. Take that drug. You really need it to calm you down and relax you from a busy day. Have another and another, it will be okay and make you feel good." Or, he may be telling you, "That person you work with is so much nicer and understands you much better than your own spouse. There is a real chemistry here. You need to check it out." What Satan didn't tell you is the last part of 1 Corinthians 6:12 that says, "...But not everything is beneficial. Everything is permissible for me – but I will not be mastered by anything." Don't let Satan trick you into a life of pain and suffering. Be strong and recognize temptation for what it is, a trap set by Satan.

Prayer: God, help me to recognize temptation and have the strength to avoid it.

> Luke 4:43 But He said to them, "I must preach the kingdom of God to the other cities also, because for this purpose I have been sent."

Jesus was in the City of Capernaum, teaching weekly in the synagogue. His ministry was thriving and He was reaching a lot of people there. Luke tells us He was casting out demons and had healed Simon Peter's mother who had a very high fever. Things were going well, and Jesus could have stayed there and been very successful. However, Jesus knew His calling was more than preaching and teaching in Capernaum. In Luke 4:18-19 Jesus proclaims His purpose, quoting Isaiah 61:1-2 saying, "The Spirit of the Lord is upon Me, Because He has anointed Me to preach the gospel to the poor; He has sent Me to heal the brokenhearted, to proclaim liberty to the captives and recovery of sight to the blind, to set at liberty those who are oppressed; to proclaim the acceptable year of the Lord." Jesus was obedient to God's call in His life and told the people He must go to preach to other cities as well. How often do we find ourselves in the same place as Jesus? Things are going well and life is good; yet, God has other plans for us. His plans require us to move out of our comfort zone into territory we have never been before. Do we trust God and take that first step, or do we stay in the place where we are most comfortable? Speaking from experience, I can assure you trusting God and following Him out of your comfort zone will fill you with peace and a real sense of purpose. Several years ago, God opened the door for Vivian and I to lead mission teams from our church to Nicaragua. This is something we had never done before. It was challenging, it stretched us, and it was hard work. However, it not only changed our lives, but the lives of those who went on those trips. We made lifelong friendships, saw God work miracle upon miracle, and grew our faith to levels we had never experienced. I look back now and wonder what our lives would have looked like had we not been obedient to God. I wonder who God would have chosen to take our place. My friend, don't miss out on God's calling upon your life. Don't hand over your blessing to someone else. Say yes to God when He begins to move you out of your comfort zone.

Prayer: God, send me.

> *Luke 5:4 When He had stopped speaking, He said to Simon, "Launch out into the deep and let down your nets for a catch."*

Simon Peter was an experienced fisherman. He and his crew had finished a long night of fishing and were in the process of cleaning their nets when Jesus comes along and asks to borrow his boat. Jesus tells Peter to push off from the shore so He could teach the crowd that had gathered on the beach. As Jesus was finishing up, He told Peter to go out deeper to catch some fish. It just so happened the night before was one of those fishing trips you would prefer to forget. They didn't catch a thing. Peter's reply in Luke 5:5 tells us a lot about Peter, "Master, we've worked hard all night and haven't caught anything. But because You say so, I will let down the nets." From Peter's perspective, Jesus didn't know a thing about fishing and could he could have easily said, "Jesus we are tired, and it is just not worth the trouble." Or, "Jesus I'm the expert here, and the tide is not right for fishing." So why did Peter decide to launch out deeper? Because he had heard Jesus speak and knew there was something different about Him. Even though Jesus' command may have sounded foolish, Peter decided to trust Jesus. Through his obedience, Peter learned several valuable lessons. First, God never gives us foolish commands. They may sound foolish at the time, but God has a purpose in mind. Secondly, God blesses those who obey Him. When Peter and his crew lowered the nets, they caught so many fish that their nets began to break. The fish had been in the Sea of Galilee the entire time, but Peter couldn't find them the night before. With Jesus in the boat, everything changed. Lastly, being obedient to God requires some type of action on our part. What is Jesus calling you to do? In most cases it falls into one of three categories. He may want you to plant seeds of His word, sharing the good news of salvation with someone. Or, maybe it is to water the seeds that have been planted by someone else. Perhaps He is calling you to reap the harvest of the seeds that were planted and nourished by others. No matter the call, it will require obedience and work on your part. What will be your response when Jesus asks you to do something?

Prayer: God, help my answer always to be, but because You say so.

> Luke 5:10 And so also were James and John, the sons of Zebedee, who were partners with Simon. And Jesus said to Simon, "Do not be afraid. From now on you will catch men."

James and John were working nearby when Peter pushed out to deeper water at Jesus' command. When his nets began to tear due to the number of fish being caught, Peter frantically signaled for them to come help. Luke tells us when both boats began to sink due to the weight of all the fish, Peter said to Jesus, "Go away from me Lord; I am a sinful man!" In that moment, Peter came to the realization who was in the boat with him. He had witnessed Jesus' power and became acutely aware of his own sinfulness and need for a Savior. The good news is that Peter's story doesn't end there. Peter wants more of Christ, so he drops his nets, leaves the fish behind, and follows Jesus. Peter spends the next several years with Jesus, learning and growing in faith. Later, when Jesus asks the disciples who are the people saying He is, it is Peter who boldly speaks up, "The Christ, the Son of the Living God." This is very commendable, because many see Jesus as Elijah, John the Baptist, or an old prophet that has returned from the dead, not the Messiah. At this moment, Peter only has a head knowledge of who Jesus is. He has spent several years getting to know Jesus, listen to His words, and witness His miracles, but he still lacks a heart knowledge. It is not until Jesus' death and resurrection that Peter really became aware who Jesus was. Peter began to see Jesus as His Lord and Savior, the One who died on the cross to pay the penalty for this "sinful man" Jesus had met three years earlier. At that moment, Jesus' call for Peter to come "catch men" became a reality. Where are you on this journey with Christ? Have you recognized your sinfulness and need for a Savior? Perhaps you have even acknowledged Jesus as the Son of God. James 2:19 tells us, "You believe there is one God. Good! Even the demons believe that – and shudder." We must take it one step further, confessing our sins and asking Jesus into our hearts as Lord and Savior. That is when salvation and our call to serve Him begin. My prayer is that you have already taken that step and are following Jesus daily. If not, ask Jesus into your heart this very moment.

Prayer: God, help me to follow You.

> Luke 15:11-14 Then He said, "A certain man had two sons. And the younger of them said to his father, 'Father, give me the portion of goods that falls to me.' So he divided to them his livelihood. And not many days after, the younger son gathered all together, journeyed to a far country, and there wasted his possessions with prodigal living."

In Luke 15:11-31, we find the Parable of the Lost or Prodigal Son. This parable tells the story of two sons and the relationship they had with their father. In the parable, the younger son asks for his share of the estate while his father is still alive. A request like that in Jesus' day is saying to the father, "I wish you were dead, so I can get my share of the inheritance." Surprisingly, the father goes along with the request and divides his estate between the two brothers. The older brother receives two thirds, and the younger one third. The estate was primarily land, so the younger brother would have had to liquidate his share by selling off his father's property to friends and relatives. The younger brother leaves and pretty quickly squanders his money on extravagant living. Finding himself in a foreign land without any money or friends, the young man resorts to looking after someone's pigs. Hungry and destitute, the young man comes to his senses. Realizing his foolishness, he makes a plan to go back to his father, saying, "I have sinned against heaven and before you, and I am no longer worthy to be called your son. Make me like one of your hired servants." On the surface, it sounds like the younger son has the right attitude. However, his repentance comes with conditions. Basically, he is just sorry that he got himself into a mess. However, the son never has the chance to finish his rehearsed speech. The father runs to him, embraces him, and welcomes him back into the family. He plans a big party and invites the entire village. The older son, returning from the field hears the celebration and asks one of the servants what is going on. When the servant told the older brother the story of his brother's return, he became angry and would not join the party. The father comes out and pleads with him to celebrate his brother's return. Instead, the older son unloads years of frustration on the father. Although insulted by his son, the father is patient and forgiving of him, saying, "Son, you are always with me, and all that I have is yours." Jesus doesn't tell us how the story ends, because we get to write it. You and I are those two sons. Which son are you?

Prayer: God, I am thankful You are a loving Father.

> *Luke 16:19-20 There was a certain rich man who was clothed in purple and fine linen and fared sumptuously every day. But there was a certain beggar named Lazarus, full of sores, who was laid at his gate.*

Jesus shares a parable in Luke 16:19-31 about the Rich Man who lived a life of extreme luxury, and Lazarus who was very poor and ate the scraps off the Rich Man's table. Sadly, the Rich Man was indifferent to poor Lazarus sitting at his gate, showing him no love or compassion. Both men soon die, with Lazarus being carried by the angels to heaven and the Rich Man sent to hell. Jesus describes hell as a real place of continual torment. Adding to the torment, the Rich Man could look up and see Lazarus resting in peace in heaven. Appealing to Father Abraham, the Rich Man asks if Lazarus could dip the tip of his finger in water and come cool his tongue, "for I am tormented in this flame." Jesus lets us know that hell is also a place of continual flame and unbearable heat. Father Abraham replies to the Rich Man telling him, "Son, remember that in your lifetime you received your good things, and likewise Lazarus evil things; but now he is comforted and you are tormented. And besides all this, between us and you there is a great gulf fixed, so that those who want to pass from here to you cannot, nor can those from there pass to us." Another thing we learn is that hell is a one-way trip. There is no return. Then the Rich Man asks if Father Abraham would send Lazarus back from the dead to warn his five brothers to repent so they would not join him in hell. Father Abraham tells him, if his brothers didn't believe the scriptures, they wouldn't be persuaded by someone who came back to life. How many people have doubted the death and resurrection of Jesus? How many have not accepted the truth of His Word? Hell is a real place prepared for those who do not believe. James 4:4 says, "Yet you do not know what tomorrow may bring. What is your life? For you are a mist that appears for a little time and then vanishes." When it is our time to die, it doesn't matter the amount of wealth we have accumulated or our social status. All that matters is our relationship with Jesus Christ. The moral of the story is, it is better to be poor in material things and rich in faith, than rich, and poor in faith.

Prayer: God, help me to be always rich in faith.

Luke 17:17 *So Jesus answered and said, "Were there not ten cleansed? But where are the nine?"*

Jesus and the disciples are on their way to Jerusalem when they encounter a group of lepers outside a village. Remaining some distance away, the lepers began shouting out to Jesus saying, "Jesus, Master, have mercy on us." This was their normal cry for help to anyone passing by in hopes of getting food or clothing. Since they called Jesus by name, they knew who He was; however, instead of asking for healing they will take anything Jesus would give them. Jesus replies back the lepers, "Go, show yourselves to the priests." Although this may sound like an odd response, Jesus is essentially instructing them to get a certificate of release from the priests indicating they no longer had leprosy. Jesus is following the guidelines for cleansing from an infectious skin disease found in Leviticus 14. There was also a test of faith in Jesus' command. In this situation, Jesus did not immediately heal the lepers. James 2:17, "In the same way, faith by itself, if it is not accompanied by action, is dead." Often times, the blessings Jesus has in store for us are just one step away. He doesn't say, "here is your blessing," but wants us to step out in faith to receive it. The lepers had nothing to lose, so they start walking. Luke tells us, "And so it was that as they went, they were cleansed." Imagine the surprise and joy as they begin to notice the changes in their skin. Then an odd thing happens. Only one of the ten, a Samaritan, turns around and goes back to thank Jesus. Luke 17:15-16, "And one of them, when he saw that he was healed, returned, and with a loud voice glorified God, and fell down on his face at His feet, giving Him thanks. And he was a Samaritan." Jesus concludes His encounter with the leper by saying in Luke 17:19, "Arise, go your way. Your faith has made you well." Yes, the Samaritan was healed of his leprosy, so were the nine other lepers. However, the Samaritan's faith and his return to thank Jesus for healing gained him much more. His faith gained him salvation and the ability to understand the full meaning of what has happened. Are we grateful for what God has done in our lives? Fall at His feet today and loudly give Him praise.

Prayer: God, I thank You for what You have done in my life.

> *Luke 18:2 Saying: "There was in a certain city a judge who did not fear God nor regard man. Now there was a widow in that city; and she came to him, saying, 'Get justice for me from my adversary.'"*

In his memorable speech at the 1993 ESPY's, Jim Valvano said these words, "Don't give up, don't ever give up." Two months later he would lose his battle with cancer, but his fight has continued on through the V Foundation for Cancer Research. According to Jesus, those seven words should be the foundation of our prayer life. Jesus tells the disciples a parable about a widow who kept going to a judge for justice against her adversary. He describes the judge as one who had no fear of God, nor regard for man, basically doing as he chooses. Although the widow kept coming to the judge for help, he kept denying her request. After a while, the judge began to change his opinion. Luke 18:4-5, "For some time he refused. But finally he said to himself. 'Even though I don't fear God or care about men, yet because this widow keeps bothering me, I will see that she gets justice, so that she won't eventually wear me out with her coming!'" Jesus then tells the disciples, in verses 7-8, "And will not God bring about justice for His chosen ones, who cry out to Him day and night? Will He keep putting them off? I tell you, He will see that they get justice, and quickly. However, when the Son of Man comes, will He find faith on the earth?" God hears our every prayer and knows the burdens on our heart. He hears our prayers for our lost child, spouse, or relative. He hears our prayers about the grip an addiction has on us. He hears our prayers for physical, mental, and emotional healing. He knows about the persecution and injustice many pray for relief from each day. However, God does not operate by keeping a score card and sending an answer to our prayers when we reach a certain number. His answers come at just the right moment, never early, never too late. We have to trust God's timing and sovereignty. Don't become discouraged if your prayers are not getting answered. According to James, they are powerful and effective. James 5:16 "...The prayer of a righteous person is powerful and effective." Jesus asked if He will find faith when He returns. The answer is yes. Keep praying, keep bringing your burdens to Him. Most importantly, don't give up, don't ever give up.

Prayer: God, thank You for hearing and answering my prayers.

> Luke 19:5-6 And when Jesus came to the place, He looked up and saw him, and said to him, "Zacchaeus, make haste and come down, for today I must stay at your house."

"Zacchaeus was a wee little man and wee little man was he, He climbed up in a sycamore tree for the Lord he wanted to see. And as the Savior passed that way, He looked up in the tree, and He said, 'Zacchaeus, you come down, for I'm going to your house today! For I'm going to your house today!'" The story of Zacchaeus, is one of my favorite Bible stories, because it demonstrates Jesus' love for the worst of sinners, and how He radically transforms our lives when we trust in Him. Luke tells us that Zacchaeus was a chief tax collector. His position made him very rich, but also a lonely man. Zacchaeus heard that Jesus was coming into Jericho that day and wanted to see Him. Being short in stature, he was unable to see over the crowds lining the streets. If you have ever been at Disney World and tried to get a spot where your three-year old could see the Mickey Mouse Parade, you know exactly how Zacchaeus felt. Like many parents, we would put our children on our shoulders so they could see. Zacchaeus' plan was to run ahead of the crowd and climb up in a sycamore tree. Walking by, Jesus sees Zacchaeus and calls him by name and tells him, "I must stay at your house today." Overjoyed, Zacchaeus climbs down and welcomed Him to his home. Each one of us will have or has had that type of defining encounter with Jesus. It is that moment when you know that He is calling you to receive Him as Lord and Savior. For me, my heart was pounding as I heard the word of God being preached and I couldn't stay still when our pastor invited anyone to come receive Christ as Lord and Savior. For others, the calling may have started with seeds that were planted years before, that later germinated and reached a point where it became crystal clear you needed a Savior. However, like Zacchaeus we also have a choice whether or not to accept His invitation. He could have easily said, Lord, I am not ready for You to come to my house. It is a mess, and I need to clean it up before You can come in. Jesus doesn't care what shape your house is in, accept His invitation today.

Prayer: God, I receive You as my Lord and Savior today.

> *Luke 19:40 But He answered and said to them, "I tell you that if these should keep silent, the stones would immediately cry out."*

What a great day this had to be. Jesus, riding a colt nears Jerusalem when the disciples and the crowds begin to line the road with palm branches and coats, shouting, "Blessed is the King who comes in the name of the Lord! Peace in heaven and glory in the highest!" Luke tells us they were praising God with a loud voice for all the mighty works they had seen. Naturally all this commotion got the attention of Pharisees who called out to Jesus, "Teacher, rebuke Your disciples," and tell them to be quiet. Jesus responds, "if these should keep silent, the stones would immediately cry out." This encouraged the crowds to cry out even louder; because, who would want to let a "rock cry out in their place?" All creation including mankind was created to praise God. Psalm 19:1-4, "The heavens declare the glory of God; And the skies proclaim the work of His hands. Day after day they pour forth speech; night after night they display knowledge. There is no speech or language where their voice is not heard. Their voice goes out into all the earth, their words to the ends of the world." We may not hear or understand their voices, but day after day all of creation is declaring His glory and giving Him praise. What about you? Are you praising God, or have you let the rocks take your place? David said in Psalm 34:1, "I will extol the Lord at all times; His praise will always be on my lips" No matter our circumstances, we can find reasons to praise Him. First, God commands that we praise Him. Psalm 150:6, "Let everything that has breath praise the Lord." Secondly, He desires our praise and inhabits them. Psalm 22:3, "But You are holy, Enthroned on the praises of Israel." Thirdly, our praise gives us direct access to the throne of God. Psalm 100:4, "Enter His gates with thanksgiving and His courts with praise; give thanks to Him and praise His name." Next, praise replaces our despair with hope and comfort from God. 2 Corinthians 1:3, "Praise be to the God and Father of our Lord Jesus Christ, the Father of compassion and the God of all comfort." Lastly, God is worthy of it. He sent His only Son to pay the penalty for our sin and give us eternal life with Him.

Prayer: God, I give You praise for all Your great works.

> Luke 19:46 Saying to them, "It is written, 'My house is a house of prayer,' but you have made it a 'den of thieves.'"

In Jesus' day, animal sacrifices were the primary form of worship and atonement for sins. During the celebration of Passover, people would travel for miles to Jerusalem to offer their annual sacrifice to the Lord. Because of the travel distance, many would wait until they reached Jerusalem to purchase an animal to sacrifice. Seizing the opportunity, the priests had set up a lucrative business in the temple courtyard of selling sheep and other animals to those who needed one. As someone entered the temple, the noise of people haggling over the price of bleating animals was overwhelming. The scene was total chaos. All this was taking place in an area of the temple that had been set aside for the Gentiles or non-Jews to come and worship. Essentially, worship in that part of the temple had been replaced with commercialism. Three years earlier, Jesus had entered the Temple and drove out the ones who were doing business with a whip of cords, telling them, "Get out of here! How dare you turn My Father's house into a market!" Today, Jesus returns to the Temple to find business as usual and becomes angry. He overturns tables and drives out those who were buying and selling, quoting scripture from Isaiah 56:7 and Jeremiah 7:11, saying, "My house is a house of prayer, but you have made it a den of thieves." If Jesus were to walk into your church on Sunday morning, what would He find? My hope is that He would find it a place of prayer and worship, not a social gathering for entertainment purposes. What attracted you to the church you attend? Was it the type of music they sing, your kid's friends attend there, an energetic service, or a charismatic leader? If so, you may have lost sight of what is most important. Sadly, worship becomes a production in many churches today. There is no doubt it attracts people to a church; however, is God there? Is His word being read and taught or is the sermon a motivational speech that makes you feel good? Church should lead you to an encounter with the truth of God's word. It should be a place where prayer and worship are prioritized. It should be a place where God is welcome. If your church doesn't have those qualities, find one that does.

Prayer: God, help me to find a place to worship where Your word is prioritized.

Luke 23:34 Then Jesus said, "Father, forgive them, for they do not know what they do."

Jesus is hanging on the cross, surrounded by two thieves and a mob of people making fun of Him when He utters this prayer, "Father, forgive them, for they do not know what they do." In their minds, they knew exactly what they were doing. In fact, they were pros at crucifying someone. Jesus has been beaten beyond recognition, had nails strategically driven in His hands and feet, His flesh torn open by a whip, yet He asked the Father to forgive them. There was no resentment, bitterness, or anger in His heart. He readily forgave all who were involved in His crucifixion. If it were me hanging on that cross, my prayer would likely have been, "Father get them," not, "Father forgive them." Although you and I were not there, Jesus' words on the cross were meant for us as well; because, it was for our sins that He hung upon that cross. Even if you live a near perfect life, that is still enough sin to make His sacrifice necessary. Thankfully, Jesus paid our penalty and remembers our transgressions no more. Isaiah 43:25, "I, even I, am He who blots out your transgressions, for My own sake, and remembers your sins no more." Once we receive God's grace and forgiveness, Jesus tells us we should forgive others. Matthew 6:14, "For if you forgive men when they sin against you, your heavenly Father will also forgive you." Ephesians 4:32, "Be kind and compassionate to one another, forgiving each other, just as in Christ God forgave you." Forgiveness heals and restores relationships, but most importantly it heals the person who forgives. Unforgiveness eats away at a person like cancer. Bitterness, thoughts of revenge, and anger begin to control your life. Unforgiveness affects your mental and physical health, causes you to lose sleep, hinders your relationship with God, and destroys your witness as a Christian. Nothing good comes from unforgiveness. I am not saying forgiveness is easy. It takes a lot of time and prayer to get beyond some offenses. In many cases, the offending person has moved on and clueless they even need to ask forgiveness, leaving you with a decision to forgive or not forgive. Decide today to forgive. Begin by taking small incremental steps of letting your resentment go. Each day, ask God to replace it with His love and mercy.

Prayer: God, help me to forgive as You forgave me.

> *Luke 23:43 And Jesus said to him, "Assuredly, I say to you, today you will be with Me in Paradise."*

Below Him, the soldiers are casting lots for His clothes and mocking Him. The religious leaders are shouting at Him, "He saved others; let Him save Himself if He is the Christ, the chosen of God." On either side of Him, hang two criminals condemned to death for their crimes. Luke 23:39 says, "Then one of the criminals who were hanged blasphemed Him, saying, 'If You are the Christ, save Yourself and us.'" Isaiah 53:3 and Psalm 22:7-8, come to life in this moment, "He was despised and rejected by men, a man of sorrows, and familiar with suffering. Like one from whom men hide their faces. He was despised, and we esteemed Him not." "All who see Me mock Me; they hurl insults, shaking their heads: He trusts on the Lord; let the Lord rescue Him. Let Him deliver Him since He delights in Him." Taking all this in, the other criminal speaks up saying in Luke 23:40-42, "But the other, answering, rebuked him, saying, 'Do you not even fear God, seeing you are under the same sentence? We are punished justly, for we are getting what our deeds deserve. But this Man has done nothing wrong.' Then he said, 'Jesus remember me when You come into Your kingdom.'" On one side of Jesus, you have a person who is defiant and cursing Jesus to his grave. On the other, one who acknowledges his guilt, knew he deserved to die, but reached out to Jesus for forgiveness. Can you imagine the joy in this man's heart when he hears the words, "Assuredly, I say to you, today you will be with Me in Paradise." He had no time to be baptized or to perform some good deed. He only had time to believe in Jesus. Ephesians 2:8-9, "For it is by grace you have been saved, through faith – and this not from yourselves, it is the gift of God – not by works, so that no one can boast." No matter how bad your sins may be, Jesus' promise to the thief hanging beside Him applies to anyone who has trusted Him as their Lord and Savior. What a joy to know that Heaven awaits all who believe in Him. We can rest assured of eternal life with Him and join our loved ones there one day.

Prayer: God, thank You for Your promise of salvation to all who trust in You.

> *Luke 24:17 And He said to them, "What kind of conversation is this that you have with one another as you walk and are sad?"*

It is human nature to put our hopes in a person, maybe a minister or elected official, to effect change for the good. I recall many Christians trusted Jim Bakker and the PTL Club in the 1970's and '80's, investing their money and believing in his ministry. The same with Jimmy Swaggart. Both men eventually had a moral failure and lost their ministries and the trust of a lot of people. Presidential elections are no different. People support a candidate who they believe will change our country for the good, only to be discouraged when things don't work out like they think it should. This is the attitude of two of Jesus' followers who were traveling back to Emmaus the Sunday morning Jesus arose. They were discussing the events of the weekend, when Jesus joins them on their journey and asks them what they are talking about. Luke 24:18, "Then the one whose name was Cleopas answered and said to Him, 'Are you the only stranger in Jerusalem, and have You not known the things which happened there in these days?'" They begin to explain that Jesus of Nazareth was a mighty Prophet who was condemned to die on a cross. He was to be the great redeemer of Israel who would deliver them from the oppression of the Romans. However, their hopes died on that cross with Jesus. Although they were present when the women reported that Jesus was not in the tomb earlier that morning and heard Peter and John tell the same story of their experience, they didn't understand Jesus' purpose here on earth. Jesus then begins to explain to them what was said about Him in the scriptures. As they neared Emmaus, Cleopas and his friend still have not recognized Jesus and invited the stranger to stay with them. Then as they sat down at their table to eat, Jesus broke bread and blessed it. It was at this moment their eyes were opened to know who He was. As soon as they recognized Jesus, He vanished from their sight. What are you looking for Jesus to be, simply your provider, healer, comforter? If so, you will easily become disillusioned like Cleopas and his friend. Jesus is so much more. Take time today to break the bread of life with Him and discover who He really is.

Prayer: God, open the eyes of my heart to who You are.

> Luke 24:38 And He said to them, "Why are you troubled? And why do doubts arise in your hearts?"

On their way home from Jerusalem to Emmaus, Jesus appeared to Cleopas and his friend. However, it was not until later when Jesus broke bread and blessed it with them, did they realize who He is. Then, just as soon as they recognized Him, Jesus vanished from their sight. But something was different now. They had seen and met Jesus, their risen Savior. Luke 24:32, "And they said to one another, 'Did not our heart burn within us while He talked with us on the road, and while He opened the scriptures to us?'" Do you remember that moment when Jesus was speaking to you and your heart was burning inside? The moment He revealed Himself to you and you accepted Him as your Lord and Savior? I still remember the excitement, joy, happiness, and even relief at that moment. I also remember wanting to share that experience with someone else. Cleopas and his friend had the same feelings. Luke 24:33-35, "So they rose up that very hour and returned to Jerusalem, and found the eleven and those who were with them gathered together, saying, 'The Lord is risen indeed, and has appeared to Simon!' And they told about the things that had happened on the road, and how He was known to them in the breaking of the bread." As they were sharing their story, Jesus appears in the midst of the group and says, "Peace to you." Jesus will always be there when you share your story about Him to others. He is there to give you boldness, the right words, and to speak peace over your life. However, the disciples thinking they had seen a ghost were terrified and in a state of confusion. This is very likely the same reaction the person you are sharing your story of salvation will have, especially if they have never heard the good news before. They are not ready to grasp the full understanding of the gospel. Luke 24:41 says, "But while they still did not believe for joy, and marveled..." The disciples felt great joy, but the truth had not yet created faith in their hearts. In the same way, the seed of truth you have planted must take root and grow. It is up to that person to accept it by faith. Be a seed planter, tell your story to others.

Prayer: God, help me to share the good news of Your salvation.

> Luke 24:46 Then He said to them, "Thus it is written, and thus it was necessary for the Christ to suffer and rise from the dead the third day."

Jesus' death and resurrection is one of the key foundations of our faith. It is what separates Christianity from any other religion in the world. Yet for some, it is a difficult concept to comprehend. Many people would prefer just to have a set of rules to follow. Give me a list of "do's and don'ts" and I will do my best to live according to them. Or, as some prefer today to create their own standards of right and wrong. But that is not Jesus' way. Christianity is about a relationship with a living God who was crucified, buried, and three days later rose from the grave. His death and resurrection should have been no surprise. On several occasions He told His disciples He would die and be raised on the third day. Matthew 16:21, "From that time on Jesus began to explain to His disciples that He must go to Jerusalem and suffer many things at the hands of the elders, chief priests and teachers of the law, and that He must be killed and on the third day be raised to life." There is no mistaking, that He rose from the dead. 1 Corinthians 15:6, "After that, He appeared to more than 500 of the brothers at the same time, most of whom are still living, though some have fallen asleep." It could be easy to fabricate a story between a few disciples that had seen the resurrected Jesus. However, it would be very difficult to refute the testimony of 500 people who saw Him at one time. Jesus' death and resurrection were written about, hundreds of years before it happened. The prophet Isaiah describes Jesus' crucifixion in great detail. Isaiah 53:5,7,11, "But He was pierced for our transgressions, He was crushed for our iniquities; the punishment that brought us peace was upon Him, and by His wounds we are healed. He was oppressed and afflicted, yet He did not open His mouth; He was led like a lamb to the slaughter, and as a sheep before her shearers is silent, so He did not open His mouth. After the suffering of His soul, He will see the light of life and be satisfied; by His knowledge my righteous servant will justify many, and He will bear their iniquities." Give Him praise today. We serve a risen Savior who suffered and died for our sins.

Prayer: God, thank You for Your death and resurrection.

John 1:38 *Then Jesus turned and seeing them following, said to them, "What do you seek?"*

John the Baptist and several of his disciples are together as Jesus was walking nearby. John points at Jesus and tells them, "Look, the Lamb of God." Intrigued, the two disciples start following Jesus. One of them happened to be Andrew, Simon Peter's brother and would soon introduce him to Jesus. Jesus notices the two following Him, and asks, "What do you seek?" Or, what are you looking for? Wanting to know more about Jesus, they answered, "Rabbi, where are You staying?" Jesus told them, "Come and see." From that encounter, Andrew was convinced that Jesus was the Messiah and became one of Jesus' 12 disciples and followed Him. It is interesting to note that not much else is written about Andrew in the Bible. He was the disciple who found the young boy who had five loaves and two fishes which led to the miracle of feeding the 5,000. However, Andrew was more comfortable being a behind the scenes type of person who faithfully served God his entire life. There will be a lot of Andrew's in heaven. Jesus is asking the same challenging question to you and I, "What are you looking for?" Why have you decided to follow Him? Are you seeking Him as Jehovah Jireh, the Provider just to fulfill your wish list of wants and needs? Or perhaps, you are seeking Him as Jehovah Rapha, a God who heals your sicknesses. Maybe you are looking for peace in your troubled life from Jehovah Shalom. In and of themselves, none of these are bad things to be following God for. But these should not be our main reasons for doing so. Like Andrew, we need to recognize Jesus as the Messiah, our Lord and Savior and want to serve Him. We should want to learn more about His word each day and follow it. We should want to share the good news of the Gospel to others. Following Jesus also means becoming a servant to others. It requires the sacrifice of our own desires and shifts them to a heavenly or eternal perspective. Things such as trusting God, walking in obedience with Him, and perseverance through trials become second nature to us. As 2 Corinthians 4:18 says, "So we fix our eyes not on what is seen, but on what is unseen. For what is seen is temporary, but what is unseen is eternal."

Prayer: God, help me to follow You each day.

> John 1:39 He said to them, "Come and see."

There are some things in life you just have to see for yourself; such was the case for Andrew and his friend. Jesus had just asked them, "What do you seek?" Perhaps wanting to have more than a casual conversation in the middle of the street, they replied, "Where are You staying?" Jesus, who has time for everyone told them, "Come and see." John writes that it was about the 10th hour of the day, or 4pm, two hours before sunset. John does not record their conversation, but it made an impact on Andrew's life. The same day he introduced his brother Peter to Jesus and began to follow Him from that day. A few verses later, we read where Jesus found Philip and said to him, "Follow Me." That is all it took for Philip to trust in Jesus. Right after that, we find Philip introducing Nathanael to Jesus. John 1:45-46, "Philip found Nathanael and said to him, 'We have found Him of whom Moses in the law, and also the prophets, wrote – Jesus of Nazareth, the son of Joseph. And Nathanael said to him, 'Can anything good come out of Nazareth?' Philip said to him, 'Come and see.'" Knowing Jesus as your Lord and Savior begins with an invitation to come and see who He is. In the case of Andrew, he was seeking the Savior and found Jesus. But it was the words of Jesus that convinced him that He was the Messiah. For Peter, it was the concern and witness shared by a family member that led him to Christ. Philip simply had a powerful encounter with Christ. Nathanael was led to Christ by the testimony of his friend Philip. How were you introduced to Jesus? More importantly, are you an Andrew or Philip, introducing Christ to others? Jesus is depending on those who already know Him to bring others to Him. Jesus wants everyone to have a chance to come and see just as Andrew and his friend. Matthew 11:28-29 assures us that Jesus will take great care of those who are introduced to Him, "Come to Me, all you who are weary and burdened, and I will give you rest. Take My yoke upon you and learn from Me, for I am gentle and humble in heart, and you will find rest for your souls. For My yoke is easy and My burden in light."

Prayer: God, help me to lead others to You.

> *John 1:42 And he brought him to Jesus. Now when Jesus looked at him, He said, "You are Simon the son of Jonah. You shall be called Cephas" (which is translated, A Stone).*

Andrew was excited. He had met Jesus and trusted Him as his Lord and Savior and could not keep the news to himself. He immediately introduces his brother Simon to Jesus. John 1:41-42, "He first found his own brother Simon, and said to him, 'We have found the Messiah' (which is translated, the Christ). And he brought him to Jesus." I remember when I received Jesus as Lord and Savior. It was impossible for me to keep the news to myself. I wanted to tell everyone about Jesus. But now, the challenge for me has been to keep that level of excitement and willingness to share Jesus with others. I know I should be telling others, but I have lost some of that boldness over the years. I continue to look for ways to rekindle that excitement I had when I was first saved. If you are feeling the same, ask God to rekindle the passion you first had when you were saved. 1 Timothy 1:6, "For God did not give us a spirit of timidity, but a spirit of power, of love and of self-discipline." Next, when Jesus and Simon meet, Jesus looks at Simon and changes his name to Cephas which means a stone. Peter is a hard-core fisherman who was strong-willed, out-spoken, and impulsive. Yet Jesus knows Peter's potential and the plans He has for him. God used this uneducated, ordinary, and reckless fisherman to become a leader of His disciples and bold preacher of the good news. God knows every detail about you. He also knows your potential and has a plan just for you. He can take a retired grandfather who had a difficult time writing a three-page report in school, and transform him to writing a 365-page devotional book. Better yet, He can take someone whose life is a complete mess and make something beautiful of it. Jesus is saying to you today, "I know what you are and the mess your life is in now; but I know what I can make your life to be! Trust me." 2 Corinthians 5:17, "Therefore, if anyone is in Christ, he is a new creation; the old has gone, the new has come." God has a wonderful plan for your life. Surrender your life to Him today and let Him use you.

Prayer: God, transform my life into something beautiful.

> John 1:50 Jesus answered and said to him, "Because I said to you, 'I saw you under the fig tree,' do you believe? You will see greater things than these."

In the movie series, "*The Chosen*," Nathanael's life was in ruins as he found himself sitting under a fig tree contemplating a disaster that had just taken place at a construction site he had designed. It makes for a great story, but the Bible doesn't tell us why Nathanael was under the tree. Most importantly, it is where Phillip found him, and brought him to Jesus. John 1:47, "Jesus saw Nathanael coming toward Him, and said of him, 'Behold, an Israelite indeed, in whom is no deceit.'" Nathanael is blown away by Jesus' comment and asks Him, "How do you know me?" Jesus replied in John 1:48, "...Before Phillip called you, when you were under the fig tree, I saw you." Nathanael answered Jesus in verse 49, "Rabbi, You are the Son of God! You are the King of Israel!" Jesus told Nathanael he would see greater things than these. Verse 51, "And He said to him, 'Most assuredly, I say to you, hereafter you shall see heaven open, and the angels of God ascending and descending upon the Son of Man.'" Have you ever wondered if God really cared about you and knew what you were going through? Nathanael's story should leave you no doubt. Jesus knew exactly where Nathanael was long before they met. More importantly, Jesus knew Nathanael's heart. By Nathanael asking Jesus, "How do you know me?", confirms Jesus' assessment of him. God created us and knows us both inside and out. Jeremiah 1:5, "Before I formed you in the womb, I knew you, before you were born I set you apart; I appointed you as a prophet to the nations." Psalm 139:1 also says, "O Lord, You have searched me and You know me." God knows our strengths and weaknesses, our character, our family history, our genetic makeup, and our going and coming. In spite of all this, God loves us and has a plan for our lives. He can use our past failures to turn our lives into something useful for Him. Serving Him is what we were created for. Is Jesus inviting you to come and see today? He wants to transform your life from bad to good, good to great, great to spectacular, and spectacular to miraculous. Just as Jesus promised Nathanael, come and see the greater things when we chose to truly follow Him.

Prayer: God, thank You for loving me in spite of knowing who I really am.

> John 2:4 Jesus said to her, "Woman, what does your concern have to do with Me? My hour has not yet come."

Jesus and His disciples were attending a wedding in the small town of Cana in Galilee. His mother Mary was also a guest at the wedding. At some point during the week-long wedding celebration, the wine began to run out. Not having enough wine for the entire celebration would have been a terrible embarrassment for the groom's family. Mary learns about the family's predicament and tells Jesus, "They have no wine," expecting Him to do something about it. Jesus is now 30 years old, but according to John, He has yet to begin His public ministry. In fact, He tells Mary, "My hour has not yet come." Although Jesus only has three short years to accomplish His mission on earth; He doesn't want to reveal Himself and His power sooner than God the Father intended. Jesus also takes this opportunity to begin separating Himself as simply being known as Mary's son. While it may sound rude, He asks Mary, "Woman, what does your concern have to do with Me?" The NIV Bible states it this way, "Dear woman, why do you involve Me?" In a kind way, He is telling Mary she has no right to determine the time or manner in which He reveals Himself to others. Jesus always does the right thing with the right motive. Unknown to those at the party except Mary, a couple of servants, and His disciples, Jesus turned six waterpots containing twenty to thirty gallons of water each into wine. John 2:9-10, "When the master of the feast had tasted the water that was made wine, and did not know where it came from (but the servants who had drawn the water knew), the master of the feast called the bridegroom. And he said to him, 'Every man at the beginning sets out the good wine, and when the guests have well drunk, then the inferior. You have kept the good wine until now.'" Isn't that what Jesus does for those who trust Him? Before we ask Him into our lives, we are a plain jar of water. But once we accept Him as Lord and Savior, He transforms us into the very best for His kingdom. 2 Corinthians 5:17, "Therefore, if anyone is in Christ, he is a new creation; the old has gone, the new has come!" Thank God today for His transforming power in your life.

Prayer: God, thank You for transforming me.

> John 3:3 *Jesus answered and said to him, "Most assuredly, I say to you, unless one is born again, he cannot see the kingdom of God."*

Jesus' teaching began to get the attention of the religious leaders of the day. Nicodemus, a leading Pharisee, came to Jesus one night and said to Him, "Rabbi, we know that You are a teacher come from God; for no one can do these signs that You do unless God is with him." Like many others, Nicodemus was curious, but unsure of who Jesus was. He seemed to be more focused on learning more about the person rather than His message, viewing Jesus simply as a teacher sent by God. Jesus bypasses the entire conversation by replying, "Unless one is born again, he cannot see the kingdom of God," which really confused Nicodemus and shattered a cornerstone of the Jewish faith. Basically, the Jews felt as God's chosen people, their racial identity by birth guaranteed them entry into heaven. They had the 10 Commandments to live by and a system of offering sacrifices to atone for their sins. They believed the Messiah's purpose for coming was to set up His kingdom on earth and putting them in charge. Essentially, Jesus was telling Nicodemus, your birth into a Jewish family isn't a guarantee of eternal life in heaven. Only by being born again, can a person receive eternal life. Nicodemus replied, "How can a man be born when he is old? Can he enter into his mother's womb and be born?" Jesus answered him in John 3:5-6, "Most assuredly, I say to you, unless one is born of water and of the spirit, he cannot enter the kingdom of God. That which is born of the flesh is flesh, and that which is born of the Spirit is spirit." Jesus' words apply to us as well. We were all born into sin with a sinful nature. This sinful nature separates us from God and eternal life with Him. To receive eternal life, we must die to our sinful nature and be reborn into the family of God allowing Him to transform our hearts to a desire for righteousness and holiness. 1 Peter 1:23, "For you have been born again, not of perishable seed, but of imperishable, through the living and enduring word of God." Being reborn also makes us a new person in Christ. 2 Corinthians 5:17, "Therefore, if anyone is in Christ, he is a new creation; the old has gone, the new has come!" Have you been reborn?

Prayer: God, thank You for making me a new creation.

> John 3:11 *Most assuredly, I say to you, "We speak what We know and testify to what We have seen, and you do not receive Our witness."*

Jesus and Nicodemus' conversation continues in John 3:7-11, "'You should not be surprised at My saying, you must be born again. The wind blows wherever it pleases. You can hear its sound, but you cannot tell where it comes from or where it is going. So it is with everyone born of the Spirit.' 'How can this be?' Nicodemus asked. 'You are Israel's teacher,' said Jesus, 'and you do not understand these things? We speak what We know and testify to what We have seen, and you do not receive Our witness.'" Nicodemus, the teacher, is getting schooled by Jesus in a good way. He is having a hard time understanding what Jesus is talking about, but keeps asking questions to better understand. In his defense, Nicodemus has not experienced the moving of the Holy Spirit in one's life. His beliefs have him following a long list of "do's and don'ts" to achieve a right relationship with God. Jesus came to replace that path to salvation. Being born again requires the repentance of our sins and putting our faith and trust in Jesus Christ. Titus 3:5, "He saved us, not because of righteous things we had done, but because of His mercy. He saved us through the washing of rebirth and renewal by the Holy Spirit." When we accept Jesus as Lord and Savior, the Holy Spirit moves into our heart and begins to transform us into a new person. Jesus compared the work of the Holy Spirit to the wind. We can't see the wind or where it comes from. We can only feel and see the effects of where it has been. Just like the wind, we can't see the Holy Spirit, but we can see the changed lives where it dwells. 1 Corinthians 2:12, "We have not received the spirit of the world but the Spirit of who is from God, that we may understand what God has freely given us." Most importantly, Jesus tells Nicodemus, I know what I am talking about. You can count on it. Jesus' words are for you today as well. What is the Holy Spirit speaking into your life right now? Like Nicodemus, you may be unsure of things and have more questions than answers. Listen to the Holy Spirit speaking to you. He knows the plans God has for you. Trust Him.

Prayer: God thank You for the Holy Spirit and His work in my life.

John 3:12 If I have told you earthly things and you do not believe, how will you believe if I tell you heavenly things?

The more I learn about following Jesus, the more I find out there is to know. Poor old Nicodemus was still struggling with the concept of being born again. Like many, he wanted to make it more difficult than God designed it. We want to add stipulations about cleaning up our lives and following the rules, before we can be saved. Paul makes it clear in Romans 10: 9-10 that salvation is simply confession and belief, "That if you confess with your mouth, 'Jesus is Lord,' and believe in your heart that God raised Him from the dead, you will be saved. For it is with your heart that you believe and are justified, and it is with your mouth that you confess and are saved." Jesus then asks Nicodemus, "How will you believe if I tell you heavenly things?" If Nicodemus can't grasp the basics of salvation and the privileges of the children of God here on earth, how in the world will he understand heavenly things like eternity, the Holy Spirit, and angels? A number of Christians find themselves caught up in this 'post salvation' stage. They know Jesus as their Lord and Savior, but have not grown in their faith. Paul describes it this way in 1 Corinthians 3: 1-3, "Brothers, I could not address you as spiritual but as worldly – mere infants in Christ. I gave you milk, not solid food, for you were not ready for it. Indeed, you are still not ready. You are still worldly. For since there is jealousy and quarreling among you, are you not worldly? Are you not acting like mere men?" How do we move past the 'post salvation' stage and get into the deeper things of Christ? The key is spiritual growth. 2 Peter 3:18, "But grow in the grace and knowledge of our Lord and Savior Jesus Christ. To Him be glory both now and forever! Amen." Peter also lays out the steps of spiritual growth in 2 Peter 1:5-8, "For this very reason, make every effort to add to your faith goodness; and to goodness, knowledge; and to knowledge, self-control; and to self-control, perseverance; and to perseverance, godliness; and to godliness, brotherly kindness; and to brotherly kindness; love. For if you possess these qualities in increasing measure, they will keep you from being ineffective and unproductive in your knowledge of our Lord Jesus Christ."

Prayer: God, help me to add to my faith each day.

> John 3:14 And as Moses lifted up the serpent in the wilderness, even so must the Son of Man be lifted up.

Why did Moses lift up a snake in the wilderness and how does this apply to Jesus? We find the story in Numbers 21: 4-9, "They traveled from Mount Hor along the route to the Red Sea, to go around Edom. But the people grew impatient on the way; they spoke against God and against Moses, and said, 'Why have you brought us up out of Egypt to die in the desert? There is no bread! There is no water! And we detest this miserable food!' Then the Lord sent venomous snakes among them; they bit the people and many Israelites died. The people came to Moses and said, 'We sinned when we spoke against the Lord and against you. Pray that the Lord will take the snakes away from us.' So Moses prayed for the people. The Lord said to Moses, 'Make a snake and put it up on a pole, anyone who is bitten can look at it and live.' So Moses made a bronze snake and put it up on a pole. Then when anyone was bitten by a snake and looked at the bronze snake, he lived." Because of their rebellion, God sent venomous snakes to punish the Israelites. They quickly realized their sin and asked for forgiveness. However, instead of sending the snakes away, God did something that would teach them another lesson about faith. They had to trust that God would do what He said. I can only imagine how the first person who had a viper hanging on to his leg felt when he looked up at the bronze snake. My reaction would be, I hope this really works. If not, I'm a goner. This image was kept for many years by the Israelites and is mentioned again in 2 Kings 18:4 when King Hezekiah had it destroyed because the people had begun to worship it. By mentioning this image, Jesus is foreshadowing His death. From the very beginning of time, the serpent has represented sin and rebellion. Jesus knew that He would take upon himself the sin and judgment of the world and be hung on a cross. 2 Corinthians 5:21, "God made Him who had no sin to be sin for us, so that in Him we might become the righteousness of God." Give Him thanks today for taking your sin to the cross.

Prayer: God, thank You for sending Your Son to pay the penalty for my sin.

> John 3:16 For God so loved the world that He gave His only begotten Son, that whoever believes in Him should not perish but have everlasting life.

Perhaps the most quoted, memorized, and loved verse in the Bible, John 3:16 is the core of our faith. It was the first Bible verse I ever learned. It has been shared in a number of ways. In the 1980's there was a man with a rainbow-colored wig who would show up at most every major sporting event and hold up a sign that read "John 3:16." Tim Tebow, a college and professional football player would have "John 3:16" written in his eye black so when the cameras focused in on him, the world would see it. Billy Graham would preach countless sermons from John 3:16. What is so special about John 3:16? It is the gospel, the good news, wrapped up in 25 powerful words. Let's dig deeper into the meaning of this verse. I have always thought that the phrase, "For God so loved the world," meant "God loved the world so much." This is not incorrect, but it also can mean, "God loved the world in this way," emphasizing what God did rather than why. 1 John 4:9-10, "This is how God showed His love among us: He sent His one and only Son into the world that we might live through Him. This is love: not that we loved God, but that He loved us, and sent His Son as an atoning sacrifice for our sins." We know that Jesus the Son, and Holy Spirit, have existed from the very beginning. So, when Jesus continues with "His only begotten Son," He is stating that He was not brought into existence at His birth in Bethlehem, but that He is and has been of the same nature as God the Father. John 1:1, "In the beginning was the Word, and the Word was with God, and the Word was God, He was with God in the beginning." Jesus concludes with a promise of eternal life for whoever believes in Him. *Mirriam-Webster* defines "whoever" as "whatever person, no matter who." What a great promise. No one has to perish. Anyone, no matter how troubled their life has been, no matter how far away from God they have traveled, can have eternal life. All that is required is that we believe in Him and that He died on a cross for our sins and raised on the third day.

Prayer: God, thank You for sending Your Son, so that I can have eternal life with You.

> John 3:17 For God did not send His Son into the world to condemn
> the world, but that the world through Him might be saved.

Early in the history of the world, God's heart was filled with pain because of the sin and depravity of mankind. Things had gotten so bad, God decided to destroy the world and everything in it except Noah and his family. Genesis 6: 5-8, "The Lord saw how great man's wickedness on the earth had become, and that every inclination of the thoughts of his heart was only evil all the time. The Lord was grieved that He had made man on the earth, and His heart was filled with pain. So the Lord said, 'I will wipe out mankind, whom I have created, from the face of the earth – men and animals, and creatures that move along the ground, and birds of the air – for I am grieved that I have made them. But Noah found favor in the eyes of the Lord.'" Noah, his sons and their wives began a fresh new start. However, there is only one problem, the flood did not change their sinful nature. Genesis 8:21, "The Lord smelled the pleasing aroma and said in His heart: 'Never again will I curse the ground because of man, even though every inclination of his heart is evil from childhood. And never again will I destroy all living creatures as I have done.'" This sinful nature has continued to be passed down from generation to generation. Sadly, people are no better than they were before the flood. The good news is that God honors His covenants. Instead of condemning the world and destroying it again, He sent His Son to save all who would trust in Him. It is His desire that all would be saved. 2 Peter 3:9, "The Lord is not slow in keeping His promise, as some understand slowness. He is patient with you, not wanting anyone to perish, but everyone to come to repentance." Salvation is for everyone through Christ. 1 Timothy 2:4, "Who wants all to be saved and to come to a knowledge of the truth." Sadly, many who have accepted Jesus as Lord and Savior are still living under condemnation. They view God as a God of wrath and judgment, waiting for them to make a mistake so He can punish them. Trust God at His word. He longs to save, forgive, and restore, not condemn.

Prayer: God, thank You for sending Your Son to save us, not condemn us.

> John 3:18 He who believes in Him is not condemned; but he who does not believe is condemned already, because he has not believed in the name of the only begotten Son of God.

According to Jesus, there are two types of people in the world, saved and condemned. *Dictionary.com* defines condemned as "sentenced to a particular punishment, especially death," and "officially declared unfit for use." Both of those definitions hold true for anyone who has not received Christ as their Savior. Without Christ we are condemned to death in hell for eternity. But also, while we are living, an unsaved person is unfit for use in His kingdom. His very purpose for coming to the earth was to save anyone who would believe in Him and transform them into someone who He can use for His Glory. However, those who do not believe are already condemned by their own choice. Because of Adam and Eve's disobedience in the Garden of Eden, everyone has been born with a sinful nature that separates us from God. Romans 3:23, "For all have sinned and fall short of the Glory of God." The penalty for our sin is death and separation from God. Romans 6:23, "For the wages of sin is death, but the gift of God is eternal life through Christ Jesus our Lord." No matter how hard we try, we can't work our way into heaven. In fact, any good works we do are overshadowed by the works of our sinful nature which leads to death. God loves us and knew we couldn't bridge the gap between our sinful nature and His holiness. So, He sent His only Son to pay the penalty for our sin. Romans 5:8, "But God demonstrated His own love for us in this: While we were still sinners, Christ died for us." However, God knows our hearts and that not everyone will believe in Him. Jeremiah 7:10, "I the Lord search the heart and examine the mind, to reward those according to their conduct, according to what their deeds deserve." King David, speaking to his son Solomon, gave him this advice in 1 Chronicles 28:9, "As for you, my son Solomon, know the God of your father, and serve Him with a whole heart and a willing mind; for the Lord searches all hearts, and understands every intent of the thoughts. If you seek Him, He will let you find Him, but if you forsake Him, He will reject you forever." What is in your heart? My prayer is that you are seeking Him each day.

Prayer: God, help me to be fit for Your kingdom work.

> John 3:19 And this is the condemnation, that the light has come into the world, and men loved darkness rather than light, because their deeds were evil.

Merriam-Webster.com defines light as, "Something that makes vision possible." Without light, there is total darkness. Perhaps the most vivid illustration of total darkness I have experienced, is when our family went to visit the Linville Caverns, near Marion, NC. The guide leads you to a room deep underground and then turns off all the lights. The darkness immediately surrounds you. After a few moments of complete darkness, the guide lights a small match and the darkness disappears. It was amazing to see how much light that one match provided. That is the way the world is without God, total darkness. What does darkness look like without God? Jesus said in Mark 7:21-22, "For from within, out of a person's heart, comes evil thoughts, sexual immorality, theft, murder, adultery, greed, malice, deceit, lewdness, envy, slander, arrogance and folly." Jesus said in John 8:12, "I am the light of the world." John 1:4-9 tells us, "In Him was life, and that life was the light of men. The light shines in the darkness, but the darkness had not understood it. There came a man who was sent from God; his name was John. He came as a witness to testify concerning the light, so that through Him everyone might believe. He himself was not the light; he came only as a witness to the light. The true light that gives light to everyone was coming into the world." The light of Christ reveals the truth and exposes what is hidden in our hearts. Sadly, many people prefer living in darkness rather than having their lives exposed by the light. Jesus said, they have condemned themselves by choosing to continue living in darkness. This is the answer to those who like to argue that how could a loving God send someone to hell. He doesn't. Everyone has a choice whether or not to admit they are a sinner, repent of their sins, and accept Jesus as Lord and Savior. However, the person who loves their life the way it is and hates the exposure the light of Christ shines on their lives, condemns themselves. John 12:25, "The person who loves their life will lose it, while the person who hates their life in this world will keep it for eternal life." God gives us a choice. Choose wisely.

Prayer: God, help me to love the Light who has come into the world to save us from condemnation.

> John 3:20 For everyone practicing evil hates the light and does not come to the light, lest his deeds should be exposed.

Jesus tells us there are some who hate the light and will reject Him as their Lord and Savior. Today we are going to dig deeper into several reasons why they do. The Bible tells us clearly in Acts 4:12, "Salvation is found in no one else, for there is no other name under heaven given to men by which we must be saved." It is His desire that all should be saved and come to a knowledge of Him. 1 Timothy 2:3-4, "This is good, and pleases God our Savior, who wants everyone to be saved and to come to a knowledge of the truth." However, God has given us the ability to make choices in life. He created us to have eternal fellowship with Him. Only those who truly love Him and choose to have a relationship with Him through His Son, Jesus Christ will do so. Some people reject Jesus because they don't think they need a savior. By their moral standards, they are a good person and their good deeds should be enough to get them to heaven. But God doesn't see us as righteous and holy because of a few good deeds. Isaiah 64:6, "All of us have become like one who is unclean, and all our righteousness acts are like filthy rags..." Others decide not to follow Jesus because of rejection from their family and friends. "What will my friends think?" "Will they still be my friend if I become a Christian?" Will my family disown me?" Peer pressure can be overwhelming and in someone's mind not worth it. We see an example of peer pressure in John 12:42, "Yet at the same time many even among the leaders believed in Him. But because of the Pharisees they would not confess their faith for fear they would be put out of the synagogue." Others are too busy chasing what the world has to offer. They enjoy the material things of life and have dedicated their lives to acquiring and holding on to them. A good example is the story of the rich young ruler found in Matthew 19:16-22. Lastly, others resist the pull of the Holy Spirit drawing them to faith in Jesus. Although convicted of their sins, they keep putting off that inner urge to surrender their life to Christ. Pray for those struggling with a decision to follow Christ.

Prayer: God, I pray that everyone would come to the light.

> *John 3:21 But he who does the truth comes to the light, that his deeds may be clearly seen, that they have been done in God.*

Yesterday, Jesus said those who practice evil hate the light and try to stay away from it so their deeds will not be exposed. It is very much like the persons who are breaking into parked cars in our area. They sneak around late at night while everyone is sleeping and plunder through unlocked cars looking for money and other valuables. They would never try something like that during the day when they could be seen. Jesus said, "but those who live by the truth, come to the light, so their deeds can be seen." Those who live by the truth are not ashamed of their actions. First, we need to understand what living by the truth means. In today's world, the truth for many is whatever they think it to be. Your truth may be different from what I consider to be true. Essentially, there is no standard for truth. Although many prefer to make up their own truth, Jesus said in John 14:6, "I am the way, the truth, and the life. No one comes to the Father except through Me." Jesus is the model for truth. His word is the truth and it sets the standard for us to live by. When we strive to follow His word and do things that please Him, we don't have to sneak around in the darkness. More importantly, He created us to do good works that He prepared before we were born. Ephesians 2:10, "For we are God's workmanship, created in Christ Jesus to do good works, which God prepared in advance for us to do." Paul writing to Timothy in 2 Timothy 2:15 said, "Do your best to present yourself to God as one approved, a workman who does not need to be ashamed and correctly handles the word of truth." According to Paul, our focus should be doing things that please God, rather than making people happy. It is important to understand that while we were created to do good works, they have nothing to do with our salvation. Ephesians 2:8-10, "For it is by grace you have been saved, through faith – and this not of yourselves, it is the gift of God – not by works, so that no one can boast." What kind of works are you doing? My prayer is that you are following God's plan for your life.

Prayer: God, help me to do good works in Your name.

> John 4:10 Jesus answered and said to her, "If you knew the gift of God, and who it is who says to you, 'Give me a drink.' You would have asked Him, and He would have given you living water."

Jesus on His way to Galilee, stopped in the city of Samaria. The story is found in John 4:5-8, "So He came to the City of Samaria which is called Sychar, near the plot of ground that Jacob gave his son Joseph. Now Jacob's well was there. Jesus therefore being weary from His journey, sat by the well. It was about noon. When a Samaritan woman came to draw water, Jesus said to her, 'Give Me a drink.' His disciples had gone into town to buy food." The woman replied to Jesus, "How is it that You, being a Jew, ask a drink from me, a Samaritan woman? For the Jews have no dealings with Samaritans?" Jesus has traveled a long distance and reached this particular well at the same time a Samaritan woman arrives to draw water. Jesus offers the woman living water which sparks a conversation that leads to her salvation and the salvation of many others in that city. This meeting was not accidental, but a divine appointment arranged by God. A divine appointment is a meeting with another person that God has unmistakably set up. The Holy Spirit arranges the encounter because someone needs what He can offer through you. They can happen at the most unlikely time and place. We just need to listen and follow the leading of the Holy Spirit. Vivian and I walk most every day in our neighborhood. One day as she and I were walking, we met two neighbors we had never seen before. One was a lady in her mid-80's whose husband was crippled because of a massive stroke. The other a widow with Parkinson's, who was looking after her 90-year-old mother. This chance meeting has led to a new friendship and a deeper walk with the Lord for her. It also led to her baptism which I was blessed to participate in. God arranges these chance meetings for us all the time. It is up to us whether or not we keep them. Sadly, we avoid some because they will push us out of our comfort zone or cost us time and money. Is there a divine appointment waiting for you today? Don't be afraid to follow that still, small voice, that says speak to that person. They are hungry for a touch from God. You have the privilege of being the one God choses to help someone. What a blessing.

Prayer: God, give me a divine appointment today.

> John 4:14 But whoever drinks of the water that I shall give him will never thirst. But the water that I shall give him will become in him a fountain of water springing up into everlasting life.

Jesus is a master at using earthly examples to explain heavenly things. He asked the Samaritan woman for a drink of water from Jacob's well, and wound up offering her living water. She still doesn't understand what Jesus is talking about and said in verses 11-12, "'Sir, You have nothing to draw with and the well is deep. Where can You get this living water? Are You greater than our father Jacob, who gave us this well and drank from it himself, as did also his sons and his flocks and herds?" Jesus tells her the water He is speaking about comes from Him and will become a fountain that continuously springs up within a person. Obviously, Jesus is not talking about a physical thirst, but a spiritual one that sends each one of us on a quest to find the true meaning of life. For this woman, her quest led her into a promiscuous lifestyle. For others, it could be seeking fame and fortune. Still, others get caught up in addictions that numb themselves and take them out of reality. We are all searching for something. Jesus said that those who drink of the water He gives, will never thirst again. Jesus is promising that He will give the Holy Spirit to those who trust Him, and the Spirit will fill their lives with the knowledge of the one true God. We will never thirst again for the meaning of life because we have been given eternal life in Him. Jesus said it this way in John 7:37-39, "...If anyone is thirsty, let him come to Me and drink. Whoever believes in Me, as the Scripture has said, streams of living water will flow from within him." Jesus offers this living water to anyone who is thirsty and longing to receive it. This water is free and satisfies your soul. Revelation 21:6-7, "And He said to me: 'It is done, I am the Alpha and Omega, the Beginning and the End. To him who is thirsty I will give to drink without cost from the spring of the water of life. He who overcomes will inherit all this, and I will be their God and they will be My child." The next time you hear someone say they are thirsty, tell them to try the living water Jesus offers and they will never thirst again.

Prayer: God, thank You for offering us Your living water.

> John 4:17-18 *The woman answered and said, "I have no husband." Jesus said to her, "You have well said, 'I have no husband,' for you have had five husbands, and the one whom you now have is not your husband; in that you spoke truly."*

The Samaritan woman asks Jesus for this living water He has told her about so she won't have to keep coming back to Jacob's well to draw water. Jesus tells her in verse 16, "Go, call your husband and come back." This opens up a "can of worms" for the woman, because she has been married five times and is currently living with another man. The surprise is that she did not have to tell Jesus her life history. He told it to her. More surprisingly, Jesus did not accuse her of wrongdoing or judge her behavior. However, in order for the Samaritan woman to find the secret of living water, she would have to involve the man she was living with and together come to Him. The lesson today is Jesus knows every little detail of our lives. There are no hidden sins, nothing He can't see. There have been moments in my life, I wished He was looking the other way. In fact, I would be embarrassed if anyone else knew about those moments. But Jesus knows each one of them. Thankfully, He loves the sinner, but hates the sin. Why? Because sin dishonors Him, grieves the Holy Spirit, and damages us. That is why we need a daily filling of the living water, the Holy Spirit, moving in our hearts and lives to keep us from sin. Ephesians 4:30-31, "And do not grieve the Holy Spirit of God, with whom you were sealed for the day of redemption. Get rid of all bitterness, rage and anger, brawling and slander, along with every kind of malice." For those who are not saved, God is compassionate and forgiving wanting them to come to a knowledge of Him. He is not judgmental or condemning. Numbers 14:18, "The Lord is slow to anger, abounding in love and forgiving sin and rebellion. Yet He does not leave the guilty unpunished..." For those who come to know Christ as Savior, there is no punishment or penalty to pay for our sins. Jesus has already paid the penalty for us. Instead, there is a celebration in heaven. Luke 15:7, "I tell you that in the same way there will be rejoicing in heaven over on sinner who repents than over ninety-nine righteous persons who do not need to repent." I am so thankful for a God who forgives our sins.

Prayer: God, thank You for loving me in spite of my shortcomings.

> John 4:23 But the hour is coming, and now is, when the true worshipers will worship the Father in spirit and truth; for the Father is seeking such to worship Him.

Having her life story told to her, the Samaritan woman recognizes that Jesus is no average person. Verse 19, "Sir, I can see that You are a prophet." She understands that only a prophet would be able to know that much about her. She then does what any normal person would do when their "dirty laundry" is being talked about. She tries to change the subject by having Jesus resolve an old spiritual argument between the Jews and the Samaritans. Verse 20, "Our fathers worshipped on this mountain, but you Jews claim the place where we must worship is in Jerusalem." This sounds pretty surprising coming from someone whose lifestyle doesn't demonstrate that she would be interested in worshipping God. She had filled the void in her life with promiscuity and a long list of failed relationships. People are no different today. Until a person is truly repentant and ready to turn their life over to Christ, they will make up all types of excuses of why they don't need God. Some will cast doubt about the validity of the Bible. Others will claim a loving God would not send anyone to hell. Still others play the comparison game where they think they are no worse than someone who goes to church. While others claim they are okay because they go to church. However, Jesus cuts through our smokescreen and gets to the heart of the matter. In answering the Samaritan woman's question, He tells her the place where someone worships is not important. The Jews worshipped in the Temple built by Solomon. There, in the Holy of Holies, sat the Ark of the Covenant which represented God's presence. Exodus 25:22, "There, above the cover between the two cherubim that are over the ark of the Testimony, I will meet with you and give you all My commands for the Israelites." The Samaritans believed that God's presence was on Mount Gerizim in Samaria, because that is where Abraham and Jacob had met with God and built altars there. Jesus told her, God is spirit, and those who worship Him, will now worship in spirit and truth. Worship is no longer wrapped up in rituals and location. Worship is all about the condition of our hearts and minds. Our excuses for not worshipping Him are just that, excuses.

Prayer: God, help me to be a true worshipper, one who worships in "Spirit and in Truth."

> John 4:24 *God is Spirit, and those who worship Him must worship in spirit and truth.*

The concept of worshipping God in spirit and truth is a major departure from the norm of that day. Jesus explains to the Samaritan woman that God is Spirit and not restricted to being in a single location, like the false gods others worship. He also repeats His comment from verse 23, "those who worship Him must worship in spirit and truth." Part of worshipping in spirit means the place of worship is no longer important. Today, we see believers worshipping God all over the world. However, worshipping God in spirit and truth is more than the freedom to worship God anywhere, anytime. Worship comes from a heart of love for God. Until we understand who God is, what He has done, and how much He loves us, it is difficult to worship Him. Moses wrote in Deuteronomy 6:5, "Love the Lord your God with all your heart and with all your soul and with all your strength." Jesus speaking to one of the teachers of the law in Mark 12:30 added one more component to loving God. He said, "Love the Lord your God with all your heart and with all your mind and with all your strength." This engages our entire being in worship. Left by itself, worshipping God in spirit sends you on an emotional roller coaster with its highs and lows. I have been in worship services where the presence of the Lord has been very powerful and real. You don't want to ever leave. Psalm 16:11 says, "You have made known to me the path of life; You will fill me with joy in Your presence, with eternal pleasures at Your right hand." To balance the emotional side of worship, Jesus said we must also worship in truth. He said in John 14:6, "I am the way, the truth and the life. No one comes to the Father except through Me." Talking to Pilate at His trial, Jesus also spoke about truth. John 18:37, "...In fact, for this reason I was born, and for this I came into the world, to testify to the truth. Everyone on the side of truth listens to Me." Real truth is our foundation for worship. It teaches us who God is. The more we get to know God, the deeper our passion for Him grows and deepens our worship of Him.

Prayer: God, thank You for the truth of Your word which deepens our worship of You.

> John 4:35 *Do you not say, "There are still four months and then comes the harvest?" Behold, I say to you, lift up your eyes and look at the fields, for they are already white for harvest!*

The disciples return from town and are surprised to see Jesus talking to the Samaritan woman because the Jews and Samaritans had little to do with each other. The woman, understanding who Jesus is, heads back into town full of excitement. She tells everyone, "Come, see a Man who told me everything I ever did. Could this be the Christ?" Her shame and embarrassment are now gone. Her sins have been forgiven and her guilt replaced with a boldness to share the good news with others. The people in town recognize something different in the woman and follow her to Jesus. Meanwhile, the disciples are urging Jesus to eat. Verse 32, "But He said to them, 'I have food to eat that you know nothing about.'" The disciples are wondering who could have brought Jesus some food. But He explains to them in verse 34, "My food is to do the will of Him who sent Me and to finish His work." About that same time, they look up and see an entire town coming towards them. The disciples recognize many of them because they had just bought food from them. However, Jesus looks and sees souls that are ripe for harvest. The disciples had missed it. They had an opportunity to share the good news about Jesus while they were in town, but did not. Before we come down too hard on the disciples, how many opportunities have we missed to share the good news about Jesus. Maybe we are afraid of offending someone or we do not know what to say. Or, maybe we are too wrapped up in our own lives and don't want to get involved in someone else's life. As Christians we are all called to share what Christ has done for us. Don't worry about what to say. God will equip you with the right words at the right time. Start by being kind to someone. Kindness goes a long way and will open doors for a deeper conversation about Jesus. Leave your spiritual persona at home and just be honest with them. People relate to honesty and can see through a facade. Lastly, have ordinary conversations with people that build up to sharing the gospel with them. Although it may take some time, God will do the rest. Don't miss out on your opportunity.

Prayer: God, help me to see the fields that are ready for harvest.

> John 4:36 *And he who reaps receives wages, and gathers fruit for eternal life, that both he who sows and he who reaps may rejoice together.*

Jesus is overjoyed with the response from the Samaritans and celebrates the harvest of souls brought into the Kingdom. He then introduces the concept of sowing and reaping and that the one who sows may not be the one who reaps. However, they both will share the reward of the souls brought into the Kingdom of God. Daniel describes someone who leads another to righteousness as a wise person and an all-star in God's Kingdom. Daniel 12:3, "Those who are wise will shine like the brightness of the heavens, and those who lead many to righteousness, like the stars for ever and ever." Jesus refers to the righteous as light that shines as bright as the sun. Matthew 13:43, "Then the righteous will shine like the sun in the kingdom of their Father." Those who sow, those who reap, and those who are saved will all rejoice together throughout eternity. One can only imagine what kind of celebration that will be. However, there is more. Jesus promises us wages or a reward for sowing and reaping. Paul writing in Thessalonians and Philippians defines this reward as a crown. 1 Thessalonians 2:19, "For what is our hope, our joy, or the crown in which we glory in the presence of our Lord Jesus when He comes? Is it not you?" Philippians 4:1, "Therefore my brothers, you whom I love and long for, my joy and crown, that is how you should stand firm in the Lord, dear friends." This crown is one of five crowns mentioned in the Bible and is known as the "Crown of Rejoicing." These crowns are imperishable, or will endure forever. They are awarded at the Judgment Seat of Christ where our service to Him will be judged. This judgment is not to determine whether one enters heaven or not, but to reward believers for their faithfulness. 1 Corinthians 3:10-15 explains this judgment as one where our service will be put to the test. Only the acts that withstand God's evaluation will be rewarded. 1 Corinthians 3:13, "His work will be shown for what it is, because the Day will bring it to light. It will be revealed with fire, and the fire will test quality of each man's work." My prayer is that whether you plant seeds or lead someone to Christ, your works are motivated by a love, and receive your crown.

Prayer: God, give me opportunities to earn the Crown of Rejoicing.

> John 4:37 For in this the saying is true: "One sows and another reaps."

Everyone has a role in the Kingdom of God. Some sow seeds while others reap. Neither is more important than the other and both need each other. Paul writes in 1 Corinthians 3:5-7, "What, after all, is Apollos? And what is Paul? Only servants, through whom you came to believe – as the Lord has assigned to each his task. I planted the seed, Apollos watered it, but God made it grow. So neither he who plants nor he who waters is anything, but only God, who makes things grow." As a Christian, sowing seeds of faith should be part of our daily routine. But, like a farmer who sows seeds there are different ways to go about it. In Jesus' day, farmers would take seeds and cast them out into a field. Today, farmers prepare the soil by plowing it up and making rows before planting. Like the method used by farmers in Jesus' day, casting seeds of our faith would include offering encouragement, being kind, and listening to someone. These types of seeds let people know you care about them and opens the door for you to share your faith with them at a later time. However, there are times when sowing seeds requires more effort and planning. Things such as inviting someone for coffee or a meal, sending a card, inviting and taking them to church, taking a meal to someone who is sick are just a few examples of ways to plant seeds. The list of possibilities is endless, but the point is we all need to do what we can to plant seeds for the Kingdom of God. Another key point is don't try to be someone you are not. My strengths are in helping someone, while Vivian is great at sending cards and reaching out to people. God has given you unique skills and abilities to use for His Kingdom. Take the time to discover what they are and start sowing seeds. While sowing seeds we should also be ready to lead someone to Christ. You never know when that person is ready to surrender their life to Him. Hosea 10:12 says, "I said, 'plant the good seeds of righteousness, and you will harvest a crop of love. Plow up the hard ground of your hearts, for now is the time to seek the Lord, that He may come and shower righteousness upon you.'"

Prayer: God, help me to sow seeds of faith.

> *John 4:48 Then Jesus said to him, "Unless you people see signs and wonders, you will by no means believe."*

I was in a church service recently where the pastor opened the service by allowing the congregation to ask questions they had about their faith and the Bible. One person asked, why do we not see the manifestation of the Holy Spirit in our worship services any longer? The pastor had a great four-word answer, "I do not know." He then followed up with when and how God choses to move is a mystery only known to Him. However, He is moving when someone comes to Christ. He is moving when our hearts are open to worship Him. It may not look exactly like we expect it to, but the Holy Spirit is still active and working in our church. In today's verse, Jesus is in Cana where He had recently turned water into wine. While He was there, a royal official who lived 16 miles away in Capernaum came to Jesus because his son was very sick. Verse 47 says, "...He went to Him and begged Him to come and heal his son, who was close to death." Jesus' response in our verse today was directed not only to the man, but to the many others who were following Him. John 6:2 tells us, "And a great crowd of people followed Him because they saw the miraculous signs He had performed on the sick." Many following Jesus were just thrill seekers. Verse 49, "The royal official said, 'Sir, come before my child dies.'" Jesus replies, "You may go. Your son will live." Jesus has set up a spiritual challenge for the man. Was he willing to trust Jesus without seeing proof? What would you do? Would you continue to beg Jesus to come and lay hands on your son or trust Him enough to head back home? Verse 50-53 tells us, "The man took Jesus at His word and departed. While he was still on his way, his servants met him with the news that his boy was living. When he inquired as to the time when his son got better, they said to him, 'The fever left him yesterday at the seventh hour.' Then the father realized that this was the exact time at which Jesus had said to him, 'Your son will live.' So he and all his household believed." Trust God even when you don't see the evidence of it yet.

Prayer: God, help me to trust You at Your word.

> John 5:24 *Most assuredly, I say to you, "he who hears My word and believes in Him who sent Me has everlasting life, and shall not come into judgement, but has passed from death into life."*

Jesus is speaking to the Pharisees who were furious at Him for healing a crippled man on the Sabbath, and saying God was His Father, making Him equal with God. Jesus defends His actions by telling them He can't do anything on His own initiative, but only what He sees the Father do. Jesus then speaks about avoiding judgement, receiving eternal life, and passing from death to life. Let's start with eternal life. Jesus said, "Anyone who hears My word and believes in Him who sent Me has everlasting life." Eternal life begins the moment you accept Jesus as your Lord and Savior. 1 John 5:11, "And this is the testimony: God has given us eternal life, and this life is in His Son. In John 10:10, Jesus calls our life in Him the abundant life; a life filled with purpose, hope, and love. Paul writes in 1 Corinthians 13:13, "And now these three remain: faith, hope and love. But the greatest of these is love." Why is love so important? 1 John 3:14, "We know that we have passed from death to life, because we love our brothers. Anyone who does not love remains in death." When we move from death to life, we become people who love. John 13:35, "By this all will know that you are My disciples, if you have love for one another." In contrast, eternal death awaits those who remain in their sin and disobedience. Daniel 12:2, "Multitudes who sleep in the dust of the earth will awake; some to everlasting life, others to shame and everlasting contempt." We were all facing eternal death, until Jesus came to show us the way to eternal life. Sadly, judgment day is coming for those who have not accepted Christ as their Lord and Savior. Revelation 20:11-15 speaks about this judgment day for the unsaved. This is a judgment on the evil works of the unsaved, including the rejection of Christ. Their fate is found in Revelation 20:15, "If anyone's name was not found in the Book of Life, they were thrown into the lake of fire." But, perhaps the greatest punishment of eternal death is separation from God. 2 Thessalonians 1:9, "They will be punished with everlasting destruction and shut out from the presence of the Lord and from the majesty of His power." Eternal life or death? Your choice.

Prayer: God, thank You for Your gift of eternal life.

> John 5:25 Most assuredly, I say to you, "the hour is coming, and now is, when the dead will hear the voice of the Son of God; and those who hear will live."

There are several ways of interpreting what Jesus is saying today. Jesus said, "the hour has come when the dead will hear the voice of the Son of God." In other words, the time is now and anyone who responds to His voice will have eternal life. We learned yesterday, that we are all dead in our sins. However, those who hear and respond to the voice of God calling them to salvation will receive eternal life. But Jesus also included this statement, "the hour is coming." Jesus explains further in John 5:28-29, "Do not be amazed at this, for a time is coming when all who are in their graves will hear His voice and come out – those who have done good will rise to live, and those who have done evil will rise to be condemned." This is what we read about in Daniel 12:2, and Paul writes about in Acts 24:15, "And I have the same hope in God as these men, that there will be a resurrection of both the righteous and the wicked." Everyone, without exception will be raised from the dead by Jesus. That should give the believer great hope, and fear to the unbeliever. With this resurrection, everyone who was ever born will be given a new resurrected body suited for eternity. Paul writes about our resurrected bodies in 1 Corinthians 15:35-58. He tells us we will receive our resurrected bodies at the return of Jesus. Our bodies will go from perishable to imperishable. We will never again experience death. 1 Corinthians 15:54-57, "When the perishable had been clothed with the imperishable, and the mortal with immortality, then the saying that is written will come true: 'Death has been swallowed up in victory.' 'Where, O death, is your victory? Where, O death is your sting?' The sting of death is sin, and the power of sin is the law. But thanks be to God! He gives us the victory through our Lord Jesus Christ." Christ has conquered the grave and offers us eternal life with Him. The important question for you and I is "where will our resurrected bodies spend eternity?" Will it be with Him in heaven or experiencing eternal punishment in hell? My prayer today is that you will rise to eternal life with Christ our Savior.

Prayer: God, help me to make the right choice.

> *John 5:36 But I have a greater witness than John's; for the works which the Father has given Me to finish—the very works that I do – bear witness of Me, that the Father has sent Me.*

How do we know that Jesus is the Son of God, the Messiah, the way to eternal life? Jesus presents irrefutable evidence in John 5:31-40. Following the Jewish law that required the testimony of two or three witnesses to establish any fact, He provides three pieces of evidence. Deuteronomy 19:15, "One witness is not enough to convict a person accused of any crime or offense he may have committed. A matter must be established by the testimony of two to three witnesses." The first piece of evidence Jesus mentions is John the Baptist, who preached repentance and the coming of the Messiah. Mark 1:7, "After me will come one more powerful than I, the thongs of whose sandals I am not worthy to stoop down and untie." Isaiah had prophesied about John the Baptist and his purpose in Isaiah 40:3, "A voice of one calling: 'In the desert prepare the way for the Lord; make straight in the wilderness a highway for our God.'" No one could deny John the Baptist's message and powerful ministry because of the many who repented and were baptized by him. Yet Jesus said, He had a "greater witness than John;" look at My works, the miracles I have done. When John the Baptist was in prison and having doubts about Jesus, he (John the Baptist) sent his disciples to ask Jesus if He was the Messiah. Jesus' reply found in Matthew 11:5 is not only for John the Baptist, but for us as well. "The blind receive sight, the lame walk, those who have leprosy are cured, the deaf hear, the dead are raised, and the good news is preached to the poor." These works were given to Jesus by the Father to do and bear witness that the Father had sent Him. Lastly, Jesus points out that the scriptures testify about Him. John 5:39, "You diligently study the Scriptures because you think that by them you possess eternal life. These are the Scriptures that testify about Me." Conservatively, there are over 300 prophesies in the Old Testament that Jesus fulfilled. Yet with all this evidence, the religious leaders refused to come to Jesus. John 5:40, "Yet you refuse to come to Me to have life." Are you still trying to decide that Jesus is the way to salvation and eternal life? The evidence is overwhelming.

Prayer: God, thank You for making it clear You are the way to eternal life.

> John 5:46-47 For if you believed Moses, you would believe Me; for he wrote about Me. But if you do not believe his writings, how will you believe My words?

To the Jews, Moses was "The Man." He wrote the first five books of the Bible, led the children of Israel out of slavery from Egypt, met face to face with God, and inscribed the Ten Commandments on stone tablets. God performed many miracles through Moses. The religious leaders had dedicated their lives to studying the scriptures and committing themselves to following every aspect of the law written by Moses. They were experts in knowing the scriptures, but didn't believe in what they had learned. Jesus tells the religious leaders, "If you believed what Moses wrote, you would believe Me; because he wrote about Me." You may be thinking, where does the Old Testament mention the name of Jesus. It doesn't but it describes His life and purpose through prophesy and imagery. A good example is the deliverance of the Israelites from slavery. The Israelites had been in bondage for over 400 years in Egypt. Moses approached Pharoah a number of times asking him to let the Israelites go. Pharoah refused even though God had sent nine plagues on the people of Egypt. However, the tenth and final plague was to unleash God's judgment by killing every first born not covered by the blood of the sacrificial lamb. It was the sacrifice of a lamb without blemish that freed them from their bondage of slavery. For the Passover Celebration, each family was to take a lamb, without defect, and put its blood on the sides and tops of their doorframe. They were also instructed not to break the bones of the lamb. When the angel of death saw the blood on the doorframe, it passed over that house sparing the first born inside. Those not covered by the blood of the lamb were killed by the Angel of Death. You and I are the Israelites living in bondage to sin. There is no escaping the Day of Judgment to come. However, Jesus, the sacrificial lamb, perfect, without blemish, was sacrificed on the cross to pay the penalty for our sins. His blood covers our sins and gives us eternal life with Him. Just as the blood of the sacrificial lamb spared the children of Israel, the blood of the Lamb of God spares you and I. The story of the Passover is found in Exodus 12. Take time to read about God's deliverance.

Prayer: God, thank You for the sacrifice of Your Son, Jesus, who paid the penalty for my sin.

> *John 6:32-33 Then Jesus said to them, "Most assuredly, I say to you, Moses did not give you the bread from heaven, but My Father gives you true bread from heaven. For the bread of God is He who comes down from heaven and gives life to the world."*

Just the day before, Jesus fed the five thousand with five loaves of bread and two fish. Many of them began to follow Him because He fed them bread in the wilderness. Jesus told those who had started following him in John 6:26, "Most assuredly, I say to you, you seek Me, not because you saw the signs, but because you ate of the loaves and were filled." Jesus saw through their motives. They wanted to fill their earthly desires, not their spiritual hunger. Even so, they continued by pressing Jesus to give them a sign, asking Him, "Moses gave our forefathers manna in the desert to eat, what other miracle will You perform for us to see and believe?" In other words, what big miracle are You going to do for us so that we will believe You are who You say You are? People are no different today. Many seek God for what He can do for them, rather than for who He is. They are seeking the gift, not the Giver. The true test of one's reason for following God is revealed when life's trials come along. How does a person react when a financial hardship, health problems, or attack by the evil one occurs? Do they trust Him regardless of their circumstances or do they give up on God? Still others seek God for the emotional experience. They tend to base their spiritual condition on their feelings. I admit, it is wonderful when God shows up at a worship service and the presence of the Holy Spirit is moving in the room. However, this emotional experience is a temporary high that shortly wears off. Those who seek God just for the emotional experience are on a spiritual roller coaster, with its highs and lows, and no spiritual growth. Following Christ requires our complete faith and trust Him. It also requires spiritual growth and not just signs and gifts. Jesus told those who were looking for signs and gifts, "Moses didn't give you the bread from heaven, but My Father gives you true bread from heaven." The gift of bread that God gave through Moses satisfied their hunger for a few hours; however, the bread Jesus offers satisfies our hungry souls for eternity. Which bread are you seeking, the bread from heaven that satisfies forever, or the bread of signs and gifts?

Prayer: God, thank You for the bread from heaven.

> John 6:35 And Jesus said to them, "I am the bread of life. He who comes to Me shall never hunger, and he who believes in Me shall never thirst."

Jesus told the thrill seekers who were following Him, "My Father gives you true bread from heaven. For the bread of God is He who comes down from heaven and gives life to the world." They replied in verse 34, "Lord, give us this bread always." Their only reference to the bread and water God supplies is the manna and water provided during the Israelites 40-year journey through the wilderness. Each morning manna would appear like dew on the ground. The people would gather as much as they needed to fulfill their needs for one day. When water was needed, Moses would strike a rock, and God would send it gushing out. God's provision sustained them for that day, but the very next day, they were hungry and thirsty all over again. The people following Jesus wanted a taste of the bread sent from God thinking it would nourish their physical bodies. Shifting the conversation from physical food to spiritual, Jesus declares, "I am that bread, the bread of life." I am what nourishes your soul, who satisfies your cravings, who strengthens you. Anything else in life will leave you wanting for more. They may satisfy your longings for a moment, but will not last. That hunger in your soul will send you searching deeper and deeper into all the wrong places. Jesus has promised us something that can satisfy our deepest needs by simply coming to Him. However, coming to Him means more than just believing in Him. James 2:19, "You believe that there is one God. Good! Even the demons believe that – and shudder." Believing in Jesus is more than head knowledge. It requires a change of heart. He becomes the center of our lives. We trust Him, have a relationship with Him, spend time with Him and listen to Him. We stop chasing after the things of the world we thought made us happy. We stop listening to the world that is telling us pleasure and power are the keys to happiness. Even for Christians, these voices can get in our heads and occasionally steer us off course. We must keep our eyes on what is most important. Jesus said in Matthew 24:35, "Heaven and earth will pass away, but My words will never pass away." Stay in God's word and daily eat from the bread of life.

Prayer: God, help me to come to You each day for Your bread of life.

> John 6:38 *For I have come down from heaven, not to do My own will, but the will of Him who sent Me.*

Jesus continues to share with the crowd who He is, where He is from, and His purpose for being here. He plainly tells them He has come from heaven to do the will of God who sent Him. From the people's perspective, this man Jesus is either crazy or very bold to put Himself on the same level as God. The Pharisees called it blasphemy, having a total disrespect of God, and later arrested Jesus for it. Doing the will of God was not easy for Jesus. As a fully human person, He had to overcome the daily temptations and emotions you and I experience. He faced rejection and ridicule. He was falsely accused, arrested, beaten beyond recognition, and crucified on a Roman cross. Knowing all this, He still came to do the will of God by bringing redemption to a lost and dying world. John 3:17, "For God did not send His Son into the world to condemn the world, but to save the world through Him." Just as God had a plan for Jesus' life, He has one for you and I. Jeremiah 29:11, "'For I know the plans I have for you,' declares the Lord, 'plans to prosper you and not harm you, plans to give you hope and a future.'" It is wonderful to know that the God of the universe has a plan and purpose for my life. But knowing God has a plan and living out that plan are two different things. All too often, we want to do our own thing. Being a Christian doesn't make us immune to yielding to our selfish nature. Our selfish nature loves to take over and life becomes all about me. Romans 7:15, "I do not understand what I do. For what I want to do I do not do, but what I hate to do." How do we overcome that inner battle and live a life that pleases God? First, ask God to show you the areas in your life where He is not welcome. Ask Him to reveal your selfish thoughts and motivations. Most importantly, be willing to change and turn those areas over to Him. Ask Him to fulfill His purpose in your life. Psalm 138:8, "The Lord will fulfill His purpose for me; Your love, O Lord, endures forever – do not abandon the works of Your hand."

Prayer: God, help me to seek and do Your will for my life.

> John 6:39 *This is the will of the Father who sent Me, that of all He has given Me I should lose nothing, but should raise it up at the last day.*

Jesus continues to share more about the will of the Father who sent Him. In verse 37 Jesus uses the phrase, "all that He (The Father) has given Me." This phrase is also found in Jesus' prayer for all believers in John 17:24, "Father, I want those You have given Me to be with Me where I am, and to see My glory, the glory You have given Me because You loved Me before the creation of the world." We know John 17:24 is about all believers because Jesus began His prayer with, "I do not pray for these alone (the 12), but also for those who will believe in Me through their word." A few verses later in John 18:9, Jesus declared during His arrest, "This happened so that the words He had spoken would be fulfilled: 'I have not lost one of those You gave Me.'" In John 18:9, Jesus is referring to the twelve disciples He had chosen to follow Him, minus Judas who betrayed Him. So, who is Jesus speaking about in today's verse and why is it important? If He is simply speaking about the disciples, then Jesus' words in John 6:39 were fulfilled upon His arrest and crucifixion. The disciples stayed together and soon after became the driving force behind the spreading of the gospel. However, if Jesus is speaking about all believers, then no believer would ever be lost, and all would be raised on the last day. This makes a very convincing argument for "once saved, always saved." However, Jesus does say in Matthew 7:21-23, not everyone who calls Me, Lord, Lord shall enter the kingdom of heaven. This is a subject you should research and talk about with your pastor. However, whether Jesus is only talking about the disciples or all believers to come, there is hope in this verse. God loves you and me. It was His will that sent Jesus to the cross to save us from the eternal punishment we deserve. Just as Jesus was raised from the dead, those who are dead in their sins have the assurance of a new life in Him. We are also assured that no one who truly comes to Christ will be lost.

Prayer: God, thank You for keeping Your promise of a new life in Christ.

> John 6:40 And this is the will of Him who sent Me, that everyone who sees the Son and believes in Him may have everlasting life; and I will raise him up on the last day.

Often times our concept of God is one of a supreme being that is waiting and watching for us to mess up so He can punish us. However, God is not about the business of trying to right every wrong and zap us for making a mistake. Jesus tells us the will of God is just the opposite. It is God's will that we would receive eternal life through Christ and be with Him for eternity. God knew before He created Adam and Eve, they would choose to disobey Him and eat from the fruit of the tree of the knowledge. Through their disobedience, everyone has been born with a sinful nature separating us from God. However, God already had a plan to send His Son, Jesus, to be the sacrificial lamb. He would take upon Himself the sins of the world and die on the cross, resurrecting to eternal life with the Father. Paying the penalty for our sins, Jesus becomes the bridge between God and us. He said, "anyone who sees the Son and believes in Him may have everlasting life; and I will raise him up on the last day." Jesus shares the same promise He gave in John 3:16, "...that whoever believes in Him shall not perish but have eternal life." What is a promise? It is a commitment by someone to either do or not do something. The thing about promises is that some are kept and some are not. Promises are made with good intentions, but quite often circumstances change and our promises are forgotten. Our pastor made a comment last Sunday about the promises of God that I had never really considered. He said, "God cannot break a promise." Simply stated, it is impossible for God not to keep His promises. No matter the circumstances, God keeps His promises. Even better, He doesn't forget them and passes them from generation to generation. Deuteronomy 7:9, "Know therefore that the Lord your God is God; He is the faithful God, keeping His covenant of love to a thousand generations of those who love Him and keep His commands." Have you seen who Jesus is and believed in Him as your Lord and Savior? This is God's will for you. He wants you to be raised to life and spend eternity with Him. If you have taken this step, pass it to the next generation.

Prayer: God, thank You for always keeping Your promises.

> *John 6:47 Most assuredly, I say to you, "he who believes in Me has everlasting life."*

Everything Jesus has spoken about in John 6 regarding the Bread of Life and Him being the path to eternal life was set up by the feeding of the 5,000 with the five loaves and two fish. Was the feeding of the 5,000 just a good opportunity for Jesus to take advantage of and use as a teaching moment, or was the feeding something planned long before it ever happened? As believers, we know nothing is a surprise to God. Paul writing in 1 Corinthians 2:7, "No, we speak of God's secret wisdom, a wisdom that has been hidden and that God destined for our glory before time began." Peter speaking in Acts 2:23, "This Man (Jesus) was handed over to you by God's set purpose and foreknowledge; and you, with the help of wicked men, put Him to death by nailing Him to the cross." The feeding of the 5,000 and the entire conversation in John 6 has led to this point where Jesus plainly and emphatically tells them, "He who believes in Me has everlasting life," and verse 48, "I am the bread of life." The people complained, saying, "Is this not Jesus, the son of Joseph, whose father and mother we know? How can He now say, 'I have come down from heaven.'" They only recognized Jesus as Mary and Joseph's son, expecting the Messiah to be someone great and powerful who would defeat their earthly enemies. The very key to salvation was their stumbling block. Some 2,000+ years later and Jesus is still a stumbling block to some and a cornerstone of their faith to others. 1 Peter 2:7-8, "Now to you who believe, this stone is precious. But to those who do not believe, 'The stone the builders rejected has become the capstone,' and, 'A stone that causes some to stumble and a rock that makes them fall.' They stumble because they disobey the message – which is also what they were destined for." In other words, those who understand and believe in Jesus as the way to salvation have the hope of eternal life with Him. However, those who willfully reject Him are saying, I have the ultimate power and say over my life. I am choosing my own destiny and it doesn't include Jesus. Jesus said, "Trust Me, I am the One who offers eternal life."

Prayer: God, thank You for being the cornerstone of my faith.

> John 6:61 When Jesus knew in Himself that His disciples complained about this, He said to them, "Does this offend you?"

Some who had started following Jesus found His teaching hard to understand and completely opposite of what they had been taught all their lives in the synagogue. Talking among themselves, they said, "This is a hard saying; who can accept it?" The Bible tells us, to understand spiritual things, you must be led by the Spirit of God. 1 Corinthians 2:14, "The person without the Spirit does not accept the things that come from the Spirit of God, for they are foolishness to them, and they cannot discern them, because they are spiritually discerned." Jesus' teaching was getting too uncomfortable for them and they were ready to bail out. Their motto was, "When the going gets tough, it is time to go." People are no different today. Many who hear the Word of God don't understand it and think it is foolishness; while others get it and the Word transforms their lives. What is the difference? It comes down to how we react to and treat the Holy Spirit working in our lives. Some choose to ignore the Holy Spirit working through their conscience and suppress any knowledge of God. They continue to push back and ignore long enough until God gives them over to their own depravity. Others quench the Spirit by trying to silence what God is saying to them. They fill their lives with noise and the busyness of life to where they cannot hear God. Still others hear God speaking to them and know what they should do, but resist God in some area of their lives. Today's verse makes it very clear that Jesus knows our thoughts and the condition of our hearts. Nothing is hidden from Him. What is the condition of your heart? Are you offended by the Word of God preached every Sunday morning, leaving church mumbling and complaining? Be careful what you say, God hears it as well. Perhaps God is trying to teach you something that will cause you to grow deeper in your faith. Unless we open our hearts and minds to the leading of the Holy Spirit, we will never grow. Remove any pride that may be holding you back from receiving His Word. Allow the Holy Spirit to speak to you and lead you into a deeper relationship with God. It is time to grow, not go.

Prayer: God, help me to grow deeper in my faith with You.

> John 6:64 *"But there are some of you who do not believe." For Jesus knew from the beginning who they were who did not believe, and who would betray Him.*

Jesus' teaching continues to get more complicated. John tells us, "Jesus knew from the beginning which of them did not believe and who would betray Him." God is omniscient, knowing every detail about everyone. He knows what is going to happen before it happens. He knows our very thoughts before we speak them. Psalm 139:4, "Before a word is on my tongue You know it completely, O Lord." This raises a big question. Since God is all knowing, why would He allow those who were unsaved follow Him as disciples, especially Judas who would later betray Him? The answer lies in Jesus' mission found in Luke 19:10, "For the Son of Man came to seek and to save what was lost." As long as Judas and the others were listening to Jesus' teaching day after day, He could seek them and show them how much He loved them. Although some will choose not to follow Jesus, it is His desire that none should perish. 2 Peter 3:9, "The Lord is not slow in keeping His promise, as some understand slowness. He is patient with you, not wanting anyone to perish, but everyone to come to repentance." Then Jesus said in verse 65, "This is why I told you that no one can come to Me unless the Father has enabled him." Coming to Christ for salvation is not something we can accomplish on our own. Jeremiah 31:3 says it this way, "The Lord appeared to us in the past, saying: 'I have loved you with an everlasting love; I have drawn you with loving-kindness.'" We are drawn by the Holy Spirit to receive Jesus as our Lord and Savior. He is that still small voice that speaks to our conscience, saying Jesus is the answer. I believe the Holy Spirit speaks to everyone at some point in their lives. He may speak to someone for years and others just a few days. However, the longer we resist, the fainter the Holy Spirit's call is upon our lives. Judas resisted God's intense drawing for three years sitting under Jesus' teaching and betrayed Him. Like Judas, attending church and listening to preaching doesn't mean we are saved. However, it could be part of the work of the Holy Spirit in drawing us to Christ. Have you responded to the Holy Spirit's call in your life?

Prayer: God, thank You for sending Your Holy Spirit to draw us to Christ.

> *John 6:66-67 From that time many of His disciples went back and walked with Him no more. Then Jesus said to the twelve, "Do you also want to go away?"*

John 1:14 describes Jesus as one who was, "...full of grace and truth." Sadly, many of those who had started to follow Jesus couldn't accept the truth of His words and walked away. Jesus turns and asks the twelve disciples, His closest companions, "Do you also want to go away?" Peter speaking for the group answered Jesus in verse 68, "Lord, to whom shall we go? You have the words of eternal life. We believe and know that You are the Holy One of God." Peter's response is the same as anyone who comes to Christ in faith, accepting Him as their Lord and Savior. He didn't have all the answers, but Jesus' words had spoken to his heart. He understood enough to know that Jesus was the Son of God and He offered eternal life. The first step to salvation is hearing the Word of God. Paul writing in Romans 10:17 said, "So then faith comes by hearing, and hearing by the Word of God." Many had heard Jesus and witnessed the miracles He had done. It wasn't too difficult for them to understand, but it was much too difficult for them to accept. How many people hear the Word of God today, but walk away because it is too difficult to accept? Sadly, when faced with a choice of what they like and what is truth, the tendency is to hold on to the things we like. Taking the step of faith to follow Jesus requires changes in our lifestyle and can push us out of our comfort zone. Many are fearful and walk away. Some who hear the Word of God can identify with Peter when he said, "To whom shall we go? You have the words of eternal life." They have tried everything in the search for the meaning of life. Just as Solomon wrote in Ecclesiastes 1:2, they had given up and said, "meaningless, everything is meaningless," until the Words of Jesus speaks to their heart. They accept by faith a new life in Christ where they find true meaning. Where are you in your walk with Christ? Perhaps the daily challenges of life have caused you to walk away as many did when Jesus' teaching got hard. Can I tell you, there is nowhere else to go. Jesus words offer not only an abundant life, but an eternal life with Him.

Prayer: God, to whom else shall we go?

> John 7:18 *He who speaks from himself seeks his own glory; but He who seeks the glory of the One who sent Him is true, and no unrighteousness is in Him.*

The people began to question where Jesus obtained His vast knowledge about scripture and the kingdom of God. Verses 15-16, "The Jews were amazed and asked, 'How did this Man get such learning without having studied?'" Jesus tells them, 'My teaching is not My own. It comes from Him who sent Me.'" Jesus makes it known; His knowledge comes directly from the Father who sent Him and not some earthly Rabbi. In verse 17 Jesus then tells them, "If anyone who chooses to do God's will, he will find out whether My teaching comes from God or whether I speak on My own." We tend to do just the opposite. We focus on learning God's word so that it will teach us how we are to live in obedience to Him. Jesus turned that teaching around by saying, our willingness to obey God is what determines our understanding. In other words, obedience leads to greater understanding. The deeper we walk in obedience to God's word; the clearer God's word becomes to us. Jesus also points out that His teaching comes directly from God. His desire was to glorify God by teaching the Words given to Him by the Father. Everything Jesus taught, was true and consistent with God's word. This angered the religious leaders because they could find no argument against Him. Following Jesus' example, we are to act and live differently from the world and in a way that honors God's Word. Titus 2:7-8, "In everything set them an example by doing what is good. In your teaching show integrity, seriousness and soundness of speech that cannot be condemned, so that those who oppose you may be ashamed because they have nothing bad to say about us." As Christians, someone is always watching us. They would love nothing more than to catch us doing something wrong. 1 Peter 3:15-16, "But in your hearts set apart Christ as Lord. Always be prepared to give an answer to everyone who asks you to give the reason for the hope that you have. But do this with gentleness and respect, keeping a clear conscience so that those who speak maliciously against your good behavior may be ashamed of their slander." Watch your step. Allow God to guide you each day, walking in obedience to God's Word. Be an example for others to follow.

Prayer: God, help me to walk in obedience to Your Word.

> John 7:24 Do not judge according to appearance, but judge with righteous judgement.

On Day 36, we read from Matthew 7 where Jesus taught on judging. He said, "Do not judge, or you too will be judged. For with what judgement you judge, you will be judged: and with the measure you use, it will be measured back to you." We learned that Jesus didn't forbid us from judging, but not to judge hypocritically and self-righteously. The occasions when it is necessary to make judgments, we should be careful and prayerful in how we go about it. Today, Jesus cautions us about judging on appearances, rather than truth. I can't tell you the times when I have seen a situation and drawn the wrong conclusion. It happens quite frequently with our grandchildren. Vivian will give them permission to do something or have a snack, while I am not present. I come in and see them doing something I didn't think they were supposed to be doing and call them out on it. Instead of assuming they wouldn't do what they were doing without permission, I jump to the conclusion they are breaking the rules. Jesus said we are to judge correctly. So how do we go about judging fairly and correctly? First, we should know and understand the situation before we judge. Too often our assumptions are based on incomplete information. When that occurs, we tend to slant our judgment toward the negative side of the situation. We assume the worst-case scenario instead of giving someone the benefit of the doubt. Get all the facts. Second, avoid assigning labels to others based on their economic status, race, education, religion, gender, appearance, etc. It is human nature to want to fit everyone into the boxes we have identified in our minds and shape our judgments around them. Don't stereotype. Next, seek God as your source for wisdom and knowledge. Trust Him, and ask for His insight and perspective into the events, people, and problems you are trying to understand. Ask God for spiritual discernment so that your motives and decisions are according to His will. Listen to what God is telling you. Lastly, guard your heart from selfish thoughts and motives. Proverbs 4:23, "Above all else guard your heart, for it is the wellspring of life." Too often we allow our favorite person, "me, myself, and I" to influence our decisions. Ask God to remove our selfish thoughts and motives.

Prayer: God, give me discernment so I can make righteous judgments.

> John 7:33-34 Then Jesus said to them, "I shall be with you a little while longer, and then I go to Him who sent Me. You will seek Me and not find Me, and where I am you cannot come."

Jesus was teaching in the synagogue and drawing large crowds. The Pharisees were getting concerned and sent Temple guards to arrest Jesus. Jesus tells them He will not be with them very much longer because He is returning to the One who sent Him, and they would not be able to find Him. Instead of arresting Jesus, the guards began to question where could Jesus be going and assumed their problem would soon be solved. However, Jesus knew He was headed to the cross to die and rise to eternal life with the Father. He told them they would look for Him but not find Him, and they couldn't go where He going. Jesus was going back to heaven to be with the Father and yet they could not go where He was going? Jesus tells us why in John 14:6, "I am the way, the truth and the life. No one comes to the Father except through Me." Salvation is through Jesus alone. The religious leaders saw Jesus as a threat, not the Messiah. Sadly, they were more concerned about their popularity with the people than understanding who Jesus is. Jesus' words, "I shall be with you a little while longer," are for us as well. Life is short and opportunities to live for Him pass us by each day. How many opportunities have we let slip away? Please don't waste them because one day there may not be any more. The older I get, the more I realize how important the opportunities are. You are never too old to serve Jesus. In fact, age should be a motivation to do more rather than sitting back and letting others take over. I want to follow my father's example, who at age 90 is teaching a Sunday School class of over 50 people. I want to follow Vivian's mother's example of having a vital leadership role in her church at age 87. God has a plan and a purpose for you. Don't allow yourself to slip into church every Sunday to sit on the back pew and leave without getting involved. Don't miss out on the opportunity to help someone in need, speak a kind word, or lift someone up in prayer. The opportunities are endless. Our time is not. "Today is the first day of the rest of your life," make the best of it.

Prayer: God, give me an opportunity to serve You today.

> John 7:37-38 *If anyone thirsts, let him come to Me and drink. He who believes in Me, as the Scripture has said, out of his heart will flow rivers of living water.*

Jesus is in Jerusalem celebrating the Feast of Tabernacles which was an annual event instituted by God to remind the Israelites of their deliverance from the bondage of slavery in Egypt. The last day of the festival included a water ceremony where the Priest would draw water from a pool and pour it into a funnel high above the altar. At some point during this ceremony, Jesus stands up and cries out, "If anyone thirsts, let him come to Me and drink. He who believes in Me, as the scripture has said, out of his heart will flow rivers of living water." If you recall, Jesus had told the Samaritan woman about this "living water" He offers. Water represents the Spirit of God. Anyone who believes in Jesus, receives His life changing Spirit and an abundant life. What difference does water make? You can look at my lawn and understand. I use an irrigation system to water my lawn. However, there are a couple places where the sprinklers miss. Those areas are dry and brown, while the areas that receive water are a healthy green color. Without the Spirit of God living in our lives, we are like the brown areas in my yard, dry and unfruitful. However, with the abundance of water comes the ability to grow and flourish. Jesus promised that "rivers of living water would flow from out of our hearts." The best way I can describe this flow of water is a white-water rafting trip. You launch a rubber raft into the water and start paddling. The flow of the water begins to get faster and faster until you find yourself in a rapid. There is no stopping or turning around and you quickly realize the power of the moving water. Not only that, it just keeps coming. There is no end to it. Have you experienced this life changing encounter with Jesus? Are you living the abundant life Christ offers you? Perhaps you have allowed the daily problems of life or some unforgiven sin to block the flow of God's Spirit in your life. His life giving, life fulfilling water is there waiting for you to open the flow. Ask Jesus to remove the sin, the doubt, and the things that have taken His place in your life. He is willing to forgive and to bless you with "rivers of living water."

Prayer: God, open the flow of Your living water within my life.

> John 8:7 So when they continued asking Him, He raised Himself up and said to them, "He who is without sin among you, let him throw a stone at her first."

The Scribes and Pharisees have brought a woman to Jesus who had been caught in the act of adultery. They said to Him, "Teacher, this woman was caught in adultery, the very act. Now Moses, in the law, commanded us that such should be stoned." Leviticus 20:10 says, "If a man commits adultery with another man's wife – with the wife of his neighbor – both the adulterer and the adulteress must be put to death." The Scribes and Pharisees are setting what they think to be the perfect trap for Jesus. It was an obvious trap since the religious leaders only brought the woman and not the man with her to be judged as the Law required. If Jesus were to answer to stone the woman according to the requirements of the Law, He would be breaking Roman law which forbid the Jews from executing someone. If He answered to spare her life, then He would be breaking the Law of Moses which was given to Moses by God. Instead of immediately answering, Jesus stoops down and begins writing on the ground with His finger. Not letting Jesus off the hook, the religious leaders press Him for an answer. Jesus stands up and says to them, "He who is without sin among you, let him cast the first stone." Jesus stoops back down to write. One by one, the religious leaders drop their rocks and leave until all have left. If you or I were in the crowd that day, we would have dropped our rocks and left as well. We are as guilty of sin as the person beside us. However, we have a problem when we begin rationalizing that our sins are not quite as bad as someone else's. In essence, we are saying that I am a pretty good person and don't need Christ's forgiveness. But Jesus is saying that no sin is greater than another. We are all sinners. We simply sin in different ways and decide which commands to follow and which ones to ignore. James 2:10 says, "For whoever keeps the whole law and yet stumbles at just one point is guilty of breaking all of it." Because we are not perfect, Jesus died on the cross for our sins. He offers forgiveness, not condemnation, life, not death. Praise Him today for paying the penalty for our sins.

Prayer: God, thank You for dying on the cross for my sins.

> *John 8:11 She said, "No one Lord." And Jesus said to her, "Neither do I condemn you; go and sin no more."*

After a few minutes, Jesus stands up to find that everyone had left except the woman who was accused of adultery. He said to her, "Woman, where are those accusers of yours? Has no one condemned you?" She replied, "No one Lord." Then Jesus does something pretty amazing. Although He was the only sinless person there and had every right to condemn the woman for her sin, Jesus offers her mercy and grace. What are mercy and grace? God's mercy is not punishing us as we deserve. God's grace is His kindness to us, blessing us with things we don't deserve. Note that Jesus doesn't try to make excuses for the woman's behavior or condone her sin. She was guilty. He tells her, "Neither do I condemn you; go and sin no more," or from now on, stop this life of sin. Was Jesus talking about living a life of sinless perfection. Of course not, He knows that would be impossible for anyone. He is saying, you have been pardoned, change your sinful lifestyle. The Bible doesn't tell us what happened to the woman. But one thing is for sure, she had met Jesus, and her life would never be the same. Jesus offers this very same mercy and grace to us. Before coming to Christ, we were as guilty as the woman caught in adultery. However, His mercy and grace changed our life. It exposed the sin and ugliness for what it is. It changed our motivation for doing things. Sin doesn't have the control over us as it used to. Romans 6:1-2 says, "What shall we say, then? Shall we go on sinning so that grace may increase? By no means! We died to sin; how can we live in it any longer?" It should be our goal as Christians to not sin anymore although we are human and will stumble. The point is we shouldn't make a habit of it. 1 John 3:9-10, "No one who is born of God will continue to sin, because God's seed remains in him; he cannot go on sinning, because he has been born of God. This is how we know who the children of God are and who the children of the devil are: Anyone who does not do what is right is not a child of God; nor is anyone who does not love his brother."

Prayer: God, help me to go and sin no more.

> John 8:12 Then Jesus spoke to them again, saying, "I am the light of the world. He who follows Me shall not walk in darkness, but have the light of life."

Jesus has just forgiven the woman brought to Him who had been caught in adultery. He turns to those who are left and tells them, "I am the light of the world. He who follows Me shall not walk in darkness, but have the light of life." This is the second "I Am" declaration made by Jesus. The first was in John 6:35 when Jesus said, "I am the bread of life," after feeding the 5,000 with five loaves and two fishes. We will discover several more in the days to come. Why are these "I am" declarations by Jesus so important? When God appeared to Moses in the burning bush, He told Moses in Exodus 3:14, "I Am who I Am. This is what you are to say to the Israelites: 'I Am has sent me to you.'" Jesus is providing an answer to the question, who is this "I Am." Jesus also uses the symbolism of the rituals of the festival to identify Himself as the Messiah. According to www.jewishroots.net, there was a great ceremony during the Feast of Tabernacles called the "Illumination of the Temple." During this ceremony, four 75' tall oil lamps were lighted at night to remind the people of the pillar of fire that had led the Israelites through the wilderness. During this ceremony, the priests would use their worn-out clothing as wicks to light the lamps. Many believe the light to represent the Shekinah or dwelling presence of God that once filled the Temple. Amid this backdrop, Jesus said, "I am the light of the world." He is declaring Himself to be the one and only source of spiritual light. There is no other way to salvation except through Jesus. Whoever believes in Him will have the light that comes from God's presence and eternal life. He also makes two promises for those who follow Him. The first promise is, His followers will never walk in darkness or will be apart from God. When we accept Jesus as our Lord and Savior, we are set free and are no longer slaves to the sin and darkness that controlled our lives. The second promise, is that we have the light of Jesus living in us. Like the moon that reflects the light of the sun, we are to reflect the light of Christ living in us. Enjoy the presence of His light today.

Prayer: God, help me to reflect Your light to others.

> John 8:17-18 *It is also written in your law that the testimony of two men is true. I am One who bears witness of Myself, and the Father who sent Me bears witness of Me.*

The Pharisees challenged Jesus' authority and claim of being the Messiah. They said, "Here You are appearing as Your own witness; Your testimony is not valid." The very ones who supposedly knew the scriptures and taught it in the synagogues don't accept Jesus for who He is. Jesus told them, "Even if I testify on My own behalf, My testimony is valid, for I know where I came from and where I am going." He also told them His second witness is the Father who sent Him. According to Jewish law, the testimony of two witnesses was required to establish a fact. Still not understanding who Jesus is, the Pharisees ask Him, "Where is Your Father?" Jesus told them, "You do not know Me or My Father. If you knew Me, you would know My Father also." Jesus is telling them based on the testimony of the witnesses, you should have enough evidence to know who I am. In a court case, there are typically three types of witnesses. The first is an eyewitness, who has first-hand knowledge of the facts of a case and testifies to what they have seen or know. Jesus is the eye witness. The second is a character witness, who knows the individual involved in a case and provides information about the character and traits of that person. God, the Father, is the character witness. He sent Jesus, His one and only Son to save us from our sins. Lastly, there is the expert witness. This witness has specialized knowledge in a particular field that is relevant to the case. The scriptures provide expert testimony of who Jesus is and why He came. Jesus speaking to the disciples just before His ascension in Acts 1:8 commanded them, "But you will receive power when the Holy Spirit comes on you; and you will be My witnesses in Jerusalem, and in all Judea and Samaria, and to the ends of the earth." If you have had an encounter with Jesus and have accepted Him as your Lord and Savior, you are an eyewitness. You have first-hand knowledge of Jesus and can testify to others how He has changed your life. Your testimony is not only the words you use, but the love you have for others, the life you live, and the choices you make. Share your testimony with someone today.

Prayer: God, help me to be a witness of Your love and mercy to others.

> John 8:24 *Therefore I said to you that you will die in your sins; for if you do not believe that I am He, you will die in your sins.*

People use different methods for communicating an idea or stating a thought. Some like to provide a lot of detail and supporting information, while others prefer to get directly to the point. Many pastors I know, have the gift of taking 30 minutes to say the same thing several different ways, following the old adage, "tell them what you are going to tell them, tell them, and tell them what you told them." There are times when it is helpful to spend several minutes explaining a thought or idea because people hear things differently. However, there are times when getting to the point is necessary. I recall a time in my career with Progress Energy when our company was reorganizing and I had to meet with our Vice President about my future with the company. He did an excellent job in describing the circumstances and reasoning behind the reorganization. He took some time to tell how I had done a good job and the changes were not performance related. However, all during the conversation my thoughts were, "cut to the chase, just tell me if I have a job or not." He finally got around to telling me I had a position at our new Customer Service Center in Raleigh. This was a blessing because several of my peers lost their jobs due to the reorganization. However, the wait to hear the verdict seemed like an eternity. In today's verse, Jesus tells the Pharisees, they will die in their sins if they do not believe in Him. Using a quote from my favorite character in the Andy Griffeth Show, Ernest T. Bass, "I don't chew my cabbage twice," Jesus is very blunt and direct with Pharisees. He can't make it any simpler than this. The same holds true for you and I. We are all born into sin and will die in our sins unless we believe in the One who came to bear our sins on the cross, paying the penalty for them. Believing in Christ is the key to having eternal life with Him. Not believing in Him, condemns us to a Christless eternity in hell. We condemn ourselves by not believing. However, 2 Peter 3:9 tells us, "The Lord is not slow in keeping His promise, as some understand slowness. He is patient with you, not wanting anyone to perish, but everyone come to repentance."

Prayer: God, thank You for paying the price for my sins.

> John 8:31-32 Then Jesus said to those Jews who believed Him, "If you abide in My word, you are My disciples indeed. And you shall know the truth, and the truth shall make you free."

Jesus turns His attention away from the Pharisees who were challenging Him, and begins speaking to those who believe in Him. He tells them how to be His disciples and to live a life that God created us for. He speaks about abiding, knowing the truth, and living in freedom. According to Jesus, the foundation of being a Christian is to abide in His word. What exactly does that mean? To abide in His word means to reside in, remain in, or to stay in God's word. How much time are you spending in God's word each day? If the only Word you hear each week is the scripture being read at church on Sunday, then you are not abiding in His Word. If you pick up a Bible and randomly read a few verses once or twice a week, then you are not abiding in His Word. Daily devotionals are helpful, but should not be a substitute for digging deeper into God's word. God instructed Joshua in Joshua 1:8, "Do not let this Book of the Law depart from your mouth; meditate on it day and night, so that you may be careful to do everything written in it. Then you will be prosperous and successful." There are several ways to get into God's word on a more consistent and deeper level. However, it takes self-discipline and sacrifice. One way is to read through the Bible each year. There are several reading plans on the Bible app, which makes it very convenient and easy to do. This is something I have committed myself to do ever since Pastor Roland Stone challenged our church to do many years ago. Another option is to join a weekly Bible study; such as the Bible Study Fellowship, that requires you to research and dig deeper in God's word during the week. As we spend more time in God's word, it changes us, affecting our lives, our choices, and our conversations. It draws us closer to Him and makes us more like Him. It draws us closer to the truth. Jesus said in John 14:6, "I am the way, the truth, and the life..." Knowing the truth sets us free from our slavery to sin. We are able to live in freedom, experiencing life according to God's design for us. Get into God's word today and start abiding in Him.

Prayer: God, help me to abide in Your word.

> John 8:34,36 Jesus answered them, "Most assuredly, I say to you, whoever commits a sin is a slave of sin. Therefore if the Son makes you free, you shall be free indeed."

In response to Jesus telling them, "You shall know the truth and the truth will set you free," the people asked, "We are Abraham's descendants, and have never been in bondage to anyone. How can You say, 'You will be made free?'" Jesus tells them, "Most assuredly, whoever commits a sin is a slave to sin." How can committing one sin make us a slave to sin? That is the nature of sin. As Christian author, Kay Arthur once said, "Sin will take you farther than you ever expected to go, it will keep you longer than you intended to stay, and it will cost you more than you ever expected to pay." Often times, one sin leads to another, which leads to another and to another. The merry-go-round of sin never stops. Some sins are addictive such as drugs, alcohol, sexual sins, and pornography. Once hooked, it is almost impossible to stop. The desire for another hit, another drink, another look, another relationship is overwhelming. Other sins are emotional such as anger, bitterness, selfishness, and jealousy. If not careful, our emotions will rule and ruin our lives. There are two sides to sin. One, it becomes our master and we are unable to resist it. The other is we hold on to it because we enjoy it. In either case, it has us in bondage. Jesus went on to say, "If the Son makes you free, you shall be free indeed." The freedom that Jesus offers is threefold. He offers us freedom from the penalty of sin. Romans 8:1, "Therefore, there is now no condemnation for those who are in Christ Jesus." Next, we are free from the power of sin. Sin no longer has control of our lives. We may slip up from time to time, but sin no longer dominates our lives. Romans 6:11-12, "In the same way, count yourselves dead to sin but alive to God in Christ Jesus. Therefore do not let sin reign in your mortal body so that you obey its evil desires." Lastly, one day we will be free from the presence of sin. 1 Corinthians 15:51-52, "Listen, I tell you a mystery: We will not all sleep, but we will all be changed – In a flash, in the twinkling of an eye, at the last trumpet. For the trumpet will sound, and the dead will be raised to imperishable, and will be changed."

Prayer: God, set me free from sin.

> *John 8:47 He who is of God hears God's words; therefore you do not hear, because you are not of God.*

Although we may not like to admit it, we inherit the nature of our fathers. A friend of mine in his 60's was telling how he had unconsciously begun to hang a used paper towel to dry and reuse just as his father had done years before. He actually didn't remember his father doing it, but was reminded by his wife of that habit. Kidding around, my brother-in-law started calling me 'Little Mel' because I was doing things just like my father. However, just as we have an earthly father, we also have a spiritual father. We are either a child of God or a child of Satan. You can identify whose child you are by the fruit you produce and the nature you inherited. Acts 13:6-10 describes an encounter Paul and Barnabas had with a child of Satan. Here the Holy Spirit guided Paul to know the true identity of Elymas. "Now when they had gone through the island to Paphos, they found a certain sorcerer, a false prophet, a Jew whose name was Bar-Jesus, who was with the proconsul, Sergius Paulus, an intelligent man. This man called for Barnabus and Saul (Paul) and sought to hear the word of God. But Elymas (Bar-Jesus) the sorcerer withstood them, seeking to turn the proconsul away from the faith. Then Saul, who also is called Paul, filled with the Holy Spirit, looked intently at him and said, "O full of all deceit and all fraud, you son of the devil, you enemy of righteousness, will you not cease perverting the straight ways of the Lord?" Paul also told Elymas that the Hand of God was upon him and that he would be temporarily blinded. Elymas who was spiritually blinded was now physically blinded in hopes that he would see the light of God. In 2 Timothy 3:2-5 Paul provides the traits of those who are not children of God. "People will be lovers of themselves, lovers of money, boastful, proud, abusive, disobedient to their parents, ungrateful, unholy, without love, unforgiving, slanderous, without self-control, brutal, not lovers of the good, treacherous, rash, conceited, lovers of pleasure rather than lovers of God – having a form of godliness but denying its power. Have nothing to do with them." In Galatians 5, Paul says a child of God produces love, joy, peace, patience, kindness, goodness, faithfulness, gentleness and self-control. Whose child, are you?

Prayer: God, I want to be Your child.

> John 8:58 Jesus said to them, "Most assuredly, I say to you, before Abraham was , I AM."

If there was ever any doubt that Jesus is God, He ends that discussion today by declaring He is the "I AM." We read in Exodus chapter 3 where God appears to Moses in the burning bush and calls him to lead the people of Israel out of the bondage of slavery from Egypt. During that conversation, Moses asks God, "Suppose I go to the Israelites and say to them, 'The God of your fathers has sent me to you,' and they ask me, 'What is His name?' Then what shall I tell them?'" Exodus 3:14 says, "God said to Moses, 'I AM WHO I AM.' This is what you are to say to the Israelites: 'I AM' has sent me to you." In today's verse, Jesus declares "Before Abraham was, I AM." In other words, I AM the I AM spoken about in Exodus. I existed long before Abraham who is considered to be the father of the Jewish nation. Jesus is the great "I AM." This statement "rocked the Jews' world." How can that be possible? They said to Jesus, "You are not yet 50 years old, and have You seen Abraham?" John 8:59 says it made them very mad, "Then they took up stones to throw at Him; but Jesus hid Himself and went out of the temple, going through the midst of them, and so passed by." By declaring that He is the I AM, Jesus is God. He is also not limiting Himself to be just the God of salvation. He is all that we need Him to be. When we are sick and need healing, He is Jehovah Rapha, our healer. When we are in need, He is Jehovah Jireh, our provider. When our life is in turmoil, He is Jehovah Shalom, our peace. He is Jehovah Nissi, the banner that goes before us. He is Jehovah Rohi, the good shepherd that takes care of us. He is Jehovah Elohim, the God strong and mighty. He is Jehovah Elyon, the God most high. He is Jehovah Shammah, the God who is always there. These names barely scratch the surface of who Jesus and God are. What type of need do you have today? Maybe you need peace in your life, healing, salvation, or help with your finances? Our God is more than able to meet your needs. Call out to Him today.

Prayer: God, thank You for being the great I AM.

> John 9:3 Jesus answered, "Neither this man nor his parents sinned, but that the works of God should be revealed in him."

Jesus and the disciples are walking along and come upon a man who was blind from birth. This was not an accidental or by chance meeting. Anything Jesus did and the people He encountered were all because of God's providence. This still holds true for today. Trying to sound theological, the disciples ask Jesus in John 9:2, "Rabbi, who sinned, this man or his parents, for he was born blind?" They wanted an explanation for the man's blindness. What was the cause? The rule of thumb in Jesus' day was that the punishment for sin was passed down to the next generation. Numbers 14:18, "The Lord is slow to anger, abounding in love and forgiving sin and rebellion. Yet He does not leave the guilty unpunished; He punishes the children for the sin of the fathers to the third and fourth generation." However, Jesus' answer speaks to the purpose, not the cause. "The disciples didn't understand this distinction, it seems that the existence of sin in the world is the cause of suffering in the world, but specific sins in the world are usually not the cause of specific sufferings in the world." John Piper[18] For this man, the purpose of his blindness was that the works of God would be displayed in his life. Just to be clear, this is not the sole answer to suffering and disabilities in the world today. Some we may never understand. Our seventh grandchild, Gracie was born this summer. She is a healthy baby girl. While some friends' grandchild was born around the same time with a cleft palate and lip. According to the CDC, this is not an uncommon occurrence with approximately 1 in approximately 1,600 babies born each year with this condition. Thankfully, there are services and treatments available to correct this condition. However, the question comes to my mind, why this child and not Gracie? Why are children born with disabilities and diseases that will affect them their entire lives? I couldn't begin to explain the cause or the purpose. Many things in life will make no sense until God becomes our complete focus. All I know is that Jesus saw the blind man and had compassion for him. If you are living with a disability, Jesus sees you and cares about you. He will not leave you to face life's challenges on your own.

Prayer: God, help me to care about others who are living with disabilities.

> John 10:1 *Most assuredly, I say to you, "he who does not enter the sheepfold by the door, but climbs up some other way, the same is a thief and a robber."*

In John chapter 10, Jesus uses several examples to illustrate He is the "Good Shepherd." In verses 1 – 10, He describes Himself as the True shepherd who loves and cares for His sheep. They will follow Him because they know His voice. Anyone else who tries to get the sheep to come to them are a thief and a robber whose motives are purely for personal gain. Because they are false shepherds, they have to sneak around the gate and get into the sheepfold by any means possible. Jesus is referring to the Pharisees and other religious leaders as false shepherds. Ezekiel 34:1-6 speaks about the lost sheep and motives of the false shepherds. "The word of the Lord came to me: 'Son of man, prophesy against the shepherds of Israel; prophesy and say to them: This is what the Sovereign Lord says: Woe to the shepherds of Israel who only take care of themselves! Should not the shepherds take care of the flock? You eat the curds, clothe yourselves with the wool and slaughter the choice animals, but you do not take care of the flock. You have not strengthened the weak or healed the sick or bound up the injured. You have not brought back the strays or searched for the lost. You have ruled them harshly and brutally. So they were scattered because there was no shepherd, and when they were scattered they became the food for all the wild animals. My sheep wandered over all the mountains and on every high hill. They were scattered over the whole earth, and no one searched or looked for them.'" Doesn't Ezekiel's description of the lost sheep sound like many people today? I see them every day. They are ones who wander aimlessly around with no purpose in life, sick, hurting, vulnerable to attacks by wild animals. They need the Good Shepherd, not someone who wants to take advantage of them. They need the Shepherd, David wrote about in Psalm 23, "The Lord is my shepherd, I shall not want." Perhaps you are one of the lost sheep without a shepherd, or have been led astray by a false shepherd. Jesus is saying to you today, "Come to Me, all you who are weary and burdened, and I will give you rest." Matthew 11:28. Listen to the Good Shepherd, hear His voice calling you.

Prayer: God, thank You for sending the Good Shepherd to save us.

> John 10:10 *The thief does not come except to steal, and to kill, and to destroy. I have come that they may have life and that they may have it more abundantly.*

Jesus continues His illustration about the good shepherd and contrasts His motives with those of the thief. A thief does not care about anyone except themselves and satisfying their own selfish gain. Most often, we identify Satan as the thief who comes to steal, kill, and destroy our lives. His purpose is to get us to serve him by offering immediate pleasure and gratification. However, the things he offers has a hook in them. Once we take the bait, they will take us down a path of misery and destruction, eventually leading to an eternity in hell. Satan is not the only thief we have to look out for. Some are disguised as well-intentioned preachers and evangelists who do not preach the gospel, but are doing it for selfish gain. 2 Peter 2:1-3, "But there were also false prophets among the people, just as there will be false teachers among you. They will secretly introduce destructive heresies, even denying the sovereign Lord who bought them – bringing swift destruction on themselves. Many will follow their shameful ways and will bring the way of truth into disrepute. In their greed these teachers will exploit you with stories they have made up. Their condemnation has long been hanging over them, and their destruction has not been sleeping." Jesus promises us an abundant life, saying, "I have come that you may have life and have it more abundantly." What is this abundant life Jesus has promised? First, abundant life is something that is plentiful, beyond measure, more than anyone would expect. Does the abundant life Jesus offers include a huge bank account, large home, and expensive cars? Maybe for a few people, but abundant life is more about spiritual abundance, not material. Both eternal and abundant life begins when we accept Christ as our Lord and Savior. God wants us to have the best life possible in this broken world. He wants us to experience love, joy, peace, patience, kindness, goodness, faithfulness, gentleness, and self-control in a world that is far from perfect. Abundant life is not dependent upon our circumstances, but based on a knowledge that our heavenly Father has something much better in store for us. Living an abundant life is a continual learning process of growing, failing, recovering, overcoming and drawing closer to a God who is with us every step of the way.

Prayer: God, thank You for giving me an abundant life in You.

> *John 10:11 I am the good shepherd. The good shepherd gives His life for the sheep.*

Jesus declares, "I am the good shepherd," which is the fourth of the seven "I AM" sayings of Jesus. To understand the attributes of a good shepherd, we are going to straight to Psalm 23. David writes, **"The Lord is my shepherd I shall not want."** A good shepherd supplies all our needs. We should want nothing more than what the Lord our Shepherd gives us. **"He makes me lie down in green pastures, He leads me beside still waters."** In this busy and chaotic world, the good shepherd takes you to places of peacefulness where you can find rest in the middle of life's storms. **"He restores my soul. He guides me in paths of righteousness for His name's sake."** When we wander away from the Lord, He brings us back to where we need to be. When we are down, He lifts us up. When we are discouraged, He encourages us. He is constantly pursuing us to bring us closer to Himself. He guides our every step along His path of righteousness, never leading us into sin. When we choose to go our own way, we quickly wander off His path of righteousness. However, He is there to lead us and restore us for His name's sake, so that His name will be glorified. **"Even though I walk through the valley of the shadow of death, I will fear no evil, for You are with me; Your rod and Your staff, they comfort me."** One of the harsh realities of life is that at some time in our lives we are going to go through a deep dark valley. It could be a financial, emotional, relational, or a physical valley. During those times, the feelings of aloneness can overwhelm you. Take heart, God is not waiting to join you on the other side. He is with you all the way, using His rod and His staff to comfort and protect you. **"You prepare a table before me in the presence of my enemies. You anoint my head with oil; my cup overflows."** God invites us to a banquet where we do not have to fear our enemies. We can sit down in confidence, knowing our enemies cannot harm us. He anoints our heads with oil, giving us a purpose in life. He fills our cup until it is overflowing. How well do you know the good shepherd?

Prayer: God, thank You for being the good shepherd.

> John 10:17-18 *Therefore My Father loves Me, because I lay down My life that I may take it up again. No one takes it from Me, but I lay it down of Myself. I have power to lay it down, and I have power to take it again. This command I have received from My Father.*

For you and I, eternal life is a gift from God. Ephesians 2:8-9, "For it is by grace you have been saved, through faith – and this not from yourselves, it is the gift of God – not by works, so that no one can boast." When we fully understand the cost of that gift, it becomes even more precious to us. Because it is a gift, salvation cannot be earned by trying to live right and doing good works. No matter how close we come to living a perfect life, we are still sinners in need of God's grace. On the other hand, Jesus was born into this world having eternal life. However, He gave up His right to eternal life by coming to die on the cross, paying the penalty for our sins. He said the Father loves Him because He was willing to forfeit His life. Following the command of the Father, Christ obediently chose to die. No Roman soldier could take His life, because He willingly gave it up. Yet, Jesus didn't have to go through the pain and suffering of the cross. He could have avoided the 39 lashes, the crown of thorns, the nails driven into His hands and feet. He could have called 10,000 angels to deliver Him. However, He chose to go to the cross for you and I. Moreover, He had complete faith the Father would give His life back to Him. Yet as Jesus was hanging on the cross, taking His last breath, Matthew 27:46 tells us, "…Jesus cried out in a loud voice, 'Eloi, Eloi, lama sabachthani?' Which means, 'My God, My God, why have You forsaken Me?'" At this moment, all the past, present, and future sins of the world were placed upon Him. He became the final and complete sacrifice for our sins. It was at this instant, Jesus was banished from the presence of God, because sin cannot exist in God's presence. His death was certain and God had turned away. Maybe what was not completely certain to Jesus, was God really going to fulfill the plan and bring Him back to life? However, we know the rest of the story. God fulfilled His plan by raising Jesus to life on the third day, conquering death and the grave, paving the way for us to have eternal life.

Prayer: God, thank You for Jesus who was willing to lay His life down for my sins.

> *John 10:32 Jesus answered them, "Many good works I have shown you from My Father. For which of those works do you stone Me?"*

Jesus has just said, "I and My Father are one." Once again, He is declaring that He and the Father are unified and are equal to each other. They are distinct persons, but share the same spirit and attributes. This infuriates many of the Jews including the Pharisees who heard Jesus say this. They picked up stones, ready to stone Him. Although Jesus knew why they wanted to stone Him, He stops them in their tracks by asking, "Which one of the good works that I have done are you stoning Me for? They couldn't deny the miracles He had done and realize no one without divine support from God could have done them. They answered Jesus, "It is not for a good work that we are going to stone You but for blasphemy, because You, being a man, make Yourself God." By claiming to be God, Jesus is messing up their lives, their livelihood, and their religion. The Pharisees had it all together. They had the law given by Moses and even created their own set of rules and regulations to add to the law. They were leaders in the synagogues and popular with the people, who considered them the highest religious authority. Jesus' teaching, His miracles, and His claim to be God have completely disrupted the Pharisees lives. Sadly, their response was not to listen and accept what Jesus said, but to accuse Him of something they could legally kill Him for. Jesus is still disrupting lives today. When we accept Him as Lord and Savior, our lives change. The bad habits and sinful lifestyle are gone. Our selfish nature is replaced with one of love and kindness for others. Jesus becomes first place in our lives. He replaces our traditions and religious rituals by demanding we take up our cross and follow Him. He sends us to places we would have never gone and to people we would have never met. Why does Jesus disrupt our lives? Unless He does, we would continue to follow sin to our graves. By disrupting our lives, He offers us a new, everlasting, and abundant life in Him. This disruption is not a one-time thing. God is continually pushing us out of our comfort zone to serve Him. Age does not matter to God. You are never too young or too old to be used by Him.

Prayer: God, thank You for disrupting my life.

> John 11:4 When Jesus heard that, He said, "This sickness is not unto death, but for the glory of God, that the Son of God may be glorified through it."

Lazarus, the brother of Mary and Martha who lived in Bethany about 20 miles from where Jesus was staying in Bethabara, became very sick. Knowing Jesus' power to heal, Mary and Martha sent word to Jesus that His good friend Lazarus was ill, in hopes He would come quickly and heal him. John tells us, "Jesus loved Martha and her sister and Lazarus." But strangely, when Jesus heard that Lazarus was sick, He stayed two more days in Bethabara. However, He sends the messenger back with this reply, "This sickness is not unto death, but for the glory of God, that the Son of God may be glorified through it." Later in John, we read that Lazarus had been in the grave for four days when Jesus finally arrives in Bethany. This would mean that Lazarus had probably died shortly after the messenger left to get Jesus. Jesus, knowing of Lazarus' death, sends the messenger back with what sounds like an encouraging and comforting reply. I can only imagine how Mary and Martha felt after burying their brother, receiving word from Jesus that Lazarus' sickness will not end in death. I'm sure there was confusion, pain, grief, hurt and plenty of tears. In fact, Martha tells Jesus when He arrives, "Lord if You had been here, my brother would not have died." How many times when troubles overwhelm us, have we asked God, where are You? Or ask Him why are You not helping me? Our problems keep growing while God seems to be miles away. But Martha didn't end her conversation questioning Jesus about why He allowed her brother to die. She continued saying, "But I know that even now God will give You whatever You ask." Even though her brother had died, she still had faith in Jesus. She may not have understood why God allowed all this to happen, but she had faith and hope that He would work it out. In this instance, Jesus raises Lazarus back to life so that the "Son of God may be glorified through it." Often times we pray believing for healing and deliverance and God chooses not to heal. We may never understand why, but we can trust that God is in control. If He chooses not to heal, then He has a reason and a purpose, one that will draw us closer to Him and ultimately bring Him glory.

Prayer: God, be glorified in me.

> John 11:14 The Jesus said to them plainly, "Lazarus is dead."

Two days after the messenger had brought word that Lazarus was sick, Jesus tells the disciples, "Let's go back to Judea." Remembering the people wanted to stone Him there, the disciples asked, "Rabbi, a short while ago, the Jews sought to stone You, and You are going there again?" Jesus doesn't simply say, "It will be alright. I got this." He responds by saying, "Are there not twelve hours in the day? If anyone walks in the day, he does not stumble, because he sees the light of this world. It is when he walks by night that he stumbles, for he has no light." Although it sounds like Jesus is telling the disciples everything will be okay as long as they stay in at night, that is not the case. His comments have a much deeper meaning related to walking in the light of God's will. Although following God's will may seem dangerous at times, nothing can stop God's ultimate purpose from being accomplished. I recall reading the story of David Wilkerson in the book, "The Cross and the Switchblade." Called by God, David Wilkerson went into some of the most dangerous neighborhoods in Brooklyn, NY in the 1950's to share the gospel. There he met and led the feared Mau - Maus Gang leader, Niki Cruz to Christ. Yet, there are other examples of Christian missionaries martyred for their faith. I can only say that God's ways are a mystery. But one thing is for certain, there is no reason to serve Him living in fear of what might happen to us. God is in control of our lives. Jesus tells the disciples, "Our friend Lazarus sleeps, but I go that I may wake him up." The disciples breathe a sigh of relief and tell Jesus Lazarus should get better when he wakes up, hoping Jesus will cancel the trip. Jesus plainly tells them, "Lazarus is dead. And I am glad for your sakes that I was not there, that you may believe. Nevertheless, let us go to him." Jesus gives us a little insight into the purpose of Lazarus' death. Although the disciples have witnessed many miracles, raising someone to life was to help grow their faith. They were going to need it in the days to come. God does the same for you and I, providing opportunities to grow our faith.

Prayer: God, help me to see the faith opportunities You give me.

> John 11:25 Jesus said to her, "I am the resurrection and the life. He who believes in Me, though he may die, he shall live."

Lazarus' sister, Martha, heard that Jesus was on the way and left to go meet Him. She said to Jesus, "Lord, if You had been here, my brother would not have died. But even now I know that whatever You ask of God, God will give You." Is Martha giving Jesus a subtle hint that He could bring Lazarus back to life? It certainly sounds like it. However, Jesus doesn't directly respond to her hint, but tells her, "Your brother will rise again." Martha assumes Jesus is talking about the resurrection of the believers He had taught in John 6:39-40, "And this is the will of Him who sent Me, that I should lose nothing of all that He has given Me, but raise it up on the last day. For this is the will of My Father, that everyone who looks on the Son and believes in Him should have eternal life, and I will raise Him up on the last day." So, Martha responds, "I know that he will rise again in the resurrection on the last day." Jesus then announces, "I Am the resurrection and the life. He who believes in Me, though he may die, he shall live." This is the fifth of the seven "I AM" statements. Jesus is stating He is the source of both our resurrection and life. There is no eternal life apart from Him. 1 John 5:11-12, "And this is the testimony: God has given us eternal life, and this life is in His Son. He who has the Son has life; he who does not have the Son of God does not have life." What a great promise to all who believe in Him. Even though we are going to die, we live. Our physical bodies will eventually give out and die, but our spirit lives on forever. The only thing found in a casket is a perishable shell. Earlier this year, I watched my mother struggle for life in her last hours on earth. Our bodies don't want to give up its life. Although we were sad, her death was a relief because of the way her health had deteriorated over the last months of her life. However, for Mama it was a celebration. She experienced the resurrection and received a new life with Christ in heaven. One day as believers, we will experience that same celebration.

Prayer: God, thank You for being my resurrection and life.

> *John 11:26 And whoever lives and believes in Me shall never die.*
> *Do you believe this?*

Jesus has just told Martha, "I am the resurrection and the life. He who believes in Me, though he may die, he shall live, and whoever believes in Me shall never die." Then He poses the million-dollar question, "Do you believe this?" Jesus' question is just as relevant today as it was 2,000 years ago. Before we learn how Martha answered Jesus' question, how would you answer it? The answers are pretty simple, "yes," "no," or "I don't know." However, those answers lead to the next question, "What do you believe?" Perhaps you believe Jesus was just another great prophet, who taught us how to live a good life, and going to heaven is simply about how we live our lives on this earth. You may lean towards agnosticism, believing the existence of God is unknowable and unwilling to make a decision for or against God's existence. You may doubt there is a God because you do not understand or agree with some of the things He allows to happen. You may fall into the growing number of people who claim to be atheists, who don't believe there is a God and life ends when we die. Then there are those who agree with Martha. She answered Jesus saying, "Yes, Lord, I believe that You are the Christ, the Son of God, who is come into the world." What information did Martha have that leads her to know and believe that Jesus is the Christ, the Son of God? You could make the argument that she actually has less information than we have today. Martha didn't have the entire Bible at her disposal. She hasn't seen Jesus raise Lazarus from the dead. She hasn't witnessed Jesus' death, burial, and resurrection. She hasn't seen Him appear to over 500 people after His resurrection. However, Martha had what many of us need more of, faith. Hebrews 11:6, "And without faith it is impossible to please God because anyone who comes to Him must believe that He exists and that He rewards those who earnestly seek Him." We must believe God by faith, and trust His ways by faith. How do we grow in faith? Romans 10:17, "Consequently, faith comes from hearing the message, and the message is heard through the word of Christ."

Prayer: God, I believe that Jesus is the Christ, the Son of God, who died to pay the penalty for my sins.

> John 11:43 Now when He had said these things, He cried with a loud voice, "Lazarus, come forth!"

If you have ever doubted that God cares for you, read John 11:33-36. Mary has come to Jesus, weeping and falling at His feet. When Jesus saw her and many others weeping, "He was deeply moved in spirit and troubled. 'Where have you laid him?' He asked. 'Come and see, Lord,' they replied. Jesus wept." Jesus is about to display His glory and power by raising Lazarus from the dead, yet He is deeply moved by the grief expressed by Lazarus' friends and family. He identified with their pain and sorrow and wept with them. Isn't it comforting to know we have a God who understands what it means to lose someone we love. Because He cares, He can offer comfort and peace in our darkest moments. I experienced this peace and strength first hand when I had to speak at my Mother's funeral, earlier this year. I woke up the morning of the funeral with a stomach bug and was unsure I would be able to go, much less stand before a church full of people and speak. Without a doubt, it was only by God's strength and healing touch, that I was able to do it. However, the story of God's love for us doesn't end here. Jesus goes to the tomb where Lazarus is buried and prays loudly and clearly, "Father, I thank You that You have heard Me. And I know that You always hear Me, but because of the people who are standing by I said this, that they may believe that You sent Me." Then He cried out in a loud voice, "Lazarus, come forth!" Lazarus comes stumbling out of the grave, wrapped from head to toe in strips of linen. Jesus then tells those close by Lazarus, "Take off his graveclothes and let him go." Before coming to Christ, we were all dead and rotting in our sins like Lazarus. Then one day, we hear the voice of our Savior calling us to come out of the grave of sin and death. At that moment, we have a choice of staying there or stepping out into the light. As we step out, Jesus removes the sin that is wrapped around us, keeping us in the grave. Lazarus' life completely changed that day. So will yours the day you accept Jesus as Lord and Savior of your life.

Prayer: God, thank You for calling me out of the grave of sin and death.

> *John 12:8 For the poor you have with you always, but Me you do not have always.*

Jesus is at the home of Mary, Martha, and Lazarus, whom He raised from the dead, enjoying a dinner held in His honor. At the dinner, Mary takes a jar of very costly perfume and pours it on Jesus' feet, wiping them with her hair. Judas, the group treasurer, speaks up and says, "Why wasn't this perfume sold and the money given to the poor?" This would have been a reasonable question, had Judas' motives for saying it were in the right place. John writes that Judas did not say that because he cared for the poor, but because he was a thief and helped himself to the treasury. Mary's actions had much more meaning than anyone knew at the time. Unknown to everyone except Jesus, in about a week He would be crucified, buried, and raised from the dead. Little did Mary know that her act of love and devotion would foreshadow Jesus washing the disciples' feet at the Last Supper. It also was her moment to worship Jesus and anoint His body. She would not have that opportunity later when the women go to Jesus' tomb to prepare His body for burial. Jesus defends her actions, saying, "Leave her alone, it was intended that she should save this perfume for the day of My burial. You will always have the poor among you, but you will not always have Me." Let's be clear, Jesus is not saying the poor should be ignored or He is more important. Deuteronomy 15:11 says, "There will always be poor people in the land. Therefore I command you to be open handed towards your brothers and toward the poor and needy in your land." I can recall growing up in the 1960's, programs being put in place to end poverty. Since then, there have been decades of investments into Social Security, Medicare, unemployment insurance, nutrition assistance, low-income tax credits and many other anti-poverty programs. The result, according to *www.americanprogress.org*, is that there are still 35 million people living in poverty today in the United States alone. Since COVID, this number is rising. It seems the more we do, the further behind we get. God has His own plan for helping the poor. It is through His church. We may not be able to save the world, but we can at least help one person. They are not very hard to find.

Prayer: God, show me ways to help those in need.

> John 12:24 Most assuredly, I say to you, "unless a grain of wheat falls into the ground and dies, it remains alone; but if it dies, it produces much grain."

Jesus, speaking to Andrew and Peter, uses the example of a grain of wheat to explain a kingdom principle. Unless a grain of wheat is planted, it has no value other than being added to more wheat to be ground for flour. However, once it is planted, one grain can produce over 100 more grains of wheat. This one tiny seed dies to its current state. Yet, when the right conditions are present, it begins to transform into a beautiful plant that produces 100 times more than when it started. Before coming to Christ, we are very much like this grain of wheat. We have no value other than being thrown into this world to be ground up by life with the other kernels of grain. However, when we accept Christ as our Savior, we die to our old way of life and the things we want to do. We die to our sinful desires, thoughts, words and actions. This is a daily process. I wake up each morning with my selfish nature wanting to take over. In Luke 9:23, Jesus said, "If anyone would come after Me, he must deny himself and take up his cross daily and follow Me." Not only does this dying process take out the bad, it replaces what was taken out with Christ's nature. Paul said in Galatians 2:20, "For I have been crucified with Christ and I no longer live, but Christ lives in me. The life I live in the body, I live by faith in the Son of God who loved me and gave Himself for me." We take on a new nature, and become a new person in Christ. 2 Corinthians 5:17, "Therefore, if anyone is in Christ, he is a new creation; the old is gone, the new has come!" That old seed has now become a beautiful productive plant. What stage is your seed in? Are you still in the ground waiting to grow or have you sprouted roots and begun to produce more seeds? God's purpose for our lives is for us to grow and expand His kingdom. If you are not producing more seeds, ask Him to show You how. Get into His word and grow your faith. Allow Him to guide you to opportunities to share His love to others.

Prayer: God, help me to produce much grain in Your kingdom.

> John 12:26 *If anyone serves Me, Let him follow Me; and where I am, there My servant will be also. If anyone serves Me, him My Father will honor.*

Three times in this verse, Jesus mentions either serving or being a servant. Jesus speaking about Himself in Mark 10:45 said, "For even the Son of Man did not come to be served, but to serve and to give His life as a ransom for many." Paul writing in Galatians 5:13 said, "You my brothers were called to be free. But do not use your freedom to indulge in sinful nature; rather, serve one another in love." Peter also wrote in 1 Peter 4:10, "Each one should use whatever gift he has received to serve others, faithfully, administering God's grace in its various forms." By now, you should be getting the picture that as followers of Christ, we are called to be His servants, not simply church goers. Since we are called to be a servant, it might be helpful to understand what that looks like. Acts of servanthood will be different from person to person but they all begin with an attitude of humbleness and self-sacrifice. It is impossible to be a servant if you are constantly seeking to fulfill your own wants and desires. Secondly, a servant's perspective is an eternal one with heavenly goals and Christlike values. Devoting your time to serving certain people in hopes of personal gain is not following Jesus' example. Lastly, a servant finds more joy and blessing from hearing "Well done My good and faithful servant," than seeking the praises and accolades from others. Servanthood is not about personal recognition and acts of service that make us feel good about ourselves. True servanthood is following Jesus wherever that takes you. Matthew 16:24, "If anyone would come after Me, he must deny himself and take up his cross and follow Me." The good news is that as we follow Him, He is with us. Hebrews 13:5, "...Never will I leave you; never will I forsake you." Our reward for serving Christ is honor. Not just any honor, but true and lasting honor. The highest honor that anyone could receive, the honor that comes from God. Romans 8:18, "I consider that our present sufferings are not worth comparing with the glory that will be revealed in us." In the movie, "Jeremiah Johnson," he is asked, "You've come far pilgrim, were it worth the trouble?" To which Jeremiah Johnson replied, "What trouble?" Let that be our answer to those who ask if serving Christ is hard.

Prayer: God, help me to follow You.

> *John 12:27-28 Now My soul is troubled, and what shall I say? "Father, save Me from this hour?" But for this purpose I came to this hour. Father, glorify Your name.*

I love watching the life of Jesus depicted in the TV series, "*The Chosen.*" In an episode from Season 3, Jesus, Peter, John, and Matthew are walking to Jerusalem for an encounter with a crippled man at the Pool of Bethesda. As they approach Jerusalem, Roman soldiers are crucifying several criminals outside the city gates. Walking by, Jesus stares intently at the men being crucified. Without a word being spoken, you knew what Jesus was thinking by the look on His face. Just like Jesus' comment in today's verse, we get a glimpse of the human side of Jesus. He experienced the same emotions, hurt, disappointments, temptations, trials, and physical pain that we have. Yet through all He faced, Jesus was sinless. Hebrews 4:15, "For we do not have a high priest who is unable to sympathize with our weaknesses, but we have one who has been tempted in every way, just as we are – yet without sin." Days away from His crucifixion, Jesus shares His feelings saying, "My soul is troubled, what shall I say? Father, save Me from this hour?" This is very similar to His prayer in the Garden of Gethsemane found in Mark 14:34-36. If there were any other way, Jesus is asking the Father to change His circumstances. Yet He knew this was the very reason He came. So instead of ending His prayer at "Save Me from this hour," He continued saying, "But for this purpose I came to this hour. Father, glorify Your name." No matter how dreadful things were going to get, Jesus prayed that the Father be glorified. In other words, God's will be done, not mine. What do you pray when you are facing difficult circumstances? Do you pray for God to move mountains, part the Red Sea, and make a way for you to get to the other side or do you pray for His will to be done in your life? All too often, I am looking for relief and a path out of life's problems, when I should be focused on God's plan for my life. I will even provide Him solutions I think will work best. Jesus models the prayer He taught us to pray in Matthew 6:9-13, "Your kingdom come, Your will be done." If you feel your prayers have become ineffective, you may need to change the way you are praying.

Prayer: God, I pray that Your will be done in my life.

> John 12:32 And I, if I am lifted up from the earth, will draw all peoples to Myself.

Jesus has just said, "But for this purpose I came to this hour. Father, glorify Your name." John then writes, "A voice came from heaven saying, 'I have both glorified it and will glorify it again.' Therefore, when the people who stood by heard it and said that it had thundered. Others said, 'An angel has spoken to Him.'" This is the second time God has audibly spoken to Jesus. The first was at His baptism when God said, "This is My Son, whom I love; with Him I am well pleased." Jesus told the crowd the voice was for their benefit. It was another among the long list of signs He was the Messiah. Jesus is headed to the cross. He knows it and makes it clear that He has come to offer salvation to both the Jews and non-Jews alike. Jesus isn't implying that every person would put their faith in Him for salvation. Obviously, there are many who don't. However, through His death and resurrection, eternal life is made available to anyone who believes. 1 Peter 3:18, "For Christ died for sins once for all, the righteous for the unrighteous, to bring you to God. He was put to death in the body but made alive by the Spirit." Sadly, I think we as Christians lose focus on the significance of Jesus being lifted up on the cross. Jesus stressed this very act will "draw all peoples" to Himself; because, it is at the cross where we find God's judgment for sin. But the cross is also where we find God's mercy through the forgiveness of our sins. The cross can also be a stumbling block to many. 1 Corinthians 1:23, "But we preach Christ crucified: a stumbling block to the Jews and foolishness to the Gentiles." Questions like, "Why would someone chose to die a horrible death on the cross?" "Wouldn't it be easier to set up an earthly kingdom and wipe out all the non-believers?" However, the cross was God's plan for saving us from our sins. He can't overlook them or let us remain in them and have an eternal relationship with Him. For that reason, forgiveness has a price, and that price was God's only Son, Jesus, who bore them on the cross. Have you been drawn to the cross? If not, allow the Holy Spirit to lead you there today.

Prayer: God, thank You for the cross.

> John 12:46 I have come as a light into the world, that whoever believes in Me should not abide in darkness.

You don't have to look very hard to see that a great number of people in this world are living in darkness. It shows up on our TV screens, in the movie theatres, and in the lyrics to many popular songs. It is also readily available on your mobile device through various social media platforms. While the methods and technology have changed, nothing is really new about the darkness that covers this world. The reality is that we are born into it with a sinful nature. It doesn't have to be taught. It is what makes a child who is too young to know how to lie, tell a lie. We grow up with it inside us, becoming accustomed to the darkness of sin and its lifestyle of greed, selfishness, sexual immorality, hatred, drunkenness, envy, and idolatry. The Bible tells us that not only are we born with a sinful nature, we become slaves to it. Romans 6:6, "For we know that our old self was crucified with Him so that the body of sin might be done away with, that we should no longer be slaves to sin." No matter how hard we try, there is no escaping the darkness of sin on our own. For those who think they are okay and don't have a problem with living in darkness, we learn in 1 John 1:8, "If we claim to be without sin, we deceive ourselves and the truth is not in us." How do we escape our slavery to sin and darkness? Today's verse is the answer. This is the second time Jesus refers to Himself as the light of the world. He also spoke about it in John 8:12. In both scriptures, Jesus tells us, He is the only way out of the darkness of sin, "I have come as a light into the world, that whoever believes in Me should not abide in darkness." Anyone who believes in Jesus is delivered from the bondage of sin and darkness. They are enabled by the Holy Spirit to walk in spiritual light and life where there is freedom. Why would anyone want to want to remain in bondage to sin if they could have freedom and life eternal? Maybe they have not been led to the light. Do you know someone who is living in darkness? Tell them about Jesus. Let Him do the rest.

Prayer: God, help me to lead someone to Your light.

> John 12:47 *And if anyone hears My words and does not believe, I do not judge him; for I did not come to judge the world but to save the world.*

Yesterday, we talked about the sinful nature we were born with that causes us to rebel against God and which leads us down a path of ugliness. Sin has plagued everyone who has ever been born, except Jesus, the Son of God, who never sinned. Yet, He never looked down on anyone or condemned them because of their sin. In John 8:1-11, we read about the woman caught in the act of adultery who was brought before Jesus. The Pharisees wanted to trap Jesus into breaking either the Law of Moses that said she should be stoned, or Roman law that said the Jews were not allowed to punish someone by death. In His conversation with the woman, Jesus didn't tell her what a mess she had made of her life and that she wasn't going to heaven. He didn't condemn her for breaking the 7th commandment of the Law. He said to her, "Woman, where are they that accused you? Has no one condemned you? Then neither do I condemn you, go now and leave your life of sin." More than anything else, Jesus had compassion for the lost, the hurting, and unsaved. We find that throughout the Bible. Matthew 14:14, "When Jesus landed and saw a large crowd, He had compassion on them and healed their sick." Matthew 9:36, "When He saw the crowds, He had compassion on them..." Luke 7:13, "When the Lord saw her, He had compassion on her..." Mark 1:41, "Filled with compassion, Jesus reached out His hand and touched the man." Jesus said today, "I did not come to judge the world, but to save the world." Jesus announced His purpose for coming to the world early in His ministry when he read from Isaiah 61:1-2, "The Spirit of the Lord is upon Me, because He has anointed Me to preach the good news to the poor. He has sent Me to proclaim freedom for the prisoners and recovery of sight for the blind, to release the oppressed, to proclaim the year of the Lord's favor." If you are feeling condemnation today, it is not from Jesus. He loves you and has compassion for you. He came to save you from your sins, not condemn you for them. Jesus offers forgiveness and a new life in Him. Listen to His voice of love and compassion. Start a new life with Him today.

Prayer: God, thank You for coming to save us, not condemn us.

> John 12:48 *He who rejects Me, and does not receive My words, has that which judges him – the word that I have spoken will judge him in the last day.*

The first time Jesus came into the world, His purpose was to save the world. John 3:17, "For God did not send His Son into the world to condemn the world, but to save the world through Him." Jesus' second coming will be completely different. Instead of being born in a lowly manger, Jesus will return to earth, riding on the clouds with glory and power. Matthew 24:30, "At that time the sign of the Son of Man will appear in the sky, and all the nations of the earth will mourn. They will see the Son of Man coming on the clouds of the sky, with power and great glory." When He returns, Jesus will defeat Satan and his followers, bless His children, and set up His Kingdom on earth. Jesus will also sit as judge over every one who did not receive His word. Anyone's name not found written in the Book of Life will be thrown into the lake of fire. (Revelation 20:15) Jesus said the evidence which will be used against those who deny Him are His words. Jesus' words are simple and easy to understand. His words are the words that God the Father has given Him to speak. God has revealed Himself and the path to salvation through the words of Jesus. Yet so many people find them hard to accept and a stumbling block to receiving salvation. 1 Corinthians 1:23, "But we preach Christ crucified; a stumbling block to Jews and foolishness to Gentiles." Others just flat out deny the truth of God's word, thinking they know more than God. Paul writes in Romans 1:18-19,21-22, "The wrath of God is being revealed from heaven against all the godlessness and wickedness of those who suppress the truth by their wickedness, since what may be known about God is plain to them because God has made it plain to them. For although they knew God, they neither glorified Him as God nor gave thanks to Him, but their thinking became futile and their foolish hearts were darkened. Although they claimed to be wise, they became fools." Jesus' words are truth and will stand the test of time and man's challenges. Eventually, everyone will have to reckon with the invincible reality of the Word of Christ. My prayer for you is that you have already come to that conclusion.

Prayer: God, I receive Your words into my life. Help me to live them each day.

> *John 13:7 Jesus answered and said to him, "What I am doing you do not understand now, but you will know after this."*

Jesus' public ministry has ended. He and the disciples are now in the upper room, celebrating the Feast of the Passover, which we know as "The Last Supper." After they had finished eating, Jesus got up, took off His outer garment and wrapped a towel around Himself. Jesus poured water into a bowl and began, one by one, washing and drying the disciples' feet. The disciples needed a lesson in humility. Luke 22:24 tells us they had been arguing among themselves at dinner who was greatest. When Jesus gets around to Peter, he objects to Jesus stooping to do a lowly servant's task saying, "Lord, are You washing my feet?" In Jewish culture, washing another person's feet was not the job of the typical household servant. It was reserved for the lowest of the low. As guests would enter a person's home, the servant would kneel down, remove the guest's sandals, wash and dry their feet and put their sandals back on. Jesus answers Peter, "What I am doing you do not understand now, but you will know after this." Peter didn't know in a couple of hours, he would deny Jesus three times, abandon Him while He was being crucified, and doubt the resurrection until he saw the empty tomb for himself. Jesus understood that Peter and the other disciples needed to experience His unconditional love and teach them the importance of humility. Jesus' statement applies just as much to you and I today. Perhaps you have it all together and understand God and know what He is doing in your life. However, there are many of us who are struggling and need help figuring life out. Life can be going along just fine, then out of nowhere you get bad news from your doctor. Your company downsizes and you lose your job, leaving your finances in shambles. Problems develop between you and your spouse. We may never understand the reason for life's twists and turns, but our only hope is in trusting God. He knows the end before the beginning and is in control. Romans 8:28, "And we know that in all things God works for the good of those who love Him, who have been called according to His purpose." But how can these things work for my good? Jesus said, 'You do not realize now what I am doing, but later you will.

Prayer: God, help me to trust You in all circumstances.

John 13:14 *If I then your Lord and Teacher, have washed your feet, you also ought to wash one another's feet.*

Thankfully, washing feet is not a decree or religious observance like communion, issued by Jesus that we should do periodically at church. However, some churches will schedule a foot washing service from time to time to teach humbleness and servanthood. I recall the first foot washing service, I ever attended. Brother Roy Woodard who is at least 10 years older than me, knelt down before me, took off my shoes and socks, and began to wash my feet. There is a reason we wear shoes and socks. They hide our ugly looking toe nails, smelly feet, and the dirt between our toes. My first reaction was embarrassment. Brother Roy didn't complain or make some wise comment about the condition of my feet. Maybe he was holding his breath, trying to get through it. I didn't ask when it was over. But as I sat there, I began to think about the significance of the moment. Here was a leader of our church, someone older than me, teaching me how to serve others. After he finished, we switched places and it was my turn to wash his feet. My normal reaction would have been to make a joke or funny comment to lighten the situation. Instead, I thought about Jesus washing the disciples' feet and how much the Savior of the world, God himself, must have loved us to do what He did. For me, one of the hardest things to accept as a follower of Christ is the fact that we are to put others ahead of ourselves. Jesus said, if we want to be first in the kingdom of God, we should be a servant. Mark 9:35, "If anyone wants to be first, he must be the very last, and the servant of all." Christ can't use our selfish ambition and pride in His Kingdom. They will not work. How do we replace those with a spirit of giving and humility? We follow Jesus' example by becoming a foot washer. How do I put that into practice? First, start by thinking of one way that you can serve someone else in love. It may be a family member, a neighbor, or fellow church member. Then do it. Not for reward or recognition, but because you love others like Christ loved you. Once you have finished, start the process all over again.

Prayer: God, help, me to be a foot washer in Your kingdom.

> John 13:16-17 Most assuredly, I say to you, "a servant is not greater that his master; nor is he who is sent greater than he who sent him. If you know these things, blessed are you if you do them."

Jesus has just finished washing the disciples' feet, including Judas who was minutes away from betraying Him. He tells the disciples in John 13:15, "For I have given you an example, that you should do as I have done to you." Jesus, the Son of God, lowered Himself to take on the role of a servant and washed their feet. Then, He tells the disciples they should follow His example because, "a servant is not greater than his master, nor is he who is sent greater than he who sent him." Jesus is not teaching them to go around washing everybody's feet. But He is giving them an example of how a servant leader should live. Also, being His followers made them no better than He. They were not too important to humble themselves to serve others. Then He tells the disciples, now that you have learned this lesson, you will be blessed by following it. Jesus was the ultimate servant leader, leading by example. If you are a Christian, then Jesus expects you to be a servant leader. This does not mean you are required to be a small group leader or in charge of some ministry at your church. He just wants you to follow His example. What exactly does that look like? First, put others first. Philippians 2:3-4, "Do nothing out of selfish ambition or vain conceit, but in humility consider others better than yourselves. Each of you should look not only to your own interests, but also to the interests of others." Second, genuinely care for others. Be kind and have concern for others. Galatians 6:9-10, "Let us not become weary in doing good, for at the proper time we will reap a harvest if we do not give up. Therefore, as we have opportunity, let us do good to all people, especially to those who belong to the family of believers." Lastly, we should value people and appreciate them for who they are; while, challenging them to be what God has called them to be. When Jesus was speaking to the woman caught in adultery, He didn't rake her over the coals for her behavior. Jesus said in John 7:11, "Then neither do I condemn you. Go now and leave your life of sin." While serving others, we can't condone their sin, but neither should we be condemning them for it either.

Prayer: God, help me to follow Your example.

Day 282

John 13:19 Now I tell you before it comes, that when it does come to pass, you may believe that I am He.

After washing the disciples' feet, Jesus tells them about His upcoming betrayal, primarily to make the disciples aware of what was about to happen. It was also to prove He was who He said He was. Jesus told them in John 13:18, "I am not referring to all of you, I know those I have chosen. But this is to fulfill the scripture; 'He who shares my bread has lifted up his heel against me.'" Jesus is referencing Psalm 41:9 where David writes, "Even my close friend, whom I trusted, he who shared my bread, has lifted up his heel against me." If you have ever been kicked by a horse, you know exactly what Jesus means by "lifting his heel against me." A horse will raise its back leg and kick if they feel they are in danger from something behind them. Their kick is so powerful, it can injure or even kill anything in its path. Jesus likens Judas betrayal, to being kicked by a horse. Judas was one of the twelve disciples chosen by Jesus. Although he wasn't very honest with the ministry funds, Judas was their treasurer and a member of the team. He is right there listening as Jesus tells them He will be betrayed and the pain it will cause. Judas has the opportunity to change his mind and repent. Yet on his own volition, he leaves shortly after Jesus shares a piece of bread with him to lead the religious leaders to where Jesus will be. Jesus' words are a word of warning for us as well. 2 Timothy 3: 12, "In fact, everyone who wants to live a godly life in Christ Jesus will be persecuted." God knows that we are going to experience rejection and hardship because of our faith in Him. It may even come from our closest friends or family. When that time comes, we shouldn't be surprised, but should trust God who is in control. 2 Corinthians 1:9, "Indeed, in our hearts we felt the sentence of death. But this happened that we might not rely on ourselves but on God who raises the dead." People will abandon us and even stop loving us, but Jesus never will. Trust in the one who raises the dead.

Prayer: God, I believe You are He who raises the dead.

> John 13:34 *A new commandment I give to you, that you love one another; as I have loved you, that you also love another.*

Having set the example of washing the disciples' feet, Jesus gives them a new commandment. Jesus tells them to love one another, as He loved them. Jesus has added a new twist to an old commandment that said you should love your neighbor as yourself. Leviticus 19:18, "Do not seek revenge or bear a grudge against one of your people, but love your neighbor as yourself. I am the Lord." Very soon, the disciples would experience the very depth of Jesus' love, by Him willingly going to the cross to die for our sins. He would later say in John 15:13, "Greater love has no one than this, that he lay down his life for his friends." The thing so special about Jesus is that He doesn't require anything of us, that He has not already done Himself. Jesus' command is very simple and easy to understand, but sometimes very difficult to live out. Loving other people is hard work. It is not easy to love your spouse when they have hurt you. Who wants to love a friend who has betrayed you? How easy is it to love someone at work who is constantly putting you down to gain favor with the boss? Even as children, it is hard to love the school bully who takes advantage of those smaller than them. There have been times when I wanted to ask, "God are you sure I am supposed to love this person?" Of course, I know the answer is going to be, "I loved you, didn't I?" The only difference between me and those I am supposed to love is God's grace. How do we love others as Christ loved us? We start by praying for them. I have found the more you pray for someone, the more compassion you have for them. Prayer leads you into wanting to understand that person and the reasons why they are so hard to love. Prayer breaks through our focus on behaviors and places it on the person. Next, loving others isn't giving them what they deserve, but what they need. People need kindness and forgiveness, not retaliation. Loving others requires self-restraint, not lashing out at them when they do things we don't approve of. Lastly, loving others isn't rejoicing when they are hurting, but having sympathy for them and hurt when they hurt.

Prayer: God, help me to love others as You have loved me.

> John 13:35 *By this all will know that you are My disciples, if you have love for one another.*

We live in a crazy mixed-up world. Being a Christian is no longer viewed as someone who is kind and compassionate to others, but someone who is intolerant of others lifestyle choices. What was once considered loving your neighbor as yourself is now viewed as hatred and bigotry. I feel we have gotten to this point partly because we as Christians have not followed Jesus' command to love one another, and because many people today do not want to accept the truth of God's word. Anyone who shares God's word in love, contradicts what others believe to be truth; and are therefore not considered loving and accepting. Before throwing up your hands and saying, what's the use, Jesus reminds us, "By this all will know that you are My disciples, if you have love for one another." As Christians we should follow Jesus' example. Jesus loved people who were not like Him and disagreed with Him. He loved the sick, the poor, and the lame. He loved tax collectors, prostitutes, and people of all races. There is no one that Jesus did not love. However, it doesn't mean He didn't challenge people, get frustrated with them, and throw some of them out of the temple. If we look closely at Jesus' interactions with people, we see He met them where they were, but didn't leave them there. He never accepted or agreed with what they were doing. Jesus called them to repentance. He offered forgiveness and invited them to change their ways. I don't want to make it sound like Jesus had it easy and all together. He loved the soldiers who had torn His back open with a whip. He loved those who had Him nailed to a cross. He loved the disciples who deserted Him. Loving as Jesus loved is not going to be easy. Loving unconditionally makes us vulnerable to be hurt. It is safe to say, at some time in our lives, we all have been hurt by someone we love. I can assure you, unless you are completely sold out to God, you will slip up and fail at loving them back. The good news is that God will love you anyway. Pray today that God will give you grace to follow His command to love one another and grace for when we fail. Go and be a disciple today.

Prayer: God, I want others to know I am Your disciple.

> *John 14:1 Let not your heart be troubled; you believe in God, believe also in Me.*

The disciples were troubled and confused. Jesus has just told them He was leaving them and where He was going, they could not go. Peter speaks up and asks, "Lord where are You going?" Jesus replied, "Where I am going, you cannot follow now, but you will follow later." Peter then asked, "Lord, why can't I follow You now? I will lay down my life for You." Making matters worse, Jesus answered Peter saying, "Will you really lay down your life for Me? I tell you the truth, before the rooster crows, you will deny Me three times." Jesus has just rocked Peter's world. No doubt this created even more concern among the disciples. Peter, the rock, is going to deny Jesus three times tonight? How can that happen? Amidst the confusion, Jesus speaks these words of comfort and peace to the disciples, "Do not let your hearts be troubled, you believe in God, believe also in Me." These words of Jesus are often read at someone's funeral. They are read to comfort the grieving family and friends. We read them and hold fast to them because we live in a world filled with trouble. It knocks on our door every day. Today, we are witnessing the atrocities of terrorism by Hamas towards Israel. Hundreds of innocent people attending a festival, murdered by the Hamas terrorists. Hundreds more in the neighboring towns taken as hostages, tortured, and beheaded. More innocent lives will be lost in the upcoming days because of hatred and evil in this world. In the midst of all the chaos and confusion in our lives and throughout the world, how do we keep our hearts from being troubled? Jesus knew our hearts were going to be troubled and gave us this word, "trust in God, trust also in Me." Will that automatically stop the madness? Will it keep us safe from all danger? Not likely, but it will change our perspective of it. God will give you inner peace and strength to face the day. Isaiah 26:3-4, "You will keep in perfect peace him whose mind is steadfast because he trusts in You. Trust in the Lord forever, for the Lord, the Lord, is the Rock eternal." Be intentional each day, keeping your mind fixed on Jesus and His word. Allow His peace to fill your life.

Prayer: God, I put my faith and trust in You.

> John 14:2 In My Father's house are many mansions, if it were not so, I would have told you. I go to prepare a place for you.

My father used to sing in a quartet when he was in his 20's. The group would travel around and sing at different churches in the area. One Sunday evening, they were singing one of their favorite songs, "Lord Build Me a Cabin," written by Curtis Stewart, and sung by Hank Williams. The chorus goes, "Yes, *just build me a cabin in the corner of Glory Land, In the shade of the tree of life that it may ever stand, Where I can just hear the angels sing and shake Jesus' hand. Lord build me a cabin in the corner of glory land.*" Papa said as they were singing, an elderly man in bib overalls came walking down the aisle, shouting at them to stop singing. The music stopped and everyone was waiting to see what the old man was going to do. He told them, "Boys, I ain't looking for some old cabin in the corner of heaven, I live in one of them right now. Jesus has a mansion prepared for me. So don't be singing about some old cabin." Papa said, they quickly started singing, "*Let Us Have a Little Talk With Jesus.*" From then on, they never sang "Lord Build Me a Cabin," and replaced it with "*Build My Mansion Next Door to Jesus.*" Jesus tells the disciples, that He is going to prepare a place for them in His Father's house. What that looks like is up for debate. The Bible translates it as "mansions," but it could also mean a dwelling place. The important point is there is room for all who trust in Jesus. However, in order for Jesus to prepare a place for us, He had to go to the cross at Calvary. Once Jesus conquered death and the grave, eternal life begins for all who believe in Him. Our bodies then become a temple or dwelling place for God. 1 Corinthians 6:19, "Do you not know that your body is a temple of the Holy Spirit, who is in you, whom you have received from God. You are not your own." Ephesians 2:22, "And in Him, you too are being built together to become a dwelling in which God lives by His Spirit. One day our earthly bodies will die and Jesus will transport us to a glorious dwelling place He has prepared for us.

Prayer: God, thank You for preparing a place for me.

> *John 14:3 And if I go and prepare a place for you, I will come again and receive you to Myself; that where I am, there you may be also.*

Jesus has just told the disciples there are many mansions in His Father's house and He was going to prepare a place for them. Then He promises them, "I will come back and take you to be with Me that you also may be where I am." The disciples are still confused and unaware of the significance of what is about to take place. Jesus knows He is headed to the cross and will be raised back to life on the third day. He will spend 40 days on earth with the disciples and appearing to many other believers. However, He will return to heaven. Mark 16:19, "After the Lord Jesus had spoken to them, He was taken up into heaven and He sat at the right hand of God." Paul tells us in Romans 8:34, that Jesus is at the right hand of God, interceding for us. For almost 2,000 years, Jesus has sat at the right hand of the Father, waiting for the moment of His triumphal return to earth. Prior to His return, Jesus will call to Himself, both dead and alive, those who have believed in Him. 1 Thessalonians 4:14-18, "We believe that Jesus died and rose again and so we believe that God will bring with Jesus those who have fallen asleep in Him. According to the Lord's own word, we tell you that we who are still alive, who are left till the coming of the Lord, will certainly not precede those who have fallen asleep. For the Lord Himself will come down from heaven, with a loud command, and with the voice of the archangel and with the trumpet call of God, and the dead in Christ will rise first. After that, we who are still alive and are left will be caught up together with them in the clouds to meet the Lord in the air. And so we will be with the Lord forever. Therefore encourage each other with these words." You may be like the disciples, confused and unaware of what is going to happen next. Let these words encourage you. Jesus is coming back very soon, for you and me to be with Him forever. We may not live to see the rapture, but that doesn't matter. Everyone who has trusted Jesus as their Lord and Savior, will be with Him in heaven.

Prayer: God, thank You for Your promised return.

> *John 14:6 Jesus said to him, "I am the way, the truth, and the life. No one comes to the Father except through Me."*

Jesus has just told the disciples in John 14:5, "You know the way to the place where I am going." Thomas then asks a very reasonable question, "Lord, we don't know where You are going, so how can we know the way?" Jesus has just been talking about His Father's house, mansions, and preparing a place for them, but the disciples were not thinking in those terms. Jesus' answer to Thomas was the sixth of seven "I Am" declarations made by Jesus. He said, "I am the way, the truth, and the life. No one comes to the Father except through Me." His answer leaves no doubt there is only one path to God. Salvation is by the grace of God, through our faith in Jesus. Ephesians 2:8-9, "For it is by grace you have been saved, through faith – and this not from yourselves, it is the gift of God – not by works, so that no one can boast." However, many object to the idea that only those who believe in Christ will be saved. Why is Jesus the only way to salvation? First, He was sent by God to pay the penalty for our sins. 1 John 2:2, "He is the atoning sacrifice for our sins, and not only for ours but for the sins of the whole world." Second, He was the only person who has lived a perfect life. Hebrews 4:15, "For we do not have a high priest who is unable to sympathize with our weaknesses, but we have one who has been tempted in every way, just as we are – yet was without sin." Third, He is the only person to conquer death and the grave. Romans 6:9, "For we know that since Christ was raised from the dead, He cannot die again; death no longer has mastery over Him." Not only is Jesus the way, He is the source of all truth and the standard to which all things are judged to be true or not. Jesus testifying before Pilate said in John 18:37, "...In fact, for this reason I was born, and for this reason I came into the world, to testify to the truth. Everyone on the side of truth listens to Me." Lastly, Jesus offers eternal life. John 11:25, "I am the resurrection and the life. He who believes in Me will never die..."

Prayer: God, thank You for showing us the way to eternal life.

> *John 14:7 If you had known Me, you would have known My Father also; and from now on you know Him and have seen Him.*

It is one thing to know about someone, and quite another to truly know them. How well do you know Jesus? How often do you speak with Him and read His word? I have come to realize, the more I read and study His word, there is so much more to learn about Him. I'm not sure I will ever fully know Jesus until I get to heaven. However, that is not going to stop me from trying. 2 Peter 3:18 tells us, "But grow in the grace and knowledge of our Lord and Savior Jesus Christ. To Him be the glory both now and forever! Amen." One thing I have learned is that only having a head knowledge of who Jesus is and what He did is not enough. Simply knowing the facts about Jesus doesn't save us. James 2:19, "You believe there is a God. Good! Even the demons believe that – and shudder." Quite often, I will meet people who say they know Jesus, but their lives say otherwise. They don't live any differently before they knew Christ. Knowing Christ changes us from the inside out, and transforms us into a new person. Paul said in Philippians 3:8, "What is more, I consider everything a loss compared to the surpassing greatness of knowing Christ Jesus my Lord, for whose sake I have lost all things. I consider them rubbish, that I may gain Christ." Paul understood the "why" behind who Jesus was and turned his life upside down to follow Him. Jesus became real to him. For Paul, it took a blinding light and the voice of Jesus speaking to him on the Road to Damascus to change his heart. Mostly likely, God is not going to speak to you in that way. So, how do we move from having a head knowledge of Christ to a heart knowledge? God needs to become real to us. If you are reading His word, going to church, and praying out of an obligation to check off the boxes of religious activity, then you are struggling to have a heart knowledge of Christ. This does not mean doing these things are wrong, but our attitude for doing them needs adjusting. Transfer your head knowledge to your heart by taking time to grasp the love of God and what He has done for you. Take time each day to get to know Him better.

Prayer: God, help me to know You better.

> John 14:13-14 And whatever you ask in My name, that I will do, that the Father may be glorified in the Son. If you ask anything in My name, I will do it.

These may be two of the most misused verses in the Bible. We are led to believe if you are sick, ask in Jesus' name and He will heal you. If you are having financial problems, ask in Jesus' name and He will provide. Or maybe you have prayed, "In Jesus name, get me out of this mess I have made of my life." All we have to do is include, "in the name of Jesus" to our prayers and they will automatically be answered. If you have prayed similar prayers, then you know they simply don't work. When our prayers are not aligned with the will of God, we will be waiting a long time for them to be answered. How do we genuinely pray in the name of Jesus to have a productive prayer life? First, pray according to God's will. Jesus taught us that in the Lord's prayer. He said, "Your kingdom come, Your will be done on earth as it is in heaven." Secondly, our prayers reach the throne of God when they are made in Jesus' name and in line with His will. Romans 5:1-2, "Therefore, since we have been justified through faith, we have peace with God through our Lord Jesus Christ, through whom we have gained access by faith into the grace in which we now stand..." Lastly, when we pray according to God's will and in Jesus' name, we can pray with confidence our prayers will be heard, and answered as God deems best for us. 1 John 5:14-15, "This is the confidence we have in approaching God: that if we ask anything according to His will, He hears us. And if we know that He hears us – whatever we ask – we know that we have what we asked of Him." However, sandwiched between Jesus saying to ask for anything in His name are the words, "that the Father may be glorified in the Son." The purpose of our prayers should be to glorify the Father. If your prayer life is not very effective, ask yourself before praying, "How can God receive the glory through this request?" Your prayers will become more powerful as you begin aligning them to His will and purpose, and where He receives the glory. Then as you ask in Jesus' name, you can have the assurance God will act on your behalf in accordance to His will.

Prayer: God, help me to pray according to Your will.

> *John 14:15 If you love Me, keep My commandments.*

Is Jesus saying we should keep His commandments to show that we love Him, or should our love for Him compel us to keep His commands? This is not a trick question. You will find some Christians who think loving Jesus is just about following the rules. They feel it is their moral duty to be obedient to God and focus solely on obeying His commands. To be clear, anyone who follows Christ should keep His commands. 1 John 2:3-5, "We know that we have come to know Him if we obey His commands. The person who says, "I know Him," but does not do what He commands is a liar, and the truth is not in him. But if anyone obeys His word, God's love is truly made complete in Him. This is how we know we are in Him." If our motivation for keeping His commands and doing good works is to help keep our salvation or to check off the boxes of do's and don'ts, then our hearts may not be in the right place. Romans 11:6, "And if by grace, then it is no longer by works; if it were, grace would no longer be grace." Salvation is through the grace of God. There is nothing we can do to work our way closer to Him. Jesus tells us in Matthew 22:36 what our motivation should be for obeying Him. He was asked by an expert of the law, "Teacher, which is the greatest commandment of the Law?" Jesus responded, "Love the Lord your God with all your heart and with all your soul and with all your mind. This is the first and greatest commandment. And the second is like it: 'Love your neighbor as yourself.' All the Law and the Prophets hang on these two commandments." We start by obeying the greatest commandment given by Jesus, to love the Lord God with all our heart, mind, and soul giving Him praise and thanksgiving continually. When we get that right, following the other commandments become a desire not a moral duty. Loving our neighbor, forgiving others, and avoiding temptations and the desire to sin becomes easier. God's commands are designed for us to have an abundant life in Him. Get to know and love Him more each day.

Prayer: God, help me to love You more each day. I want to obey Your commands.

John 14:16 And I will pray the Father, and He will give you another Helper, that He may abide with you forever.

As a Christian, can you imagine what life would be like without the Holy Spirit? Coming to Christ would be almost impossible. Without the Holy Spirit convicting us of our sins, how would we realize we need a Savior? It is through His work that we are drawn to know Jesus is the answer to forgiveness and salvation. John 16:8, "And when He (the Holy Spirit) comes, He will convict the world of its guilt in regard to sin and righteousness and judgment." Not only coming to salvation would be difficult, but we would have no assurance of being saved. Without the presence of God living within us, we have no moral compass to guide us. No internal voice teaching us right from wrong. Truth becomes what we believe it to be. We are left to figure life out on our own. The Holy Spirit on the other hand leads and guides us to know the truth. John 16:13, "But when He, the Spirit of Truth, comes, He will guide you into all truth. He will not speak on His own; He will speak only what He hears, and He will tell you what is yet to come." But that is not all the Holy Spirit does for us. He is our advocate, offering support, strength and counsel. The Holy Spirit reminds us what Jesus taught so we can depend on His word. Romans 8:16, "The Spirit Himself testifies with our spirit that we are God's children." The Holy Spirit is also our comforter. Life is full of ups and downs, challenges, failures, good and painful times. The Holy Spirit doesn't desert us when life gets hard. The Holy Spirit is with us and gives us peace during those times. Romans 8:26, "In the same way, the Spirit helps us in our weakness. We do not know what we ought to pray for, but the Spirit Himself intercedes for us with groans that words cannot express." Lastly, the Holy Spirit encourages us to let Him guide and direct our lives. Romans 8:9, "You, however, are not controlled by the sinful nature but by the Spirit, if the Spirit of God lives in you. And if anyone does not have the Spirit of Christ, he does not belong to Christ." Jesus promised our advocate, comforter, and encourager would abide with us forever. How well do you know Him?

Prayer: God, thank You send sending the Holy Spirit.

> John 14:17 *The Spirit of truth, whom the world cannot receive, because it neither sees Him or knows Him; but you know Him, for He dwells with you and will be in you.*

Yesterday Jesus told us the Father would send a Helper that would abide with us forever. This Helper, the Holy Spirit would be an advocate for us, a comforter to us, and an encourager to guide us. Today, Jesus identifies the Holy Spirit as the Spirit of Truth. He also tells us the world "neither sees Him or knows Him." The Holy Spirit will only dwell with those who have accepted Jesus as their Lord and Savior. To the non-believer, Christianity and the Holy Spirit are foolishness. 1 Corinthians 2:14, "The person without the Spirit does not accept the things that come from the Spirit of God, for they are foolishness to them, and they cannot understand them, because they are spiritually discerned." Christianity to the non-Christian is like someone who is watching a football game for the first time. That person only sees a bunch of men dressed up with helmets and pads, fighting over an odd-shaped ball. However, when someone helps explain the rules and the reason why the teams try to get the ball over the goal line, the game takes on more meaning. The role of the Holy Spirit is to explain, equip, and guide the believer. Jesus identifies the Holy Spirit as the Spirit of Truth. We can trust what the Holy Spirit is teaching us. It is sad to watch so many people who are confused and struggling to identify what is truth. I attended an event last month where author/apologist, Dr. Frank Turek spoke on his book, "I Don't Have Enough Faith To Be An Atheist." He touched on the concept of there being no truth and there is no absolute truth. His reply to someone who says there is no truth, "Is that true? Is it true that there is no truth? Because if it is true that there is no truth, then the claim that there is no truth can't be true even though it claims to be true." His response to the statement, "There is no absolute truth," is very similar. He asks, "Is that an absolute truth? Are you absolutely sure? Isn't that an absolute truth?" If you are like me, I had to reread those statements several times before they sunk in. That is why I am thankful for the Spirit of Truth who lives in the heart of every believer.

Prayer: God, thank You for sending Your Holy Spirit, the Spirit of Truth to teach me what is truth.

> John 14:21 He who has My commandments and keeps them, it is he who loves Me. And he who loves Me will be loved by My Father, and I will love him and manifest Myself to him.

Jesus said our love for Him is demonstrated by keeping His commandments. He knows obedience flowing from love looks very different from obedience performed out of obligation. For example, in a marriage, both spouses should want to do things for each other. If those actions are being done out of obligation, the marriage is more of a contract than a commitment. Love is the foundation of any good relationship. Keeping Jesus' commandments demonstrates our love for Him. As we look into the reasons for keeping His commandments, it is important to understand; first, doing good works does not earn our salvation. Titus 3:5, "He saved us, not because of righteous things we had done, but because of His mercy. He saved us through the washing of rebirth and renewal by the Holy Spirit." Jesus said in Matthew 7:22, "Many will say to Me on that day, 'Lord, Lord, did we not prophesy in Your name, and in Your name cast out demons and perform many miracles?" Those things didn't matter to Jesus. He said, "I never knew you. Away from Me you evildoers!" Secondly, the reason for keeping the commandments of Jesus should not be because we are fearful of punishment or want to gain His favor. John said the reason we should love Him and keep His commandments is because He first loved us. (1 John 4:19) Jesus died on the cross to pay the penalty for our sins. He wants to abide with us. The deeper relationship we have with Him, the more we become like Him and want to serve Him. James 2:14-18 says, "What good is it, my brothers, if a man claims to have faith but has no deeds? Can such faith save him? Suppose a brother or sister is without clothes and daily food. If one of you says to him, 'Go, I wish you well; keep warm and well fed,' but does nothing about his physical needs, what good is it? In the same way, faith by itself, if it is not accompanied by action is dead. But someone will say, 'You have faith; I have deeds.' Show me your faith without deeds, and I will show you my faith by what I do." Lastly, Jesus promises the more we love Him and keep His commandments, the more He reveals Himself to us. Want more of Jesus, love and serve Him.

Prayer: God, help me to love You and keep Your commandments.

> *John 14:24 He who does not love Me does not keep My words; and the word which you hear is not Mine but the Father's who sent Me.*

As Christians we know salvation is not the result of our obedience, but rather obedience is the result of salvation. With salvation comes a personal relationship with Christ. He created us with a specific plan for our lives. Ephesians 2:10, "For we are God's workmanship, created in Christ Jesus to do good works, which God prepared in advance for us to do." Because of our love for Jesus and His sacrifice for our sins, we should serve and obey Him. Like all relationships, our relationship with Christ is not static. Jesus told us yesterday the more we "Keep His commandments, the more He reveals Himself to us." However, to keep His commandments we need to know what they are. They just don't pop up in our minds each day. God's commandments are found in His word. Only when we read and study it each day will He reveal His truths to us. Reading and studying God's word and applying it to our daily lives represents a growing and healthy relationship. But there are some whose relationship with Him never develops, as He points out in the Parable of the Sower found in Matthew 13. In the parable, some of the seed of God's word fell along the path and the birds came and ate the seeds. Other seed was sown on rocky soil. Because of the shallowness of the soil, the roots didn't grow very deeply and the plant withered away. Today so many people's lives are shaped by the world and social media instead of God's word. We see our favorite social media star endorsing and doing things and we want to emulate them. Things that God's word says we should avoid and disapprove of are now considered okay because everyone is doing it. Things such as: It's okay to live together before you are married. How else are you going to know if you are compatible? It's okay for a man to say he is a woman, and a woman to say she is a man, because that is how they identify themselves. It's okay to have a same sex relationship because that's the way God made me. It's okay to cheat, steal, and tell lies because it is the only way to get ahead. As harsh as this may sound, those are not the words of God. Learn His words and follow them.

Prayer: God, help me to apply Your word to my heart.

> John 14:26 But the Helper, the Holy Spirit, whom the Father will send in My name, He will teach you all things, and bring to your remembrance all things that I said to you.

Jesus said in John 14:16, He would pray to the Father that He would give us another Helper to abide with us forever. Today Jesus identifies the Helper as the Holy Spirit, who will teach and bring to remembrance all things Jesus has spoken to them. This very same Holy Spirit is the third person of the Trinity, God the Father, the Son, and the Holy Spirit, who were present when the world was created. Genesis 1:2, "Now the earth was formless and empty, darkness was over the surface of the deep, and the Spirit of God was hovering over the waters." The importance of the Holy Spirit working in the lives of the disciples is played out in the book of Acts. Before the Day of Pentecost, the disciples simply met together and prayed. Afterwards, they were emboldened to preach the good news to everyone. Three thousand people were saved that day after hearing Peter's message of repentance. The Holy Spirit was also instrumental in guiding Matthew, Mark, Luke, and John in writing their gospels. Most scholars believe the gospels were not written until 20 – 30 years after Jesus' death. It was by the guidance of the Holy Spirit they could remember and record the details they have in their gospels. This very same person is living within you and I today, indwelling the hearts of all those who have put their trust in Christ as their Savior. He is there enabling us to understand and apply God's word to our lives. 1 Corinthians 2:13-14, "This is what we speak, not in words taught us by human wisdom but in words taught us by the Spirit, expressing spiritual truths in spiritual words. The person without the Spirit does not accept things that come from the Spirit of God, for they are foolishness to him, and he cannot understand them, because they are not spiritually discerned." It's wonderful we have the Holy Spirit guiding us, but how do we discern between our own thinking and His leading? Honestly, I have never heard the Holy Spirit audibly speak to me. His method of speaking to us is through our conscience and other subtle ways. Paul said in Romans 9:1, "I speak the truth in Christ – I am not lying, my conscience confirms it in the Holy Spirit." Take time today to listen to the Holy Spirit speaking to you.

Prayer: God, thank You for sending the Holy Spirit to teach and guide us.

> John 14:27 *Peace I leave with you, My peace I give to you; not as the world gives do I give to you. Let not your heart be troubled, neither let it be afraid.*

Many people are looking for peace in their troubled lives, seeking freedom from life's worries and problems. The sad thing is, this kind of peace is temporary and lasts until another one of life's troubles comes along. Jesus knew the disciples were going to face some very difficult and challenging days after His death and resurrection. He tells them, "Peace I leave with you, My peace I give to you." What kind of peace does Jesus offer? Paul describes it very well in Philippians 4:7, "And the peace of God, which transcends all understanding, will guard your hearts and minds in Christ Jesus." We learn three things from Paul about the peace of God. First, it is supernatural and unexplainable. I can tell you from experience, when the peace of God comes over you, it can take you out of the deepest hole, and bring calmness to your life. It doesn't make sense, because our circumstances have not changed. We just have to accept that God is in control. Secondly, God's peace will guard our hearts in Christ Jesus. Why is it important to guard our hearts? Because that is where the motives for everything we do originates. Proverbs 4:23, "Above all else, guard your heart, for it is the wellspring of life." Lastly, God's peace will guard our minds. Anxiety and fear love to take residence in our minds, playing cruel tricks on us. Our minds will make up a worst-case scenario to our situation and then make it ten times worse. Philippians 4:6 says, "Do not be anxious about anything, but in everything, by prayer and petition, with thanksgiving, present your requests to God." Paul said to chase away fear and anxiety, we need to take them to God in prayer, with thanksgiving, knowing that He will answer. This all sounds very good until a major crisis arises in our lives. When it does, we have two choices, trust God and His word, or panic and let our minds take over. When my mind wants to take over and make up junk, I love to sing the following chorus, "Wonderful Peace," written by W. D. Cornell. "Peace, peace, wonderful peace, coming down from the Father above; Sweep over my spirit, forever I pray, In fathomless billows of love." Is your life full of trouble and worry? Seek the peace of God that passes all understanding.

Prayer: God, thank You for Your peace that passes all understanding.

> John 15:1-2 I am the true vine, and My Father is the vinedresser. Every branch in Me that does not bear fruit He takes away; and every branch that bears fruit He prunes, that it may bear more fruit.

My father transplanted a grape vine in his yard from my uncle's farm many years ago. This grape vine has been fertilized, cut back, pruned, and relocated but has yet to produce any grapes. What is even more frustrating, there are some wild grape vines in the nearby woods producing grapes. Essentially, that vine is good for nothing. It should be dug up and thrown away since it isn't producing anything. In the Old Testament, Israel is often referred to as a vine. Psalm 80:8, "You brought a vine out of Egypt; You drove out the nations and planted it." Today, Jesus talking to the disciples, uses a metaphor to describe Himself as the "True Vine," and the Father as the "Vinedresser." As the True Vine, Jesus replaces the old way of being born into the family of God from simply being Jewish, to being born again in Him. He describes the role of the Father as the vinedresser, tending the vine, removing unfruitful branches, and pruning the fruitful ones so they will bear more fruit. Again, we cross paths with the question of eternal security. If a branch is connected to the vine, but not bearing fruit, the Vinedresser or God will take that branch away. Some will argue that this is a warning to Christians about falling away from the faith. They ask, if a believer cannot lose salvation, why warn about falling away? Others on the side of eternal security will argue that these warnings are directed toward professing Christians who appear to be connected to the Vine, but have no relationship with Him. This would be someone like Judas who was called to be a disciple and followed Jesus, but turned away and betrayed Him. For me, the key to knowing if someone has truly accepted Christ is the type of fruit they produce. 1 John 3:9-10, "No one who is born of God will continue to sin, because God's seed remains in him; he cannot go on sinning, because he has been born of God. This is how we know who the children of God are and who the children of the devil are: Anyone who does not do what is right is not a child of God; nor is anyone who does not love his brother." Ask God to prune you today, so you can bear more fruit for Him.

Prayer: God, help me to bear much fruit for Your kingdom.

> John 15:4 Abide in Me, and I in you. As the branch cannot bear fruit of itself, unless it abides in the vine, neither can you, unless you abide in Me.

The 15th Chapter of John records Jesus' conversation with the disciples about the vine and the branches. Today, Jesus tells us, "Abide in Me, and I in you," because it is impossible to bear fruit unless the vine and the branch are connected. Jesus didn't make this an "if/then" statement. Abiding in Christ is a command for all believers. Therefore, we need to understand what Jesus is commanding us to do, and what that looks like in the life of a believer. Some translations use the phrase, "remain in Me," in place of abide. Abide also means to live, reside, or continue in Christ. It describes a close, intimate relationship, not just a casual acquaintance with Him. Abiding means to have a growing relationship with Christ, where we are learning more about Him and making changes in our lives to emulate Him. It means we continue to seek after Christ in spite of life's hardships. Abiding increases our faith in Christ, helping us to push through the doubts and fears of life. Lastly, abiding helps us to bear fruit. Colossians 1:10, "And we pray this in order that you may live a life worthy of the Lord and may please Him in every way; bearing fruit in every good work, growing in the knowledge of God." The keys to abiding in Christ are actually very simple. As you read them, you are going to think, I know all that. But the question is, how much time and effort do you put into them? The first step in abiding is to pray. Set aside time each day to spend time in prayer. Talk to God, tell Him about the things that are going on in your life. Admit your faults and sins, seeking His forgiveness. Allow Him time to speak to you. Second step, spend time in God's word. Often times, God will answer many of your prayers and questions through His written word. His word will also encourage you, challenge you, and change you. Third, spend time with other believers either in church, a Bible Study, or small group. Hebrews 10:25, "Let us not give up meeting together, as some are in the habit of doing, but let us encourage one another – and all the more as you see the day approaching." My prayer is that you will make abiding in Christ a priority in your life today.

Prayer: God, help me to abide in You.

> *John 15:5 I am the vine, you are the branches. He who abides in Me, and I in him, bears much fruit; for without Me you can do nothing.*

We have learned that we must abide in Christ because a branch cannot bear fruit if it is not attached to the vine. Jesus goes on to say in verse 8, "By this My Father is glorified, that you bear much fruit; so you will be My disciples." Our connection to the vine also helps us to produce a lot of fruit, which glorifies the Father. But just as important, our connection to Christ allows us to produce the right kind of fruit. Not all fruit is good. Take for instance the Pharisees, they were great at appearing to be righteous by following the law. However, their motivation was not out of love for God and others, but of self-righteousness and wanting to lift themselves up. Being a fruitful Christian works from the inside out. 2 Peter 1:5-8, "For this very reason, make every effort to add to your faith goodness; and to goodness, knowledge; and to knowledge, self-control; and to self-control, perseverance; and to perseverance, godliness; and to godliness, brotherly kindness; and to brotherly kindness, love. For if you possess these qualities in increasing measure, they will keep you from being ineffective and unproductive in your knowledge of our Lord Jesus Christ." God changes our character to be more like His. The outward result is a change in our lives from the acts of our sinful nature found in Galatians 5:19-21, to the fruits of the Spirit, love, joy, peace, patience, kindness, goodness, faithfulness, gentleness and self-control. Not only does abiding in Christ change our character, it changes the fruit of our conduct. We no longer live like the world, but as Christ has called us to live. Romans 12:2, "Do not conform any longer to the pattern of this world, but be transformed by the renewing of your mind. Then you will be able to test and approve what God's will is – His good, pleasing and perfect will." Lastly, bearing fruit should result in others coming to know Christ as their Lord and Savior. Occasionally, the changes in our character and conduct will draw others to Christ. Matthew 5:16, "In the same way, let your light shine before men, that they may see your good deeds and praise your Father in heaven." However, God commanded us to go and make disciples. We should be sharing the love of Christ with others. How much fruit are you bearing?

Prayer: God, help me to bear much fruit.

> John 15:7 *If you abide in Me, and My words abide in you, you will ask what you desire, and it shall be done for you.*

In today's verse, Jesus said, "Ask what you desire, and it shall be done for you." This is not the first time He has promised to answer our prayers in this way. Matthew 21:22, "And whatever you ask in prayer, you will receive, if you have faith." John 14:14, "You may ask Me for anything in My name, and I will do it." Mark 11:24, "Therefore I tell you, whatever you ask for in prayer, believe that you have received it, and it will be yours." John 16:24, "Until now you have not asked for anything in My name. Ask and you will receive, and your joy will be complete." A new Christian or someone outside the faith could interpret these to say, God will give me anything I ask for. Prayer becomes a pursuit of things. In the early 70's, Janis Joplin wrote a song, "*Mercedes Benz*," about the search for happiness in the pursuit of things. The first verse says, "O Lord won't You buy me a Mercedes Benz, My friends all drive Porsches, I must make amends. Worked hard all my lifetime, no help from my friends. So, oh Lord won't you buy me a Mercedes Benz." However, we know that is not the meaning of Jesus' teaching in these verses. Jesus has been speaking about abiding in Him. When we abide in Him, and His words abide in us, we are not going to ask for selfish things, but what His word leads us to ask for. The key to a powerful prayer life is through His words living in us. This means we welcome Jesus into our lives and allow His words to guide us. I can give you an example of what that doesn't look like. Has a friend ever asked you for your advice on a particular decision they had to make? You thoughtfully give them what you know to be solid advice, only to watch them do the complete opposite. If Jesus abides in us, then His views, His principles, His commandments, and His promises also abide in us. We didn't invite Him into our lives just to put Him in a corner of our hearts, and to call on Him when we get in trouble. As David wrote in Psalm 119:105, "Your word is a lamp to my feet, and a light for my path." Are His words abiding in you?

Prayer: God, let Your words abide in me.

> John 15:10 *If you keep My commandments, you will abide in My love, just as I have kept My Father's commandments and abide in His love.*

Is Jesus saying we need to obey His commands to be loved? Absolutely not. His love is unconditional. Romans 5:8, "But God demonstrates His own love for us in this: While we were still sinners, Christ died for us." 1 John 3:1, "How great is the love the Father has lavished on us, that we should be called children of God." I could list many more verses about God's unconditional love for us. But to borrow a few words from an old children's hymn, "Jesus loves me this I know, for the Bible tells me so." There are many believers who are caught up in trying to follow the rules rather than abiding in His love, missing out on the abundant life Christ has for us. Obedience is important. Jesus has just said in John 14:15, "If you love Me, you will obey what I command." However, if we remain (abide) in His love, we will want to keep His commandments. We are taught as young children to obey our parents. Why? Because they love us and only want what is best for our lives. Some of their rules were to protect us from harm, and others were to teach us how to function in the world on our own. There were times I thought I knew more than my parents and disobeyed their rules. That is when I received a lesson on discipline. Our relationship with Christ is much the same. He loves us and wants what's best for us. As a result, we should want to remain in that love, and follow His commands. The Old Testament Law was given so we could understand what God considered to be sin. Jesus' commandments are nothing like the Ten Commandments. His centered around love. For example, Matthew 22:37-39, "Love the Lord your God with all your heart and with all your soul and with all your mind...Love your neighbor as yourself." Matthew 7:12, "So in everything, do to others what you would have them do to you..." Mathew 5:16, "...Let your light shine before men, that they may see your good deeds and praise your Father in heaven." Jesus' intention was not to make following Him difficult. He said in Matthew 11:30, "For My yoke is easy, and My burden is light." Following Him will bring joy and peace to our lives.

Prayer: God, I want to abide in Your love, help me keep Your commandments.

> *John 15:11 These things I have spoken to you, that My joy may remain in you, and that your joy may be full.*

In Acts chapter 16, Paul and Silas are in the City of Philippi preaching the good news of Jesus. While there, they cast out a spirit from a young slave girl that gave her the ability to predict the future. When her owners realized their source of income was gone, they hauled Paul and Silas before the magistrate and made all sorts of false accusations against them. A crowd gathered and joined in the attacks against them. The magistrate then ordered Paul and Silas to be flogged or beaten with sticks and put in jail. Verse 23 says, "After they had been severely flogged, they were thrown into prison." Having been ordered to guard them carefully, the jailer put them into an inner cell and fastened their feet in stocks. Putting it mildly, Paul and Silas had a bad day. They were falsely accused, beaten with rods, put in prison, and locked in stocks where they couldn't move. They had every reason to moan and complain to God for allowing this to happen to them. They could have easily given up their ministry and said, I quit. However, Acts 16:25 tells us, "About midnight Paul and Silas were praying and singing hymns to God, and the other prisoners were listening to them." In the midst of all their troubles, Paul and Silas, full of joy, were singing and praying to God. We all have experienced some bad days, but very likely, none as bad as Paul and Silas. I am ashamed to admit my attitude is not like Paul and Silas' on many of my bad days. Jesus said, "I have told you this so that My joy may be in you and that your joy may be complete." He wants us to experience the fullness of His joy continually, so that our joy is unaffected by the circumstances of life. James 1:2 tells us, "Consider it pure joy, my brothers, whenever you face trials of many kinds." Where do we find this kind of joy? 1 Peter 1:8 says, "Though you have not seen Him, you love Him; and even though you do not see Him now, you believe in Him and are filled with an inexpressible and glorious joy." The answer is very simple, the closer we draw to Christ, the more of His joy we will have in our lives.

Prayer: God, I want my joy to be full.

John 15:12 *This is My commandment, that you love one another as I have loved you.*

Two days ago, we read John 15:10, "If you keep My commandments, you will abide in My love, just as I have kept My Father's commandments and abide in His love." We learned that Jesus' love was unconditional, and that many of His commandments are centered around loving others. Today's verse is a direct command from Jesus to love one another as He has loved us. It must be a very important command, because He repeats it a few verses later in verse 17. You may be thinking, there are a lot of people I really don't like, this isn't going to be easy. How am I supposed to feel happy and have loving thoughts about others all the time? Before feeling overwhelmed, the type of love Jesus is commanding us to have towards others is not based on our feelings or emotions. It is a practical love, where our actions align to show others that we genuinely care about them. Also, in the context of who Jesus is talking to, our love for others starts with our brothers and sisters in Christ. If we can't learn how to love a fellow believer, how are we going to love an unbeliever and share Christ with them? Also, what would draw anyone to Christ if there were bitterness and hatred between Christians? Loving one another as Christ loved us also means we are to mimic the nature of His love. The qualities of Jesus' love are humility, sacrifice, and service. Our approach to others should be characterized by those traits. **Humility**: Philippians 2:3 tells us, "Do nothing out of selfish ambition or vain conceit, but in humility consider others better than yourselves." Ephesians 4:2, "Be completely humble and gentle; be patient, bearing one another in love." **Sacrifice**: Luke 9:23, "If anyone would come after Me, he must deny himself and take up his cross daily and follow Me." **Service**: 1 Peter 4:10-11, "Each one should use whatever gift he has received to serve others, faithfully administering God's grace in its various forms. If anyone speaks, he should do it as one speaking the very words of God. If anyone serves, he should do it with the strength God provides, so that in all things God may be praised through Jesus Christ..." Ask God today to show you ways to put humbleness, sacrifice, and service into action.

Prayer: God help me to love others as You have loved me.

Day 305

John 15:13 Greater love has no one than this, than to lay down one's life for his friends.

Jesus has just given the disciples a new commandment, "Love one another as I have loved you." In today's verse, He foreshadows His death by telling them how much He loves them. Jesus knows He is hours away from being betrayed and nailed to a cross to die. He will not only lay down His life for His friends but for you and I as well. Romans 5:8 tells us, "But God demonstrated His own love for us in this: While we were yet sinners, Christ died for us." The concept of caring enough for another person to die for them is hard for me to comprehend. The first thought that comes to my mind, is the sacrifice of the men and women of our armed services who have given their lives for our country. I am thankful for the bravery and courage of these men and women. One of the highest awards of military decoration is the Medal of Honor. "Over, 3,520 military personnel have been awarded the Medal of Honor award since the inception of the award in the 1800's. The recipient must have distinguished themselves at the risk of their own life above and beyond the call of duty in action against and enemy of the United States."[19] Due to the nature of this medal, most are awarded posthumously. You and I may never be called upon to physically give our lives for someone else. However, that does not release us from following Jesus' example to lay down our lives for others. 1 John 3:16, "This is how we know what love is: Jesus Christ laid down His life for us. And we ought to lay down our lives for our brothers." Perhaps the best teaching on how to love others is found in 1 Corinthians 13:4-8, "Love is patient, love is kind. It does not envy, it does not boast, it is not proud. It is not rude, it is not self-seeking, it is not easily angered, it keeps no record of wrongs. Love does not delight in evil but rejoices with the truth. It always protects, always trusts, always hopes, always perseveres. Love never fails..." This is how we are to lay our lives down for others. Is it easy? Absolutely not. Will some people take advantage of you? More than likely, yes. Jesus never said following Him would be easy.

Prayer: God, thank You for laying down Your life for me.

John 15:14 You are My friends if you do whatever I command you.

Proverbs 18:24 says, "A person of many companions may come to ruin, but there is a friend who sticks closer than a brother." Solomon makes the point that having a large number of friends does not necessarily mean they can be counted on when times get tough. Some who call themselves friends simply hang around for popularity, personal gain, or to use you as a stepping stone to someone else. These types of friends come and go. But to find one or two friends who are closer than a brother is priceless. They will stick with you in hard times and never give up on you. Jesus has been talking to the disciples about abiding in Him and keeping His commandments. Today, He calls them friends. Jesus said, "You are My Friends if you do whatever I command you." A friendship is a two-way relationship where both enjoy spending time together. They share interests, and know and understand each other. They help and look out for each other. However, friendship with Jesus is conditional. Salvation is a free gift, but having a close relationship with Jesus depends on obeying His commands. Abraham was considered a friend of God. James 2:23, "And the scripture was fulfilled that says, 'Abraham believed God, and it was credited to him as righteousness, and he was called God's friend.'" Why was Abraham a friend of God, because he listened and obeyed God's commands. God speaking to Abraham's son, Isaac said in Genesis 26:4-5, "I will make your descendants as numerous as the stars in the sky and will give them all these lands, and through your offspring all nations on earth will be blessed, because Abraham obeyed Me and kept My requirements, My commands, My decrees and My laws." Because of the obedience of one man, Abraham, all the nations of the earth will be blessed by his offspring. With obedience comes blessings. However, many of us want the blessings without the obedience. It doesn't work that way. What are the benefits of having a friendship with Jesus? The words to this old hymn, "*What a Friend We Have in Jesus*" sums it up. "What a friend we have in Jesus, All our sins and griefs to bear! What a privilege to carry, everything to God in prayer." My prayer is that you are seeking a closer relationship with Him.

Prayer: God, I want Your friendship, help me to obey Your commands.

> John 15:16 *You did not choose Me, but I chose you and appointed you that you should go and bear fruit, and that your fruit should remain, that whatever you ask the Father in My name He may give you.*

Jesus' disciples came from all walks of life. Matthew was a tax collector and Peter was a fisherman. Yet, Jesus knew their potential and the impact they would have on the world after His death. Although Jesus had a specific purpose in mind for each disciple, each one had to accept His calling. Some of the disciples were approached by Jesus, and others began following Him out of curiosity. Andrew and John who were originally disciples of John the Baptist, were present when he pointed to Jesus, saying "Look, the Lamb of God who takes away the sin of the world. John 1:37-38 says, "When the two disciples heard him say this, they followed Jesus. Turning around, Jesus saw them following and asked, 'What do you want?' They said 'Rabbi, where are You staying.'" The very next day, Andrew introduced his brother Peter to Jesus. Jesus' calling was not like being drafted into the army. He didn't say, "Peter you are now My disciple whether you like it or not." He simply said, "Follow Me, I will make you fishers of men." Jesus' calling on our lives is the same. He has a plan and a purpose for your life. However, you are not forced by Him to accept it. 2 Timothy 1:9, "Who has saved us and called us with a holy calling, not according to our works, but according to His own purpose and grace which was given to us in Christ Jesus before time began." His purpose or holy calling for our lives is for us to go and bear fruit. The go part is easy. We just need to engage the world wherever God puts us. That place may be your own home, your place of work, your school, your neighborhood, or on a mission field. As we go, we should be bearing fruit that remains. In other words, what we do and how we live as Christians should have a lasting impact on those around us. All along, Jesus has been telling us how to do it, "Love one another." Too often, we ask Jesus for the things we need for ourselves. However, His promise is to give us what we need to accomplish His call to produce fruit. How do I bear fruit? Jesus said, "That whatever you ask the Father in My name, He may give it to you."

Prayer: God, help me to go and produce fruit that remains.

> *John 15:17 These things I command you, that you love one another.*

According to *www.Bible.knowing-jesus.com/topics/Loving-One-Another*, there are 36 verses in the Bible about loving one another. I am not going to list them all, but will share a few. Romans 13:8, "Let no debt remain outstanding, except the continuing debt to love one another, for he who loves his fellowman has fulfilled the law." 1 Peter 4:8, "Above all, love each other deeply, because love covers a multitude of sins." 1 John 4:11-12, "Dear friends, since God so loved us, we also ought to love one another. No one has ever seen God; but if we love one another, God lives in us and His love is made complete in us." God's message to us is pretty clear. We are supposed to love one another. Why? Because God is love and it is His love shining through us that sets us apart from the world. How are we able to love others? Because He first loved us. Several days ago, we read about the characteristics of love from 1 Corinthians 13:4-8. Paul concludes his writing on love, saying, "And now these three remain: faith, hope and love. But the greatest of these is love." Love will last throughout eternity, but faith and hope are equally important while we are waiting for Christ's return. Faith is the instrument of our salvation. Without faith in Christ, we cannot be saved. Faith is also trust in God and His word, that what He says is true. Hope is the perseverance of faith. Hope is not wishful thinking, but the confident assurance God will fulfill His promises no matter our circumstances. Isaiah 40:31, "But those who hope in the Lord will renew their strength. They will soar on wings like eagles; they will run and not grow weary, they will walk and not be faint." How do we apply faith and hope to our daily lives to love others? When we love others, we will believe in them. Whatever the situation, love is ready to trust that person. True love is also able to look past another's faults to meet their needs. Hope is having a positive attitude towards others. With the hope of Christ living within us, we are able to help people reach their full potential. True love looks past the disappointments and failures, and doesn't give up. Jesus doesn't give up on us, neither should we give up on love.

Prayer: God, help me to incorporate faith and hope in my love for others.

John 15:18-19 *If the world hates you, you know that it hated Me before it hated you. If you were of the world, the world would love its own. Yet because you are not of the world, but I chose you out of the world, therefore the world hates you.*

Michael Johnson, a congressman from Louisiana, was recently elected as Speaker of the House of Representatives after a long and contentious process to elect a speaker. Johnson is a devout Christian whose beliefs are reflected in his personal and political stances. This should be a breath of fresh air to Congress and our nation, considering the direction our country has been headed. However, just the opposite is true. A former White House Press Secretary made the following comments about Mr. Johnson: "It's not just his political ideology that should scare us. He believes America is a Christian nation, and those values should be reflected in our interpretation of the Constitution. Johnson's ideas are completely out of line with what America actually is, making him the opposite of harmless."[20] The day has arrived when someone with Christian values is considered a threat to our country. We should not be shocked by this. The world hates Christians because we are not a part of it. If we were, we would be loved by the world. Because of our faith, we should expect trouble. Although this is not a message we like to hear, it is the reality of following Christ. Jesus was met with hostility and hatred because He was a threat to the religious leaders of His day. Jesus said, "If the world hates you, you know that it hated Me before it hated you." The opposition to Jesus led to His death. While serving Christ may not lead to our death, we can expect to be ridiculed, slandered, insulted, and ostracized. But choosing to be a part of the world has worse consequences. James 4:4, "You adulterous people, don't you know that friendship with the world is hatred towards God? Anyone who chooses to be a friend of the world becomes an enemy of God." Peter tells us we should not be surprised when we are hated by the world, but should celebrate it. 1 Peter 4:12-14, "Dear friends, do not be surprised at the painful trial you are suffering, as though something strange were happening to you. But rejoice that you participate in the sufferings of Christ, so that you may be overjoyed when His glory is revealed. You are insulted because of the name of Christ, you are blessed, for the Spirit of glory and of God rests on you." Have you experienced the hatred of the world?

Prayer: God, help me to rejoice in suffering for You.

> *John 15:26-27 But when the Helper comes, whom I shall send to you from the Father, the Spirit of Truth who proceeds from the Father, He will testify of Me. And you also will bear witness, because you have been with Me from the beginning.*

We touched on several roles of the Holy Spirit earlier in John 14. Today, Jesus identifies the Holy Spirit as the "Helper" and the "Spirit of Truth sent out by the Father." A key role of the Holy Spirit is to give evidence of Jesus. We can trust the Holy Spirit's testimony, because He is the Spirit of Truth. I heard an evangelist recently say, "there are facts, then there is the truth." Knowing that Jesus was the Son of God who died on a cross for our sins is a fact. But knowing Him as your personal Lord and Savior is knowing the truth of His word. It is a fact that I woke up this morning. The truth is I woke up this morning with the Spirit of God living within me. Knowing the truth behind the facts is very important to our relationship with Christ. Jesus said in John 8:32, "Then you will know the truth, and the truth will set you free." Knowing Jesus sets us free from the bondage of sin, condemnation and death. It is the work of the Holy Spirit, or Spirit of Truth, that leads us to Jesus. He will also direct others to Jesus through us by our bearing witness of Christ. Paul said in 1 Corinthians 12:3, "So I want you to know that no one speaking by the Spirit of God will curse Jesus, and no one can say Jesus is Lord, except by the Holy Spirit." Our words and deeds reflect our true nature. Unless the Holy Spirit resides in us, we have not truly accepted Christ as Lord and Savior. 1 Corinthians 6:19-20, "Do you not know that your body is the temple of the Holy Spirit, who is in you, whom you have received from God? You are not your own; you were bought with a price. Therefore, honor God with your body." When we are saved, the Holy Spirit takes up permanent residence in our lives. This indwelling of the Holy Spirit is different from being repeatedly filled with the Spirit. The indwelling secures us as a child of God, and begins to change our lives to reflect Christ. Our attitude, our behavior, and our choices change because of the Holy Spirit living within us. He bears witness to the change in our lives.

Prayer: God, thank You for sending the Spirit of Truth who constantly testifies of You.

> *John 16:2 They will put you out of the synagogues; yes, the time is coming that whoever kills you will think that he offers God service.*

It would be bad enough to face persecution from an Islamic jihadist or a Hindu nationalist who is opposed to Christianity. But to face persecution by the very religious leaders who are supposed to be serving the same God as you, would be much more painful. Betrayal at the hands of someone you have looked up to hurts much worse and has many lasting consequences. Jesus tells the disciples in John 16:1, "These things I have spoken to you, that you should not be made to stumble." Jesus is warning them about the difficult days ahead at the hands of the Pharisees. In verse 2, Jesus said, "They (the religious leaders) will put you out of the synagogues; yes, the time is coming that whoever kills you will think that he offers God service." The Bible doesn't record the fate of every disciple, but it is believed that everyone except John was martyred for their belief in Jesus. John did not get off easy. Some historical reports say John was thrown into a pot of boiling oil, before being exiled to the Isle of Patmos where he wrote the Book of Revelation. Fortunately for us living the 21st century, persecution by the church is not a concern. However, that doesn't mean someone cannot be hurt by or scarred for life by the church. Over the last 20 years, the news has been filled with reports of sexual abuse of children by predatory priests and nuns in the Catholic Church. Sadly, sexual abuse within the church is not just limited to the Catholic Church. In a 2018 Lifeway Research Study reports, "1 in 8 protestant pastors said a church staff member had sexually harassed a member of the congregation at some point in the past."[21] The church should be a safe place where we are free from abuse, conflict, and pain. Unfortunately, that is not the case in all churches. If you are a victim of abuse whether at home, church, or at work, you should report it. The Lifeway Research Study indicated only 30% of all abuse cases are reported. The first step to healing is to make someone aware and get help. Don't try to hide that kind of information deep within your heart, because it will consume you. Solomon said in Proverbs 4:23, "Above all else, guard your heart, for it is the wellspring of life."

Prayer: God, help me to guard my heart.

> John 16:4 But these things I have told you, that when the time comes, you may remember that I told you of them.

As a supervisor, I heard the following phrases many times and used them myself on occasion: "What you don't know won't hurt you," and "You are better off not knowing." These phrases are used when something doesn't go as planned and knowing the truth would cause more trouble and distress than not knowing it. Jesus didn't operate that way. He wanted to give the disciples plenty of warning of what was going to take place. He knew it was better for them to have that understanding than to blindly face the upcoming events. Although they may not recall Jesus' exact words during the moment of crisis, they could look back with assurance knowing Jesus had forewarned them. Speaking of His arrest and execution, Jesus tells them, "These things I have told you, that when the time comes, you may remember that I told you of them." He wants the disciples to know and remember what is about to take place. He is also warning them of the impending persecution they will face for being His followers. Following Christ is no different today. Many who accept Christ as Lord and Savior, come to Him expecting a trouble-free life, only to find the opposite is true. Often times, our troubles seem to get worse instead of better. Peter writes about the sufferings of Christians in 1 Peter 4:12-16, "Dear friends, do not be surprised at the painful trial you are suffering, as though something strange were happening to you. But rejoice that you participate in the sufferings of Christ, so that you may be overjoyed when His glory is revealed. If you are insulted because of the name of Christ, you are blessed, for the Spirit of glory and of God rests on you. If you suffer, it should not be as a murderer or thief or any other kind of criminal, or even as a meddler. However, if you suffer as a Christian, do not be ashamed, but praise God that you bear His name." Satan wants to use our troubles to discourage us and lead us away from God. Jesus wants us to have His peace and trust Him in our trials. Philippians 4:7, "And the peace of God which transcends all understanding, will guard your hearts and minds in Christ Jesus." We can find His peace through prayer and preparation because He has forewarned us.

Prayer: God, help me to remember Your words when trouble comes.

> John 16:7 Nevertheless I tell you the truth. "It is to your advantage that I go away; for if I do not go away, the Helper will not come to you; but if I depart, I will send Him to you."

The Bible uses several words to describe the Holy Spirit: Helper, Comforter, Counselor, Advocate, Teacher, Spirit of Truth, and Witness. Jesus said, "It is to your advantage that I go away; for if I do not go away, the Helper will not come to you; but if I depart, I will send Him to you." For the Holy Spirit to fulfill the roles Jesus describes, it was necessary for Him to die on the cross. But, wasn't the Holy Spirit in the world before Jesus' death and resurrection? The answer is yes, but in a much different role. The Holy Spirit would come to indwell and empower someone for a specific purpose. For example, Judges 6:34, "Then the Spirit of the Lord came upon Gideon..." 2 Chronicles 24:20, "Then the Spirit of God came upon Zechariah son of Jehoiada..." The Holy Spirit would also leave someone as well. 1 Samuel 16:14, "Now the Spirit of the Lord had departed from Saul..." The Holy Spirit also gifted people with special talents and abilities to accomplish His work. Exodus 31:2-3, "See, I have chosen Bezalel son of Uri, the son of Hur, of the tribe of Judah, and I have filled him with the Spirit of God, with skill, ability and knowledge in all kinds of crafts." Over the next two days we will continue to dig deeper into the roles of the Holy Spirit. However, it is important for us to know the Holy Spirit is real and came to fill us with His presence, so we can glorify Jesus. In Acts 1, Jesus tells the disciples to stay in Jerusalem and wait for the gift of the Holy Spirit. Acts 2:1-4 describes the day the Holy Spirit filled the disciples, "When the day of Pentecost came, they were all together in one place. Suddenly a sound like the blowing of a violent wind came from heaven and filled the whole house where they were sitting. They saw what seemed to be tongues of fire that separated and came to rest of each of them. All of them were filled with the Holy Spirit and began to speak in other tongues as the Spirit enabled them." This very same Holy Spirit is available to every believer. God wants to infill us with His Holy Spirit to empower us to serve Him with boldness. Ask Him to fill you with His Spirit.

Prayer: God, fill me with Your Holy Spirit.

> *John 16:8 And when He has come, He will convict the world of sin, and of righteousness, and of judgment.*

The Holy Spirit fills us with power and gifts to serve God. He will also take up residence or indwell within us when we accept Christ as Lord and Savior. This indwelling by the Holy Spirit removes our sinful ways and replaces them with a desire to serve God. Without the Holy Spirit living within us, our witness and work for Christ would be completely ineffective. These are very important roles of the Holy Spirit in the life of a believer. Jesus tells us today, the Holy Spirit is also at work, bringing awareness to the world of their sin and need for a Savior. The Holy Spirit does this by working through our consciences to expose the sin in our lives. Jesus said, "He, (the Holy Spirit) will convict the world of sin, and of righteousness, and of judgment." Jesus continued in verses 9-11 saying, "Of sin, because they do not believe in Me; of righteousness, because I go to My Father and you see Me no more; of judgment, because the ruler of this world is judged." The Holy Spirit's role in convicting the world of sin is to bring awareness of our sin and unbelief, motivating us to admit our guilt before God. 2 Corinthians 7:10, "Godly sorrow brings repentance that leads to salvation and leaves no regret, but worldly sorrow brings death." Without the convicting role of the Holy Spirit there is no guilt for our sin. Sin being our rejection or unbelief in Christ as our Lord and Savior. Sins (plural) are the by-products of sin. Next, the Holy Spirit convicts us of our perceived righteousness and our rejection of Jesus as the standard of righteousness. Isaiah 64:6, "All of us have become like one who is unclean, and all our righteousness acts are like filthy rags..." Jesus is the spotless, sinless Lamb of God. He is the only one who has lived a perfect and righteous life. 1 Peter 2:21-22, "To this you were called, because Christ suffered for you, leaving you an example, that you should follow in His steps. He committed no sin, and no deceit was found in His mouth." Lastly, the Holy Spirit convicts us of our denial of a coming judgment for our sins. Numbers 32:23, "But if you fail to do this, you will be sinning against the Lord; and you may be sure that your sin will find you out."

Prayer: God, thank You for the convicting work of the Holy Spirit.

> John 16:13 However, when He, the Spirit of truth, has come, He will guide you into all truth; for He will not speak on His own authority, but whatever He hears He will speak; and He will tell you things to come.

Several days ago, we learned there is a difference between facts and truth. Truth is deeper than fact. Facts can be interpreted and twisted to be what we want them to be. Truth is God's way of viewing things. The only way to know the truth is to know God. Today, Jesus identifies the Holy Spirit as the Spirit of Truth. His role is to help us understand the truth of God's word. 1 Corinthians 2:10-11, "But God has revealed it to us by His Spirit. The Spirit searches all things, even the deep things of God. For who among men knows the thoughts of a man except the man's spirit within him? In the same way no one knows the thoughts of God except the Spirit of God." The Holy Spirit is God in spirit form. He is co-equal and co-exists with God the Father, and God the Son. Since the Holy Spirit is God, He knows the thoughts of God and is the One who reveals the truth of God's word, even to those who wrote it. 2 Peter 1:21, "For prophecy never had its origin in the will of man, but men spoke from God as they were carried along by the Holy Spirit." Unfortunately, the Holy Spirit doesn't automatically fill us with wisdom and knowledge of God's word when we are saved. He also doesn't replace our thoughts or opinions. Jesus tells us the Holy Spirit will "guide" us into all truth. His influence can be ignored. That is why we sometimes make bad life choices. The Holy Spirit will reveal God's truth to our lives when we pray and ask Him for guidance. However, it is our responsibility to listen to the Holy Spirit and follow His direction. By following the leading of the Holy Spirit, we can have a closer walk with Christ. Paul writes in Ephesians 1:17-19, "I keep asking that the God of our Lord Jesus Christ, the glorious Father, may give you the Spirit of Wisdom and revelation, so that you may know Him better. I pray also that the eyes of your heart may be enlightened in order that you may know the hope to which He has called you, the riches of His glorious inheritance in the saints, and His incomparably great power for us who believe..."

Prayer: God, thank You for the Spirit of truth who guides us.

> John 16:24 *Until now you have asked nothing in My name. Ask, and you will receive, that your joy may be full.*

When Jesus taught us how to pray in Matthew 6:9-13, there was no mention of asking for anything in His name. "The Lord's Prayer" speaks directly to our Father in heaven. On Day 290, we read in John 14:13-14 where Jesus said, "Whatever you ask in My name, that I will do, that the Father may be glorified in the Son. If you ask anything in My name, I will do it." Today, Jesus confirms that we should ask for things in His name, using His authority and His will in making our requests to God. This does not necessarily mean God will automatically give us what we ask for. Attaching Jesus' name at the end of our prayers is not a magic formula for winning the lottery. When we pray in Jesus' name, we should be praying according to His will and plan for our lives. Aside from Jesus sitting at the right hand of the Father, ever interceding for us, (Romans 8:34), there are several reasons we should pray in the name of Jesus. First and foremost, there is power in the name of Jesus. Power to save us, heal us, and give us victory over death and the grave. Hebrews 1:3, "The Son is the radiance of God's glory and is the exact representation of His being, sustaining all things by His powerful word. After He had provided purification for sins, He sat down at the right hand of the Majesty in heaven." Secondly, there is salvation in the name of Jesus. Acts 4:12, "Salvation is found in no one else, for there is no other name under heaven given to men by which we must be saved." In the name of Jesus our sins are forgiven and we are promised eternal life with Him in heaven. Next, there is healing in the name of Jesus. 1 Peter 2:24, "He Himself bore our sins in His body on the tree, so that we might die to sins and live for righteousness; by His wounds you have been healed." Lastly, there is victory in the name of Jesus. Jesus conquered death and the grave and gives us eternal life with Him in heaven. 1 Corinthians 15:57, "The sting of death is sin, and the power of sin is the law. But thanks be to God! He gives us the victory through our Lord Jesus Christ."

Prayer: God, unleash the power of Your name in my prayer life.

> John 16:33 *These things I have spoken to you, that in Me you may have peace. In the world you will have tribulation; but be of good cheer, I have overcome the world.*

I doubt the words Jesus spoke about having trouble in this world come as a surprise to you. Life isn't fair, and troubles will find us all. 1 Peter 4:12 tells us, "Dear friends, do not be surprised at the painful trial you are suffering, as though something strange were happening to you." Anyone who accepts Christ as Lord and Savior with the hopes of a perfect life, good health, financial security, and problem-free relationships will be quickly disappointed. So, what are we supposed to do? Numb our feelings and press on, hoping that things will get better soon? Or do we put on our "happy face" and act like nothing is wrong. Perhaps we play the role of victim and blame others for our circumstances. The answer is found in today's verse. Jesus offers peace, confidence, and victory in overcoming the trials and tribulations of this world. I can tell you from experience, it is hard to achieve peace when your world is crashing around you. It takes true faith to trust God at His word. Faith is the confident assurance God has our situation in His hands. Romans 5:1-2, "Therefore, since we have been justified through faith, we have peace with God through our Lord Jesus Christ, through whom we have gained access by faith into this grace in which we now stand. And we rejoice in the hope of the Glory of God." Secondly, Jesus tells us to "be of good cheer." Other translations use the words, "Take heart," "Be confident," or "Be courageous." The only way we are going to have this inner peace and confidence is to abide in Him. David said in Psalm 16:11, "You have made known to me the path of life; You will fill me with joy in Your presence, with eternal pleasures at Your right hand." Lastly, we have victory because Jesus has conquered the world and its problems. Perhaps you feel like David when he wrote Psalm 31:10, "My life is consumed by anguish and my years by groaning; my strength fails because of my affliction, and my bones grow weak." But David didn't stop there. He called upon the Lord, Psalm 31:14-16, "But I trust in You, O Lord...You are my God. My times are in Your hands; deliver me from my enemies...Let Your face shine on Your servant..."

Prayer: God, help me to experience peace, confidence, and victory each day.

> John 17:3 And this is eternal life, that they may know You, the only true God, and Jesus Christ whom You have sent.

John chapter 17 records a prayer of Jesus' before He and the disciples leave for the Garden of Gethsemane. Jesus prays for Himself, His disciples, and all future believers. He opens His prayer by saying, "Father, the hour has come. Glorify Your Son, that Your Son also may glorify You." The "hour" Jesus has spent His entire earthly life working towards has finally arrived. This "hour" Jesus is about to face shows us His human side. Like anyone else who gets nervous just before a big event, Jesus was apprehensive about the trials He would soon face. Luke 22:44 tells us, "And being in anguish, He prayed more earnestly, and His sweat was like drops of blood falling to the ground." Yet, Jesus loves us so much that He took the time to pray for all who would believe in Him. Jesus continues His prayer, "For You granted Him authority over all people that He might give eternal life to all those You have given Him." Jesus is the giver of eternal life. This is the very reason He came into the world. 1 John 5:11-12, "And this is the testimony: God has given us eternal life, and this life is in His Son. He who has the Son has life; he who does not have the Son of God does not have life." Jesus continues His prayer by defining eternal life as a relationship with God, not a span of time. Because our earthly lives are finite, we look at eternity through the lens of time. Jesus said, eternity is not time, but rather a deep, intimate, relationship with the only true God. How do we get to know the only true God and have a deep, personal relationship with Him? Jesus tells us that to know God, we must first know His Son, Jesus Christ whom God sent to save us from our sins. Jesus said in John 14:6, "I am the way and the truth and the life. No one comes to the Father except through Me." Once we accept Jesus as Lord and Savior, our journey into eternal life with the Father begins. The only way we are going to know Him better and have a relationship with Him is to daily spend time with Him in prayer, read His word, fellowship with the Holy Spirit that dwells within us, and obey His commands. Enjoy the journey.

Prayer: God, I want to know You more.

> John 17:4 I have glorified You on earth. I have finished the work which You have given Me to do.

What a great testimony to be able to say, "I have finished the work which You have given Me to do." Although Jesus hasn't gone to the cross, He has accomplished what God sent Him to earth to do. He lived a sinless life, submitting to God's authority. He healed the sick and gave sight to the blind. He called the disciples who would be left to spread the gospel after His death. Most importantly, He did the will of the Father. Every person ever born has been given a work or purpose by God. These works do not secure our salvation because salvation is a gift of God. However, they are important because they all fit together as puzzle pieces in God's masterplan. Also, the more we know Him, the more we want to do His will. Ephesians 2:8-10, "For it is by grace you have been saved, through faith – and this not from yourselves, it is the gift of God – not by works, so that no one can boast. For we are God's workmanship, created in Christ Jesus to do good works, which God prepared in advance for us to do." The question we find ourselves asking is "What good works have I been created for?" The most obvious answer would be to go to church, read my Bible, pray daily, and be kind to others. These are good things and should be the basic activities of our faith. However, God's plan for our good works is much broader and deeper. It also encompasses our life outside of church activity. Jesus said in Matthew 5:16, "In the same way, let your light shine before men, that they may see your good deeds and praise your Father in heaven." In other words, good deeds should be a natural part of our lives and point others to Christ. However, God has also gifted you with skills and abilities to accomplish a work He has planned for you. He will make that plan known to you at the right time. For example, God called Vivian and I to lead mission teams to Nicaragua several years ago. He has now led me to write a second daily devotion. He has called Vivian to model godliness as a mother and grandmother. Listen to God's voice calling you and say, yes Lord. Don't look back on life and say, "I wish..."

Prayer: God, help me to finish the work You have called me to do.

> *John 17:15 I do not pray that You should take them out of the world, but that You should keep them from the evil one.*

In the early days of the church, the disciples found themselves spending a great deal of time in the daily distribution of food and neglecting the ministry of the word. To solve the problem, seven men, who were known to be full of Spirit and wisdom were given the responsibility for the food distribution. One of the seven was Stephen. Acts 6:8 tells us, "Now Stephen, a man full of God's grace and power, did great wonders and miraculous signs among the people." Stephen was sharp, highly successful, and a devout believer. Yet, that did not exempt him from trouble. It actually created problems for him. Acts 6:9-10 tells us, "Opposition arose, however, from members of the Synagogue of the Freedmen...These men began to argue with Stephen, but they could not stand up against his wisdom or the Spirit by whom he spoke." To make matters worse, the "Freedmen" convinced several men to falsely testify about Stephen. He is given a chance to defend himself before the High Priest and elders. Stephen's defense is recorded in Acts 7:1-53. At the end of his testimony, Acts 7:55 says, "But Stephen, full of the Holy Spirit, looked up to heaven and saw the glory of God, and Jesus standing at the right hand of God." Stephen couldn't have been any closer to God. Yet, he was dragged out of the city and stoned to death. The story of Stephen teaches us that God will not take believers out of persecution or hardship. Like Stephen, we can be very successful at doing the work God has called us to do. We can be walking with God daily, and filled with His Spirit; however, that does not exempt us from the difficulties of life. Jesus' prayer today is very similar to the prayer He taught us in Matthew 6:13, "And lead us not into temptation, but deliver us from the evil one." Jesus knows we are going to face trials and temptations and wants the Father to sustain us during those times. He also knows we are unable to resist the devil on our own. We should come into agreement with Jesus each day, asking God to keep us from the evil one. Ask Him to protect you from the types of trials that would result in the failing of your faith and turning your back on Him.

Prayer: God, lead me not into temptation, but deliver me from the evil one.

> *John 17:17 Sanctify them by Your truth. Your word is truth.*

Many years ago, our church would occasionally have testimony time during a Sunday Night service. The old saints of God would stand up and begin their testimony saying, "Pastor, I want to thank the Lord that I am saved, sanctified, and filled with Holy Ghost." The word sanctify is also used by Jesus in today's verse. The words sanctify or sanctification, the process of being sanctified are very important to our daily walk with Christ. However, they are not mentioned very often in churches today. The word sanctification is one of those religious words like justification and regeneration that tend to confuse people. Sanctification is simply the process of setting something or someone apart for God's special use. Leviticus 20:7-8, "Consecrate yourselves and be holy, because I am the Lord your God. Keep My decrees and follow them. I am the Lord, who sanctifies you." Sanctification is associated with holiness. When we accept Christ as Lord and Savior, we are set apart (sanctified), and made Holy in God's sight. Hebrews 10:10, "By that will we have been sanctified through the offering of the body of Jesus Christ once and for all." However, sanctification does not begin and end at salvation. Sanctification is an ongoing process of becoming holy. Romans 6:19, "I put this in human terms because you are weak in your natural selves. Just as you used to offer the parts of your body to slavery to impurity and to ever-increasing wickedness, so now offer them in slavery to righteousness leading to holiness." We become holy by replacing our old evil desires with the likeness of Christ. Ephesians 4:22-24, "You were taught, with regard to your former way of life, to put off your old self, which is being corrupted by its deceitful desires; to be made new in the attitude of your minds; and to put on the new self, created to be like God in true righteousness and holiness." Sanctification is also the will of God. 1 Thessalonians 4:3, "It is God's will that you should be sanctified; that you should avoid sexual immorality." How does this sanctification process work? According to Jesus, it takes place through the application of God's word to every area of our lives. God's word is truth. It enables us to understand who God is and how He calls us to live. Dig deeper into His word each day and grow in holiness.

Prayer: God, sanctify me by Your truth.

> *John 17:18 As You sent Me into the world, I also have sent them into the world.*

Yesterday, Jesus' prayer was that the Father would sanctify His disciples by the truth of God's word. Being set apart and made holy in God's sight is a key element in Jesus sending the disciples into the world. There would be no reason to send anyone if they lived and behaved the same way the world does. The same holds true for us today. Just as Jesus sent the disciples into the world, we are also told to go. Matthew 28:19, "Therefore go and make disciples of all nations, baptizing them in the name of the Father and of the Son, and of the Holy Spirit." However, our efforts to follow Jesus' command begins with sanctification and the indwelling power of the Holy Spirit. Jesus speaks about the world all throughout the Book of John. It may be helpful to understand where it is that Jesus wants to send us. The world is not a place, but rather a host of lost and dying people. The world is where you live, work, go to school, play, and even worship. The world is your sphere of influence. For those called into ministry or mission work, your world may be far from your home. Everyone's world is different. The next important step is to figure out what God wants us to do in this world He is sending us. 1 Peter 4:7-11, gives us a good foundation for living in the world. "The end of all things is near. Therefore, **be clear minded** and **self-controlled** so that you can **pray**. Above all, **love** each other deeply, because love covers a multitude of sins. **Offer hospitality** to one another without grumbling. Each one should **use whatever gift they have received to serve others**, faithfully **administering God's grace** in its various forms. **If anyone speaks**, they should do it as one speaking the very words of God. **If anyone serves**, they should do it with the strength God provides, so that in all things God may be praised through Jesus Christ. To Him be the glory and the power for ever and ever. Amen." It can't be said enough, "Above all, love each other." Perhaps the hardest thing to do, is the most important. Jesus said in John 13:35, "By this, all will know that you are My disciples, if you love one another." God has sent us to love our neighbor.

Prayer: God, help me to love others.

> *John 17:20 I do not pray for these alone, but also for those who will believe in Me through their word.*

Jesus expands His prayer for the disciples to include everyone who would ever believe in Him because of their word. What started out as the testimony of twelve disciples has now reached the entire world. Jesus, knowing their impact, continues His prayer for all believers in verse 21, "That they all may be one, as You, Father, are in Me, and I in You; that they also may be one in Us. That the world may believe that You sent Me." Jesus is praying for unity among all who believe. Just as the Father, the Son, and the Holy Spirit are unified, His prayer is that we reach the same level of unity. Fortunately for us, this is not a command, but a prayer of Jesus. Over my 60+ years of being a part of the church, I have witnessed my share of disunity and conflict. Most of the issues have not come from biblical teachings, but rather differing opinions. The latest example is the lack of, or the excessive enforcement of COVID protocols which has caused heated arguments and many to leave the church. Fortunately, Paul gives us some guidance on how to demonstrate true love and achieve unity. He writes about the controversial issues of his day in Romans 14; determining what meat was okay to eat, and what day to worship on. First and foremost, biblical truths should not be compromised to achieve unity. However, Paul points out, our personal preferences and opinions are no more important than anyone else's and should be set aside to achieve unity. Romans 14:1-4, "Accept other believers who are weak in faith, and don't argue with them about what they think is right or wrong. For instance, one person believes it's all right to eat anything. But another believer with a sensitive conscience will eat only vegetables. Those who feel free to eat anything must not look down on those who don't. And those who don't eat certain foods must not condemn those who do, for God has accepted them. Who are you to condemn someone else's servants? Their own master will judge whether they stand or fall. And with the Lord's help, they will stand and receive His approval." Paul sums it up in Romans 14:9. "So then, let us aim for harmony in the church and try to build each other up"

Prayer: God, help me to do what leads to unity in Your church.

> *John 18:37 Pilate therefore said to Him, "Are You a king then?" Jesus answered, "You say rightly that I am a king. For this cause I was born, and for this cause I have come into the world, that I should bear witness to the truth. Everyone who is of the truth hears My voice."*

Jesus has been brought to Pilate by the Jewish religious leaders to stand trial. Ironically, when Pilate asked what accusations they were bringing against Jesus, the religious leaders said, "If He were not an evil doer, we would not have delivered Him up to you." In other words, they had nothing to accuse Jesus of. They just wanted Pilate to do their bidding and have Jesus executed. Pilate pushes back and tells the religious leaders to judge Jesus according to Jewish law. However, they replied, "We can't put anyone to death." They wanted Jesus crucified and out of their lives. Pilate then goes to Jesus and asks Him, "Are You the King of the Jews?" He follows up and asks a second time, "Are You a king then?" Jesus told Pilate, "You rightly say I am a king." Little did Pilate know he was standing before the one true King. He may have considered Jesus as a King of Jews, having inscribed the sign on Jesus' cross to say, "Jesus of Nazareth, The King of the Jews." However, Pilate never recognized Jesus as the King of Kings and Lord of Lords. The Bible reveals to us that Jesus is the King. When He returns to earth, Jesus will reign eternally as King. Revelation 19:16, "On His robe and on His thigh He has this name written: King of Kings and Lord of Lords." At Jesus' birth, the Magi recognized a King had been born. Matthew 2:1-2, "After Jesus was born in Bethlehem in Judea, during the time of King Herod, Magi from the east came to Jerusalem and asked, 'Where is the one who has been born King of the Jews? We saw His star in the east and have come to worship Him.'" David recognized Him as the King of Glory. Psalm 24:7-8, "Lift up your heads, O you gates; be lifted up, you ancient doors, that the King of Glory may come in. Who is this King of Glory? The Lord strong and mighty, the Lord mighty in battle." Zechariah writes that He is the King over all the earth. Zechariah 4:9, "The Lord will be King over the whole earth. On that day there will be one Lord and His name the only one." How well do you know the soon coming King? Make Him Lord of your life today. Don't be like Pilate and miss your opportunity.

Prayer: God, please be the Lord of my life.

> John 19:11 Jesus answered, "You could have no power at all against Me unless it had been given you from above. Therefore the one who delivered Me to you has the greater sin."

Pilate could find no fault in Jesus and wanted to release Him. However, to appease the angry mob, he gave them a choice of who he should release, Jesus or Barabbas. When the mob shouted "give us Barabbas", Pilate had Jesus scourged. The soldiers twisted a crown of thorns and pressed it on His head, beat Him, put a purple robe on Jesus, and mocked Him. Pilate then brought Jesus back out to the crowd, hoping the beating would satisfy them. However, they began to shout, "crucify Him, crucify Him!" Pilate knew Jesus was innocent, but became afraid of the defiant mob. Pilate went back and questioned Jesus again. But Jesus didn't answer. Pilate then said, "Are You not speaking to me? Do You not know that I have the power to crucify You, and power to release You?" In answering Pilate, Jesus reminds us that all governing authorities are put into place by God. "You could have no power at all against Me unless it had been given from above." Romans 13:1 tells us, "Everyone must submit themselves to the governing authorities, for there is no authority except that which God has established. The authorities that exist have been established by God." Daniel 2:21, "He changes times and seasons, He sets up kings and deposes them. He gives wisdom to the wise and knowledge to the discerning." As much as we may like or dislike our governing authorities, they were put in place by God's hand and for His ultimate purpose. Although Pilate was responsible for deciding Jesus' fate on the cross, Jesus also points out that the religious leaders are guilty of a greater sin. All sins are equal in that they separate us from God. At the same time, it is obvious that some sins are worse than others. For example, murder is much worse than stealing a pack of gum. But God views our sins from a different perspective. Pilate's sin was out of ignorance to who Jesus was. However, those who handed Jesus over to Pilate knew the Law of Moses. They had the writings of David and the prophets. Their sin was greater, because they knew better. Jesus speaking in Luke 12:48 said, "...From everyone who has been given much, much will be demanded; and from the one who has been entrusted with much, much more will be asked."

Prayer: God, I repent of my sins and receive Your gift of forgiveness.

John 19:26-27 *When Jesus therefore saw His mother, and the disciple whom He loved standing by, He said to His mother, "Woman, behold your son!" The He said to the disciple, "Behold your mother."*

Jesus, nearing death has been on the cross for several hours. John 29:25 tells us, "Now there stood by the cross of Jesus, His mother, and His mother's sister, Mary the wife of Clopas, and Mary Magdalene." I can only imagine the heartache and despair Mary must have felt. There is a special bond between a mother and her son. To watch your first-born son be ridiculed, mocked, beaten beyond recognition and nailed to a cross would be heartbreaking. To add to the heaviness of the moment, Mary had known something would happen in Jesus' life that would cause her to suffer deep anguish. When Jesus was eight days old, Mary and Joseph, following the Law of Moses, took Jesus to the temple to be presented to the Lord. While there, Simeon, a righteous and devout man spoke a word of prophecy to Mary about Jesus. Luke 2:34-35 tells us, "Then Simeon blessed them and said to Mary, His mother; 'This Child is destined to cause the falling and rising of many in Israel, and to be a sign that will be spoken against, so that the thought of many hearts will be revealed. And a sword will pierce your own soul too.'" No doubt, Mary's soul was being pierced that day. Jesus looks down from the cross and sees His Mother and John. Although Mary and Joseph had four other sons and a couple of daughters, it was the responsibility of the first-born son to take care of his mother after his father's death. Jesus fulfilling His earthly responsibility of taking care of His mother, tells her, "Dear woman, behold your son!" And to John, "Behold your mother." We can only speculate why Jesus gives that responsibility to John rather than one of His half-brothers. But we do know that John was dearly loved by Jesus and even referred to himself as the disciple who Jesus loved. John has proved his loyalty, courage and faith by being the only disciple present at Jesus' crucifixion. He would honor Jesus' request and take very good care of Mary. The take away from today's scripture for me is the fact that Jesus is concerned about the smallest details of our lives and has the best in store for us. Jesus said in Matthew 6:33, "But seek first His kingdom and His righteousness, and all these things will be given to you as well."

Prayer: God, thank You for caring for me.

> John 19:30 So when Jesus had received the sour wine, He said, "It is finished!" And bowing His head, He gave up His spirit.

Jesus ends His life and earthly ministry with three short, but powerful words, "It is finished!" He has accomplished the purpose for which He came. Our debt has been paid in full. 2 Corinthians 5:21, "God made Him who had no sin to be sin for us, so that in Him we might become the righteousness of God." 1 Peter 2:24, "He Himself bore our sins in His body on the tree, so that we might die to sins and live for righteousness; by His wounds we are healed." The price that was paid for our sins was enormous, the very blood of Jesus. When I think of the cross and the sacrifice Jesus made for me, I am reminded of an old hymn written by Isaac Watts, "At the Cross." "Alas! And did my Savior bleed and did my Sovereign die? Would He devote that sacred head for sinners such as I? Was it for crimes that I had done He groaned upon that tree? Amazing pity! Grace unknown! And love beyond degree! Well might the sun in darkness hide and shut His glories in. When Christ the mighty maker died, for man the creature's sin. But drops of grief can ne'er repay, the debt of love I owe: Here Lord, I give myself away, tis all that I can do. At the cross, at the cross where I first saw the light, and the burden of my heart rolled away. It was there by faith I received my sight, and now I am happy all the day!" When you think about the cross what comes to mind? Are you reminded of the price that was paid for your redemption? Jesus willingly went to the cross for you and I. He finished the work He was sent to do. However, Jesus' life was not taken from Him. It was His choice to willingly give it up. Not only did Jesus freely go to the cross, John writes, "And bowing His head, He gave up His Spirit." In a last act of worship, Jesus bows His head before heaven and dismisses His Spirit. He releases His spirit from His body. My prayer is that the cross will take a new and deeper meaning in your walk with Christ. Let the cross be a vivid reminder of the sacrifice that was made for you.

Prayer: God, I surrender my life to You, tis all that I can do.

John 20:15 *Jesus said to her, "Woman, why are you weeping? Whom are you seeking?"*

It is very early Sunday morning and Mary Magdalene is on her way to Jesus' tomb to finish preparing His body for burial. She arrives at the grave and finds the huge stone that covered the entrance to Jesus' tomb had been rolled away. Assuming someone had taken the body, she runs back to find Peter and John and said to them, "They have taken away the Lord out of the tomb, and we do not know where they have laid Him." Peter and John take off running to the empty tomb. John doesn't enter the tomb, but looks in and sees the empty linen cloths lying there. Peter goes right inside and sees the empty grave cloths and a neatly folded handkerchief that had been placed around Jesus' head. Peter and John hang around for a few minutes pondering what has happened, then leave and go back to their homes. Mary is back at the tomb, but doesn't leave. John 20:11 tells us, "But Mary stood outside the tomb weeping, and as she wept she stooped down and looked into the tomb." Inside the tomb were two angels, one sitting at the head and the other at the feet of where Jesus' body had been placed. They ask Mary, "Woman, why are you weeping?" She said to them, "Because they have taken away my Lord, and I do not know where they have laid Him?" The stone rolled away, an empty tomb, and talking to angels is not enough evidence for Mary to understand what has happened. She turns around and finds Jesus standing behind her. He asks her why she is weeping. Mary doesn't recognize Jesus and assumes He is the gardener. She asks Him, "Sir, if You have carried Him away, tell me where You have laid Him, and I will take Him away." Jesus replies, "Mary!" It is at this moment; Mary recognizes the risen Savior. Yet, it was not until Jesus called Mary by name, did she recognize who He was. Do you remember the day Jesus called you by name? Did you recognize the risen Savior? Revelation 3:20 says, "Here I am! I stand at the door and knock. If anyone hears My voice and opens the door, I will come in and eat with him and he with Me." If you haven't already, open the door and let Him into your life today.

Prayer: God, thank You for calling me by name.

> John 20:27 Then He said to Thomas, "Reach your finger here, and look at My hands; and reach your hand here, and put it into My side. Do not be unbelieving, but believing."

The Bible doesn't have a lot to say about Thomas. However, from one brief incident after the resurrection of Christ, he has been branded with the nickname "Doubting Thomas." On the evening of His resurrection, Jesus appeared to the disciples. They were overjoyed and convinced of Jesus' resurrection. However, Thomas was not present with the other disciples that evening. When the disciples told him they had seen the risen Lord, Thomas replied, "Unless I see in His hands the print of the nails, and put my finger into the print of the nails and put my hand into His side, I will not believe." Was Thomas skeptical of what the disciples had told him, or did he just want to confirm for himself that Jesus was alive? Eight days later he gets his chance to find out. All the disciples have gathered together again behind locked doors in fear of the Jews. While they are there, Jesus appeared in the midst of them, saying, "Peace be with you." Guess who would be the very first person Jesus speaks to? Jesus then tells Thomas, "Reach your finger here, and look at My hands; and reach your hand here, and put it into My side. Do not be unbelieving, but believing." Jesus didn't chastise Thomas for wanting to see for himself. Jesus lovingly showed him. Haven't we all experienced moments in our lives just like Thomas? We find ourselves doubting the promises of God's word. Our prayers seemingly go unanswered, and God seems a million miles away. Self-doubt, fear, anxiety begin to take over. All the while, Jesus is there telling us to seek and trust Him. "Do not be unbelieving, but believing." How do we erase those doubts and fears? First, like Thomas, we need to seek the presence of the Lord. Thomas happened to be huddled with the disciples when Jesus appeared again; however, seeking the Lord's presence can be done in corporate worship or alone in your prayer time. Next, Thomas had made known his doubts. Tell the Lord your doubts and fears. He is not going to rebuke you for your feelings. Then reach out and take hold of His outstretched hand. That touch erased all doubt for Thomas who proclaimed, "My Lord and my God." Jesus' touch will do the same for you. As the old hymn says, "Place your hand in the nail scared hand."

Prayer: God, thank You for helping my unbelief.

> John 21:17 He said to him the third time, "Simon, son of Jonah, do you love Me?" Peter was grieved because He said to him a third time, "Do you love Me?"

If you have made a mess of your life and feel like you have completely ruined your relationship with God, today's encounter between Jesus and Peter should give you hope. We know the night that Jesus was betrayed, Peter had denied knowing Jesus three times. Upon hearing the rooster crow, Peter left weeping bitterly for his failure. It is now over a week later and the resurrected Lord has appeared to the disciples twice. The last time was for Thomas' benefit so he could see and touch the scars of Jesus. Several days have passed since then and Jesus hasn't appeared to the disciples. Peter says to the group, "I'm going fishing." The other disciples join him and they fish all night without catching a thing. It is early morning and Jesus standing on the shore calls to them and asks, "Children have you any food?" They answer "no." Jesus then tells them to throw their nets on right side of the boat and they will find some. Although they had not recognized it was Jesus, they complied and their net was filled with fish. John would later record the exact number of fish as 153. As the nets were filling up, John says, to Peter, "It is the Lord." Immediately Peter jumps into the water and swims to shore to meet Jesus. The other disciples make it to shore and share a meal that Jesus had prepared. After breakfast, Jesus and Peter have a conversation that restores and reinstalls Peter as one of His disciples. Jesus asks Peter the same question, three times, "Simon, son of Jonah, do you love Me?" To which Peter replies, "Yes, Lord: You know that I love You." Why would Jesus ask Peter three times if he loved Him in front of the other disciples? Was it to rub it in Peter's face that he had denied the Lord three times? Thankfully, God does not treat us that way when we fail. He doesn't ask us if we are sorry. He doesn't make us promise we won't do whatever we did again. Like Peter, Jesus challenges us to love Him. Jesus wants the same from you and I as He did Peter. Jesus is concerned about the condition of our heart. He will make us face the reality of our failures, but He also challenges us to move forward. Do you love Him?

Prayer: God, You know all things; You know that I love You.

> Acts 1:5 For John truly baptized with water, but you shall be baptized with the Holy Spirit not many days from now.

Before the crucifixion, Jesus told the disciples, "Nevertheless I tell you the truth. It is to your advantage that I go away; for if I do not go away, the Helper will not come to you; but if I depart, I will send Him to you." Jesus is now with the disciples giving them some last-minute instructions and encouragement prior to His ascension to heaven. He tells them the Helper that He promised would come is now only days away. They would know when He arrived because they will be baptized or fully immersed in the Holy Spirit. This immersion would be different from the Holy Spirit indwelling us when we receive Christ as Lord and Savior as Paul writes about in 1 Corinthians 12:13. "For we were all baptized by one Spirit into one body – whether Jews or Greeks, slave or free – and we were all given the one Spirit to drink." This baptism is an empowerment of supernatural power and abilities to accomplish the work Christ has planned for us. Joel 2:28 tells us, "And afterward, I will pour out My Spirit on all people. Your sons and daughters will prophesy, your old men will dream dreams, your young men will see visions." It is by this kind of power given to us by the Holy Spirit that we have a boldness and desire to serve God. 2 Peter 1:3, "His divine power has given us everything we need for life and godliness through our knowledge of Him who called us by His own glory and goodness." This type of baptism or anointing of the Holy Spirit is also not a one and done type of experience. Believers will have multiple encounters and experiences with the Holy Spirit. For example, Peter was filled with the Holy Spirit on the Day of Pentecost and preached a sermon that caused 3,000 people to be saved. Later in the Book of Acts, Peter was led by the Holy Spirit to go to the home of Cornelius, a Roman Centurion. Acts 10:44 says, "While Peter was still speaking these words, the Holy Spirit fell upon all those who heard the word." Our walk with Christ would be boring and unproductive without the anointing of the Holy Spirit. If you have not experienced His anointing, walk in obedience to God's word and ask Him to daily fill you with His Spirit.

Prayer: God, fill me with Your Holy Spirit.

> Acts 1:7 And He said to them, "It is not for you to know times or seasons which the Father has put in His own authority."

Jesus has just told the disciples they are days away from the outpouring of the Holy Spirit. Still thinking in terms of Jesus setting up an earthly Kingdom, they ask Jesus, "Lord, will You at this time restore the kingdom to Israel?" Throughout Jesus' ministry, the disciples have anxiously waited for Him to free Israel from Roman rule. They also had aspirations of ruling with Jesus. Matthew 19:28, "Jesus said to them, 'I tell you the truth, at the renewal of all things, when the Son of Man sits on His glorious throne, you who have followed Me will also sit on twelve thrones, judging the twelve tribes of Israel.'" The disciples had it all figured out. This would be the perfect time for Jesus to set up His earthly kingdom and they could help Him rule. We are no different from the disciples. We think we have God's plan and timing for our lives all figured out and then we learn we don't. Isaiah 55:8-9 tells us, "For My thoughts are not your thoughts, neither are your ways My ways, declares the Lord. As the heavens are higher than the earth, so are My ways higher than your ways and My thoughts than your thoughts." I have also learned that God's plan and timing are so much better than mine. In the latter part of my career with Progress Energy, I had interviewed for another management position at our Call Center. I knew the job was mine and was terribly disappointed when I learned that it was given to someone else. Little did I know that God had a better plan. Less than a year later, Duke Energy and Progress Energy merged. Because of the merger, I was given the opportunity to retire several years earlier than I had planned and received a generous out-placement package to go along with it. God's path to retirement was vastly different and much better than I could have ever imagined. There are so many events in God's timing we would like to know about; things regarding our personal life, the lives of our family, and the kingdom of God. Jesus said, "It is not for you to know the times or seasons which the Father has put in His own authority." We have to live by faith, knowing God is in control and His timing is perfect.

Prayer: God, thank You, for Your ways are much better than mine.

> Acts 1:8 *But you shall receive power when the Holy Spirit has come upon you; and you shall be witnesses to Me in Jerusalem, and in all Judea and Samaria, and to the end of the earth.*

These are the last words spoken by Jesus before He ascended to heaven. He tells us the means by which the gospel would spread throughout the earth will be by the power of the Holy Spirit. We read in Acts chapter 2 where the Holy Spirit filled the disciples with a boldness to begin spreading the good news of Christ. Along with this boldness, the Holy Spirit also gives each believer spiritual gifts so that we can better serve God. These gifts are simply God empowering us to do what He has called us to do. 2 Peter 1:3, "His divine power has given us everything we need for life and godliness through our knowledge of Him who called us by His own glory and goodness." Paul writes about the gifts of the Holy Spirit in 1 Corinthians 12. He emphasizes we do not have every gift, nor do we all have the same gift. Our gifts should complement each other's gifts and help us work together. Let's take a look at the gifts of the Spirit. **1. The Gift of Wisdom** – The gift to make wise choices and give direction in accordance to God's will. **2. The Gift of Knowledge** – The gift to understand and comprehend physical and spiritual issues. **3. The Gift of Faith** – The gift to trust God and encourage others to trust Him, no matter the circumstances. **4. The Gift of Healing** - The gift of using God's healing power to heal a person who is sick or suffering. **5. The Gift of Miracles** – The gift to display signs and miracles that give glory to God. **6. The Gift of Prophecy** – The gift to declare a message from God. **7. The Gift of Discerning Spirits** – The gift to recognize if something is truly from God or of the world. **8. The Gift of Tongues** – The gift to speak in a language you have had no experience or training in. **9. The Gift of Interpreting Tongues** – The ability to interpret a word or message given in tongues. **10. The Gift of Administration** – The gift to keep things in order and agreement with God's principles. **11. The Gift of Helps** – The gift of wanting to serve others. **12. The Gift of Giving** – The gift of joyfully sharing with others. My prayer is that you are faithfully using the spiritual gifts God has given you.

Prayer: God, help me to faithfully use the gifts You have given me.

> Acts 9:5 And he said, "Who are You Lord?" Then the Lord said, "I am Jesus, whom you are persecuting. It is hard for you to kick against the goads."

Saul has been to the high priest in Jerusalem, asking for letters of approval to arrest and bring back for trial anyone found believing in Jesus Christ. He is on the way to Damascus to arrest the believers there, when a great light from heaven blinds him. He falls to the ground and hears a voice saying, "Saul, Saul, why are you persecuting Me?" Saul replies, "Who are You Lord?" Jesus replied, "I am Jesus, whom you are persecuting. It is hard for you to kick against the goads." The very same person Saul is trying to wipe out any knowledge of has just spoken to him and basically tells him he is only hurting himself. How is persecuting the church hurting Saul? Like many of us before we came to know Christ, Saul is fighting against God. The sad reality is that he thinks he is doing the right thing. Yet the Christians he has arrested and had killed displayed faith, forgiveness, and confidence much the way Stephen did. Likely their behavior struck a nerve with Saul's conscience. The more their faith in Christ did not waiver, the angrier it would make Saul causing him to go after other Christians even harder. The same is true for us today. Many people will take up a cause and think they are doing good. All the while, they are in complete opposition to God's word. Yet they press on, fighting against God and persecuting His church, only to suffer the consequences. Jesus likens the consequences to a goad. A goad is a stick that has a sharp metal point and is used for prodding cattle. A farmer would poke an ox or cow with the sharp point in order to get them moving or change directions. When the animal was poked with a goad, often times it would kick back causing itself more pain. God's word has been given to us as a guide. Ecclesiastes 12:11, "The words of the wise are like goads, their collected sayings like firmly embedded nails – given by one Shepherd." Jesus' words have application for Christians as well. How often do we choose to do the opposite of what God's word tells us to do? Whenever we do, we are kicking against the goads. There will be a price of some type to pay. "Trust and obey, for there's no other way to be happy in Jesus."

Prayer: God, help me to follow Your word.

> Acts 9:15 But the Lord said to him, "Go, for he is a chosen vessel of Mine to bear My name before Gentiles, kings, and the children of Israel."

After being blinded by a great light, Saul is led into Damascus where he spends the next three days praying and fasting. At the end of the three days, Jesus appears to a man named Ananias, who lived in Damascus and tells him, "Arise, and go to the street called Straight, and inquire at the house of Judas for one called Saul of Tarsus, for behold, he is praying. And in a vision he has seen a man named Ananias coming in and putting his hand on him, so that he might receive his sight." Ananias' response is understandable based on Saul's reputation. He replies to the Lord, Lord I have heard about this guy. He is a bad dude and has come to Damascus to arrest any of Your followers he can find. Are You sure about this? Jesus tells Ananias that Saul is a "chosen vessel" of His to take the name of Jesus to the Gentiles, their kings, and the Jews. Can I tell you; we are all chosen vessels in God's kingdom. Before we were born, we were a chosen vessel. While our life was a total trainwreck and before we came to know Jesus as Lord and Savior, we were a chosen vessel. He has a specific plan and purpose for each one of us. Jeremiah 1:5 says, "Before I formed you in the womb I knew you, before you were born I set you apart. I appointed you as a prophet to the nations." He chose Jeremiah to be a prophet. He chose Paul to take His name to the Gentiles. What has God chosen you for? Just like Paul we are chosen to bear His name. God takes us out of the darkness and exposes us to the light of His salvation. Then He sends us back to the darkness to share the light we have received. Unfortunately, He doesn't make us a perfect vessel without flaws and weaknesses. However, it is most often through our flaws that others can see how Christ can put the pieces of our lives back together and use us for His Kingdom. God's plan for us will not likely lead to fame and fortune. But we can count on His blessings of mercy and grace to help us each step of the way.

Prayer: God, help me to be like Ananias and not hesitate when You call me to do something for You.

> Corinthians 12:9 And He said to me. "My grace is sufficient for you, for My strength is made perfect in weakness."

Satan does a very good job of creating obstacles in our lives to prevent us from serving God. In 2 Corinthians 2:7, Paul refers to these obstacles as a "Thorn in the flesh, and a messenger from Satan to torment him." All too often, these obstacles can be easily turned into excuses for not doing what God has called us to do. While God, on the other hand, wants to use our shortcomings as a means to increase our dependency on Him, so our inabilities become His strengths. Jesus reminded Paul after he had prayed three times for God to remove the thorn in his flesh, "My grace is sufficient for you, for My strength is made perfect in weakness." God doesn't promise to make our lives easy. His goal is that we fully trust Him no matter our circumstances. This means to allow Christ to be strong in the areas where we are weak. How do we allow Christ to be strong in our lives? Hopefully this example will help you understand. Vivian attends Bible Study Fellowship and takes our 18-month-old grandson with her. She became friends with one of the ladies who faithfully serves in the children's area. This lady had lost her only son to a tragic accident just prior to COVID. Naturally, her life was devastated by this loss. A year or two later, she felt God leading her to serve in the nursery at Bible Study Fellowship. She kept telling God, she really didn't feel it and to find someone else. However, God kept impressing upon her to serve, telling her, "My grace is sufficient for you, My strength is made perfect in weakness." She listened to God and stepped out of a life of sorrow and mourning, into a life of joy and happiness taking care of little children every week. If you have ever served in a church, then you know how hard it is to find qualified nursery workers. Vivian tells me she is the most loving and caring person with children she has ever seen. Although nothing will replace the loss of her son, God has used the ministry of serving and teaching young children about Jesus to give her new life. What excuses are you using not to serve God? No matter what you are facing, God's grace is sufficient. Turn your weaknesses into triumphs.

Prayer: God, turn my excuses into strengths to serve You.

> *Revelation 1:8 "I am the Alpha and the Omega, the Beginning and the End," says the Lord, "who is and who was and who is to come, the Almighty."*

John has been exiled to the Ise of Patmos, where he receives the words of Revelation from Jesus. Revelation 1:1, "The Revelation of Jesus Christ, which God gave Him to show His servants – things which must shortly take place. And He sent and signified it by His angel to His servant John." It seems very appropriate that Jesus would begin His words to John with a "I Am" declaration. If you recall, John recorded seven "I Am" sayings of Jesus. "I Am the bread of life, I Am the light of the world, I Am the door, I Am the good shepherd, I Am the resurrection and the life, I Am the way the truth and the life, and I Am the true vine." Jesus, being fully God declares He is, "the Alpha and the Omega, the Beginning and the End, who is and who was and who is to come, the Almighty." He is the visible image of the invisible God who was with God in the beginning. John 1:1, "In the beginning was the Word, and the Word was with God, and the Word was God. He was with God in the beginning." Jesus has also been given authority by God to rule the world. Daniel 7:13 says, "He (The Son of Man) was given authority, glory and sovereign power; all peoples, nations and men of every language worshipped Him. His dominion is an everlasting dominion that will not pass away, and His kingdom is one that will not be destroyed." God, Jesus, and the Holy Spirit have always existed, there is no beginning or end for them. God's eternal existence is hope to the believer and a stumbling block for the unbeliever. Without an eternal God, what hope and guarantee of a life after death with Him would we have? We view life as a timeline. At the end of the timeline, we are no longer here. However, for those who know the Alpha and Omega, we have the promise of eternal life. This same Jesus is returning soon to set up His kingdom on earth. Revelation 1:7, "Behold, He is coming on the clouds, and every eye will see Him, even they who pierced Him. And all the tribes of the earth will mourn because of Him. Even so. Amen." Remain faithful, and look to the clouds for His return.

Prayer: God, thank You for making a way for us to spend eternity with You.

> *Revelation 1:18 I am He who lives, and was dead, and behold, I am alive forevermore. Amen. And I have the keys of Hades and of Death.*

The entire foundation of our faith in Christ is that He came to earth, lived a sinless life, was crucified on a cross for our sins, and three days later rose from the dead. We know He rose from the dead because of the empty tomb and the numerous eyewitness accounts of His appearance. Jesus appeared to John on the Isle of Patmos. However, Jesus looks entirely different from the last time he had seen Jesus. Revelation 1:12-16, "I turned around to see the voice that was speaking to me. And when I turned I saw seven golden lampstands, and among the lampstands was someone 'like the Son of Man,' dressed in a robe reaching down to His feet and with a golden sash around His chest. His head and hair were white like wool, as white as snow, and His eyes were like blazing fire. His feet were like bronze glowing in a furnace, and His voice was like the sound of rushing waters. In His right hand He held seven stars, and out of His mouth came a sharp double-edged sword. His face was like the sun shining in all its brilliance." John, paralyzed with fear, said, "When I saw Him, I fell at His feet as though dead." Jesus then places His right hand on John and said, "Do not be afraid, I am the First and the Last. I am He who lives, and was dead, and behold, I am alive forevermore. Amen. And I have the keys of Hades and Death." This is a dumb question, but can a dead person say they lived, died, and are now living forever? Of course not. Jesus is alive. He willingly went to the cross, gave up His spirit, and rose from the dead. By conquering death and the grave, He now holds the keys to Death and Hades. Jesus has the power and authority over our eternal destiny. Prior to accepting Christ as Lord and Savior, we were all bound for Hades at our death to await our final judgment. However, Christ has unlocked the door of Death and Hades and will take us to be in Paradise with Him. As Paul writes in 1 Corinthians 15:55, "Where, O death, is your victory? Where, O death, is your sting?" Our victory is in Christ Jesus.

Prayer: God, thank You for our resurrected Savior who holds the keys of Death and Hades.

> Revelation 1:19 *Write the things which you have seen, and the things which are, and the things which will take place after this.*

Jesus gives John an outline for the Book of Revelation. He breaks it down into three sections, "things which you have seen, the things that are, and the things which will take place." John is writing this book to the seven churches in Asia: Ephesus, Smyrna, Pergamum, Thyatira, Sardis, Philadelphia, and Laodicea. To each church is a message of encouragement and warning from Jesus. These messages are "the things that are" and we will look at them over the next several days. Yesterday, we read about the things John saw, which was the Son of Man, Jesus, clothed in all His glory. Beginning in chapter 4, John describes the things that will take place. He is given a panoramic view of the end times which is so overwhelming that John describes them using symbols and images. The Book of Revelation is "fun reading," but very difficult to comprehend. However, for those who take the time to read and learn from it, God promises a special blessing. Revelation 1:3, "Blessed is he who reads and those who hear the words of this prophecy, and keep those things which are written in it; for the time is near." There is also a warning to anyone who would add to or take away from the words of this book. Revelation 22:18-19, "For I testify to everyone who hears the words of the prophecy of this book: If anyone adds to these things, God will add to him the plagues that are written in this book; and if anyone takes away from the words of the book of this prophecy, God shall take away his part from the Book of Life, from the holy city, and from the things which are written in this book." What is the message of Revelation to the church? Simply, Christ wins and Satan loses. No matter how difficult life may get, there is hope for a joyous beginning of eternal life with Christ here on earth. There will be no more sickness, sorrow and death. God will wipe away all tears. There will be a new heaven and a new earth. When will all this take place? Only God knows. However, John writes in Revelation 22:20, "He who testifies to these things says, 'Surely I am coming quickly," Amen. Even so, come, Lord Jesus! Are you ready for His return?

Prayer: God, thank You for letting us know the things which will take place.

> *Revelation 2:2 I know your works, your labor, your patience, and that you cannot bear those who are evil. And you have tested those who say they are apostles and are not, and have found them liars.*

If you have ever wondered if God keeps track of what is going on in the earth, the letters John records to the churches in Revelation should give you a clear answer. Today, Jesus is speaking to the church at Ephesus which was founded by Paul. Located near a harbor, Ephesus was a center for trade and the capital city of a providence in the Roman empire. It was known for its huge amphitheater which could seat 50,000 people and its worship of the god, Artemis or Diana. Paul spent approximately two years growing the church in Ephesus. Much of his time there is recorded in Acts 19-20. The Ephesians faced many of the same challenges Christians face today. They were surrounded by a community of people who didn't know God and who worshipped knowledge and idols. There were also false teachers who came in and slanted the gospel of Jesus Christ for their personal gain. Jesus commends the church at Ephesus for their works, patience, hatred of evil, and their ability to identify false teachers. Paul commends the Ephesians for their faith and love for others. Ephesians 1:15, "For this reason, ever since I heard about your faith in the Lord Jesus and your love for all the saints, I have not stopped giving thanks for you." Paul also encouraged the church at Ephesus to be strong in the Lord and equip them to stand against the evil one. Ephesians 6:10-11, "Finally, be strong in the Lord and in His mighty power. Put on the full armor of God, so that you can take your stand against the devil's schemes." The Ephesians were good at identifying evil and not allowing themselves to be dragged into it. 1 Corinthians 15:33 tells us, "Do not be misled: Bad company corrupts good character." They were also mature in their faith, able to distinguish good from evil. Hebrews 5:14, "But solid food is for the mature, who by constant use have trained themselves to distinguish good from evil." How we live, serve others, and conduct ourselves as Christians is important in God's sight. It doesn't assure us of our salvation, but it glorifies God. Matthew 5:16, "In the same way, let your light shine among men, that they may see your good deeds and praise your Father in heaven." Be strong in the Lord and work for Him daily.

Prayer: God, I pray that my works are pleasing to You.

> *Revelation 2:4 Nevertheless I have this against you, that you have left your first love.*

Jesus has just commended the Ephesians for their good works and discerning spirit. They were very good at following instructions and working hard. However, they had become more focused on the busyness of ministry and church work and forgot their true passion for serving. Jesus calls them out on it saying, "You have left your first love." Somewhere in their passion for serving Christ, the Ephesians lost the true reason for their service. They found themselves going through the motions of worship and good works, rather than being motivated by a love for Christ. They had entered a stage of complacency and were headed towards burnout. Paul challenges us in 1 Corinthians 15:58, "Therefore, my dear brothers, stand firm. Let nothing move you. Always give yourselves fully to the work of the Lord, because you know that your labor in the Lord is not in vain." How do we give ourselves fully to the work of the Lord and not get weary or even worse, lose our love for Christ? Secondly, how do we recognize the symptoms of burnout and take action before they overwhelm us, leaving us feeling worn out and unable to carry on? In many churches, there is a shortage of members who will work. The members that do, spread themselves thin, by volunteering to serve in more areas than they can handle. According to Thomas Ranier, Founder of *www.ChurchAnswers.com*, approximately 90% of church ministry is done by 30% of the members. Also, many of the programs and ministries of the church either lack a clear vision or their purpose has not been adequately explained. Churches also get into the habit of doing the same things each year because that's what they have always done, whether useful or not. All the while, the work becomes either overwhelming or boring, leading to exhaustion and a lack of motivation. It affects a person's, physical, emotional, and spiritual life. Sadly, many who experience burnout, will gradually become less involved and leave the church never to return. If you are sensing a feeling of spiritual dryness and a lack of motivation for serving, then you may be headed for burnout. Are you serving out of a sense of duty or a love for Christ and others? Take time today to evaluate where your heart is for service.

Prayer: God, help me to run and not grow weary and walk and not be faint.

> Revelation 2:5 Remember therefore from where you have fallen; repent and do the first works, or else I will come to you quickly and remove your lampstand from its place – unless you repent.

The church at Ephesus had abandoned their first love and was in spiritual decline. The motivation they once experienced had been replaced with a sense a duty. Their hard work and patient endurance had turned into unfulfilling, monotonous tasks. Jesus recognized their decline and commanded them to remember where they had been spiritually, repent, and return to doing their first works. His command also comes with a strong warning. Jesus threatens to remove their lampstand. The significance of the lampstand is found in Revelation 1:20, "The mystery of the seven stars that you saw in My right hand and of the seven golden lampstands is this: The seven stars are the angels of the seven churches, and the seven lampstands are the seven churches." If the church at Ephesus doesn't repent, they will cease to exist. This is a chilling warning to all believers. We can get so caught up in doing church work and lose our passion for Christ. Jesus' instructions to the church at Ephesus are appropriate for us today. First, we are to remember where we were. Meditate on what your relationship was like when you were first saved. Recall the days when you were excited about being a newborn Christian and the enthusiasm you had for telling others. Think about how you relied on Jesus to meet your needs. Psalm 77:12 tells us, "I will meditate on all Your works and consider all Your mighty deeds." Next, we are to repent. Repentance requires confession and commitment. 1 John 1:9, "If we confess our sins, He is faithful and just and will forgive our sins and purify us from all unrighteousness." After repenting, we commit to turning our hearts towards Him. Psalm 37:5, "Commit your way to the Lord; trust in Him and He will do this." Lastly, we are to return to our first works, doing the same things we did as new believers. Just as a marriage counselor will advise couples to do things for each other they did when they were first married, we should do as Christians. Our feelings will begin to catch up with our actions and we will find ourselves with a renewed spirit of love and devotion for Christ. You may be wondering what happened to the Church at Ephesus. It no longer exists and the area in Turkey where it was once located is predominately Muslim.

Prayer: God, help me to return to my first love for You.

> *Revelation 2:7 He who has an ear, let him hear what the Spirit says to the churches. To him who overcomes, I will give to eat from the tree of life, which is in the midst of Paradise of God.*

The Church at Ephesus was in spiritual decline. They had lost their love for God. In His call for repentance, God issued a dire warning to the Ephesians. Their lamp or light as a church would be snuffed out and removed unless they came back to their first love. Today, Jesus offers hope and a reward for those who repent and overcome the sin in their lives. "To him who overcomes, I will give to eat from the tree of life, which is in the midst of Paradise of God." Yes, this is the same tree of life which was planted in the Garden of Eden. Genesis 2:9, "And the Lord God made all kinds of trees grow out of the ground – trees that were pleasing to the eye and good for food. In the middle of the garden were the tree of life and the tree of the knowledge of good and evil." God gave Adam and Eve permission to eat from all the trees, except the tree of the knowledge of good and evil. Once Adam and Eve tasted the fruit from that tree, life forevermore changed. God banished them from having access to the Garden of Eden and the tree of life. Genesis 3:22-24, "And the Lord God said, 'The man has now become like one of Us, knowing good and evil. He must not be allowed to reach out his hand and take also from the tree of life and eat, and live forever.' So the Lord God banished him from the Garden of Eden to work the ground from which he had been taken. After He drove the man out, He placed on the east side of the Garden of Eden cherubim and a flaming sword, flashing back and forth to guard the way to the tree of life." Jesus' promise of access to the tree of life applies to anyone who overcomes their sinful state. Revelation 22:1-2, "Then the angel showed me the river of the water of life, as clear as crystal, flowing from the throne of God and of the Lamb down the middle of the great street of the city. On each side of the river stood the tree of life, bearing twelve crops of fruit, yielding its fruit every month. And the leaves of the tree are for the healing of the nations." Be an overcomer.

Prayer: God, thank You for the fruit of the tree of life.

> *Revelation 2:9 I know your works, tribulation, and poverty (but you are rich); and I know the blasphemy of those who say they are Jews and are not, but are a synagogue of Satan.*

Located approximately 35 miles north of Ephesus, Jesus' next letter is to the church at Smyrna. Smyrna was a large city on the coast of Asia Minor. There, worship of any other god other than the Roman emperor was forbidden with the exception of Judaism. This set the church up at Smyrna for trouble not only from the Jews, but the Romans as well. Smyrna is one of two churches that Jesus had nothing critical to say about it. Jesus told them, "I know your works, tribulation and poverty (but you are rich)." Unlike the Ephesians, their works were done with the right motives and spirit. Yet they faced tribulation and poverty. Serving God and doing the right things doesn't necessarily lead to riches and fame. In fact, it is often just the opposite. However, Jesus said they were rich. They had a spiritual wealth, that no one could take away. Matthew 6:20, "But store up for yourselves treasures in heaven, where moth and rust do not destroy, and where thieves do not break in and steal." Then Jesus said, "I know the blasphemy of those who say they are Jews and are not, but are a synagogue of Satan." Jesus uses the term, "synagogue of Satan" with the church at Smyrna and Philadelphia. Both churches faced a group of unbelieving Jews who were determined to persecute the believers there. The very people who were looking for the Messiah were persecuting their fellow Jews who believed Jesus was the Messiah. In their zeal to protect the Jewish faith, the Jews were accomplishing Satan's work of destroying the church. Today, how many people who call themselves Christians are actually doing more harm to the church than good? Their intentions are in the right place, but their hearts have been led astray by false teachings of tolerance and the rejection of absolute truth. They adhere to the belief that anyone who is sincere in their faith will go to heaven. All one needs to do is be a good person, live a good life, and be kind to others to get there. Jesus tells us in John 14:6, "I am the way, the truth, and the life. No one comes to the Father except through Me." Stand strong, and don't be led astray by those who are distorting the truth of salvation and doing the work of Satan.

Prayer: God, help me to store up treasures in heaven.

> Revelation 2:10 Do not fear any of those things which you are about to suffer. Indeed, the devil is about to throw some of you into prison, that you may be tested, and you will have tribulation ten days. Be faithful until death, and I will give you the crown of life.

How would you like to receive a letter from God that said, "Do not fear any of those things which you are about to suffer?" Would you find that to be an encouragement or a reason to dread what was coming? The church at Smyrna was already facing persecution, now God is saying it is going to get worse. The devil, who is responsible for the persecution of Christians, was going to throw some of them in prison for their faith. They were going to be tested and have tribulation for ten days. Many Bible scholars do not believe this is a literal ten-day period of intense persecution, but a period of persecutions that began with the Roman Emperor Nero, 54 AD and ended with Emperor Diocletian in 305 AD. Either way, the believers at Smyrna remained faithful. Persecution is a daily reality for many Christians around the world. Although the physical persecution of Christians hasn't reached the United States it does come in the form of being ostracized, harassed, insulted, and labeled extremists. During the pandemic, churches in many states were not allowed to meet even with distancing protocols, while rioters filled the streets of these same states without masks. As we get closer to the end times, the persecution of Christians will increase. Matthew 24:9, "Then you will be handed over to be persecuted and put to death, and you will be hated by all nations because of Me." Why does God allow all this to happen to His people? God uses it to refine and purify the church. 1 Peter 4:17, "For it is time for judgment to begin with the family of God; and if it begins with us, what will the outcome be for those who do not obey the gospel of God?" In the face of persecution, I can assure you anyone who has not totally committed their lives to Christ will be revealed. They are the people Jesus spoke of in Matthew 13:20-21, "The one who received the seed that fell on rocky places is the person who hears the word and at once receives it with joy. But since they have no root, they lost only a short time. When trouble or persecution comes because of the word, they quickly fall away." For those who remain faithful, Jesus promises to each one, a crown of life.

Prayer: God, help me to be faithful until death.

> *Revelation 2:11 He who has an ear, let him hear what the Spirit says to the churches. He who overcomes shall not be hurt by the second death.*

Jesus had only good things to say about the church at Smyrna. Although they were poor and faced many trials, the Christians there didn't waiver and remained strong in their faith. Jesus said they were spiritually rich. They knew God, trusted Him, and kept their eyes on what was most important. Many of the believers in Smyrna would likely face death at the hands of their persecutors. Jesus encourages them today saying, "He who overcomes shall not be hurt by the second death." Every believer who makes it to heaven is an overcomer. They have successfully resisted the power of sin and temptation, and remained faithful to Christ through all circumstances. An overcomer is not sinless, but relies on God's grace and mercy for forgiveness. Even when things get difficult, their faith remains strong. 1 John 5:4-5, "For everyone born of God overcomes the world. This is the victory that has overcome the world, even our faith. Who is it that overcomes the world? Only he who believes that Jesus is the Son of God." You may be thinking, I am not so sure I am an overcomer. I seem to mess up more than I overcome. Jesus doesn't expect us to do anything He has not already paved the way for us. John 16:33, "I have told you these things, so that in Me you may have peace. In this world you will have trouble. But take heart! I have overcome the world." God has also given us the Holy Spirit to help us. John 14:26, "But the Counselor, the Holy Spirit, whom the Father will send in My name, will teach you all things and will remind you of everything I have said to you." Overcoming is enduring to the end. Hebrews 3:14, "We have come to share in Christ if we hold firmly till the end the confidence we had at first." God's promise today to those who overcome is that they will not be hurt by the second death. The second death is mentioned in Revelation 20:14-15, "Then Death and Hades were thrown into the lake of fire. This is the second death, the lake of fire. If anyone's name was not found written in the Book of Life, they were thrown into the lake of fire." A time of testing is coming for every believer. My prayer is that you will be an overcomer.

Prayer: God, help me to be an overcomer.

> *Revelation 2:13 I know your works, and where you dwell, where Satan's throne is. And you hold fast to My name, and did not deny My faith even in the last days in which Antipas was My faithful martyr, who was killed among you, where Satan dwells.*

Jesus is speaking to the church at Pergamos which is located approximately 50 miles north of Smyrna. He tells the church, "I know your works, and where you dwell, where Satan's throne is." We know that Satan is the "prince of this world." Jesus speaking in John 12:31 said, "Now is the time for judgment on this world; now the prince of this world will be driven out." Although we associate Satan's home as hell, it is really the earth. Hell is where Satan will be confined to at the end of times. For some reason, Satan decided to set up his headquarters in Pergamos. How would you like to live in the very place where Satan has set up his throne? Ephesians 6:12 tells us, "For our struggle is not against flesh and blood, but against the rulers, against the authorities, against the powers of this dark world and against the spiritual forces of evil in the heavenly realms." Can you imagine the demonic influence in every aspect of life there? Yet, in this dark, pagan city where the forces of evil have gathered, a church was established. Like the church at Smyrna, the church of Pergamos faced persecution. Yet they held fast to Christ's name and did not waiver in their faith because of persecution. Jesus said, even as they watched their fellow brother in Christ, Antipas, be martyred for his faith, they never turned back. It is said that Antipas was placed inside a huge brass bull that had been hollowed out. A raging fire was built under the bull until it became red hot. Knowing the same fate potentially awaited them, they still remained faithful. I often wonder how I would have reacted in that type of situation. The day is coming where we may have that opportunity. However, physical persecution is not the only tactic Satan uses to discourage us and cause us to lose faith. If that doesn't work, he has other tactics that are just as effective. Often times he puts us in situations where we have to decide to remain faithful to Christ or follow the crowd. The weight of peer pressure can be just as powerful as the fear of persecution. No matter Satan's tactics, God expects us to remain faithful to Him. Tomorrow we will learn if the church at Pergamos continued to remain faithful.

Prayer: God, help me to hold fast to Your name in all situations.

Day 348

> Revelation 2:14 But I have a few things against you, because you have there those who hold the doctrine of Balaam, who taught Balak to put a stumbling block before the children of Israel, to eat things sacrificed to idols, and to commit sexual immorality.

After commending the church at Pergamos for their faithfulness in the face of persecution, Jesus said, "But I have a few things against you." The church at Pergamos had compromised their beliefs with the world. Jesus said they had allowed "Those who hold to the doctrine of Balaam" into the church. The story of Balaam is found in Numbers 22 – 25. Balak, the King of Moab, asked the prophet Balaam to come and curse the Israelites who were passing through his country on the way to the promised land. Several times, Balaam refused King Balak's offer for his help. However, King Balak kept upping the reward and finally Balaam relents, but said he could only say what God tells him to say. Three different times, Balaam speaks blessings instead of curses over the Israelites, making King Balak furious. However, Balaam offers King Balak some advice on how to bring down the nation of Israel. Numbers 31:16, "They were the ones who followed Balaam's advice and were the means of turning the Israelites away from the Lord in what happened at Peor, so that a plague struck the Lord's people." Balaam's plan was to have the Moabite women to intermingle with the Israelite men and marry them. The influence of the Moabite wives would eventually cause the Israelites to pick up the Moabite pagan rituals and abandon their devotion to God. Numbers 25:3, "So Israel joined in worshipping the Baal of Peor. And the Lord's anger burned against them." God is a jealous God. He said, "You shall have no other gods before Me." The doctrine of Balaam says, it's okay to be like the world. God calls us to be separate and holy. The doctrine of Balaam says, it's okay to compromise our morals for the sake of being accepted. James 4:17, "Anyone, then, who knows the good he ought to do and doesn't do it, sins." The doctrine of Balaam says we shouldn't speak out against sin, while God expects us to speak the truth of His word to others. Ephesians 5:11, "Have nothing to do with the fruitless deeds of darkness, but rather expose them." Tolerance and compromise are dangerous tools of Satan which have infiltrated many churches today. No longer do they take a stand against sin, but rather embrace it. God is not pleased with what He sees.

Prayer: God, help me to stand firm in Your word.

> *Revelation 2:16 Repent, or else I will come to you quickly and will fight against them with the sword of My mouth.*

The church at Pergamos had compromised to worldly ideas. They didn't deny Jesus, but had begun to allow teachings in the church that were in direct conflict with God's word. Jesus calls them to repentance and warns that He will judge them according to "the sword of My mouth." We can easily point fingers at many churches today who have compromised to the world and look no different from a social club. You may even be attending a church where every sermon is a feel-good sermon, or where the worship sounds more like a rock concert than church. Or perhaps you attend a church where it is taught that any way you chose to live is okay in God's sight. No church is perfect. I heard someone once say, if you find the perfect church, don't go there because it will no longer be perfect. God uses imperfect people and churches to accomplish His will. But that doesn't mean He will continue to tolerate compromise and sin in the church. Churches that move away from following God's word will eventually lose their effectiveness and begin to decline. Jesus says to these churches, "Repent, or else I will come to you quickly and will fight against them with the sword of My mouth." We know from Ephesians 6:17, that the sword represents the word of God. Hebrews 4:12-13 also tells us, "For the word of God is living and active. Sharper than any double-edged sword, it penetrates even to dividing soul and spirit, joints and marrow; it judges the thoughts and attitudes of the heart. Nothing in all creation is hidden from God's sight. Everything is uncovered and laid bare before the eyes of Him to whom we must give account." The word of God is not subjective. It doesn't make suggestions for us to consider whether or not we want to do them. His word exposes every bit of ugliness in our lives and lays it bare in front of Him. And even worse, we will give an account of our lives according to His word. Jesus' word to us and the church today is to confront sin and repent. We can either use His words to live by, or He will use His words in judgment against us. Have you compromised with the world, or are you living by God's word?

Prayer: God, help me not to compromise to the world's way of life.

> *Revelation 2:17 He who has an ear, let him hear what the Spirit says to the churches. To him who overcomes I will give some of the hidden manna to eat. And I will give him a white stone, and on the stone a new name written which no one knows except him who receives it.*

The church at Pergamos had compromised their beliefs by allowing worldly ideas contrary to God's word be taught and practiced there. Compromise doesn't begin and end within the doors of the church. It is a gradual process that takes place within you and me. Compromise is like a slippery slope. We don't wake up one morning and decide things we once believed were wrong are now perfectly okay. It starts by allowing others to slowly influence the way we view things. Over time, we begin to give up our core beliefs in order to be accepted and liked by others. Also, the movies and TV shows we watch, the type of music we listen to, and the people we follow on social media can shape our beliefs if we allow them to. All the while, Satan is whispering to us, the same thing he said to Eve in the garden, "Did God really say that?" He wants to convince us God's word is outdated and create doubt in our hearts that it applies to us today. Yesterday, Jesus called on those who had compromised to repent. Today, He offers two rewards to anyone who overcomes compromise. First, Jesus said, "To him who overcomes, I will give some of the hidden manna to eat." Manna was the Israelites' primary food source and sustained them for 40 years while they were in the desert. It was visible and available to be picked up every morning. So, what is hidden manna? I believe it to be the nourishment we receive from God every time we go to His word for guidance, encouragement, and instruction. It is also given to us when we pray for strength to fight those internal battles with temptation. God has an endless supply of hidden manna. Are you seeking it each day? Next, the overcomer will receive a white stone with a new name written on it. In Jesus' day, black and white stones were used to signify guilt or innocence in a court trial. A defendant given a white stone was declared not guilty. Those who overcome will be declared not guilty by Jesus and given a new name. Your new name will represent who you are in Christ. A name only known to Jesus and yourself. Are you curious as to what your new name may be? Be an overcomer and find out.

Prayer: God, help me to be an overcomer and not compromise to the world.

> Revelation 2:19 *I know your works, love, service, faith, and your patience; and as for your works, the last are more than the first.*

Jesus is speaking to the church at Thyatira which was located approximately 30 miles southeast of Pergamos. The city of Thyatira was known for its dyeing works. It is also mentioned one other time in Acts 16:11-15, where we read about the conversion of Lydia, who was a dealer in purple cloth. Jesus commends the church at Thyatira for their works. He identifies their works as love, service, faith, and patience. Jesus also points out their works are even more now than when they were first saved. While most everyone else's works tend to decline over time, the church at Thyatira was excelling in works. Jesus wants us to continue to do more and more for His kingdom. Paul writes in 1 Thessalonians 4:1, "Finally brothers, we instructed you how to live in order to please God, as in fact you are living. Now we ask you and urge you in the name of the Lord Jesus to do this more and more." As we have already learned, works do not guarantee our salvation; however, our works are important to Christ. They are a part of His master plan for our lives. The good news is that Jesus doesn't expect us to move mountains and accomplish some great feat for Him. Our works can be very simple. First, Jesus expects us to love those we are ministering to. Hebrews 6:10, "God is not unjust: He will not forget your work and the love you have shown Him as you have helped His people and continue to help them." Secondly, service to others is an essential aspect of our faith. Service is using our time, talents, and resources to help others. Ephesians 4:11-12, "It was He who gave some to be apostles, some to be prophets, some to be evangelists, and some to be pastors and teachers, to prepare God's people for works of service, so that the body of Christ may be built up." Next is faith or faithfulness, which is a desire to do good works. Titus 2:14, "Who gave Himself for us to redeem us from all wickedness and to purify for Himself a people that are His very own, eager to do what is good." Lastly, we are to serve patiently. Galatians 6:9, "Let us not become weary in doing good..." We should never run out of doing good for others.

Prayer: God, I pray my works are more now than the first.

> Revelation 2:20 Nevertheless I have a few things against you, because you allow that woman Jezebel, who calls herself a prophetess, to teach and seduce My servants to commit sexual immorality and eat things sacrificed to idols.

The church at Thyatira was not perfect. After commending the church for their good works, Jesus said, "Nevertheless, I have a few things against you." They had allowed a false prophet to come in and lead many in the church into sexual immorality and idolatry. It is unclear if the false prophet was actually named Jezebel or if Jesus is symbolizing her teaching to be like the wicked Jezebel who was married to King Ahab, approximately 900 years earlier. Jezebel, mentioned in 1 Kings, worshipped Baal and forced Baal worship on the Israelites. She had anyone who opposed her put to death including the prophets of God. She even threatened to kill the prophet Elijah after he had won a great victory over the 400 prophets of Baal on Mount Carmel. At Thyatira, Jezebel was openly promoting sexual immorality and eating meat sacrificed to idols. Unfortunately, no one in the church challenged or tried to stop her from leading the church astray. Sexual immorality and eating meat sacrificed to idols must have been the great compromises of the day as we saw the same issues in the church at Pergamos. Those issues were bad enough for Jesus to refer to her teaching as the "so-called deep secrets of Satan" in Revelation 2:24. Every generation of Christians have faced their own issues of compromise within the church. Paul said in Acts 20:29-30, "I know that after I leave, savage wolves will come in among you and will not spare the flock. Even from your own number men will arise and distort the truth in order to draw away disciples after them." Our generation is no different. Topping the list of tolerance and compromise within the church today is sexual immorality. Promoting open hearts, open minds, and open doors, churches have ordained openly gay clergy and endorsed same sex marriages. All the while, God's word is very clear on this subject. 1 Corinthians 6:9, "Do you not know that the wicked will not inherit the kingdom of God? Do not be deceived: Neither the sexually immoral nor idolaters nor adulterers nor male prostitutes nor homosexual offenders." Romans 1:27, "In the same way the men also abandoned natural relations with women and were inflamed with lust for one another. Men committed indecent acts with other men, and received in themselves the due penalty for their perversion." Beware of false teaching.

Prayer: God, help me to hold fast to Your word.

> *Revelation 2:21 And I gave her time to repent of her sexual immorality, and she did not repent.*

Contrary to what some may believe, God is not watching from above and waiting for us to mess up so He can punish us. That is not the character of God. Psalm 103:8 tells us, "The Lord is compassionate and gracious, slow to anger, abounding in love." 2 Peter 3:9, "The Lord is not slow in keeping His promise, as some understand slowness. He is patient with you, not wanting anyone to perish, but everyone to come to repentance." Even though Jezebel was leading the church at Thyatira into sexual immorality, God gave her time to repent. Sadly, Jezebel did not repent and would face God's wrath. Some translations say that Jezebel was unwilling to repent. This implies she knew right from wrong but refused to turn from her ways. As Paul writes in Romans 2:4, God's kindness and patience is to give us opportunity for repentance. "Or do you show contempt for the riches of His kindness, tolerance and patience, not realizing that God's kindness leads you toward repentance?" In other words, there must be a willingness to repent in order for true repentance to take place. Confession and repentance are not the same but both are required by God. Confession of sin is admitting to God that our actions or words were not in alignment with His. It is acknowledging to God what we have done is wrong. 1 John 1:9, "If we confess our sins, He is faithful and just and will forgive us our sins and purify us from all unrighteousness." God will forgive our sins when we confess them to Him. However, God is also looking for repentance or a change in our behavior. I can't tell you how many times I have confessed a particular sin and have found myself doing the very same thing again. It is frustrating and I know it is disappointing to God. Repentance comes down to having a change of heart. Repentance is following through with the desire to change and do differently. There will be times when we slip and fall back into sin. But we should acknowledge it, confess it, and turn away from it. This is the difference between someone who is unwilling to change and someone who wants to trust God with their lives. Are there areas in your life God is waiting for you to turn from?

Prayer: God, help me to turn from sin and trust You.

> Revelation 2:22 Indeed I will cast her into a sickbed, and those who commit adultery with her into great tribulation, unless they repent of their deeds.

Jezebel's time was up. Because she had failed to repent, God is going to cast her into a sickbed. He also promises a great tribulation to those who have committed adultery with her unless they repent. God is letting them know they are not exempt from punishment, but He is offering them more time for repentance. Sin has its consequences. Often times they are related to our sin. Galatians 6:7-8, "Do not be deceived: God cannot be mocked. A man reaps what he sows. The one who sows to please his sinful nature, from that nature will reap destruction; the one who sows to please the Spirit, from the Spirit will reap eternal life." Also, sin always has a way of finding us out. We cannot hide from its consequences. Numbers 32:23, "But if you fail to do this, you will be sinning against the Lord; and you may be sure that your sin will find you out." Jezebel's sin was sexual immorality. The Bible is pretty clear what constitutes sexual immorality. Essentially, sexual relations outside of marriage is sin. Jesus took it even further by saying in Matthew 5:28, "But I tell you that anyone who looks at a woman lustfully has already committed adultery with her in his heart." While other sins do not affect our body, sexual sins impact us physically, emotionally, and spiritually. 1 Corinthians 6:18, "Flee from sexual immorality. All other sins a person commits are outside their body, but one who sins sexually sins against their own body." What are the consequences of sexual immorality? Aside from the emotional scars of brokenness, shame, hurt, loneliness, and lost trust are sexually transmitted diseases such as syphilis, gonorrhea, and AIDS. According to the World Health Organization, over 70 million people have been infected with the HIV virus and about 35 million people have died of AIDS since the start of the pandemic. The sickbed of sin is no joke. As hard as mankind works to find cures for the diseases caused by our own sin, God has another sickbed to take its place. If you are struggling with the temptations of sexual sins, ask God to help you set up boundaries in the areas where you are weakest. Then ask Him for the strength to be able to stay within the boundaries you have set.

Prayer: God, help to me stay true to Your word and remain sexually pure.

> Revelation 2:26 And he who overcomes, and keeps My works until the end, to him I will give power of the nations.

To those at the church of Thyatira who overcome and keep His works until the end, Jesus promises to give them power over the nations. This power or rule over the nations will occur during the Millennial reign of Christ. When Christ returns, He will set up an earthly kingdom and reign for 1,000 years. Satan will be bound and the world will live in peace and harmony. Jesus' parable of the ten minas found in Luke 19:11-27 speaks about the rewards of the faithful who are given authority to rule. In the parable, a nobleman went to a distant country to be appointed king. Prior to leaving, he gives ten servants each a mina to invest. When the king returns, the first servant presents him with ten minas. The king tells this servant; "Well done my good servant, because you have been trustworthy in a very small matter, take charge of ten cities." The king also rewards the second servant whose mina earned five more by putting him in charge of five cities. But a third servant, did nothing with the mina he was given. The king was upset and told his servants, "Take his mina away and give it to the one who has ten minas." According to this parable, the greater the faithfulness, the greater the responsibility that will be given to believers. After promising to give those who persevere power over the nations, Jesus quotes Psalm 2:9 in Revelation 2:27, "You will rule them with an iron scepter; you will dash them to pieces like pottery." When Christ returns, He will smash to pieces the nations that oppose Him. Revelation 19:15, "Now out of His mouth goes a sharp sword, that with it He should strike the nations. And He Himself will rule them with a rod of iron. He Himself treads the winepress of the fierceness and wrath of the Almighty God." We are living in exciting times. Each day, brings us closer to the fulfillment of God's plan. Now is not the time to relax and become lazy in the faith. Instead, we need to keep working for Christ until the very end. Those who are faithful overcomers are given one more promise. Revelation 2:28, "And I will give him the morning star." We are promised Jesus Christ Himself, the bright and morning star. Hallelujah!

Prayer: God, help me to keep Your works until the end.

> Revelation 3:1 And to the angel of the church in Sardis write, "These things says He who has the seven Spirits of God and the seven stars: 'I know your works, that you have a name that you are alive, but you are dead.'"

Jesus turns His attention to the church at Sardis which was approximately 30 miles southeast of Thyatira. Although the church at Sardis had a good reputation, they were spiritually dead. Jesus' criticism of the church at Sardis is very similar to the way He had called out the Pharisees for being spiritually dead. Matthew 23:27, "Woe to you teachers of the law and Pharisees, you hypocrites! You are like whitewashed tombs, which look beautiful on the outside but on the inside are full of dead men's bones and everything unclean." The church at Sardis looked good on the outside, but was dead on the inside. George Eldon Ladd described the church at Sardis as "a picture of nominal Christianity, outwardly prosperous, busy with the externals of religious activity, but devoid of spiritual life and power."[21] They were simply going through the motions of church, rather than serving and worshiping God out of a love for Him. What are some characteristics of a dead or dying church and what should we do about it? The first characteristic is the replacement of the gospel with feel-good sermons on financial prosperity, boosting our self-esteem, and correcting social injustice. Church should be focused on the good news that God provided us a way to be set free from the penalty of our sins. Secondly, a dead church is more focused on teaching a strict adherence of following rules. Galatians 5:4, "You who are trying to be justified by law have been alienated from Christ; you have fallen away from grace." Or just the opposite, of believing that God's grace allows us to live any way we chose. Romans 6:15, "What then? Are we to sin because we are not under the law but grace? By no means!" Lastly, there is no love in the church. Romans 13:8, "Let no debt remain outstanding, except the continuing debt to love one another, for he who loves his fellowman has fulfilled the law." The easiest solution to dealing with a dead church is to leave. However, the death of a church is a long, slow process that evolves over a long period of time. You may not even be aware it is happening and have fallen into the death spiral yourself. Take the opportunity today to check your spiritual pulse. Are you alive and well or barely hanging on?

Prayer: God, help me to remain alive in You.

> *Revelation 3:3 Remember therefore how you have received and heard; hold fast and repent. Therefore if you will not watch, I will come upon you as a thief, and you will not know what hour I will come upon you.*

Time for repentance at the church of Sardis was running out. Jesus referred to them as a dead church. We might call them backslidden. Today, Jesus admonishes them to remember, remain firm, and repent. When we backslide, we have grown complacent in our faith. We get away from our daily communion with God. The daily struggles of life overwhelm us causing us to forget God's mercies and goodness. Or, we begin to listen to false teaching that leads us away from God's true word. Jesus tells them to, "Remember therefore how you have received and heard." They had received God's word and were saved. Yet, over time they drifted away. Maybe they stopped going to church or allowed other things to take priority over their relationship with God. For those who have fallen away, Jesus is saying to remember how you were when you first came to Me. Next, He tells us to "hold fast" or remain firm in our faith. Peter provides some excellent instructions on remaining firm in our faith. 2 Peter 1:3-9, "His divine power has given us everything we need for life and godliness through our knowledge of Him who called us by His own glory and goodness. Through these He has given us His very great and precious promises, so that through them you may participate in the divine nature and escape the corruption in the world caused by evil desires. For this very reason, make every effort to add to your faith goodness; and to goodness, knowledge; and to knowledge, self-control; and to self-control, perseverance; and to perseverance, godliness; and to godliness, brotherly kindness; and to brotherly kindness, love. For if you possess these qualities in increasing measure, they will keep you from being ineffective and unproductive in your knowledge of our Lord Jesus Christ. But if anyone does not have them, they are nearsighted and blind, and have forgotten that they have been cleansed from their past sins." Pursuit of these attributes produces a well-rounded fruitful Christian life. Lastly, Jesus tells the church at Sardis to repent. As we have learned, repentance is following through with the desire to change and do differently. Jesus makes it clear there are no more warnings. His judgment will come quickly and at a time we are not expecting. If you are living apart from God's word, don't wait another day to repent.

Prayer: God, help me to remember and hold fast to Your word.

> Revelation 3:5 *He who overcomes shall be clothed in white garments, and I will not blot out his name from the Book of Life; but I will confess his name before My Father and before His angels.*

Jesus promises the overcomers at the Church of Sardis that they will be clothed in white garments and their names not blotted out of the Book of Life. He will also confess each person's name before the Father. What is the significance of the white garments? They represent purity, holiness, and righteousness. These robes have been purified and washed in the blood of the Lamb. Revelation 7:13-14 speaks about those who come to Christ during the tribulation receiving white robes. "I answered, 'Sir, you know.' And he said, 'These are they who have come out of the great tribulation; they have washed their robes and made them white in the blood of Lamb.'" All who remain faithful will receive a new, white garment. Isaiah 61:10 says, "I delight greatly in the Lord; my soul rejoices in my God. For He has clothed me with garments of salvation and arrayed me in a robe of righteousness..." Next, Jesus promises not to blot out anyone's name from the Book of Life who have trusted Him as Lord and Savior. Every born-again believer is promised eternal life. John 5:24, "I tell you the truth, whoever hears My word and believes Him who sent Me has eternal life and will not be condemned; he has crossed over from death to life." John 10:28-29, "I give them eternal life, and they shall never perish; no one can snatch them out of My hand. My Father, who has given them to Me, is greater than all; no one can snatch them out of My Father's hand." My opinion on the Book of Life is that everyone who has ever been born will have their name written there. Their name remains in the Book of Life until that person dies. When a person without Christ dies, their names are then erased from the Book of Life, because they are no longer alive and have not received the promise of eternal life. That is why David said in Psalm 69:28, "May they be blotted out of the Book of Life and not be listed with righteous." All who come to Christ, will have their names permanently written into the Book of Life. At the end of time, anyone's name not found in the Book of Life will be thrown into the lake of fire. (Revelation 20:15.)

Prayer: God, I thank You that my name is permanently written in Your Book of Life.

> Revelation 3:8 *I know your works. See, I have set before you and open door, and no one can shut it; for you have a little strength, have kept my word, and have not denied My name.*

Jesus is speaking to the church at Philadelphia, one of two churches that He doesn't have anything negative to say about. He opens this letter quoting Isaiah 22:22 saying, "These things says He who is Holy, He who is True, 'He who has the key of David, He who opens and no one shuts, and shuts and no one opens. I know your works.'" Jesus establishes Himself as the one who opens and closes doors and has set an open door before them. Jesus also commends the church at Philadelphia for keeping His word and not denying His name. It is really fun to watch God open doors for ministry. He can use the most unlikely situations and chance meetings to grow His kingdom. For example, He led a young pastor from Tennessee who was moving to Wilmington to plant a church, speak at a graduation ceremony approximately two hours from Wilmington. By chance, Vivian's nephew attended the service and mentioned it to her. By chance, Vivian reached out to the young pastor and invited he and his family to our house for dinner. Now Vivian and I are faithfully serving in a new church plant in Wilmington. It was by chance that our son decided to go to Nicaragua for the summer of his senior year in college. It was by chance he met a young man who had recently started a ministry in Los Brasiles, Nicaragua. Our son's experience led Vivian and me to take teams from our church there for several years. I still remain connected to the ministry, providing some bookkeeping and financial reporting support. However, I do need to correct something I wrote earlier. Nothing is "by chance" with God. In each of these situations, He was opening doors. God can close doors as well. Early in my career with CP&L, I had interviewed for a job in our Fuquay office. Thinking I had the job, I was crushed when it was offered to someone else. Six months later, a job became available in the Selma office and I was offered the job there. This allowed Vivian and me to move to the same area her family lived. It was a blessing for us. God had closed the door in Fuquay knowing the Selma position would be much better for us. What doors are God opening or closing in your life?

Prayer: God, thank You that You open and close doors.

> Revelation 3:10 *Because you have kept My command to persevere, I also will keep you from the hour of trial which shall come upon the whole world, to test those who dwell on the earth.*

Jesus commends the church at Philadelphia for keeping His commands and continuing to persevere. He also tells them, "I will keep you from the hour of trial which shall come upon the whole world, to test those who dwell on earth." Let's be clear, Jesus is not promising those who are faithful to Him, a trouble-free life. Quite the opposite is true. Christians in Jesus' day were facing severe persecution. Nothing has changed. Today, Christians are facing persecution all over the world. So, what is this "hour of trial" Jesus is talking about? Most everyone believes it to be the Tribulation period. The Tribulation is a seven-year period prior to the second coming of Christ. It will be a time marked with God's judgments, natural disasters, plagues, and strange happenings in the sky. The Anti-Christ will be revealed and begin to rule the earth. Paul refers to the Anti-Christ as the lawless one in 2 Thessalonians 2:7-9, "For the secret power of the lawlessness is already at work; but the one who now holds it back will continue to do so until He is taken out of the way. And then the lawless one will be revealed, whom the Lord Jesus will overthrow with the breath of His mouth and destroy by the splendor of His coming. The coming of the lawless one will be in accordance with the work of Satan displayed in all kinds of counterfeit miracles, signs, and wonders." Jesus promises to keep His faithful church from this hour of trial. Paul said it this way in 1 Thessalonians 1:10, "And to wait for His Son from heaven, whom He raised from the dead – Jesus, who rescues us from the coming wrath." What is Jesus' plan for the church? Paul describes it in 1 Thessalonians 4:16-17, "For the Lord Himself will come down from heaven, with a loud command, with the voice of the archangel and with the trumpet call of God, and the dead in Christ will rise first. After that, we who are still alive and are left will be caught up together with them in the clouds to meet the Lord in the air. And so we will be with the Lord forever." One day soon the trumpet of the Lord is going to sound. Those in Christ will be called up into the air to be with Him. Are you ready?

Prayer: God, help me to remain faithful to the end.

> *Revelation 3:11 Behold, I am coming quickly! Hold fast what you have, that no one may take your crown.*

Jesus encourages the church at Philadelphia to hold fast to their faith and finish strong. He declares, "I am coming quickly!" In this context, it does not mean Jesus is coming back soon, but very suddenly without warning. Jesus also lets them know they have a crown waiting for them and it would be a shame to allow someone to take it away. No one can physically take away our crown. However, crowns can be taken away if our roots are not firmly planted in God's word and we allow the world to influence our lives. Deuteronomy 10:20 tells us, "Fear the Lord your God and serve Him. Hold fast to Him and take your oaths in His name." Hebrew 10:23 says, "Let us hold fast the confession of our hope without wavering, for He who promised is faithful." Paul writes about receiving a crown of righteousness in 2 Timothy 4:7-8, "I have fought the good fight, I have finished the race, I have kept the faith. Henceforth there is laid up for me the crown of righteousness, which the Lord, the righteous judge, will award to me on that day, and not only to me, but also to all who have loved His appearing." Paul's words about finishing the race brings to mind the story of John Stephen Akhwari, an Olympic marathon runner from Tanzania. During the 1968 Olympics, Akhwari fell, gashing and dislocating his knee and injuring his shoulder. He received some medical attention, but returned to the track to finish the race. Long after the race had finished and the medals awarded, Akhwari, came limping across the finish line. When asked why he didn't withdraw from the race because of his injuries, Akhwari's response should be every Christian's motto, "My country did not send me 5,000 miles to start the race, they sent me 5,000 miles to finish the race."[22] Akhwari's determination to finish the race should be our inspiration. During our lifetime, we are going to fall, get hurt, and have plenty of reasons to give up on serving Christ. In fact, you may be at one of those pivotal crossroads right now. The world is pulling you in one direction, telling you it is not worth it. Christ, on the other hand, is encouraging you to hold fast, finish strong, and receive your crown. Who are you going to listen to?

Prayer: God, help me to finish strong and receive my crown.

> *Revelation 3:15-16 I know your works, that you are neither cold nor hot. I could wish you were cold or hot. So then, because you are lukewarm, and neither cold nor hot, I will vomit you out of My mouth.*

The letter to the church of Laodicea is the last of seven letters Jesus has given John to write to the churches in Asia. Unfortunately, Jesus doesn't have anything positive to say about this church. Even worse, Jesus says because of their lukewarmness, He would spit them out of His mouth. Have you ever tasted something so disgusting that it was impossible to swallow, and immediately spit it out? This is Jesus' reaction to the works of the church at Laodicea. Jesus said they were "neither cold nor hot," using an analogy from the two water sources for the City of Laodicea. Because they lacked a natural water supply, a system of aqueducts was built to transport the cold drinking water from Colossae and hot water from the City of Hierapolis. However, by the time the waters reached Laodicea, they were lukewarm. Jesus said, "I wish you were cold or hot." We tend to think of cold and hot as a spiritual temperature, being on fire for God or unsaved, living apart from God. Jesus is using the water temperature to describe its usefulness. Hot water was useful for healing and restoration; while the cold water was refreshing and quenched people's thirst. Jesus said in Matthew 7:16-17, "By their fruit you will recognize them. Do people pick grapes from thornbushes, or figs from thistles? Likewise every good tree bears good fruit, but a bad tree bears bad fruit." Obviously, the lukewarm deeds of the Laodiceans were not bearing good fruit and were unacceptable and disgusting to Christ. It even brings into question their salvation. Paul calls it a "form of godliness" in 2 Timothy 3:5, "Having a form of godliness but denying its power. Have nothing to do with them." What are some signs of a lukewarm Christian? They attend church out of habit, putting in no effort to worship and getting nothing out of it. They only pray when they need something from God or find themselves in trouble. They are unwilling to help others or share their faith. The only time they pick up a Bible is to move it from one place another. They allow the world to influence their thinking and beliefs instead of God's word. No one would even know they are a Christian. Today is a good day to check your spiritual temperature. Are you cold, hot, or lukewarm?

Prayer: God, help me to be either cold or hot.

> Revelation 3:17 Because you say, "I am rich, have become wealthy, and have need of nothing" – and do not know that you are wretched, miserable, poor, blind, and naked.

Jesus gets right to the heart of the problem with the church at Laodicea. They saw themselves as wealthy and prosperous, but had become complacent in their faith. They had everything they needed, but were spiritually bankrupt. They thought they were doing well, but Jesus called them, "wretched, miserable, poor, blind, and naked." Where did the Laodiceans go wrong in the estimation of their spiritual condition? Like many of us, they were caught up in measuring themselves against the world's standards rather than God's standards. Their wealth gave them a false sense of security of God's favor when they compared themselves to those who were less fortunate. They had no clue of their spiritual decline. As Christians, we would rather set the bar for our faith by comparing our lives to others around us. As long as we are doing a little better than the other person, we are okay. Sadly, the more we lose focus on the true standard of living for Christ, the more we become like the world around us. Churches today, have a problem of trying to blend in with the world. They can easily become a social club where everyone is welcome and whose programs benefit themselves. The music and sermons are merely entertainment, and the culture of the church is to not offend anyone. Still other churches take on the role of a political action committee, completely focusing on the issues of the day. Churches of these types have a tendency to attract a lot of people and grow to be very large. However, they have missed the mark. Jesus called His church to be the light of the world. Matthew 5:14-16, "You are the light of the world. A city on a hill cannot be hidden. Neither do people light a lamp and put it under a bowl. Instead, they put it on its stand, and it gives light to everyone in the house. In the same way, let your light shine before men, that they may see your good deeds and praise your Father in heaven." Light chases away the darkness. It exposes the sin and ugliness of our lives. It also leads us to repentance. Have you become complacent and self-sufficient in your faith, led astray by worldly ideas? If so, allow the light of God's word to bring you back to a right relationship with Him.

Prayer: God, help me to rely on You and not my worldly possessions.

> *Revelation 3:19 As many as I love. I rebuke and chasten. Therefore be zealous and repent.*

Jesus tells the church at Laodicea to wake up and stop being lukewarm. He loves them and wants the best for them. However, they need to change their ways and be zealous for Him and repent. *www.merriam-webster.com* defines zealous as "marked by a fervent partisanship for a person, a cause, or an ideal." In other words, He wants the Laodiceans to turn away from their complacency and be the light He called them to be. Jesus also lets them know He disciplines those He loves. Like our earthly parents, God's discipline is given out of love to prevent us from hurting ourselves and not punishment for doing wrong. Hebrews 12:10-11, "Our fathers disciplined us for a little while as they thought best; but God disciplines us for our good, that we may share in His holiness. No discipline seems pleasant at the time, but painful. Later on, however, it produces a harvest of righteousness and peace for those who have been trained by it." God's discipline also includes training and education with a specific purpose in mind. Growing up, my parent's primary method of discipline was a switch. It got my attention and made lasting memories. Over the years, parents have tried many different methods of discipline, but the purpose is still the same. God uses various methods to discipline us as well. Often times His discipline simply comes through the consequences of our sins. For me, it seems to be unexpected and untimely expenditures. For you it could be trouble at work, hardships at home, or unexpected health issues. James 1:2-4 tells us, "Consider it pure joy, my brothers, whenever you face trials of many kinds, because you know that the testing of your faith develops perseverance. Perseverance must finish its work so that you may be mature and complete, not lacking anything." How do we know if what we are going through is God's discipline or His plan for helping us to mature as a Christian? David's words in Psalm 139:23-24 give us a great start, "Search me, O God, and know my heart; test me and know my anxious thoughts. See if there is any offensive way in me, and lead me in the way everlasting." God will reveal your "offensive ways" as He did to the Laodiceans. However, knowing what they are is not enough. Repent and return to God.

Prayer: God, thank You for loving me enough to rebuke and chasten me.

> *Revelation 3:20 Behold, I stand at the door and knock. If anyone hears My voice and opens the door, I will come in to him and dine with him, and he with Me.*

Congratulations, you have reached the last day. My prayer is that Jesus' words have spoken to you in a new and fresh way and have changed your life. For those who may have picked up this book out of curiosity and thumbed to the last page, this may be the very page God has led you to read. Jesus is speaking to the church of Laodicea who had essentially pushed Christ out of their lives. Their faith had become lukewarm, good for nothing. They had put their dependence on material things rather than relying on God. They were spiritually bankrupt, having no relationship with Christ. Here we find Christ patiently standing at the door of their heart, knocking. He wants to come in and have an intimate relationship with them. He wants the type of relationship where He can sit down and share a meal with them. But this will not happen unless they open the door. Christ will not force Himself on anyone. He doesn't go where He is not invited. Christ has given us a free choice to accept His love and have a relationship with Him. The Bible doesn't tell us how their story ends. However, you have a chance to write your own story today. Perhaps your relationship with Christ is not what it once was. You are feeling a little lukewarm in your faith. Maybe, you have never invited Christ into your heart and received salvation. Christ is patiently knocking on the door of your heart. There is nothing more He desires than to have a personal relationship with you. He doesn't make it hard to do. Romans 10:9-10 says, "That if you confess with your mouth, 'Jesus is Lord,' and believe in your heart that God raised Him from the dead, you will be saved. For it is with your heart that you believe and are justified, and with it is with your mouth that you confess you are saved." Ask Christ today to forgive you of your sins and invite Him into your heart.

Prayer: "I keep asking that the God of our Lord Jesus Christ, the glorious Father, may give you the Spirit of wisdom and revelation, so that you may know Him better. I pray also that the eyes of your heart may be enlightened in order that you may know the hope to which He has called you, the riches of His glorious inheritance in the saints." Ephesians 1:17-18.

Endnotes

1   Littlewood, Dave, *Heroes of the Faith*, Bunny, Nottingham, New Life Publishing, March 2021, Issue 47

2   Jeremiah, David, *The Jeremiah Study Bible*, New York, New York, Worthy Publishing, 2013, page 1291

3   *www.bing.com*, Definition of *Hallowed*

4   Bureau of Labor Statistics, www.bls.gov/opub/ted/2022, 12 Months ending June, 2022 Report

5   Franklin, Jentzen, *The Fasting Edge*, Lake Mary, Fla, Charisma House, page 1

6   *www.britanica.com/event/Jonestown*, Jonestown – History, Facts, Jim Jones, Survivors

7   Martin, Civilla, *His Eye is on the Sparrow*, 1905

8   *www.usatoday.com/story/news*, *Number of US adults who believe in God has dropped*, June 17, 2022

9   *www.statistica.com/churchattendance*, *How often do you attend church or a synagogue?* December, 2022

10 *www.takingcharge.csh.umn.edu*, *Create-Healthy-Lifestyle/Life-Purpose-and spirituality*, 2023

11 *www.christianpost.com/ashbury*, Ashbury revival moving to new sites to accommodate people arriving from around the world, Kumar, Anaugrah, February 20, 2023

12 *www.billygrahamlibrary.org*, *10 Quotes from Billy Graham about the Cross*, April 13, 2019

13 Warren, Rick, *Purpose Driven Life*, United States, Zondervan, *Attributes of a Servant*

14 *www.britanica.com/event/world-war-1*, World War I, 1914-1918

15 *www.britanica.com/event/world-war-1*, World War I, 1914-1918

16 *www.news.yahoo.com/news/martin-luther-king-jr---8-peaceful-protests-that-bolstered-civil-rights*, Mach, Andrew, Christian Science Monitor, January 16, 2022

17 *www.fee.org/articles/martin-luther-king-jr-s-6-principles-of-non-violence*, Cox, Hannah, FEE Stories, January 18, 2021

18 *www.desiringgod.org/messages/why-was-this-child-born-blind*, Piper, John, May 21, 2011

19 *www.cmons.org/medal/faqs*, Medal of Honor FAQ's, December 11, 2020

20 *www.washingtonexaminer/news/2446190/jen-psaki-calls-mike-johnson-a-wolf-in-a-suit-jacket-and-a-true-trump-believer*, Notheis, Asher, October 31, 2023

21 *www.research.lifeway.com/2019/05/21/churchgoers-split-on-existence-of-more-sexual-abuse-by-pastors*, Earls, Aaron, May 21, 2019

22 Ladd, George, *A Commentary on the Revelation of John*, Grand Rapids, Michigan, William B. Eerdmans Publishing Company, page 56

23 *www.olympics.com/en/news/marathon-man-akhwari*, Marathon Man Akhwari Demonstrates Superhuman Spirit, October 18, 1968

www.ingramcontent.com/pod-product-compliance
Lightning Source LLC
Chambersburg PA
CBHW080835120626
46553CB00009B/2445